PRESENTED TO

Name

Date / Occasion

Personal Note

A Year with Divine Mercy

A Year with Divine Mercy

Daily Meditations on God's Eternal Love

Vinny Flynn
Erin Flynn

TAN Books
Gastonia, North Carolina

A Year with Divine Mercy: Daily Meditations on God's Eternal Love

ISBN: 978-1-5051-1710-3
Kindle ISBN: 978-1-5051-1711-0
ePUB ISBN: 978-1-5051-1712-7

Published in the United States by
TAN Books
PO Box 269
Gastonia, NC 28053
www.TANBooks.com

Introduction

Many people, perhaps most people, when they hear or read the words "Divine Mercy," automatically think of the devotional elements and prayers found in the *Diary* of St. Faustina: the Divine Mercy Image, the Chaplet, the Hour of Mercy, The Feast of Mercy, and the Novena before the Feast. But as powerful and fruitful as these are, it's important not to focus so exclusively on the devotions themselves that we miss the teachings and insights they are meant to reveal—about who God is and who we are in His love. It's all about the Father's great plan of mercy to share His own life with us and to make us one with Him and each other, drawing us into the embrace of the Trinity Itself.

As St. Paul tells us, God "has made known to us the mystery of his will, according to his good pleasure that he set forth in Christ, as a plan for the fullness of time, to gather up all things in him, things in heaven and things on earth." (Ephesians 1:9–10, NRSVCE).

"Everything is grace," wrote St. Therese. And she might well have said, "Everything is mercy," because without mercy there would be no grace. The source of all grace, all blessings, all the sacraments, all the manifold ways that God works in our lives, is Divine Mercy. Indeed, Divine Mercy, as the endless outpouring of Trinitarian Love, lies at the heart of everything that is.

All of creation is an act of mercy! As I explained in *7 Secrets of Divine Mercy*, devotion to Divine Mercy is not just "a private devotion." It's *the* devotion, the "umbrella" over everything else. Every other devotion in the Church, every ritual, every activity, every teaching is under that umbrella. It's all there to help us understand and enter into Divine Mercy. Everything in our lives becomes more meaningful, more powerful, more life-changing once we understand and embrace Divine Mercy. It's the primary reality of our existence.

It's this all-encompassing reality of Divine Mercy that Erin and I have tried to keep in mind as we searched for and edited the passages we've gathered here. As you read through them, you'll certainly find selections relating to the Divine Mercy Image, the Chaplet, and the other devotional elements from the *Diary* of St. Faustina. But you'll also find excerpts from the scriptures, the *Catechism*, saints and mystics, theologians and scholars, popes and poets, prayers and hymns. You'll even find some passages that don't actually contain the word "mercy," but that we felt might help you "to understand fully the mystery," the plan of mercy and its application to you in your life. [In this context it might be of interest to recall St. Pope John Paul II's comment about the parable of the prodigal son that, "Although the word 'mercy' does not appear, it nevertheless expresses the essence of the divine mercy in a particularly clear way" (*Rich in Mercy*, #5)]

It is our prayer that this year of reflection on Divine Mercy will be a great blessing to you, a joyful, day-by-day rediscovery of the Father's love and of your own place in the Heart of the Trinity—not in an abstract way, but with a growing awareness and acceptance of how completely and personally you are loved.

—Vinny Flynn

How To Use This Book

This is not primarily a book to learn about Divine Mercy, but to encounter it. Or more specifically, to encounter the One who *is* mercy. Even the most erudite scholar at some point needs to move beyond the intellectual pursuit of God and His attributes, and be touched in the depths of his being by an *experience* of God Himself. It involves that difficult process of moving from the head to the heart; dismantling those barriers that protect the vulnerable places within. The hope is that in these pages you will not only begin to recognize the tributaries of mercy that run through your entire life, but that you will open yourself up to experience God's mercy each day in a new way. Consider these two words: *observation* and *exposure*. As you read, it can be powerful to observe the origin and action of mercy—through God's word, the saints, and contemporary writers—but the only thing that will lead to the deep personal transformation needed for holiness, is to *expose to God those places where you need mercy most.*

In this pursuit, we encourage you to use the Lectio Divina method of simply becoming aware of what has your attention. Some of these passages, especially those from the Fathers of the Church and the Catechism, can be a lot to take in as a whole. Stay where the grace is, even if you never finish reading the rest of the quote. Ask yourself "What has my attention?" as you read through, and then invite God into that place. It could be a word, a phrase, a thought that causes an affective response in you. If you are drawn to or moved by something, if you feel anything like resistance, joy, grief, or contrition, pay attention! These are often trailheads that lead to places of deep encounter and grace. They provide opportunities to pause for a moment and be present, asking God to be present there with you. And these are the very places where He wants to speak, the areas of the heart He longs to inhabit.

In the Divine Mercy Image, you see that His left foot is forward coming toward you, the rays issuing forth from a heart always open to you, His hand raised in blessing over you. When you invite Him into these deep places, this is how He comes—with the kindness and benediction of mercy.

—Erin Flynn

Acknowledgments

We would like first of all to acknowledge Conor Gallagher and his wonderful team at TAN Books for inviting us to take on this project and for their patient support and guidance throughout the process. Special thanks to Brian Kennelly (co-author of *Divine Mercy for Children*), who was our initial editor and supervisor for this book and provided invaluable direction and assistance. We owe a great debt of gratitude also to Jason Gale and John Vella, who kept us on track and worked closely with us—answering questions, offering suggestions, and giving direction, especially during the final editing stages.

There are so many pieces to compile in a book like this. Many citations have been taken from public domain sources, scripture, the *Catechism*, and Church documents. In a few instances we have modified the phrasing of certain passages from ancient sources in order to make the text more accessible or clear. We have carefully chosen excerpts that we felt would be of the greatest value to our readers, both in terms of deepening their understanding of Divine Mercy and as an introduction to inspiring authors whom they might not previously have read.

We gratefully acknowledge the Congregation of the Marians of the Immaculate Conception for their gracious permission to draw from several of their titles, most especially from *Divine Mercy in My Soul*, the *Diary* of St. Maria Faustina Kowalska. Special tribute must be paid to the contemporary writers featured here. They bring out in unique ways a more complete understanding of Divine Mercy in light of the direct revelations from Christ through St. Faustina.

We are deeply indebted to Fr. Avram Brown, a dear friend and longtime board member of MercySong Ministries of Healing, for partnering with us in co-writing some of the intros, applications, and prayers. As a scripture scholar and priest in deep communion with the Father of mercy, his input was rich and greatly appreciated.

We profoundly thank our friends and family who have supported, encouraged, and prayed us through the compilation of this book, which, for various reasons, ended up being a much lengthier process than any of us could have anticipated! May the Lord richly reward you for your patient endurance. We hope all of it has led to a work that will be a blessing to each reader.

A Year with Divine Mercy

The Daily Readings

My Special Task

On November 22, 1981, St. Pope John Paul II made his first public visit outside of Rome, following a lengthy recuperation from medical complications he had suffered in the aftermath of the attempt on his life earlier that year on May 13. He traveled on the Feast of Christ the King to the Shrine of Merciful Love in Collevalenza, Italy, where he shared with the world his conviction that the message of mercy was the special task assigned to him by God.

A year ago I published the encyclical *Dives in Misericordia*. This circumstance made me come to the Sanctuary of Merciful Love today. By my presence I wish to reconfirm, in a way, the message of that encyclical. I wish to read it again and deliver it again.

Right from the beginning of my ministry in St. Peter's See in Rome, I considered this message my special task. Providence has assigned it to me in the present situation of man, the Church and the world. It could also be said that precisely this situation assigned that message to me as my task before God, who is Providence, who is inscrutable mystery, the mystery of Love and Truth, of Truth and Love. . . .

Therefore I am praying here today together with you, dear Brothers and Sisters. I am praying to profess that merciful love is more powerful than any evil that gathers upon man and upon the world. I am praying together with you to implore that merciful love for man and the world in our difficult age.

—St. Pope John Paul II, Angelus, November 22, 1981

IN GOD'S PRESENCE, CONSIDER . . .

Compared to the amount of time I spend thinking or talking about the problems all around me, how often do I pray for it all? I consider what it would mean for me to truly join St. Pope John Paul II and implore mercy for the whole world in a time such as this.

CLOSING PRAYER

Lord, thank you for the mission of mercy you entrusted to St. Pope John Paul II. Thank you that your merciful love is greater than any evil. Remind me of this in times of discouragement, and bless my resolve to let this prayer for mercy become an enduring part of my life.

Faustina's Mission

The Diary *of St. Faustina is filled with references to her mission of mercy—a mission which would continue after her death. The Lord also granted her a great privilege, telling her to "distribute graces as you will, to whom you will and when you will" (31).*

I feel certain that my mission will not come to an end upon my death, but will begin. O doubting souls, I will draw aside for you the veils of heaven to convince you of God's goodness, so that you will no longer continue to wound with your distrust the sweetest Heart of Jesus. O my God, . . . I want to tell souls of Your goodness and encourage them to trust in Your mercy. That is my mission, which You yourself have entrusted to me, O Lord, in this life and in the life to come.

I heard a voice in my Soul: . . . My arm is supporting you; fight for the salvation of souls, exhorting them to trust in My mercy, as that is your task in this life and in the life to come.

Poor earth, I will not forget you. Although I feel that I will be immediately drowned in God as in an ocean of happiness, that will not be an obstacle to my returning to earth to encourage souls and incite them to trust in God's mercy. Indeed, this immersion in God will give me the possibility of boundless action.

Write down everything that occurs to you regarding My goodness. . . . Your thoughts are united to My thoughts, so write whatever comes to your mind. You are the secretary of My mercy. I have chosen you for that office in this life and the next life.

Despite the diligent care of my superiors and the efforts of the doctors, my health is fading and running out. But I rejoice greatly at Your call, my God, my Love, because I know that my mission will begin at the moment of my death.

—St. Faustina, *Diary* (281, 1325, 1452, 1582, 1605)

IN GOD'S PRESENCE, CONSIDER . . .

In many ways, I am a "doubting soul" in need of greater trust in God's goodness. I need help trusting in Him, yet I also want to join Faustina in her mission to tell others of His great mercy for them! She and Jesus both said that her call was for this life and the next, so I take her as my special intercessor.

CLOSING PRAYER

St. Faustina, you knew your mission would truly begin with your death. Pray for me in all the areas where I need to have greater trust in God's goodness and mercy, and help me work with you for the salvation of souls.

Love, Not Mercy

The endless exchange of love within the Trinity is not mercy, Fr. Cantalamessa explains, it's love. Mercy is when that love pours out upon us from the Trinity as a free gift of Itself.

The unique God of the Christians is . . . the Father—not, however, conceived of on his own (how can he be called "father" unless he has a son?), but as the Father always begetting the Son and giving himself to him with an infinite love that unites them both, which is the Holy Spirit. This love in the Trinity, which constitutes the Trinity, is their very *nature*. . . . *It is love, not mercy*. The Father loving the Son is not a grace or a concession; it is in a certain sense a necessity. The Father needs to love in order to exist as Father. The Son loving the Father is not a concession or a grace; it is an intrinsic necessity even if it occurs with the utmost freedom; the Son needs to be loved and to love in order to be the Son. The Father begets the Son in the Holy Spirit by loving him; the Father and the Son breathe forth the Holy Spirit in loving each other. . . .

What happens when God creates the world and human beings in it who are made in his image and likeness? *Love makes a gift of itself.* Love, like the good, by its nature "tends to pour itself out. . . . "

This love poured out is grace and no longer "love as God's nature"; it is gratuitous. It could not be otherwise and is thus a gift, a condescension. It is *hesed*, mercy.

—Raniero Cantalamessa, *The Gaze of Mercy* (Emphasis added)

IN GOD'S PRESENCE, CONSIDER . . .

When I receive God's mercy, I am receiving the endless love that exists within the Trinity. It is being poured out on me, a creature who can never do anything to deserve it. It is pure gift.

CLOSING PRAYER

Most Holy Trinity, thank you for the outpouring of Your love into my life. Let me receive everything as mercy and every mercy with gratitude.

The Gift of Love

Pope Benedict calls us beyond a superficial faith and knowledge of God to a deep, personal decision to receive and give His love.

"God is love, and he who abides in love abides in God, and God abides in him" (*1 Jn* 4:16). These words from the *First Letter of John* express with remarkable clarity the heart of the Christian faith: the Christian image of God and the resulting image of mankind and its destiny. In the same verse, Saint John also offers a kind of summary of the Christian life: "We have come to know and to believe in the love God has for us."

We have come to believe in God's love: in these words the Christian can express the fundamental decision of his life. Being Christian is not the result of an ethical choice or a lofty idea, but the encounter with an event, a person, which gives life a new horizon and a decisive direction. Saint John's Gospel describes that event in these words: "God so loved the world that he gave his only Son, that whoever believes in him should . . . have eternal life" (3:16). In acknowledging the centrality of love, Christian faith has retained the core of Israel's faith, while at the same time giving it new depth and breadth. The pious Jew prayed daily the words of the *Book of Deuteronomy* which expressed the heart of his existence: "Hear, O Israel: the Lord our God is one Lord, and you shall love the Lord your God with all your heart, and with all your soul and with all your might" (6:4–5). Jesus united into a single precept this commandment of love for God and the commandment of love for neighbour found in the *Book of Leviticus*: "You shall love your neighbour as yourself" (19:18; cf. *Mk* 12:29–31). Since God has first loved us (cf. *1 Jn* 4:10), love is now no longer a mere "command"; it is the response to the gift of love with which God draws near to us.

—Pope Benedict XVI, *Deus Caritas Est (God is Love)*, 1

IN GOD'S PRESENCE, CONSIDER . . .

In Jesus, the centrality of love is integral to the response it demands. Have I come to really know and believe in God's personal and unique love for me so that it shapes and directs the way I respond to Him and to others? Has it formed me in such a way that it gives my life a "decisive direction"?

CLOSING PRAYER

Lord, "I do believe, help my unbelief!" (Mk 9:24, NABRE). Help me to gratefully receive Your love and pass it on to others.

Trinitarian Love

There's nothing casual or haphazard about creation. It's an expression of outpouring Love. We don't exist by accident, and we don't exist because God was bored and wanted to amuse Himself by playing with clay. We were "Fathered-forth" by Love.

The Trinity—the mystery of mysteries, the greatest mystery in the Church—is all about love! It's all about Divine Love, given, received, and extended to all.

In the Trinity, God the Father is eternally loving the Son; the Son is eternally returning the love of the Father; and the Holy Spirit is the love between the Father and the Son!

In this endless cycle of self-giving love, the Son deserves the love of the Father, and the Father deserves the love of the Son. Who else deserves it? Nobody! Nobody else deserves it.

But true love longs to give of itself. So the Father decided to create more beings to love. In reality, that's what mercy is—when God, who is all-deserving, all-worthy, stoops to extend His love to mere creatures, who can't possibly deserve it.

Pope John Paul II, in his homily for the canonization of St. Faustina in 2000, explains that this extension of love, this "great wave of mercy" from the Father, comes to us through the pierced Heart of Jesus and is poured out upon us through the Holy Spirit. The entire Trinity is involved. *Mercy is the endless outflowing of Trinitarian love . . .*

—Vinny Flynn, *7 Secrets of Divine Mercy*

IN GOD'S PRESENCE, CONSIDER . . .

The Father has given us such an example of merciful love. He "stoops"—bends down toward us to pour out His love upon us, even though there's nothing we have ever done or ever could do to deserve it.

CLOSING PRAYER

Most Blessed Trinity, thank you for extending Your love to me. Father, in Jesus name, I ask you to give me, through Your Holy Spirit, the grace to offer mercy as You do—to everyone, not just to those I consider "worthy."

Receive the Blessing

Sirach is far too underappreciated in contemporary Catholicism. The early Church held this rich work in high esteem; we should join Clement, Origen, Augustine and Jerome, amongst others, in drawing upon Sirach's deep awareness of God's providence and mercy.

And the people besought the Lord Most High
in prayer before him who is merciful,
till the order of worship of the Lord was ended;
so they completed his service.
Then Simon came down, and lifted up his hands
over the whole congregation of the sons of Israel,
to pronounce the blessing of the Lord with his lips,
and to glory in his name;
and they bowed down in worship a second time,
to receive the blessing from the Most High.
And now bless the God of all,
who in every way does great things;
who exalts our days from birth,
and deals with us according to his mercy.
May he give us gladness of heart,
and grant that peace may be in our days in Israel,
as in the days of old.
May he entrust to us his mercy!
And let him deliver us in our days!

—Sirach 50:19–24 (RSVCE)

IN GOD'S PRESENCE, CONSIDER . . .

It is ridiculous for me to try to force my way through life without the one thing necessary: the blessing of my Father. My Father deeply desires to bless me and is waiting for me to accept His gifts.

CLOSING PRAYER

Heavenly Father, I bow down in worship before You. Thank you for Your blessing; thank you for Your mercy. You are my heart's desire, and I entrust myself to Your love.

Transformed by Tenderness

In her study guide for the book 7 Secrets of Divine Mercy, *Mary Flynn reflects on what happens in our lives when we truly come to know that we are beloved children of a tender Father.*

I would like to propose that as you go through this study of Divine Mercy, you reflect specifically upon the *tenderness* of God's mercy. Let your journey into this mystery be focused not just on what mercy is, or even on how much you need it, but most importantly, on the tender Heart of the all-merciful One, who longs to restore you and make you new.

This transformative tenderness of our God . . . is not simply an attribute meant to be looked at and analyzed; it is a peaceful place where our souls can rest. And in the resting, we are transformed.

Pope Francis has a great phrase that I love. At various times, stressing how much God loves us, and how this love must prompt us to then go and love others, he has said that we need a "revolution of tenderness". . . . This revolution is essentially the fruit of the knowledge of God's tenderness towards each one of us.

By coming to know the Lord's deep and tender love for us, and resting in that knowledge, we take on His tenderheartedness, and are enabled to live love in a revolutionary way. . . .

Allowing ourselves to be totally transformed by His tender mercy, we slowly become more and more able to love others with that same tenderness.

—Mary Flynn, *A Study Guide for 7 Secrets of Divine Mercy*

IN GOD'S PRESENCE, CONSIDER . . .

When I hear that God loves with tenderness, does that resonate deeply as something I long for, or is there part of me that wants to dismiss it as fluff? Do I prefer to keep Him a little more at a distance, as a strong God who is concerned with more important things than tenderness, and who isn't quite so vulnerable? Is it possible that I am the one who feels vulnerable or weak when I think of tenderness?

CLOSING PRAYER

Lord, one of the ways Your mercy comes to me is through Your tenderness, the kind of love I could never deserve, never earn. Give me the courage to open myself to You in the most vulnerable places of my soul, allowing Your gentleness, Your delight, Your tender care to heal and confirm my identity as Your beloved.

His Mercy "Gushes Forth"

Pope Francis reflects on mercy, not as an abstract concept but as a "concrete reality:" God's consistent way of responding with tenderness and compassion to all our struggles and weaknesses—even in the face of sin.

When faced with the gravity of sin, God responds with the fullness of mercy. Mercy will always be greater than any sin, and no one can place limits on the love of God who is ever ready to forgive. . . . "Patient and merciful." These words often go together in the Old Testament to describe God's nature. His being merciful is concretely demonstrated in his many actions throughout the history of salvation where his goodness prevails over punishment and destruction. In a special way the Psalms bring to the fore the grandeur of his merciful action: "He forgives all your iniquity, he heals all your diseases, he redeems your life from the pit, he crowns you with steadfast love and mercy" (*Ps* 103:3–4). Another psalm, in an even more explicit way, attests to the concrete signs of his mercy: "He executes justice for the oppressed; he gives food to the hungry. The Lord sets the prisoners free; the Lord opens the eyes of the blind. The Lord lifts up those who are bowed down; . . . (*Ps* 146:7–9)." Here are some other expressions of the Psalmist: "He heals the brokenhearted, and binds up their wounds . . . The Lord lifts up the downtrodden, he casts the wicked to the ground" (*Ps* 147:3, 6).

In short, the mercy of God is not an abstract idea, but a concrete reality with which he reveals his love as that of a father or a mother, moved to the very depths out of love for their child. It is hardly an exaggeration to say that this is a "visceral" love. It gushes forth from the depths naturally, full of tenderness and compassion, indulgence and mercy. . . . To repeat continually "for his mercy endures forever," . . . is as if to say that not only in history, but for all eternity man will always be under the merciful gaze of the Father.

—Pope Francis, *Misericordiae Vultus* (*The Face of Mercy*), 3,6,7

IN GOD'S PRESENCE, CONSIDER . . .

It's true that mercy can seem like one of many abstract theological concepts. But in reality, I see how concrete it is in my daily life when I take some time to reflect on its personal nature. God saves *me*, forgives *me*, heals *my* broken heart, binds up *my* wounds, sets *me* free from bondage, reveals Himself as the original and perfect parent to *me*.

CLOSING PRAYER

Lord, the more I dwell on Your goodness to me, the more my heart fills with gratitude and awe at who You are. Let my life be a psalm of praise to Your mercy.

God Knows My Greatest Happiness

God's mercy sometimes leads us by a strange and unexpected way. But Newman tells us we can rest assured it is the best way.

God has created all things for good; all things for their greatest good; everything for its own good. What is the good of one is not the good of another; what makes one man happy would make another unhappy. God has determined, unless I interfere with His plan, that I should reach that which will be my greatest happiness. He looks on me individually, He calls me by my name, He knows what I can do, what I can best be, what is my greatest happiness, and He means to give it to me.

God knows what is my greatest happiness, but I do not. There is no rule about what is happy and good; what suits one would not suit another. And the ways by which perfection is reached vary very much; the medicines necessary for our souls are very different from each other. Thus God leads us by strange ways; we know He wills our happiness, but we neither know what our happiness is, nor the way. We are blind; left to ourselves we should take the wrong way; we must leave it to Him.

Let us put ourselves into His hands, and not be startled though He leads us by a strange way, a *mirabilis via*, as the Church speaks. Let us be sure He will lead us right, that He will bring us to that which is, not indeed what we think best, nor what is best for another, but what is best for us.

—St. John Henry Newman, *Meditations on Christian Doctrine*, I, 1, 1–3

IN GOD'S PRESENCE, CONSIDER . . .

How often am I trying to conform to some external standard of goodness or holiness, success or competence, while God is crafting a personal journey of delight for me? Can I lean into the freedom of embracing God's gifts for me today instead of rushing past to the burdens I impose on myself?

CLOSING PRAYER

Most loving, merciful Father, You know the longings of my heart that remain hidden from my sight. Let Your gentle Spirit breathe into me, that I may awaken to the joy You hold for me.

The Loving Kindness of God

This psalm extols God's care for Jerusalem. All the good He does on earth and all the blessings He extends to His people flow from His mercy, an outpouring from His merciful Heart. These lines are, in essence, a song of praise for that mercy.

Praise the Lord for he is good;
sing to our God for he is loving:
to him our praise is due.

The Lord builds up Jerusalem
and brings back Israel's exiles,
he heals the broken-hearted,
he binds up all their wounds.
He fixes the number of the stars;
he calls each one by its name.

Our Lord is great and almighty;
his wisdom can never be measured.
The Lord raises the lowly;
he humbles the wicked to the dust.

O sing to the Lord, giving thanks;
sing psalms to our God with the harp.

He covers the heavens with clouds;
he prepares the rain for the earth,
making mountains sprout with grass
and with plants to serve man's needs.
He provides the beasts with their food
and young ravens that call upon him.

His delight is not in horses
nor his pleasure in warriors' strength.
The Lord delights in those who
revere him,
in those who wait for his love.

—Psalm 147:1–11, *Liturgy of the Hours*

IN GOD'S PRESENCE, CONSIDER . . .

Do I see and appreciate every good thing as a gift of God's mercy? He didn't have to fill our earth with beauty, pleasurable food, nature that soothes, music that stirs the soul. He doesn't need to bless my life the way He does. It is *all gift*. Maybe this week is a good time for me to write down my own song of praise to His mercy.

CLOSING PRAYER

God of creation, every good and perfect gift comes from You. And Your mercy extends farther still. Because You take even things that are hard, even suffering, even the effects of sin, and You turn all things to good for those who love You. I resolve to be more aware of Your gifts of mercy.

Architect of Mercy

St. Francis de Sales offers reassurance on the great good that God can work, even from our sins.

All things contribute to good for those who love God. And, as a matter of fact, since God can and does know how to draw good from evil, for whom should He do it, if not for those who, without reserve, have given themselves to Him?

Yes, even sins, from which God by His goodness defends us, are reduced by Divine Providence to good for those who belong to Him. Never would David have been so full of humility had he not sinned, nor would Mary Magdalene have been so full of love for her Lord if He had not remitted so many of her sins. And never could He have forgiven her these sins if she had not committed them.

You see, my daughter, this great architect of mercy: He converts our miseries into grace and makes salutary medicine for our souls from the venom of our iniquities.

Tell me, please, what could He not do with our afflictions, our sufferings and the persecutions that we endure? If, then, you are ever touched by some unpleasantness, from wherever it may come, assure your soul that, if it loves God, everything will be converted to good. And although you may not see the means by which this good will happen to you, be assured that it will happen.

—St. Francis de Sales in a letter to a novice sister

IN GOD'S PRESENCE, CONSIDER . . .

This truth of God's goodness, converting my miseries into grace, is both comforting and convicting. What a gift of His mercy—I can assure my soul that, "if it loves God, everything will be converted to good." And yet, I want to be like those great followers and lovers of God who truly allowed Him to create them anew.

CLOSING PRAYER

O God, You are the "great architect of mercy." What can You not do? Please build good and lasting things from the miseries and failings of my life. I place my trust in Your merciful and skilled hands, and leave all to You. Create beauty from the ruins and make me a living testament to Your mercy.

The Mercy through Obedience that Vanquishes Sin

The Catechism *explains that, through Christ's obedience, God's mercy is extended to us, forgiving our sins and transforming our wayward hearts.*

Sin is an offense against reason, truth, and right conscience; it is failure in genuine love for God and neighbor caused by a perverse attachment to certain goods. . . .

Sin sets itself against God's love for us and turns our hearts away from it. Like the first sin, it is disobedience, a revolt against God through the will to become "like gods,"[123] knowing and determining good and evil. Sin is thus "love of oneself even to contempt of God."[124] In this proud self-exaltation, sin is diametrically opposed to the obedience of Jesus, which achieves our salvation.[125]

It is precisely in the Passion, when the mercy of Christ is about to vanquish it, that sin most clearly manifests its violence and its many forms: unbelief, murderous hatred, shunning and mockery by the leaders and the people, Pilate's cowardice and the cruelty of the soldiers, Judas' betrayal—so bitter to Jesus, Peter's denial and the disciples' flight. However, at the very hour of darkness, the hour of the prince of this world,[126] the sacrifice of Christ secretly becomes the source from which the forgiveness of our sins will pour forth inexhaustibly.

—*Catechism of the Catholic Church*, 1849–1851

IN GOD'S PRESENCE, CONSIDER . . .

At some level every sin is a self-exaltation—and the self-emptying obedience of Christ is our way out. With that, I also know that when I begin to vanquish sin in my life, the powers of darkness will concentrate their attack. I want to remember this reality, and rely on the strength and mercy of God.

CLOSING PRAYER

Jesus, teach me obedience to the Father's will. Teach me to follow Your example of self-emptying and to not give in to discouragement or fear when my efforts are attacked by the evil one. I give thanks for Your sacrifice, rely on Your grace, and trust in Your mercy.

The Enemy's Voice

The wisdom of Venerable Bruno Lanteri is elucidated by Fr. Gallagher, showing us how the enemy seeks to destroy our confidence in God.

12. *Your affliction in regard to the past has no basis; it is simply a temptation of the enemy. I assure you of this in the name of God. Instead, therefore, of giving in to this, give glory to God and thank him from your heart for the infinite goodness with which he has forgiven everything.* . . . This same enemy, Venerable Bruno continues, will also try to afflict you regarding the future: "Look at you! Look at how little progress you made this last year, in the last years, in past months. Why do you think it will be any different now, this year? You will never make any real progress." Venerable Bruno urges us to be watchful of this! These voices also are not of God, but clearly of the enemy. We need only two gifts of grace: a humble heart and one filled with ever greater hope in God. Ask God for these two gifts today. Right now. God greatly desires to give both to us. Jesus, on the Cross, merited them for us.

13. Do you not yet see that the enemy seeks in this way to strip you of your peace and confidence in God, two dispositions we so need in order to pray well? Follow, therefore, the counsel of Saint Teresa: "Let nothing disturb you," not even your own failings, because these are the object and the foundation of the infinite mercy of God that infinitely surpasses the malice of all the sins of the world. Firmly resolved never to let yourself be troubled by anything in the world, present yourself humbly and with full confidence to the Lord in prayer, and he will not fail to have compassion on you.

God and the enemy—two contrasting approaches. The enemy seeks to strip you of your peace, to weaken your confidence in God, to burden you, to discourage you. Have you felt this? This is not God's voice. God speaks to your heart: "Let nothing disturb you, not even your own failings. My infinite mercy envelops and heals them. Do not let yourself be troubled."

—Timothy M. Gallagher, *Overcoming Spiritual Discouragement: The Wisdom and Spiritual Power of Venerable Bruno Lanteri*

IN GOD'S PRESENCE, CONSIDER . . .

From the beginning, the temptor attacked man's confidence in God. Where does he try to puff up my pride, or make me lose hope and confidence in God's goodness?

CLOSING PRAYER

Creator of all, my Father, my King, my deepest Love, I pray for "a humble heart and one filled with ever greater hope" and confidence in You. Help me to always reject the voice of the enemy. In Your infinite mercy, envelop and heal all of my failings.

The Multitude of God's Mercies

The great fourth century theologian, Cyril of Jerusalem, assures us that our offenses do not surpass the mercy of God.

God is loving to man, and loving in no small measure. For say not, I have committed fornication and adultery: I have done dreadful things, and not once only, but often: will He forgive? Will He grant pardon? Hear what the Psalmist says: *How great is the multitude of Your goodness, O Lord!*

Your accumulated offenses surpass not the multitude of God's mercies: your wounds surpass not the great Physician's skill. Only give yourself up in faith: tell the Physician your ailment: say thou also, like David: *I said, I will confess my sin unto the Lord*: and the same shall be done in your case, which he says immediately: *And you forgave the wickedness of my heart. . . . Wouldest thou see the loving-kindness of God . . . ?*

——St. Cyril of Jerusalem, 2.6, *Catechetical Lectures*

IN GOD'S PRESENCE, CONSIDER . . .

At times my sins seem to be too much, like there must be a final straw for God when it comes to how many times I can turn from Him, offend Him, fail at living the way I say I'm going to. And it's not just the fact that I sin, but as Cyril says here, the fact that I sin again and again. But there is no end to God's mercy. He wants to heal and forgive as many times as necessary. He wants my confession, my contrite heart, my trust in His goodness.

CLOSING PRAYER

O Divine Physician, I have so many ailments, so many places that need healing and strengthening. I am weak in faith, weak in virtue. But I trust that the accumulation of my offenses does not surpass the multitude of Your mercies. I will strive with Your grace to avoid sin and to live fully for You. Yet, when I fall, Jesus, I will ceaselessly return to Your Heart of mercy.

He Remembers

As Jesus tells St. Faustina, He completely wipes our sins from His memory. But He inscribes us and our story into His heart: in His steadfast love, He always remembers us.

To you, O Lord, I lift up my soul.
O my God, in you I trust;
do not let me be put to shame;
do not let my enemies exult over me. . . .

Make me to know your ways, O Lord;
teach me your paths
Lead me in your truth, and teach me,
for you are the God of my salvation;
for you I wait all day long.

Be mindful of your mercy, O Lord, and of your steadfast love,
for they have been from of old.
Do not remember the sins of my youth or my transgressions;
according to your steadfast love remember me,
for your goodness' sake, O Lord!

Good and upright is the Lord;
therefore he instructs sinners in the way.
He leads the humble in what is right,
and teaches the humble his way.
All the paths of the Lord are steadfast love and faithfulness,
for those who keep his covenant and his decrees.

—Psalm 25:1–2, 4–10 (NRSVCE)

IN GOD'S PRESENCE, CONSIDER . . .

God's mercy is a radiant light that reveals His path for me as one of steadfast love. Can I open my soul to His illumination, as He frees me from the sins of my youth and shows me that my whole story has been founded upon His faithfulness? And can I commit to a deeper faithfulness to Him?

CLOSING PRAYER

God of the New Covenant, You have sealed your children in the Blood of Christ. Lead me into the truth of my identity, and let me see that You do not forget me for even a moment. Indeed, I am held in existence by Your constant gaze of love.

And You He Made Alive

The collapsed outlook of the modern world originates in the forgetfulness that there's more to life than just us. Here St. Paul reveals that we are under spiritual attack and assault from our passions—and that God delivers us from both!

And you he made alive, when you were dead through the trespasses and sins in which you once walked, following the course of this world, following the prince of the power of the air, the spirit that is now at work in the sons of disobedience. Among these we all once lived in the passions of our flesh, following the desires of body and mind, and so we were by nature children of wrath, like the rest of mankind. But God, who is rich in mercy, out of the great love with which he loved us, even when we were dead through our trespasses, made us alive together with Christ (by grace you have been saved), and raised us up with him, and made us sit with him in the heavenly places in Christ Jesus, that in the coming ages he might show the immeasurable riches of his grace in kindness toward us in Christ Jesus.

—Ephesians 2:1–7

IN GOD'S PRESENCE, CONSIDER . . .

Do I remember the vast constellation I find myself in, with Father, Son and Spirit, brothers and sisters, angels and saints? Do I abide in this great love, or do I set out as a loner?

CLOSING PRAYER

O God, You who are Rich in Mercy, reveal to me that I am no longer under the shadow of wrath or the malice of Satan. Speak Your word of grace over me and open my eyes to the abundance of Your love.

The Cost of Mercy

In his spiritual classic, the Monk Dom Eugene Boylan describes how the cost of mercy is a love that willingly suffered.

[G]reat as were the works which He performed, His disciples were to do still greater; the one pre-eminence He seemed determined to reserve for Himself was that of suffering. . . . On that very end of our Lord's life which material standards condemn as a complete failure, the whole history of the human race hangs in eternal dependence. . . .

For His own wise reasons, to help men to understand the enormity of sin, to win their confidence and their love, and to show them His own immense love and desire for their happiness, God had decreed that the salvation of the world should be purchased by the Passion and Death of His Son. . . .

It was a short time as measured by movement of the sun; but if measured as moments of pain are really measured, by the intensity of agony, those few hours were longer than the whole duration of the world. For we cannot conceive what our Lord endured in those hours. . . . No human being ever suffered as our Lord suffered in that physical agony, and the physical agony was a mere drop in the ocean compared with the exquisite agony of His mind and heart. For the heart of the Crucified burned with a more intense love of God than the world has ever known, and the Son's heart was torn by the offenses that men offer to His heavenly Father.

And in that same heart there was a fire of love for men, of love for each man and for every man; and the Lover's heart was torn by the thought of the coldness of those whom He loved and the loss they were incurring by their refusal to love Him. . . . Truly, we must call Him, "This Tremendous Lover."

—Dom Eugene Boylan, *This Tremendous Lover*

IN GOD'S PRESENCE, CONSIDER . . .

I reflect on the intensity of the Lord's agony in those moments that were "longer than the whole duration of the world." And I ponder the immensity of what God has done for me.

CLOSING PRAYER

Father, Jesus, Holy Spirit, let me never forget the cost. Let my heart never grow cold, but burn with love and gratitude for Your mercy. May I never offend You again.

The Divine Mercy at Work

While recovering from a war injury, Ignatius of Loyola had only spiritual books to read—books that seized his imagination and allowed God in His mercy to transform the soldier's worldly heart and mind to those of a saint.

This reading led his mind to meditate on holy things, yet sometimes it wandered to thoughts which he had been accustomed to dwell upon before. . . . In the meantime the divine mercy was at work substituting for these thoughts others suggested by his recent readings. While perusing the life of Our Lord and the saints, he began to reflect, saying to himself: "What if I should do what St. Francis did?" "What if I should act like St. Dominic?". . . . These heroic resolutions remained for a time, and then other vain and worldly thoughts followed. . . . But in these thoughts there was this difference. When he thought of worldly things it gave him great pleasure, but afterward he found himself dry and sad. But when he thought of journeying to Jerusalem, and of living only on herbs, and practising austerities, he found pleasure not only while thinking of them, but also when he had ceased. . . . He learned by experience that one train of thought left him sad, the other joyful. . . . Afterward, when he began the Spiritual Exercises, he was enlightened, and understood what he afterward taught his children about the discernment of spirits. When gradually he recognized the different spirits by which he was moved, one, the spirit of God, the other, the devil . . . he began to think more seriously of his past life, and how much penance he should do to expiate his past sins.

Amid these thoughts the holy wish to imitate saintly men came to his mind. . . . The vain thoughts were gradually lessened by means of these desires . . . His brother and all in the house recognized from what appeared externally how great a change had taken place in his soul.

—*The Autobiography of St. Ignatius Loyola*

IN GOD'S PRESENCE, CONSIDER . . .

How much time do I spend thinking on and absorbing worldly things that take my attention, be it through people, news, books, or entertainment? These might bring me momentary happiness or fulfillment, and yet it never lasts. How can I create silence and habits that will allow for God to speak, to seize my imagination with zeal, and set my heart on fire to live for Him?

CLOSING PRAYER

Lord Jesus, help me to pattern my life on the heroic examples of the saints. They were weak and sinful like me, but You, Divine Mercy, transformed them into faithful servants and powerful witnesses. Grant me the deep desire and the courage to let You do the same for me.

Mercy Is Drawn By Trust

In His repeated revelations to St. Faustina, Jesus makes it unmistakably clear that there's only one way we can receive the treasures of grace He longs to pour out upon us.

The graces of My mercy are drawn by means of one vessel only, and that is—trust. The more a soul trusts, the more it will receive (1578).

Let no soul fear to draw near to Me, even though its sins be as scarlet (699). . . . I have opened My Heart as a living fountain of mercy. Let all souls draw life from it. Let them approach this sea of mercy with great trust (1520). [Urge] all souls to trust in the unfathomable abyss of My mercy, because I want to save them all. On the cross, the fountain of My mercy was opened wide by the lance for all souls—no one have I excluded! (1182)

Souls that trust boundlessly are a great comfort to Me, because I pour all the treasures of My graces into them. I rejoice that they ask for much, because it is My desire to give much, very much (1578). . . . I desire to grant unimaginable graces to those souls who trust in My mercy (687).

I am making Myself dependent upon your trust: if your trust is great, then My generosity will be without limit (548).

Let the weak, sinful soul have no fear to approach Me, for even if it had more sins than there are grains of sand in the world, all would be drowned in the unmeasurable depths of My mercy (1059) . . . No soul that has approached Me has ever gone away unconsoled. All misery gets buried in the depths of My mercy, and every saving and sanctifying grace flows from this fountain (1777) . . . Every soul believing and trusting in My mercy will obtain it (420).

I am Love and Mercy itself. When a soul approaches Me with trust, I fill it with such an abundance of graces that it cannot contain them within itself, but radiates them to other souls (1074).

—St. Faustina, *Diary* (Christ's Words)

IN GOD'S PRESENCE, CONSIDER . . .

Do I live each day with the awareness that God wants to shower me with "unimaginable graces," and yet the amount of these graces I actually receive is completely dependent upon how much I trust in Him?

CLOSING PRAYER

Jesus, I trust in you, but not enough. Give me the grace to grow in trust more and more each day until I can completely live in trust, yielding every concern, every worry, every situation, every detail of my life to You.

It Is Jesus You Seek

In his address to youth gathered in Rome for World Youth Day, 2000, St. Pope John Paul II threw out a challenge to us all—to open ourselves to a deeper experience of Christ's merciful presence in our lives.

Christ said to Thomas: "Because you have seen me, you have believed: blessed are those who have not seen and yet believe" (*Jn* 20:29). There is something of the Apostle Thomas in every human being. Each one is tempted by unbelief and each one asks the basic questions: Is it true that God exists? Is it true that he created the world? Is it true that the Son of God became man, died and rose from the dead? The answer comes as the person experiences God's presence. We have to open our eyes and our heart to the light of the Holy Spirit. Then the open wounds of the Risen Christ will speak to each of us: "Because you have seen me, you have believed: blessed are those who have not seen and yet believe". . . .

To believe in Jesus today, to follow Jesus as Peter, Thomas, and the first Apostles and witnesses did, demands of us, just as it did in the past, that we take a stand for him, almost to the point at times of a new martyrdom: the martyrdom of those who, today as yesterday, are called to go against the tide in order to follow the divine Master, to follow "the Lamb wherever he goes" (*Rev* 14:4). . . .

It is Jesus in fact that you seek when you dream of happiness; he is waiting for you when nothing else you find satisfies you; he is the beauty to which you are so attracted; it is he who provokes you with that thirst for fullness that will not let you settle for compromise; it is he who urges you to shed the masks of a false life; it is he who reads in your hearts your most genuine choices, the choices that others try to stifle. It is Jesus who stirs in you the desire to do something great with your lives, the will to follow an ideal, the refusal to allow yourselves to be grounded down by mediocrity, the courage to commit yourselves humbly and patiently to improving yourselves and society, making the world more human and more fraternal.

—St. Pope John Paul II

IN GOD'S PRESENCE, CONSIDER . . .

In what ways can I resolve to follow Jesus more completely, to take a stand for the Gospel, and to commit to improving myself and the world around me?

CLOSING PRAYER

Lord, help me to seek you above all else, knowing that you alone can satisfy, you alone can make something great of my life.

Consoler and Promiser of Abundance

Thomas à Kempis tells us that our merciful God is so close to us. He is a consoler, a helper, and our whole happiness consists in Him. We can trust in His Presence and His promises, and allow those truths to help us desire eternal things alone—even when the things of this world beckon.

Whatever I can desire or imagine for my own comfort I look for not here but hereafter. For if I alone should have all the world's comforts and could enjoy all its delights, it is certain that they could not long endure. Therefore, my soul, you cannot enjoy full consolation or perfect delight except in God, the Consoler of the poor and the Helper of the humble. Wait a little, my soul, wait for the divine promise and you will have an abundance of all good things in heaven. If you desire these present things too much, you will lose those which are everlasting and heavenly. Use temporal things but desire eternal things. You cannot be satisfied with any temporal goods. . . . Even if you possessed all created things you could not be happy and blessed; for in God, Who created all these things, your whole blessedness and happiness consists—not indeed such happiness as is seen and praised by lovers of the world, but such as that for which the good and faithful servants of Christ wait, and of which the spiritual and pure of heart, whose conversation is in heaven, sometime have a foretaste.

Vain and brief is all human consolation. But that which is received inwardly from the Truth is blessed and true. The devout man carries his Consoler, Jesus, everywhere with him, and he says to Him: "Be with me, Lord Jesus, in every place and at all times. Let this be my consolation, to be willing to forego all human comforting. And if Your consolation be wanting to me, let Your will and just trial of me be my greatest comfort."

—Thomas à Kempis, *The Imitation of Christ*

IN GOD'S PRESENCE, CONSIDER . . .

God doesn't just have mercy on me for all my sins. His mercy is so great that He longs to come close to me, this little creature. He desires to help me, console me, detach me from worldly things, and fix my eyes on eternal things. Even when there's no felt consolation, I will trust in His will and in His mercy.

CLOSING PRAYER

Though I look for it in many ways, I know I will never have full consolation or perfect delight except in You, God. Help me to seek only after the "abundance of all good things in heaven." And grant me such deep trust in Your mercy and in the goodness of Your will, that I will know You are working for my good, even when I do not feel Your consolation.

Redeemed by Love

We look to our medicines, our technology, our psychology or meditation to save us: just around the corner is the breakthrough that will make us healthy and whole. But Pope Benedict confirms that only love can save the human heart—and our whole being.

It is not science that redeems man: man is redeemed by love. This applies even in terms of this present world. When someone has the experience of a great love in his life, this is a moment of "redemption" which gives a new meaning to his life. But soon he will also realize that the love bestowed upon him cannot by itself resolve the question of his life. It is a love that remains fragile. It can be destroyed by death.

The human being needs unconditional love. He needs the certainty which makes him say: "neither death, nor life, nor angels, nor principalities, nor things present, nor things to come, nor powers, nor height, nor depth, nor anything else in all creation, will be able to separate us from the love of God in Christ Jesus our Lord" (*Rom* 8:38–39). If this absolute love exists, with its absolute certainty, then—only then—is man "redeemed", whatever should happen to him in his particular circumstances.

This is what it means to say: Jesus Christ has "redeemed" us. Through him we have become certain of God, a God who is not a remote "first cause" of the world, because his only-begotten Son has become man, and of him everyone can say: "I live by faith in the Son of God, who loved me and gave himself for me" (*Gal* 2:20). . . .

In this sense it is true that anyone who does not know God, even though he may entertain all kinds of hopes, is ultimately without hope, without the great hope that sustains the whole of life (cf. *Eph* 2:12). Man's great, true hope which holds firm in spite of all disappointments can only be God—God who has loved us and who continues to love us "to the end," until all "is accomplished" (cf. *Jn* 13:1 and 19:30).

—Pope Benedict XVI, *Spe Salvi* (*Saved in Hope*), 26–27

IN GOD'S PRESENCE, CONSIDER . . .

Can I be so vulnerable as to recognize I have no hope of rescue in myself: that I need another to love me? Can I admit that I don't have what it takes—that I need to be held in the love of another, to surrender to the certainty of the God of Mercies?

CLOSING PRAYER

Heavenly Father, Lord of love, open my heart to the gift that never ceases to flow from You, the gift of Yourself, the gift of Your infinite and unchanging love.

He Loved Them to the End

The heart-wrenching Eucharistic Prayer IV speaks poetically of the history of salvation and the God of mercy.

We give you praise, Father most holy, for you are great, and you have fashioned all your works in wisdom and in love. You formed man in your own image and entrusted the whole world to his care, so that in serving you alone, the Creator, he might have dominion over all creatures.

And when through disobedience he had lost your friendship, you did not abandon him to the domain of death. For you came in mercy to the aid of all, so that those who seek might find you. Time and again you offered them covenants and through the prophets taught them to look forward to salvation.

And you so loved the world, Father most holy, that in the fullness of time you sent your Only Begotten Son to be our Savior. Made incarnate by the Holy Spirit and born of the Virgin Mary, he shared our human nature in all things but sin. To the poor he proclaimed the good news of salvation, to prisoners, freedom, and to the sorrowful of heart, joy.

To accomplish your plan, he gave himself up to death, and, rising from the dead, he destroyed death and restored life. And that we might live no longer for ourselves but for him who died and rose again for us, he sent the Holy Spirit from you, Father, as the first fruits for those who believe, so that, bringing to perfection his work in the world, he might sanctify creation to the full.

Therefore, O Lord, we pray: may this same Holy Spirit graciously sanctify these offerings, that they may become the Body + and Blood of our Lord Jesus Christ . . . For when the hour had come for him to be glorified by you, Father most holy, having loved his own who were in the world, he loved them to the end . . .

—Eucharistic Prayer IV

IN GOD'S PRESENCE, CONSIDER . . .

The depth and beauty of this prayer cannot be appreciated in one reading. I consider reading through it again, reflecting on the great mystery and gift of salvation, and stopping on any lines that move me.

CLOSING PRAYER

Thank you for the gift of salvation, for Your faithfulness, God, to Your people. And to me.

God's Greatest Desire

The scene is the Cenacle, the Upper Room, where so much took place. The Passover meal has ended and Jesus is giving His last discourse to the disciples, just before entering into His Passion in the Garden of Gethsemane.

At the end of His instruction to the disciples, the Lord then begins praying aloud to the Father in their presence. This is the "High Priestly Prayer of Jesus," the "Prayer of Unity." It's the longest prayer recorded in the Gospels, and, to me, the most passionate. In this prayer Christ reveals his greatest desire for you and me, a desire so important to Him that He pleads with the Father for it, not once, but four times:

> Father, . . . *that they may be one*, even as we are one. . . . I do not pray for these only [the disciples], but also for those who believe in me through their word [you and me], *that they may all be one*; even as you, Father, are in me, and I in you, that they may also be in us, *that they may be one* even as we are one, I in them and you in me, *that they may become perfectly one*.
>
> Jn 17:11, 20–23; emphasis added

Christ knows that His hour has come. He knows that Judas has left the Cenacle to betray Him. He knows that, as soon as He finishes speaking to the disciples, it will be time to go to Gethsemane to take on the greatest sufferings imaginable. At this critical moment, what is He thinking about? His agony and death? No. He's thinking about you and me, and He's praying aloud to the Father so you and I will hear and understand that, to Him, we are worth dying for.

The plan of mercy, the "*plan born in the Father's Heart*" (*Catechism*, #759) from all eternity, has now, in the fullness of time, taken root in the Heart of Christ so completely that He's willing to suffer and die to accomplish that plan. The greatest wish of the Father is the greatest wish of the Son—*that you and I may become one in Them.*

—Vinny Flynn, *7 Secrets of Divine Mercy*

IN GOD'S PRESENCE, CONSIDER . . .

Scripture is the inspired Word of God, so even if something is only mentioned once, It's important. If it's repeated over and over, I really need to pay attention. God makes His desire clear here. Have I truly made His desire my own?

CLOSING PRAYER

Jesus, give me the grace to make oneness in You and the Father through the Spirit my greatest desire too. Draw me into an ever deeper union of love with You and with others in You.

Uncovering the Wound of Sin

On October 11, 1992, St. Pope John Paul II promulgated the new Catechism of the Catholic Church, *which he had called for at the Synod of Bishops in 1985, all in anticipation of the Jubilee Year 2000. As children of the Church, we are nourished and guided by this treasure for the Faithful, especially in understanding Christ's teachings about sin, repentance, and mercy.*

The Gospel is the revelation in Jesus Christ of God's mercy to sinners.[113] The angel announced to Joseph: "You shall call his name Jesus, for he will save his people from their sins."[114] The same is true of the Eucharist, the sacrament of redemption: "This is my blood of the covenant, which is poured out for many for the forgiveness of sins."[115]

"God created us without us: but he did not will to save us without us."[116] To receive his mercy, we must admit our faults. "If we say we have no sin, we deceive ourselves, and the truth is not in us. If we confess our sins, he is faithful and just, and will forgive our sins and cleanse us from all unrighteousness."[117]

As St. Paul affirms, "Where sin increased, grace abounded all the more."[118] But to do its work grace must uncover sin so as to convert our hearts . . . Like a physician who probes the wound before treating it, God, by his Word and by his Spirit, casts a living light on sin: . . .

—*Catechism of the Catholic Church*, 1846–1848

IN GOD'S PRESENCE, CONSIDER . . .

Mercy swiftly draws toward wounds: am I serious about allowing God to uncover my sin and wounds, even if it is uncomfortable and takes time and attention? Can I bring weakness, sins, failures to the light of His love?

CLOSING PRAYER

Father of Mercy, Father of Love, your Son reveals your healing light. Soften my heart to accept the tenderness of your Mercy, the ministrations that are part of Your saving grace for me.

The Bosom of Abraham

Mercy is eternal. Not only are you drawn into love and healing in this life, but are also born into it for all eternity. Don't close yourself off from love today as our unnamed lonely man does, but open your soul to the one who has passed from death to life for you.

There was a rich man, who was clothed in purple and fine linen and who feasted sumptuously every day. And at his gate lay a poor man named Laz'arus, full of sores, who desired to be fed with what fell from the rich man's table; moreover the dogs came and licked his sores. The poor man died and was carried by the angels to Abraham's bosom. The rich man also died and was buried; and in Hades, being in torment, he lifted up his eyes, and saw Abraham far off and Laz'arus in his bosom. And he called out, 'Father Abraham, have mercy upon me, and send Laz'arus to dip the end of his finger in water and cool my tongue; for I am in anguish in this flame.' But Abraham said, 'Son, remember that you in your lifetime received your good things, and Laz'arus in like manner evil things; but now he is comforted here, and you are in anguish. And besides all this, between us and you a great chasm has been fixed, in order that those who would pass from here to you may not be able, and none may cross from there to us.' And he said, 'Then I beg you, father, to send him to my father's house, for I have five brothers, so that he may warn them, lest they also come into this place of torment.' But Abraham said, 'They have Moses and the prophets; let them hear them.' And he said, 'No, father Abraham; but if someone goes to them from the dead, they will repent.' He said to him, 'If they do not hear Moses and the prophets, neither will they be convinced if some one should rise from the dead.'

—Luke 16:19–31

IN GOD'S PRESENCE, CONSIDER . . .

Have I been masking my need for God in trivial distractions, or driving efforts? Am I unwilling to be revealed truly as needy as Lazarus, and to allow my own sores and failures to be seen by God? Am I so caught up in the things of this world that I refuse eternal truths? Everything here is passing. Now is the time for acknowledging who I truly am, asking for mercy, and recognizing how imperative it is that I also show mercy.

CLOSING PRAYER

Heavenly Father, You led Abraham from his home to the Promised Land so that he could become the Father of the Multitudes, in whom all nations would bless themselves. Allow me to recognize that this blessing reaches to me also through the Son of Abraham, Son of David, King of Kings, the Resurrected One. Let me never close myself off to this blessing, Lord, and make me a blessing to others.

Rescuing Souls

In a letter to Sister Ludwina Gadzina in 1934, St. Faustina speaks of how we can participate in Christ's mission of mercy to save souls.

Dear Sister Ludwina,

I am very sorry that I have been silent for so long and that I have not written to you, Sister, but after all, our souls are united in the sweetest Heart of Jesus. We draw strength, power, and courage for the daily battle from a single source, so we are not very far from each other. . . .

Sister, what a joy I feel in my soul that the Lord Jesus called me to our Congregation, which is so closely united with the work and mission of the Lord Jesus, that is, of rescuing souls.

And if only we are faithful to this mission, then surely many souls will owe us heaven. But we must remember that our mission is sublime, resembling the mission of Jesus. We must fully possess the spirit and features of Jesus, that is, a complete self-emptying out of love for God for the sake of immortal souls, and in particular [we must take care of] those souls whom Jesus has entrusted to us. Sister dear, let us not fear a sacrifice similar to that of Jesus on the cross. Let us not fear at all because love will give us the strength and courage to offer it. What a joy it is to empty ourselves for our immortal King and Spouse. What a joy it is to be like a wild flower under the feet of Jesus, wilting slowly and delighting His divine Heart with our fragrance.

—*The Letters of Saint Faustina*

IN GOD'S PRESENCE, CONSIDER . . .

How extravagant God's mercy is! I am invited into such limitless love, that I also become a channel of mercy for others who need to know God's love! With our great apostle of mercy, St. Faustina, I can let the love of God wash over me and reach so many in need.

CLOSING PRAYER

Jesus, meek and humble of heart, make my heart like unto Thine. Transform me in Your radiance that I may also become a beacon of mercy to my brothers and sisters who cry out for Your love. I pour myself out into You, emptying myself to receive You, that You might be poured forth upon the world.

Bring to Perfection All That Is Wanting . . .

St. Augustine spent much of his life not knowing God: competent and popular, he didn't know he was missing everything. In his famous autobiography Confessions, *Augustine helps us discover the many responses of the heart to God's love.*

And then do you, Lord, in your delight at the fragrance which pervades your holy temple, have mercy on me according to your great mercy for the sake of your name. Do not, I entreat you, do not abandon your unfinished work, but bring to perfection all that is wanting in me.

So then, when I confess not what I have been but what I am now, this is the fruit to be reaped from my confessions: I confess not only before you in secret exultation tinged with fear and secret sorrow infused with hope, but also in the ears of believing men and women, the companions of my joy and sharers in my mortality, my fellow citizens still on pilgrimage with me, those who have gone before and those who will follow, and all who bear me company in my life. . . .

I love you, Lord, with no doubtful mind but with absolute certainty. You pierced my heart with your word, and I fell in love with you. But the sky and the earth too, and everything in them—all these things around me are telling me that I should love you; and since they never cease to proclaim this to everyone, those who do not hear are left without excuse. But you, far above, will show mercy to anyone . . . and will grant pity to whomsoever you choose.

—St. Augustine, *Confessions*

IN GOD'S PRESENCE, CONSIDER . . .

Saint Augustine admits to the full gamut of emotions that often war within us, speaking of his fear and secret sorrows, even as he feels joy in discovering God. And beautifully he shows us the way to this total honesty by revealing that all of creation, including us, is created and ordered to God and to love.

CLOSING PRAYER

I love You, Lord, "with no doubtful mind but with absolute certainty." Give me friends like St. Augustine and his mother, St. Monica, to confirm my heart in Your love—that You are love and always love. Let Your created world around me encompass me with Your mercy. And bring to perfection all that is wanting in me.

I Thought About You

The Church teaches that God knew and loved each of us before he formed us in our mother's womb (See Jer 1:5). And, in his first homily as pontiff, Pope Benedict XVI stressed that "each of us is the result of a thought of God." St. Faustina learned first-hand how real this is.

September 21. Having awakened several times during the night, I thanked God briefly, but with all my heart, for all the graces He has given to me and to our Congregation, [and] I reflected on His great goodness.

When I received Holy Communion, I said to Him, "Jesus, I thought about You so many times last night," and Jesus answered me, And I thought of you before I called you into being. "Jesus, in what way were You thinking about me?" In terms of admitting you to My eternal happiness. After these words, my soul was flooded with the love of God. I could not stop marveling at how much God loves us.

. . . Consider, My daughter, Who it is to whom your heart is so closely united by the vows. Before I made the world, I loved you with the love your heart is experiencing today and, throughout the centuries, My love will never change.

—St. Faustina, *Diary*, 1291,1292, 1754

IN GOD'S PRESENCE, CONSIDER . . .

Do I view myself as just another product of evolution, or do I live in the reality that God wanted me born—that He knew and loved me even before the world began?

CLOSING PRAYER

Father God, thank you for choosing life for me. Help me to live joyfully, knowing that Your love for me will never change.

Each of Us Is Loved

Elected as Holy Father five days before on April 19, 2005, Pope Benedict, in his inaugural homily, shares with us his vision for the Church, for himself as shepherd, and for each member of his flock.

When the shepherd of all humanity, the living God, himself became a lamb, he stood on the side of the lambs, with those who are downtrodden and killed. This is how he reveals himself to be the true shepherd: "I am the Good Shepherd . . . I lay down my life for the sheep," Jesus says of himself (Jn 10:14f). It is not power, but love that redeems us! This is God's sign: he himself is love.

. . . One of the basic characteristics of a shepherd must be to love the people entrusted to him, even as he loves Christ whom he serves. "Feed my sheep", says Christ to Peter, and now, at this moment, he says it to me as well. Feeding means loving, and loving also means being ready to suffer. Loving means giving the sheep what is truly good, the nourishment of God's truth, of God's word, the nourishment of his presence, which he gives us in the Blessed Sacrament. My dear friends—at this moment I can only say: pray for me, that I may learn to love the Lord more and more. Pray for me, that I may learn to love his flock more and more—in other words, you, the holy Church, each one of you and all of you together. . . .

Only when we meet the living God in Christ do we know what life is. We are not some casual and meaningless product of evolution. Each of us is the result of a thought of God. Each of us is willed, each of us is loved, each of us is necessary. There is nothing more beautiful than to be surprised by the Gospel, by the encounter with Christ. There is nothing more beautiful than to know Him and to speak to others of our friendship with Him.

—Pope Benedict XVI, Inauguration Homily, Sunday, April 24, 2005

IN GOD'S PRESENCE, CONSIDER . . .

Do I believe one of the most pernicious lies of this modern world: that random evolution has brought everything into being, and that I am a meaningless accident? Or have I met my Father who created me and loves me, the God who wanted me born and "thought" me into being? My existence is good and I am uniquely loved.

CLOSING PRAYER

Lord of Creation, Your word of love called this world into being, and Your word of love transforms me today. Let my identity be rooted in You alone, in Your will for my existence, and in the beauty of Your plan for me.

Sought and Loved . . .

St. Bernard, in his famous commentary on the Song of Songs, says that people tend not to turn to God because they have negative false images of who He is. Bernard then beautifully enlightens us on the merciful God who loves and seeks us first.

My opinion is that all those who lack knowledge of God are those who refuse to turn to Him. I am certain that they refuse because they imagine this kindly disposed God to be harsh and severe, this merciful God to be callous and inflexible, this lovable God to be cruel and oppressive. So it is that wickedness plays false to itself, setting up for itself an image that does not represent Him. . . .

"I sought Him whom my soul loves"—that is what you are urged to do by the goodness of Him who anticipates you, who sought you, who loved you before you loved Him. You would not seek Him or love Him unless you had first been sought and loved. . . . From this comes the zeal and ardor to seek Him whom your soul loves, because you cannot seek unless you are sought, and when you are sought you cannot but seek. . . .

It is so important for every soul among you who is seeking God to realize that God was in the field and was seeking you before you began to search for Him . . . You could not have sought the Word . . . if He had not sought you. . . .

Do you awake? Well, He too is awake. If you arise in the nighttime, if you anticipate to your utmost your early awaking, you will find Him awake . . . you will always be rash if you attribute any priority and predominance to yourself; for He loves both more than you love and before you love at all. . . .

She [the soul] recognizes that in loving Him, she but returns His love because He first loved her. And so indeed it is! God's love begets the soul's [love] and comes before it; His interest and care for her evoke her care for Him.

—St. Bernard of Clairvaux, "On the Song of Songs"

IN GOD'S PRESENCE, CONSIDER . . .

If I am seeking or loving God, it is only because He has sought and loved me first. It is an unfathomable mystery, but a comfort nonetheless that I am not loved by Him because of what I give to Him, what I do, or how much I love Him. No, I am loved first by Him before I can even reciprocate as feebly as I am able. Do I believe this? Or are there some negative images I have of who He is that need to be addressed?

CLOSING PRAYER

God, You love more than I love and before I love, and yet inexplicably You are content with even the smallest efforts of mine to love You. In fact, You seem to delight most in my childlike attempts and in my littleness. And so I will "seek Him whom my soul loves," knowing that You anticipate me with joy.

The Inescapable God . . .

One of the most beloved psalms reveals to us a God of love and mercy, intimately acquainted with each one of us from before our conception. He willed us and loved us into being, and is present to us no matter where we go.

O Lord, you have searched me and known me.
You know when I sit down and when I rise up; you discern my thoughts from far away.
You search out my path and my lying down, and are acquainted with all my ways.
Even before a word is on my tongue, O Lord, you know it completely. . . .
Where can I go from your spirit? Or where can I flee from your presence?
If I ascend to heaven, you are there; if I make my bed in Sheol, you are there.
If I take the wings of the morning and settle at the farthest limits of the sea,
even there your hand shall lead me, and your right hand shall hold me fast. . . .
For it was you who formed my inward parts; you knit me together in my mother's womb.
I praise you, for I am fearfully and wonderfully made. Wonderful are your works; that I know very well.
My frame was not hidden from you, when I was being made in secret, intricately woven in the depths of the earth.
Your eyes beheld my unformed substance. In your book were written all the days that were formed for me, when none of them as yet existed.
How weighty to me are your thoughts, O God! How vast is the sum of them!
I try to count them—they are more than the sand; I come to the end— I am still with you. . . .
Search me, O God, and know my heart; test me and know my thoughts.
See if there is any wicked way in me, and lead me in the way everlasting.

—Psalm 139:1–4,7–10,13–18, 23–24 (NRSVCE)

IN GOD'S PRESENCE, CONSIDER . . .

God's mercy isn't just present to me as I journey through life, but it was active from the very beginning: in choosing me, tenderly forming me, and granting me my very existence. How can I make my life a testament to His goodness?

CLOSING PRAYER

. . . *Father, Your eyes saw my unformed substance. You knew who I would be and chose to give me life! Help me remember this in times when I may be tempted toward self-condemnation or even despair, and help me respond to Your gift with a life of virtue.*

Which Will Be Poured Out for You

One of Paul's best loved letters, Philippians, invites us into a gentleness that permits our hearts to recognize the abiding presence of God's mercy and inspires imitation.

If there is any encouragement in Christ, any solace in love, any participation in the Spirit, any compassion and mercy, complete my joy by being of the same mind, with the same love, united in heart, thinking one thing. Do nothing out of selfishness or out of vainglory; rather, humbly regard others as more important than yourselves, each looking out not for his own interests, but [also] everyone for those of others. Have among yourselves the same attitude that is also yours in Christ Jesus, Who, though he was in the form of God, did not regard equality with God something to be grasped. Rather, he emptied himself, taking the form of a slave, coming in human likeness; and found human in appearance, he humbled himself, becoming obedient to death, even death on a cross. Because of this, God greatly exalted him and bestowed on him the name that is above every name, that at the name of Jesus every knee should bend, of those in heaven and on earth and under the earth, and every tongue confess that Jesus Christ is Lord, to the glory of God the Father.

—Philippians 2:1–11 (NABRE)

IN GOD'S PRESENCE, CONSIDER . . .

Jesus sees me. He knows me. And to lift me up, He pours Himself out completely. Can I find encouragement in Christ to imitate His self-emptying love?

CLOSING PRAYER

Lord Jesus Christ, You emptied Yourself out entirely. Free me from clinging to myself, and draw me into Your mind of mercy so that I, too, can pour myself out for others.

He Knows What He Is About

Mercy is Divine love overflowing from the Trinity to us who could never deserve it. And Newman says that this love is so personal that God calls each of us by name and has a particular plan for our lives.

God was all-complete, all-blessed in Himself; but it was His will to create a world for His glory. He is Almighty, and might have done all things Himself, but it has been His will to bring about His purposes by the beings He has created. We are all created to His glory—we are created to do His will. I am created to do something or to be something for which no one else is created; I have a place in God's counsels, in God's world, which no one else has; whether I be rich or poor, despised or esteemed by man, God knows me and calls me by my name.

God has created me to do Him some definite service; He has committed some work to me which He has not committed to another. I have my mission—I never may know it in this life, but I shall be told it in the next. Somehow I am necessary for His purposes, as necessary in my place as an Archangel in his—if, indeed, I fail, He can raise another, as He could make the stones children of Abraham. Yet I have a part in this great work; I am a link in a chain, a bond of connection between persons. He has not created me for naught. I shall do good, I shall do His work; I shall be an angel of peace, a preacher of truth in my own place, while not intending it, if I do but keep His commandments and serve Him in my calling.

Therefore I will trust Him. Whatever, wherever I am, I can never be thrown away. If I am in sickness, my sickness may serve Him; in perplexity, my perplexity may serve Him; if I am in sorrow, my sorrow may serve Him. My sickness, or perplexity, or sorrow may be necessary causes of some great end, which is quite beyond us. He does nothing in vain; He may prolong my life, He may shorten it; He knows what He is about. He may take away my friends, He may throw me among strangers, He may make me feel desolate, make my spirits sink, hide the future from me—still He knows what He is about.

—St. John Henry Newman, *Meditations on Christian Doctrine*, I, 2, 1–3

IN GOD'S PRESENCE, CONSIDER . . .

Mercy knows what I am about: why I am here, why I suffer, what will let me thrive. Can I trust fully in God, or, like Peter on the water, does my vision stray from Jesus?

CLOSING PRAYER

Most Loving Savior, You know the joys and longings of my heart. Reveal to me Your presence and Your providence in my life, that I may learn to rest in You.

Love Compelled You

Love is not merely an attribute of God. As St. John tells us, "love is from God" (1 Jn 4:7, NRSVCE). Love is His very nature, and He cannot act apart from that nature. Love is who He is and is the compelling motivation for all He does.

Why then, Eternal Father, did you create this creature of yours? I am truly amazed at this, and indeed I see, as you show me, that you made us for one reason only: in your light you saw yourself compelled by the fire of your charity to give us being, in spite of the evil we would commit against you, eternal Father. It was fire, then, that compelled you. O unutterable love, even though you saw all the evils that all your creatures would commit against your infinite goodness, you acted as if you did not see and set your eye only on the beauty of your creature, with whom you had fallen in love like one drunk and crazy with love. And in love you drew us out of yourself, giving us being in your own image and likeness. You, eternal Truth, have told me the truth: that love compelled you to create us.

—St. Catherine of Siena, *The Prayers of St. Catherine of Siena*

IN GOD'S PRESENCE, CONSIDER . . .

I was created because perfect love longs to give of itself. How would my life change if I could really believe that God is "crazy with love" for me?

CLOSING PRAYER

Eternal Father, help me to remember that I was not just mindlessly created, but that I exist because you longed to bestow your love on me. Help me to rejoice that I came from Love for love.

Radiance Revealed Face to Face

What is it that we build our lives around apart from the love of God? Jesus illuminates our world with His Divine Mercy, this radiant overflow of love from the Trinity, and we are meant to participate in this and reflect it in all we do. Yet, we foolishly invest ourselves in everything else, including "good works" which, apart from love, mean nothing.

If I speak in the tongues of men and of angels, but have not love, I am a noisy gong or a clanging cymbal. And if I have prophetic powers, and understand all mysteries and all knowledge, and if I have all faith, so as to remove mountains, but have not love, I am nothing. If I give away all I have, and if I deliver my body to be burned, but have not love, I gain nothing.

Love is patient and kind; love is not jealous or boastful; it is not arrogant or rude. Love does not insist on its own way; it is not irritable or resentful; it does not rejoice at wrong, but rejoices in the right. Love bears all things, believes all things, hopes all things, endures all things.

Love never ends; as for prophecies, they will pass away; as for tongues, they will cease; as for knowledge, it will pass away. For our knowledge is imperfect and our prophecy is imperfect; but when the perfect comes, the imperfect will pass away. When I was a child, I spoke like a child, I thought like a child, I reasoned like a child; when I became a man, I gave up childish ways. For now we see in a mirror dimly, but then face to face. Now I know in part; then I shall understand fully, even as I have been fully understood. So faith, hope, love abide, these three; but the greatest of these is love.

—1 Corinthians 13:1–13

IN GOD'S PRESENCE, CONSIDER . . .

How easily do I fall into a thousand traps by pouring myself into urgent things that seem good, but which have been separated from the core intention of love? Has the enemy manipulated me into pursuing a myriad of "worthy" causes that leave me feeling discouraged, resentful, or undervalued? That's a good place to start to find things that I may be doing for reasons other than love.

CLOSING PRAYER

Heavenly Father, without Your mercy I am merely a puppet whose strings are pulled by an enemy with countless masquerades—they all seem vital in the moment, but are not You, not Your love. Rid me of everything but Your love and let everything I do have its origin there.

Love Fulfills

Everything comes down to love. God is love, St. John tells us. Here, St. Paul confirms that we can be like God. With His Spirit living within us, we enter into fulfillment through love.

Owe no one anything, except to love one another; for he who loves his neighbor has fulfilled the law. The commandments, "You shall not commit adultery, You shall not kill, You shall not steal, You shall not covet," and any other commandment, are summed up in this sentence, "You shall love your neighbor as yourself." Love does no wrong to a neighbor; therefore love is the fulfilling of the law.

—Romans 13:8–10

IN GOD'S PRESENCE, CONSIDER . . .

Where have I exchanged Divine simplicity for human complexities? All answers are found in love, the Divine Mercy that rewrites our story. Today I can permit God to recast each circumstance in the light of His Divine Love. Today I can allow the love from the Trinity to overflow as mercy into my life, healing the places within that keep me from loving myself and others.

CLOSING PRAYER

Triune God: Father, Son and Holy Spirit, enlighten my heart with Your call into the fullness of life in union with You. Today let me experience the power of Your love guiding all things—and guiding me to love.

Blessed be God Forever

Jesus reveals the heart of His plan in Matthew's Gospel in the Beatitudes—blessings. Receive God's blessing today in these words of courage from Baruch. (Even the name Baruch means blessed.)

Take courage, my children, cry to God,
and he will deliver you from the power and hand of the enemy.
For I have put my hope in the Everlasting to save you,
and joy has come to me from the Holy One,
because of the mercy which soon will come to you
from your everlasting Savior.
For I sent you out with sorrow and weeping,
but God will give you back to me with joy and gladness for ever.
For as the neighbors of Zion have now seen your capture,
so they soon will see your salvation by God,
which will come to you with great glory
and with the splendor of the Everlasting.

My tender sons have traveled rough roads;
they were taken away like a flock carried off by the enemy.
Take courage, my children, and cry to God,
for you will be remembered by him who brought this upon you.
For just as you purposed to go astray from God,
return with tenfold zeal to seek him.
For he who brought these calamities upon you
will bring you everlasting joy with your salvation.
Take courage, O Jerusalem,
for he who named you will comfort you.

—Baruch 4:21–24, 26–30

IN GOD'S PRESENCE, CONSIDER . . .

Do I mistake trials and setbacks as signs that my God is far from me? Or do I recognize that my weariness and sorrow are crafted by God to fling me back into His love and mercy? God has one purpose for my life, which is total fulfillment in Him.

CLOSING PRAYER

Lord of Hosts, God of Power, open my eyes to Your Divine Providence. Your Holy Will is not lagging, is not limited, but here and now guides the course of nations, the course of world events, and the deepest paths of my own life. Allow me to recognize that all things are providentially gifted to bring me into Your joy. Nothing but my will can keep me from You.

The Prodigal Father

The word prodigal means to squander. Used in a negative sense, it means "to squander or waste money or resources, to be rashly and recklessly extravagant." But used in a positive sense, it means "to squander gifts, to be filled with great abundance and to be lavish in giving generously, freely, and profusely. In the Parable of the Prodigal Son, our focus is meant to be drawn ultimately to the father. And He, in the positive sense of the word, is prodigal.

When the prodigal son returns home, he is met by the prodigal *father*, a father who is so full of love that he gives it out freely and in abundance, not based on merit, but on relationship: "This *son of mine* was dead and is alive again."

In this father, we see God the Father, the Father who is "Rich in Mercy," the Father who is "visible" for us in the Divine Mercy Image. He is the Prodigal Father, full of love and compassion, always watching and waiting for us to come home. . . . He is always blessing, always inviting us back into His Heart, always squandering grace, squandering love, squandering mercy. . . .

The father had certainly been hurt by the behavior of both his sons, and in terms of strict justice could have responded very differently. But, as Pope John Paul II points out, "After all, it was his own son who was involved, and such a relationship could never be altered or destroyed by any sort of behavior (*Rich in Mercy*, #5).

Any sort of behavior? Does that mean that the father is condoning his son's actions? . . . No. It means that God the Father never acts apart from His fatherhood. He sees your behavior, and it wounds Him, but His focus is not on your behavior, and it's not on Himself. It's always on you and on the relationship He longs to have with you as His beloved son or daughter. He's always seeking what's best for you. Your sin wounds Him because it wounds you—it pulls you away from Him.

—Vinny Flynn, *7 Secrets of Divine Mercy*

IN GOD'S PRESENCE, CONSIDER . . .

Returning to his father, the younger son felt that he no longer deserved to be treated as a son; he had lost his right to sonship. He didn't really know his father. What about me when I've fallen into sin? Do I really know my Father? Do I know that with Him it's not about deserving, not about behavior, but about a broken relationship that can be restored in His mercy?

CLOSING PRAYER

Father God, help me to repent and turn back to You whenever I've sinned, but to do so with trust, knowing that we can never lose sonship or daughtership, that You never disown Your children. Thank you for always waiting for us to come home.

God Thinks with Mercy

God is thinking about us all the time, and He always thinks as the merciful Father, waiting for us to come back to Him.

God always thinks with mercy: do not forget this. God always thinks mercifully. He is the merciful Father! God thinks like the father waiting for the son and goes to meet him, he spots him coming when he is still far off. . . .

What does this mean? That he went every day to see if his son was coming home: this is our merciful Father. It indicates that he was waiting for him with longing on the terrace of his house. God thinks like the Samaritan who did not pass by the unfortunate man, pitying him or looking at him from the other side of the road, but helped him without asking for anything in return; without asking whether he was a Jew, a pagan or a Samaritan, whether he was rich or poor: he asked for nothing. He went to help him: God is like this. God thinks like the shepherd who lays down his life in order to defend and save his sheep.

—Pope Francis, General Audience, Wednesday, March 27, 2013

IN GOD'S PRESENCE, CONSIDER . . .

When I think about God, do I see Him as a merciful Father always thinking about me with love, always waiting for me to come closer to Him, always longing to help me along the way? And when I think about others, do I think with mercy?

CLOSING PRAYER

Lord help me to believe—and never forget—that you are thinking of me with merciful love. Make my thoughts like Yours. Make my heart like Yours.

Those Who Are Sick

Following immediately after Jesus's healing of the paralytic (Mt 9:1–8), today Jesus's mercy frees Matthew from the paralysis of his sin and alienation from God.

As Jesus passed on from there, he saw a man called Matthew sitting at the tax office; and he said to him, "Follow me." And he rose and followed him.

And as he sat at table in the house, behold, many tax collectors and sinners came and sat down with Jesus and his disciples. And when the Pharisees saw this, they said to his disciples, "Why does your teacher eat with tax collectors and sinners?" But when he heard it, he said, "Those who are well have no need of a physician, but those who are sick. Go and learn what this means, 'I desire mercy, and not sacrifice.' For I came not to call the righteous, but sinners."

—Matthew 9:9–13

IN GOD'S PRESENCE, CONSIDER . . .

Do I recognize that I am sick, or do I accept this culture's template and persist in my shallowness? I've permitted a profoundly collapsed vision of myself to define me: can I venture out into Jesus' call to follow Him and abandon the security of my old self? No matter where I'm at in the journey, there is always a deeper awareness of self and a deeper trust in Him to attain.

CLOSING PRAYER

Jesus, wherever You are, there is more. You continue to ask more of me, because You want to give me more. Help me enter into You more; without You, I can do nothing, but your radiant mercy can free me to embrace Your call more fully and follow You wholeheartedly.

Abandonment to Divine Mercy

When we awaken to the merciful love of God, we are able to abandon ourselves and all things into His hands with complete confidence.

The heart does not awaken to confidence until it awakens to love; we need to feel the gentleness and tenderness of the Heart of Jesus. This cannot be obtained except by the habit of meditative prayer, by this tender repose in God which is contemplative. Let us therefore learn to abandon ourselves, to have total confidence in God, in the big things as in the small, with the simplicity of little children. And God will manifest His tenderness, His providence and His fidelity in a manner sometimes overwhelming. If God treated us at certain moments with an apparently great harshness, He also has an unexpected delicateness, of which only a love as tender and pure as His is capable. . . . In the midst of our trials, we can experience these delicacies of Love. They are not reserved for the saints. They are for all the poor who believe that God is their Father. They can be for us a powerful encouragement to abandon ourselves to His care . . .

In abandoning myself to God, I experience in a concrete fashion that "it really works," that God makes all things work together for my good, even evil, even suffering, even my own sins. How many occasions I dreaded, when they arrived, in the final analysis proved to be supportable, and finally beneficial, after the first impact of pain. That which I believed to be working against me revealed itself to be to my benefit. Thus, I tell myself: that which God does for me in His infinite Mercy, He must do for others also; in a mysterious and hidden manner, He must do it for the entire world. We must put everything, without exception, into the hands of God, not seeking any longer to manage or "to save" ourselves by our own means . . . The measure of our interior peace will be that of our abandonment . . .

—Fr. Jacques Philippe, *Searching for and Maintaining Peace*, pp. 35–37

IN GOD'S PRESENCE, CONSIDER . . .

It is good to remember the goodness and the providence of God. Are there times where things seemed insurmountable, or where a situation or something in me seemed too broken, and yet God brought good out of it? I determine now to abandon everything to His mercy.

CLOSING PRAYER

Father, awaken my heart to Your love. Let me see more and more clearly how worthy You are of my full confidence. From this moment on I want to abandon myself and everything that happens in and around me to the transforming touch of Your mercy.

. . . Got Confidence?

We are reminded by de Caussade that nothing is beyond God. And His mercy towards us is such that everything that happens in life, even that which causes difficulty and confusion, is permitted in His Providence and will be used for our good.

[M]aking use of all our powers to love Him for Himself we shall regain with interest by this pure love all that we seem to have sacrificed; therefore, far from losing, we gain all in abandoning ourselves entirely to God by love and confidence. . . . Keep steadfast my dear daughter, in the midst of your violent interior afflictions, and never relinquish the practice of entire abandonment to God, and of perfect confidence in His goodness.

Encourage yourself with these two obvious and invariable principles: first, that God will never abandon any who have abandoned themselves entirely to Him, and who trust completely in His infinite mercy. Secondly, that nothing happens in this world that is not according to the decrees of Providence who turns all things to the advantage and greater profit of souls that are submissive and resigned. Contrary thoughts and interior combats will only serve, if you remain faithful, to strengthen in your mind, and to root more firmly in your heart, the truths and feelings so necessary for your sanctification.

—Rev. Jean-Pierre de Caussade SJ, *Abandonment to Divine Providence*

IN GOD'S PRESENCE, CONSIDER . . .

Where do I have trouble abandoning myself totally to you, Lord, the places where I want to retain some control? Is there part of me that doubts Your goodness and Your loving plan for me and those I love?

CLOSING PRAYER

Lord, I know that only when I abandon myself completely to You, will I find the deepest freedom, the deepest peace. Help me to relinquish to You all the areas where I hold onto control and where I lack trust. I speak this truth and desire to live it: You are good. You are trustworthy. I surrender myself in all things to Your Providence and to Your mercy.

The Measure of Love

The more we come to know God, the more we will love Him. Yet we busy ourselves with so many other things, which in His mercy He allows, though they grieve Him. Brother Lawrence exhorts us to increase our devotion and faith and focus solely on loving God.

God knows best what we need and everything He does is for our good; if we knew how much He loves us, we would always be ready to receive from Him, with equanimity, the sweet and the bitter, and even the most painful and most difficult of trials would be pleasing and agreeable. . . .

Let us devote ourselves entirely to knowing God; the more we know Him the more we want to know Him. Knowledge is commonly the measure of love; the deeper and wider our knowledge, the greater will be our love; and if our love of God is great, we will love Him equally in sorrow and in joy.

Let us not be satisfied with loving God because of the graces He has given us or may give us, however great they may be; these favors, great though they are, will never bring us as near to Him as does one simple act of faith. Let us seek Him often by faith. He is in the midst of us; we do not need to seek Him elsewhere. Are we not ill-mannered, even culpable, to leave Him alone, while we busy ourselves with a thousand and one trivial matters which displease Him and perhaps even offend Him? Though He tolerates them, it is to be feared that one day they will cost us dearly.

Let us begin to be devoted to Him in earnest, banishing from our hearts and minds all else. He wishes to be there alone; let us ask this grace of Him. If on our part we do the best we can, we will soon see in ourselves the changes that we are hoping for.

—Brother Lawrence, *The Practice of the Presence of God*

IN GOD'S PRESENCE, CONSIDER . . .

Do I receive whatever happens each day, joy or trial, as if it is a gift of God's mercy to me, trusting that He will work all things to good in His love? How readily I want to turn to comfort and ease! And similarly, how often am I captivated by the world, getting caught up in trivial things that are not helpful to my relationship with God and my journey to holiness?

CLOSING PRAYER

Father of mercy, banish from my mind and heart all that is not of You. Help me to spend more of my time each day coming to know You, that I might love You for Yourself and not Your gifts, and that I might surrender myself to You ever more completely.

Beauty So Ancient . . .

All God wants is my whole heart, a free gift of self, so that there can be a mutual exchange of love. No matter how much I struggle with that process, He never tires of bestowing mercy on me to this end.

Late have I loved you, Beauty so ancient and so new, late have I loved you!

Lo, you were within, but I outside, seeking there for you,
and upon the shapely things you have made I rushed headlong—I, misshapen.
You were with me, but I was not with you.
They held me back far from you, those things which would have no being,
were they not in you.

You called, shouted, broke through my deafness; you flared, blazed, banished my blindness; you lavished your fragrance, I gasped; and now I pant for you;

I tasted you, and now I hunger and thirst; you touched me, and I burned for your peace.

When at last I cling to you with my whole being there will be no more anguish or labor for me, and my life will be alive indeed, alive because filled with you. But now it is very different. Anyone whom you fill you also uplift; but I am not full of you, and so I am a burden to myself. Joys over which I ought to weep do battle with sorrows that should be matter for joy, and I do not know which will be victorious. But I also see griefs that are evil at war in me with joys that are good, and I do not know which will win the day. This is agony, Lord, have pity on me! It is agony! See, I do not hide my wounds; you are the physician and I am sick; you are merciful, I in need of mercy. . . .

On your exceedingly great mercy, and on that alone, rests all my hope.

—St. Augustine, *Confessions*, "Late have I loved Thee."

IN GOD'S PRESENCE, CONSIDER . . .

Many times I have run after the gifts and not the Giver. Mercy, Lord. Even after giving my heart to God I am at war within. He wants my whole heart. I want to give it to Him.

CLOSING PRAYER

Beauty so ancient, everything I seek is found in You. Purify my heart with Your great mercy.

The Loving Kindness of Our Savior

St. Paul gives instructions to the bishop Titus on guiding the Christian community. Everything is established in mercy.

Remind them to be submissive to rulers and authorities, to be obedient, to be ready for any honest work, to speak evil of no one, to avoid quarreling, to be gentle, and to show perfect courtesy toward all men. For we ourselves were once foolish, disobedient, led astray, slaves to various passions and pleasures, passing our days in malice and envy, hated by men and hating one another; but when the goodness and loving kindness of God our Savior appeared, he saved us, not because of deeds done by us in righteousness, but in virtue of his own mercy, by the washing of regeneration and renewal in the Holy Spirit, which he poured out upon us richly through Jesus Christ our Savior, so that we might be justified by his grace and become heirs in hope of eternal life.

—Titus 3:1–7

IN GOD'S PRESENCE, CONSIDER . . .

How long will I believe that it's what I do that earns God's love for me? What will it take for me to realize that He loves me because of who He is, and because of what He's made me for? I inherit limitless love. And, in light of the abundant mercy I have been shown, my life as a Christian is meant to reflect His love.

CLOSING PRAYER

Heavenly Father, I want to experience regeneration and renewal in the Holy Spirit. Thank you for sending St. Paul to me today; pour Your blessing richly upon me and let my life reveal Your goodness.

Hanging On a Hair of Mercy . . .

Chesterton describes the difference between the cynical lack of expectations, which results in a lack of disappointment, and a lack of expectations that creates the fertile soil for enjoying all that comes to us with awe and delight, seeing it all as a gift and, in some sense, miracle of mercy.

It is commonly in a somewhat cynical sense that men have said, "Blessed is he that expects nothing, for he shall not be disappointed". It was in a wholly happy and enthusiastic sense that St. Francis said. "Blessed is he who expects nothing, for he shall enjoy everything".

It was by this deliberate idea of starting from zero, from the dark nothingness of his own deserts, that he did come to enjoy even earthly things as few people have enjoyed them; and they are in themselves the best working example of the idea. For there is no way in which a man can earn a star or deserve a sunset. But there is more than this involved, and more indeed than is easily to be expressed in words. It is not only true that the less a man thinks of himself, the more he thinks of his good luck and of all the gifts of God. It is also true that he sees more of the things themselves when he sees more of their origin; for their origin is a part of them and indeed the most important part. . . .

Recognizing the world's awesomeness and fragility—this grandeur held together by the breath of the Creator—is seeing reality. Ordinariness is the delusion of self-sufficiency. . . .

That we all depend in every detail, at every instant, as a Christian would say upon God, as even an agnostic would say upon existence and the nature of things, is not an illusion of imagination; on the contrary, it is the fundamental fact which we cover up, as with curtains, with the illusion of ordinary life. That ordinary life is an admirable thing in itself, just as imagination is an admirable thing in itself. But it is much more the ordinary life that is made of imagination than the contemplative life. He who has seen the whole world hanging on a hair of the mercy of God has seen the truth . . .

—G.K. Chesterton, *St. Francis of Assisi*

IN GOD'S PRESENCE, CONSIDER . . .

How often do I take the things (and people) around me for granted—the wonders and beauty of creation, the things I have come to see as ordinary and so fail to treasure as gift? Do I allow the goodness around me to draw me into deeper union with God, the Origin of all goodness?

CLOSING PRAYER

Father, every good thing comes from You, and the more I can enter into that reality, the more I will find joy and delight in even the simplest thing or circumstance. Help me to focus more with gratitude on your gifts each day, to see them as reflections of Your goodness and the outpouring of Your mercy on the world.

I Am Ready

One of the great spiritual masters of the interior life, Fr. Gabriel of St Mary Magdalen gives us an advent meditation that is applicable at any time, because it speaks of our desire for union with God and our great need for Him to come into every part of our lives and beings.

O sweetest Jesus, You come to me with Your infinite love and the abundance of Your grace; You desire to engulf my soul in torrents of mercy and charity in order to draw it to You. Come, O Lord, come! I, too, wish to run to You with love, but alas! My love is so limited, weak, and imperfect! Make it strong and generous; enable me to overcome myself, so that I can give myself entirely to You, Yes, my love can become strong because "its foundation is the intimate certainty that it will be repaid by the love of God. O Lord, I cannot doubt Your tenderness, because You have given me proofs of it in so many ways, with the sole purpose of convincing me of it. Therefore, trusting in Your love, my weak love will become strong with Your strength. What a consolation it will be, O Lord, at the moment of death to think that we shall be judged by Him whom we have loved above all things! Then we can enter Your presence with confidence, despite the weight of our offenses!"

O Lord, give me love like this! I desire it ardently . . . My poor soul needs You so much! It sighs for You as for a compassionate physician, who alone can heal its wounds, draw it out of its languor and tepidity, and infuse into it new vigor, new enthusiasm, new life. Come Lord, come! I am ready to welcome Your work with a docile, humble heart, ready to let myself be healed, purified, and strengthened by You. Yes, with Your help, I will make any sacrifice, renounce everything that might hinder Your redeeming work in me. Show Your power, O Lord, and come!

Come, delay no longer!

—An Advent Meditation by Father Gabriel
of St. Mary Magdalen, OCD

IN GOD'S PRESENCE, CONSIDER . . .

Do I love God above all things? I consider whether I truly want Him more than anything else, whether His love is the most important thing in my life.

CLOSING PRAYER

Gracious God, You have given me so much and yet I have so much need of You still. But I trust that this is what You desire, to fill me with mercy and give me more and more of Yourself. Help me to give myself entirely to You.

No Worries, No Troubles

Father Stinissen comments on De Caussade's classic work and tells us that not even our troubles need to be a source of trouble for us if we see everything in light of God's mercy.

"You continue to cling to your fears and doubts", he writes to a sister who complains to him. "You study them too much, instead of despising them and abandoning yourself entirely to God as I have preached to you for a long time past. Without this happy and holy abandonment you will never enjoy a solid peace." Just as God's Providence is so all-encompassing that nothing falls outside of it and that even sin finds its proper place in it, so also, our surrender ought to be so perfect that even our worry, our troubles, and our temptations are enclosed in it and fall into place in it. Not even our troubles need to be a source of trouble. We cannot always live in total peace. "If God takes away your peace of mind, very well, let it go with the rest; God remains always, and when nothing else is left to you."

Sometimes God can seem cruel. We can get the impression that it is he who is the great tormentor. But if he tries us, it is because his mercy never gives up. He continues to believe all things, hope all things, and try all things to get us to let go and surrender. Instead of thinking that God is impossible, we ought to be thankful that he never gets discouraged. (Quotes from De Caussade, *Abandonment to Divine Providence*)

—Wilfrid Stinissen, *Into Your Hands, Father*

IN GOD'S PRESENCE, CONSIDER . . .

Do I really believe that, whatever happens, I am held in the arms of an all-merciful and all-powerful Father? Can I see everything as the merciful God trying to get me to finally let go and surrender myself to Him completely?

CLOSING PRAYER

Father, give me more faith in Your all-encompassing Providence. Help me trust that nothing falls outside of it, no temptations, no troubles, no circumstances. You are good. And You turn all things to good for those who love You. Help me live this "happy and holy abandonment."

The Incarnate Son Endures the World's Pain

Robert Stackpole reveals the extraordinary beauty of the Incarnation: now the infinite love of God reaches us through a human heart.

According to St. Thomas Aquinas, the supreme manifestation of God's mercy is the sending of His divine Son into the world to share our human nature and to make "atonement" or "satisfaction" for our sins. . . . British theologian John Saward sums up St. Thomas's viewpoint on this matter as follows:

> It is through the mercy, affective as well as effective, of his real human heart that Christ manifests the infinitely effective mercy of God. . . . In his manhood the Son of God knows by experience human misery, which as God he knew from eternity by simple knowledge. God incarnate does not just know about human misery; he has felt it ("Love's Second Name: St. Thomas on Mercy," *Canadian Catholic Review*, March, 1990, p. 92).

In fact, according to St. Thomas, our Savior experienced every general kind of human suffering. He suffered in body and soul, and in all His senses . . . suffered the greatest pain (bodily, emotional, and spiritual) that any human being could possibly experience. Saint Thomas writes:

> His body was superbly put together, for it was formed miraculously by the operation of the Holy Spirit . . . and so his sense of touch, the sense through which we experience pain, was extremely keen. His soul, likewise, by all its interior powers, perceived all the causes of sorrow with the greatest clarity (*ST* III.46.6).

Thus, through His infused and beatific knowledge, He foresaw prophetically the entire future of the human race—all human sins and miseries for which He was offering His life on the Cross. As Saward puts it: "To remove the vast burden of the world's guilt, the incarnate Son lovingly endures the vast burden of the world's pain" (p. 92).

—Dr. Robert Stackpole, *A Guide to Divine Mercy from Genesis to Benedict XVI*

IN GOD'S PRESENCE, CONSIDER . . .

Through the reality of the Incarnation, can I recognize how deeply loved I am?

CLOSING PRAYER

Jesus, from Your tiny body in the womb, to Your corpse taken down from the cross, to Your living presence in the Eucharist, You reveal that my body—and soul—are fully loved by You.

Why the Robin's Breast Was Red

Since God is not subject to time, but sees past, present, and future all at once, Jesus saw you and me from the cross; and our actions now affected Him then. What I do now either consoles Him or increases the suffering of His Passion.

The Savior, bowed beneath his cross, climbed up the dreary hill,
And from the agonizing wreath ran many a crimson rill;
The cruel Roman thrust him on with un-relenting hand,
Till, staggering slowly mid the crowd, He fell upon the sand.

A little bird that warbled near, that memorable day,
Flitted around and strove to wrench one single thorn away;
The cruel spike impaled his breast,—and thus, 't is sweetly said,
The Robin has his silver vest incarnadined with red.

Ah, Jesu! Jesu! Son of man! My dolor and my sighs.
Reveal the lesson taught by this winged Ishmael of the skies.
I, in the palace of delight or cavern of despair,
Have plucked no thorns from thy dear brow,
but planted thousands there!

—James Ryder Randall

IN GOD'S PRESENCE, CONSIDER . . .

At each moment I can choose to be either the cruel Roman or the robin. My every action either plucks a thorn from Christ's brow or pushes another in. What will I choose?

CLOSING PRAYER

Jesus, help me realize that my sins contributed to Your agony. Forgive me, Lord, for all the times and ways that I've hurt You. From now on, let me do only what will console You.

Called Out of Darkness

Our first Supreme Pontiff encourages us to let the mercy we have all received draw us into the Body of Christ, the Church. And, as the rock on whom the Church was built, he instructs us on becoming living stones and living a new life of light and belonging.

So put away all malice and all guile and insincerity and envy and all slander. Like newborn babes, long for the pure spiritual milk, that by it you may grow up to salvation; for you have tasted the kindness of the Lord.

Come to him, to that living stone, rejected by men but in God's sight chosen and precious; and like living stones be yourselves built into a spiritual house, to be a holy priesthood, to offer spiritual sacrifices acceptable to God through Jesus Christ. But you are a chosen race, a royal priesthood, a holy nation, God's own people, that you may declare the wonderful deeds of him who called you out of darkness into his marvelous light. Once you were no people but now you are God's people; once you had not received mercy but now you have received mercy.

—1 Peter 2:1–5, 9–10

IN GOD'S PRESENCE, CONSIDER . . .

After his three-fold denial, Peter had "tasted the kindness of the Lord" in the gaze of Jesus (see Lk.22:61) and the opportunity to repent and repair around a charcoal fire (see John 21:15). I, too, have been given so much, especially through the Holy Catholic Church, where I encounter the living Presence of God and receive so much of His grace and mercy. How have I strayed from living out the life He has called me to? How do I need to repent and repair so that I can be His more completely?

CLOSING PRAYER

O Lord, You called your people through the desert to enter the Promised Land. You then opened the gates of salvation to all and brought me into Your family. Pour forth Your Holy Spirit on the Church today, the Bride of Christ, and allow us to shine with Your mercy here on earth.

Believing Even in Darkness

Fr. Jean C.J. D'Elbee writes of St. Therese of Liseux's confident love.

And when Jesus conceals Himself during grievous interior trials such as dryness, aridity, anguish in darkness, when all the words of love, confidence, abandonment say nothing more to us, do not touch us, do not reach us anymore, what then? What soul has not passed through these nights?

It is then that we must push confidence to the extreme limits. These trials are graces, because they are occasions for pure faith. Pure love is realized in pure faith, and pure faith, is realized in darkness in the same way as "strength is perfected in weakness" (2 Cor. 12:9). Profit, profit from these dark hours when your nature grieves, when your heart is cold, when you believe, wrongly, that Jesus is very far from you and even, perhaps, that He is turning His eyes away from you, because you see yourself to be so imperfect and wretched; profit from them to make heroic acts of faith and confidence out of pure will. These are the most precious acts—they have immense merit because in those times they are acts of pure faith, without consolation and without sensible aid.

That is the moment to say to Jesus, "You may sleep in my boat; I shall not awaken You. You are hiding Yourself, but I know well where You are hidden: You are in my heart. I do not feel it, but I know it. I Believe in Your love for me and I believe in my love for You."

—Jean C.J. d'Elbee, *I Believe in Love,* pp. 77–78

IN GOD'S PRESENCE, CONSIDER . . .

Am I confident enough in Jesus's love for me to allow Him to continue to sleep in my boat? When I cannot feel Him close to me, do I rest in confidence knowing that He remains close?

CLOSING PRAYER

Lord Jesus, I believe in Your love for me. Help me to rest with confidence in that love even when You remain hidden or seem distant.

And Yet We Still Choose

When we naturally want to turn from suffering, and long for the times when we were more zealous, there is a way we can allow our feelings to be what they are and still enter a deep and efficacious union with Jesus.

I grew up loving the seasons in New England and the way they fit especially well with the liturgical seasons of Lent and Easter. In fact, I liked the quiet and pensive solitude of winter and the melancholy of Lent more than the mud, lilies, and lightness of spring and Easter. I wanted to fast, find big sacrifices, and meditate on the Passion. And those times of fervent prayer and consolation are always a gift. But, as I get older, I'm more easily wearied by the cold and gray, and tend to lean more towards, "Ok, Jesus, I'm ready for You and the sun to rise!" That can feel at times like I'm failing at being present to Christ in His Passion, neglecting to suffer with Him, running from the cross . . . Yet, I see that He's given me specific crosses to bear through the years that I would *not* have chosen, and so the fervor and romanticism of the early years of self-determined sacrifices, have given way to the dreadful weight of powerlessness, the necessary precursor to surrender.

My old spiritual director used to say, it's the times where if we had the "I'm done" card, we'd throw it down; when the cross feels too heavy; when we feel like we don't trust that God really does have everything under control; when doubts assail us and His loving Presence seems far off, *and* yet we still *choose* to say, "Jesus I Trust in You"—those are the most efficacious times. He wants us to come to Him in vulnerability and trust—where our misery meets His mercy. That's when we draw close to Jesus's thirsting heart and when we most resemble Him. Even if we don't feel it, the Father's loving gaze rests on us as we fall imperfectly next to the perfect suffering Jesus in the Garden, who begged for the Cross to be taken, while simultaneously offering His yes to the Father. That's when we say, "I can't do this, I don't want to do this, but I trust in You; Your will be done." That's when we have died to our own persistent will and have emptied ourselves of everything but Him.

—Erin Flynn

IN GOD'S PRESENCE, CONSIDER . . .

Do I sometimes judge my spiritual life and growth on what's happening with my emotions? Is there shame present when I wish I could take an easier path on any given day? Is there fear when I think of suffering, because I feel abandoned by God, believe it will be too much, or that it won't end?

CLOSING PRAYER

Risen Lord, Your mercy is drawn by trust. Help me in all circumstances to allow myself to feel whatever emotions come, and simply relate them to You, inviting Your Presence into that space.

Boundless Confidence . . .

From Padre Pio comes this beautiful prayer of trust in Divine Mercy.

O Lord, we ask for a boundless confidence and trust in Your divine mercy, and the courage to accept the crosses and sufferings which bring immense goodness to our souls and that of Your Church.

Help us to love You with a pure and contrite heart, and to humble ourselves beneath Your cross, as we climb the mountain of holiness, carrying our cross that leads to heavenly glory.

May we receive You with great faith and love in Holy Communion, and allow You to act in us, as You desire, for Your greater glory.

O Jesus, most adorable heart and eternal fountain of Divine Love, may our prayer find favor before the Divine Majesty of Your Heavenly Father. Amen.

—St. Padre Pio

IN GOD'S PRESENCE, CONSIDER . . .

When do I find my trust in God's mercy waning? Are there certain areas or times in my life where I am more easily brought to doubt or mistrust? I consider that these are probably weak areas from my wounding and/or habitual sin, and so places of easy attack for the evil one, who desires to turn me from the goodness of God.

CLOSING PRAYER

Lord, I want to trust that every cross, every suffering You allow in my life can be a means of growth, holiness, and grace, even those that feel especially frightening or overwhelming, and touch something deep in me where I more easily doubt Your goodness and mercy. I resolve now to shore up those areas with Your grace, and I make an act of trust that You in Your profound kindness and mercy will help make me unwavering in trust even there. Each day—especially with every Holy Communion—let Your Presence in me fill up all the cracks of uncertainty and doubt.

My Only Desire

Contradicting the promethean autonomy of our modern age, St. Claude de la Colombière tells us to throw ourselves at the feet of Jesus and reminds us of our childlike dependence on God.

From the moment one has a real desire of giving oneself entirely to God, one enjoys great peace. I am sure that which you have found by Our Lord's mercy is the result of the sincere and fervent will which he has given you to serve him and belong to him without reserve. You would indeed be miserable if there were anything in the world that could trouble you, for there is nothing that can prevent you from becoming a saint, in fact everything may help you to become one. There is nothing, not even our sins, from which we may not gain advantage for our sanctification, through the knowledge they give us of ourselves and by the renewal of fervor with which they inspire us.

This being so, I do not see what could happen that could prevent you gaining profit if only you have enough faith to realize that nothing happens to you except by God's permission and enough submission to conform yourself to his will. If ever you have a fit of sadness or trouble, remember that it is because you are still attached to life, or health, or some comfort, or person, or thing . . . Every time your heart feels troubled, be sure that it is caused by some unmortified passion and that it is a fruit of self-love which is not yet dead. Thinking this, throw yourself at the feet of Jesus crucified, and say: My Savior, do I still desire something which is not thee? Art thou not sufficient for me, shall I not love thee alone and be content to be loved only by thee? What have I come to seek, O my God, if not thee? . . . What does it matter what they say of me, or if I am loved or despised, well or ill, occupied with this work or with that, placed with these people or with others? Provided that I am with thee, and thou with me, I am content.

—*The Spiritual Direction of Saint Claude de la Colombière*

IN GOD'S PRESENCE, CONSIDER . . .

Do I remember my Savior's words that His yoke is easy, His burden light? As I encounter afflictions and trials in this life and feel a sense of burden or overwhelm, does it immediately signal to me that I have strayed from gentle dependence on God and am trying to forge my own way?

CLOSING PRAYER

Lord of all creation, You have lovingly fashioned all things, and are at this moment directing all things, for my benefit and sanctification. Release me from the lie of self-dependence, and help me recognize that all things come from Your loving hand and that You are trustworthy.

Born Anew to a Living Hope

Through the great gift of mercy bestowed on us in Christ, we have been made new and now must live with the deep awareness of that mercy, which changes everything. Through that gift we are brought to a living hope—a hope we cling to until the end.

Blessed be the God and Father of our Lord Jesus Christ! By his great mercy we have been born anew to a living hope through the resurrection of Jesus Christ from the dead, and to an inheritance which is imperishable, undefiled, and unfading, kept in heaven for you . . . In this you rejoice, though now for a little while you may have to suffer various trials, so that the genuineness of your faith, more precious than gold which though perishable is tested by fire, may redound to praise and glory and honor at the revelation of Jesus Christ. Without having seen him you love him; though you do not now see him you believe in him and rejoice with unutterable and exalted joy. As the outcome of your faith you obtain the salvation of your souls.

Therefore gird up your minds, be sober, set your hope fully upon the grace that is coming to you at the revelation of Jesus Christ. As obedient children, do not be conformed to the passions of your former ignorance, but as he who called you is holy, be holy yourselves in all your conduct; since it is written, "You shall be holy, for I am holy." . . . You know that you were ransomed from the futile ways inherited from your fathers, not with perishable things such as silver or gold, but with the precious blood of Christ, like that of a lamb without blemish or spot. . . . Through him you have confidence in God, who raised him from the dead and gave him glory, so that your faith and hope are in God.

Having purified your souls by your obedience to the truth for a sincere love of the brethren, love one another earnestly from the heart.

—1 Peter 1:3–4, 6–9, 13–16, 18–19, 21–22

IN GOD'S PRESENCE, CONSIDER . . .

Can I accept that God always wants to do something new in me? Am I willing to have Him permeate me with mercy and rewrite my story and my destiny? Will I participate fully in this work of holiness He wants to accomplish in me?

CLOSING PRAYER

Lord Jesus Christ, pour forth Your holy Blood over me, washing me clean and making me holy in Your presence. I set my hope fully on Your grace and my confidence on Your mercy.

Wedding Garment

Reflecting on the Parable of the Wedding Banquet . . . (cf. Mt 22:1–14), Pope Francis speaks of the king who throws a marriage feast for his son as the image of God the Father, who has "prepared for the entire human family a wonderful celebration of love."

The king in the parable does not want the hall to remain empty, because he wants to offer the treasures of his kingdom. So he tells his servants: "Go therefore to the thoroughfares, and invite to the marriage feast as many as you find" (v. 9). . . .

It is to this humanity of the thoroughfares that the king in the parable sends his servants. . . . The banquet hall is filled with the "excluded," those who are "outside," those who never seemed worthy to partake in a feast. . . . The king tells the messengers: "Call everyone, both good and bad. Everyone!" God even calls those who are bad. "No, I am bad; I have done many [bad things]. . . . ". He calls you: "Come, come, come!" . . . God is not afraid of our spirits wounded by many cruelties because he loves us; he invites us. . . . He prepares his banquet for everyone: the just and sinners, good and bad, intelligent and uneducated. . . .

The Lord places one condition: to wear a wedding garment. . . . When the hall is full, the king arrives and greets the latest guests, but he sees one of them without a wedding garment. . . . The people went . . . as they were able to be dressed; they were not wearing gala attire. But at the entrance, they were given a type of capelet, a gift. That man, having rejected the free gift, excluded himself: the king could do nothing but throw him out. This man accepted the invitation but then decided that it meant nothing to him: . . . he had no desire to change or to allow the Lord to change him. The wedding garment—this capelet—symbolizes the mercy that God freely gives us; namely, grace. Without grace, we cannot take a step forward in Christian life. Everything is grace. It is not enough to accept the invitation to follow the Lord; one must be open to a journey of conversion, which changes the heart. The garment of mercy, which God offers us unceasingly, is the free gift of his love.

—Pope Francis, Angelus, October 11, 2020

IN GOD'S PRESENCE, CONSIDER . . .

Like the invited guests who refuse to attend, do I sometimes put my own interests and material things ahead of the Lord who calls me? Do I refuse His gift of grace that will transform me because part of me finds comfort in old habits?

CLOSING PRAYER

Lord, draw me deeper into daily conversion of heart. Clothe me in the garment of mercy.

Gather the Gems

In the Sermon on the Mount, Jesus urges us to store up treasures for ourselves in heaven (see Mt 6:20). He's pouring those treasures out upon us and wants us to gather as much as we can. It's okay to be greedy for grace.

Once the Lord said to me, Act like a beggar who does not back away when he gets more alms [than he asked for], but offers thanks the more fervently. You too should not back away and say that you are not worthy of receiving greater graces when I give them to you. I know you are unworthy, but rejoice all the more and take as many treasures from My Heart as you can carry, for then you will please Me more. And I will tell you one more thing: Take these graces not only for yourself, but also for others; that is, encourage the souls with whom you come in contact to trust in My infinite mercy. Oh, how I love those souls who have complete confidence in Me. I will do everything for them. . . .

The Lord said to me, I want to give myself to souls and to fill them with My love, but few there are who want to accept all the graces My love has intended for them. My grace is not lost; if the soul for whom it was intended does not accept it, another soul takes it. . . .

Today I saw the Crucified Lord Jesus. Precious pearls and diamonds were pouring forth from the wound in His Heart. I saw how a multitude of souls was gathering these gifts, but there was one soul who was closest to His Heart and she, knowing the greatness of these gifts, was gathering them with liberality, not only for herself, but for others as well. The Savior said to me, Behold, the treasures of grace that flow down upon souls, but not all souls know how to take advantage of My generosity.

—St. Faustina, *Diary*, 294, 1017, 1687

IN GOD'S PRESENCE, CONSIDER . . .

Do I really believe that the Lord wants to shower us with graces, and do I actively ask and seek them from Him, trusting that He wants to give us more and more?

CLOSING PRAYER

Jesus, help me to realize that everything is grace, and to live in joyful expectation, gathering gems of grace for myself and others.

Single-minded Focus on Virtue

Writing from the earliest days of the Church, fourth pope St. Clement of Rome guides us as one of the Apostolic Fathers, allowing us to have whole-hearted trust in a merciful Father.

The all-merciful and beneficent Father has compassion on those who fear Him, and willingly and with tender regard bestows His graces on those who approach Him single-minded. Therefore let us not be double-minded, and let not our soul mistrust . . . His gifts are all-surpassing and glorious. . . . .

Let us stand in awe of Him, and abandon any seeking after evil things: thus shall we by His mercy find shelter from the judgment to come. Indeed, where can any one of us flee from His mighty hand? What world is there to receive anyone deserting Him? For somewhere the Writing says, "Where then shall I go, and where shall I hide from Your presence? If I ascend into heaven, You are there; if I go away even to the uttermost parts of the earth, there is Your right hand; if I make my bed in the abyss, there is Your Spirit." Where, then, shall anyone go, or where shall he escape from Him who embraces the universe?

Let us, then, approach Him in holiness of soul, raising pure and unsullied hands to Him, loving our forbearing and compassionate Father, who has made us His chosen portion. . . .

Since, then, we are a holy portion, let us do nothing but what makes for holiness, shunning slander, foul and impure embraces, together with all drunkenness, rebellious desires and passions, detestable adultery, and abominable pride. . . . let us with humble minds put on the livery of concord, be self-restrained, keep ourselves free from all backbiting and slanderous talk; and let us seek justification by actions, and not just words. . . . let us unhesitatingly submit to His will: with all our strength let us achieve the work of sanctification.

—St. Clement, *First Epistle to the Corinthians*, 23–30

IN GOD'S PRESENCE, CONSIDER . . .

Am I all in? Today can I reaffirm my trust in God and fling aside any lingering doubt in His goodness? I want to be single-minded and seek holiness above all else—all with total trust in His mercy. I want to be able to say in the depths of my being, "I trust in God!"

CLOSING PRAYER

Lord of Heaven and Earth, You have guided the course of creation since the dawn of time. Watch over my life today, and allow me to experience Your providential hand, as I attempt to walk in the way of holiness.

The Abyss of Mercy

In John 15:1–8, Jesus depicts himself as the true vine and God the Father as the vine grower. He calls us to "remain in Him"; and if we do, he promises that we will "bear much fruit." Blessed Elizabeth of the Trinity reflects on this Gospel in a retreat written for her sister, speaking of how this "abiding" calls for deep solitude, entering a place where our nothingness encounters the immensity of God. It is the theme of John of the Cross, the "todo"—all or everything—of God face to face with the "nada"—nothingness—of man.

"Remain in Me." It is the Word of God who gives this order, expresses this wish. Remain in Me, not for a few moments, a few hours which must pass away, but "remain . . . " permanently, habitually. Remain in Me, pray in Me, adore in Me so that you may be able to encounter anyone or anything; penetrate further still into these depths. This is truly the "solitude into which God wants to allure the soul that He may speak to it," as the prophet sang [Hos 2:14/2:16].

In order to understand this very mysterious saying, we must not, so to speak, stop at the surface, but enter ever deeper into the divine Being through recollection. "I pursue my course," exclaimed St Paul [Phil. 3:12]; so must we descend daily this pathway of the Abyss which is God; let us slide down this slope in wholly loving confidence. "Abyss calls to abyss" [Ps 42:8/42:7]. It is there in the very depths that the divine impact takes place, where the abyss of our nothingness encounters the Abyss of mercy, the immensity of the all of God. There we will find the strength to die to ourselves and, losing all vestige of self, we will be changed into love.

—Blessed Elizabeth of the Trinity, *I Have Found God (Complete Works) or Heaven in Faith Day 2*

IN GOD'S PRESENCE, CONSIDER . . .

Our world is so busy, so loud and filled with stimuli. How have I created time and space and quiet to encounter God? How much of my focus is on truly abiding in Him at all times? And if God wants to allure my soul and lead me into the wilderness to speak to me, how am I going to carve out time so I can listen?

CLOSING PRAYER

God of mercy, I want to go to the depths, to the place where I can experience this divine impact where my emptiness meets the fullness of You, the abyss of my nothingness encounters the abyss of Your mercy. In my life, with the demands of my particular vocation, show me how to foster space within for this encounter—where I can meet You, hear You, remain in You. Change me into love.

From Misery to Mercy

Recognizing our own misery, our weakness and imperfections, shouldn't discourage us, writes St. Francis de Sales, but lead us to deeper trust in God's mercy.

You ask me if a soul sensible of its own misery can go with great confidence to God. I reply that not only can the soul that knows its misery have great confidence in God, but that unless it has such knowledge, the soul cannot have true confidence in Him; for it is this true knowledge and confession of our misery that brings us to God. . . .

The greater our knowledge of our own misery, the more profound will be our confidence in the goodness and mercy of God, for mercy and misery are so closely connected that the one cannot be exercised without the other. If God had not created man, He would still indeed have been perfect in goodness, but He would not have been actually merciful, since mercy can only be exercised toward the miserable.

You see, then, that the more miserable we know ourselves to be, the more occasion we have to confide in God, since we have nothing in ourselves in which we can trust. The mistrust of ourselves proceeds from the knowledge of our imperfections. It is a very good thing to mistrust ourselves, but how will it help us, unless we cast our whole confidence upon God and wait for His mercy? . . .

And even if you do not feel such confidence, you must still not fail to make acts of confidence, saying to our Lord, "Although, dear Lord, I have no feeling of confidence in Thee, I know all the same that Thou art my God, that I am wholly Thine, and that I have no hope but in Thy goodness; therefore I abandon myself entirely into Thy hands." . . . Neither must the consciousness of these miseries discourage us; rather it should make us raise our hearts to God by a holy confidence . . . . He is as good and merciful when we are weak and imperfect as when we are strong and perfect. . . . The throne of God's mercy is our misery; therefore the greater our misery, the greater should be our confidence.

—St. Francis de Sales, *The Art Of Loving God*

IN GOD'S PRESENCE, CONSIDER . . .

How much do I hide from myself my fragility? Do I mislead myself, pretending to be more competent, more at peace, when a more authentic glimpse would reveal the desperation I find myself in? That honesty would fling me into God's encompassing love!

CLOSING PRAYER

Heavenly Father, You look with compassion on the lost sheep, the sick in need of a physician, on me in my distress. Allow me also to recognize my need for You, that I may trust in You alone.

The God Who Grieves with Us

Jesus not only took on the sins of mankind, He hung with His broken body and grieved for the brokenness of the world. His Heart was united with our hearts—seeing the sin in them, the hurt, and all that needs mending. He won for us all the mercy we would ever need, and He wants us to let Him in to the places where we need Him most.

In the midst of dealing with life—relationships, finances, health, work—heart issues can sometimes get put on the back burner. . . . We close the doors on our anxieties, doubts, fears, and anything else unpleasant. *But they don't go away.* Instead, they remain in our souls like an untreated disease, a spiritual leprosy. . . . There are deep wounds within us that God longs to heal. . . . He wants to meet us in our broken places and open the doors we have closed, because He sees it all. From the Cross, He saw when you weren't awarded that honor in middle school; when your dad didn't have time for you; . . . when your mom died. In His then, He saw you now, struggling to pay the bills, trying to keep your marriage from growing stale, living with that addiction you hope no one finds out about, . . . wondering if the emptiness will ever go away. And as He hung on Calvary, He saw you tonight when that pregnancy test reads negative again, tomorrow when you get the news that your brother has cancer, next week as you're handed a pink slip . . .

He sees you. And your pain—even the smallest hurt—saddens Him! *He is the God who grieves with us.* How beautiful is that?! And in Christ, we have a Father who doesn't shy away from our leprosy, even when we don't want to face ourselves. Let us not be afraid to trust this God with all the details of our lives, journeying forward with Him into restoration and freedom . . .

—Mary Flynn, *A Study Guide for 7 Secrets of Divine Mercy*

IN GOD'S PRESENCE, CONSIDER . . .

What are the events or circumstances in my life that might need to be grieved? I can "offer things up" and not complain about suffering, while still recognizing that there may be pain or loss that deserves to be felt and perhaps grieved. "Jesus wept" (Jn 11:35). Can I go to those places with the Lord and allow His mercy to minister to me there?

CLOSING PRAYER

You are the God who sees. Thank you for not shying away from my mess, even when I close my eyes to it. Your sacrifice for me was already extravagant in mercy, but Your love is always more. You are always more. I invite You into every part of me. Show me the places within where I need Your Presence most.

Give Me Your Misery

No matter who we are or what our situation, we each have our own particular hardships, stresses, sufferings, struggles with sinful habits—in a word, misery. And, more than anything else, that's what the Lord wants us to offer Him.

O my Jesus, in thanksgiving for Your many graces, I offer You my body and soul, intellect and will, and all the sentiments of my heart. Through the vows, I have given myself entirely to You; I have then nothing more that I can offer You. Jesus said to me, My daughter, you have not offered Me that which is really yours. I probed deeply into myself and found that I love God with all the faculties of my soul and, unable to see what it was that I had not yet given to the Lord, I asked, "Jesus, tell me what it is, and I will give it to You at once with a generous heart." Jesus said to me with kindness, Daughter, give Me your misery, because it is your exclusive property. At that moment, a ray of light illumined my soul, and I saw the whole abyss of my misery. In that same moment I nestled close to the Most Sacred Heart of Jesus with so much trust that even if I had the sins of all the damned weighing on my conscience, I would not have doubted God's mercy but, with a heart crushed to dust, I would have thrown myself into the abyss of Your mercy. I believe, O Jesus, that You would not reject me, but would absolve me through the hand of Your representative.

—St. Faustina, *Diary*, 1318

IN GOD'S PRESENCE, CONSIDER . . .

Are there any pieces of my "exclusive property," any negative, sinful, or hurtful things in my life that I have not yet offered completely to the Lord?

CLOSING PRAYER

Jesus, give me the grace to face my sin and my sufferings head-on, without over-focusing on it all, or allowing my misery to distract me from living in Your love. Help me just to continually lift it up to You in trust, knowing that when I reveal my misery, I am met by Your mercy.

Kindness and Mercy

What if God were so good, and so powerful, and so wise, that everything He introduced into your life—what we call good and bad—was entirely from His mercy? St. Francis is famous for being one of our most joyful saints because he was so free with his heart. What we call poverty, he recognized as complete freedom in God. He offers guidance here to his brothers (and to us) on how to look upon and treat those whose sins we know, and those who seem to make our journey to holiness difficult.

I speak to you as best I can on the subject of your soul; that those things which impede you in loving the Lord God and whosoever may be a hindrance to you, whether brothers or others . . . all these things you ought to reckon as a favor . . . And love those that do such things to you . . . And by this I wish to know if you love God and me His servant and yours, to wit: that there be no brother in the world who has sinned, no matter how great his sin may be, who after he has seen your face shall ever go away without your mercy, if he seek mercy, and, if he does not seek mercy, ask him if he desires mercy. And if he afterwards appears before your face a thousand times, love him more than me, to the end that you may draw him to the Lord, and on such ones always have mercy . . .

If any brother, at the instigation of the enemy, sin mortally, let him be bound by obedience to have recourse to his guardian. And let all the brothers who know him to have sinned, not cause him shame or slander him, but let them have great mercy on him and keep very secret the sin of their brother, for they that are healthy need not a physician, but they that are ill. And let them be likewise bound by obedience to send him to his custos with a companion. And let the custos himself care for him mercifully as he himself would wish to be cared for by others if he were in a like situation.

—St. Francis of Assisi, *The Writings of Saint Francis of Assisi*

IN GOD'S PRESENCE, CONSIDER . . .

If any who have sinned look upon my face, do they find mercy there—or condescension, annoyance, judgment? Does everyone, even those who have sinned directly against me, leave my presence having encountered mercy? Do I always "keep very secret the sin" of others?

CLOSING PRAYER

Father of joy, no mercy I show can ever compare with what You have shown me. Eradicate all pride and let me only look upon those who are a "hindrance to me" or whose sin I become aware of, with great mercy. Let no one ever feel shame from my response, and may I never think in these situations of how merciful I am for showing mercy to others, but of how much less I deserve Your mercy.

Shelter

Gertrude the Great was a Benedictine nun and one of the renowned mystics of the thirteenth century. In this dialogue, she instructs the soul to see the intense love and goodness of God and respond to His mercy.

Awake, O my soul. How long will you remain asleep? Beyond the sky there is a King who wishes to possess you; He loves you immeasurably, with all His Heart. He loves you with so much kindness and faithfulness that He left His kingdom and humbled Himself for you, permitting Himself to be bound like a malefactor in order to find you. He loves you so strongly and tenderly, He is so jealous of you and has given you so many proofs of this, that He willingly gave up His Body to death. He bathed you in His Blood and redeemed you by His death. How long will you wait to love Him in return?

Make haste, then, to answer Him.

Behold, O loving Jesus, I come to You. I come, drawn by Your meekness, Your mercy, Your charity; I come with my whole heart and soul, and all my strength. . . . O Jesus, my King and my God, take me into the sweet shelter of Your divine Heart, and there unite me to Yourself in such a way that I shall live totally for You. Permit me to submerge myself henceforth in that vast sea of Your mercy, abandoning myself entirely to Your goodness, plunging into the burning furnace of Your love, and remaining there forever . . .

But what am I, O my God, I, so unlike You, the outcast of all creatures? But You are my supreme confidence, because in You can be found the supplement or rather, the abundance of all the favors I have lost. Enclose me, O Lord, in the sanctuary of Your Heart opened by the spear, establish me there, guarded by Your gentle glance, so that I may be confided to Your care forever: under the shadow of Your paternal love I shall find rest in the everlasting remembrance of Your most precious love.

—St. Gertrude of Helfta (1256–1301

IN GOD'S PRESENCE, CONSIDER . . .

I am bathed in the Blood of Jesus and made new. I am loved with such kindness and faithfulness. How long will I wait to truly love God in return and give Him everything?

CLOSING PRAYER

"O Jesus, my King and my God, take me into the sweet shelter of Your divine Heart, and there unite me to Yourself in such a way that I shall live totally for You. Permit me to submerge myself henceforth in that vast sea of Your mercy, abandoning myself entirely to Your goodness. . . . "

Perfection and Mercy

The wisdom of St. Ignatius of Loyola shines in this letter to the Fathers and Brothers studying at Coimbra, as he assures them that the perfection God asks of us is only attainable because of our cooperation with the outpouring of His mercy.

God, from whom all good things come, knows what comfort and joy it gives me to see that He so helps you, not only in your studies but in your pursuit of virtue as well. Indeed, the fragrance of these virtues has carried to very distant lands, to the encouragement and edification of many. If every Christian should rejoice because of the common obligation we all have of seeking God's honor and the welfare of His image, which has been redeemed by the blood and death of Jesus Christ, I have a special reason for rejoicing in our Lord, seeing that I have a distinct obligation of keeping you in my heart with a special affection. May our Creator and Redeemer be ever blessed and praised for all, since it is from His liberality that every blessing and grace flows, and may it please Him every day to open more and more the fountain of His mercy to increase and advance what He has already begun in your souls.

I have no doubt concerning that Supreme Goodness, who is so eager to share His blessings, or of that everlasting love which makes Him more eager to bestow perfection on us than we are to receive it. If this were not so, our Lord Jesus Christ would never encourage us to hope for what we can have only from His generous hand. For He tells us: Be you therefore perfect, as also your heavenly Father is perfect [Matt. 5:48]. Thus it is certain that for His part He is ready to bestow it, on condition that we have a vessel of humility and desire to receive His graces, and that He sees that we use well the gifts we have received and cooperate diligently and earnestly with His grace.

—St. Ignatius of Loyola

IN GOD'S PRESENCE, CONSIDER . . .

God wants all good things for me. And He is ready and willing to provide everything I need for whatever He begins in me or asks of me. There is always "more" with God. He is lavish with His graces; His mercy is a *fountain*; He is *Supreme* Goodness.

CLOSING PRAYER

Creator God, Your mercy astounds me, that You would be eager to bestow blessings on me; that You are invested in my life, my growth, my perfection. I want to always desire the "more" that You have for me, receive it with a humble and grateful heart, and do everything for Your greater glory.

O Mother of Mercy

St. Ildephonsus imagines a magnificent crown for the Blessed Virgin Mary, decorated with twelve radiant jewels. Writing about the first of these jewels, he honors her as the Mother of mercy, caring and interceding for us in every way.

O Virgin, full of every grace, wholly radiant and serene! You are the sacred and blessed resting place for the Son of God, resplendent in gold and dazzling in loveliness and glory! In the first place in your magnificent crown I shall place a topaz, excelling the sparkle of all other stones. This I do hoping to reflect the praise and glory of your singular excellence. . . . Topaz—a jewel more stunning than all other stones! For you surpass all other saints and angels in beauty of virtue, in splendor of holy charisms, and in the merits by which you are crowned. Because of the loveliness of all the good qualities you possess and the generous fruitfulness of all your mercies, you draw sinners to reconciliation. You encourage all those who struggle to fight on to the crown of their victorious reward, and you lead the just to the prize of eternal glory.

O Empress of the earth, and Queen of Heaven, when you bore your glorious Son—who was also the Son of God and our Savior—you abolished our servitude and restored our liberty! You refresh us in our anxiety; you comfort us in our adversity; you strengthen us in our weakness . . . you rescue us from demons . . . you unite us with our precious Redeemer!

O Mother of mercy, you untie that which is bound up; you lighten our afflictions; you heal the wounded; you obtain mercy for sinners; you revive those who are failing; you restore those who have fallen away; you give hope to those who despair. You renew honor; you rejuvenate faith; you pour forth grace and new strength. You alleviate anger; you restore our lost inheritance; you separate us from the devil; you purify us from sin—O most gracious Mother, you reconcile us to God himself!

—St. Ildephonsus, *Crown of the Virgin*

IN GOD'S PRESENCE, CONSIDER . . .

How loved I am by my Mother! She who bore the glorious Son of God, now leads me to discover the fullness of Divine Mercy as I draw near to her. No crown is radiant enough to reveal her excellence, her loveliness, her goodness!

CLOSING PRAYER

Most loving Mother, Queen of the Universe, gentle bride of the Holy Spirit, thank you for loving me and leading me to God. Untie with your merciful hands anything that binds me, protect me from the enemy of my soul, and keep me strong in faith.

Stumbling Towards Healing

With wisdom, and a candor few saints display, St. Isaac encourages those of us who stumble, and displays a vulnerability for us to emulate when talking to the Lord.

Do not fall into despair because of stumbling. I do not mean that you should not feel contrition for them, but that you should not think them incurable. For it is more expedient to be bruised than dead. There is, indeed, a Healer for the man who has stumbled, even He Who on the Cross asked that mercy be shown to His crucifiers, He Who pardoned His murderers while He hung on the Cross.

—The Ascetical Homilies of St. Isaac the Syrian, *Homily* 64

At the door of Your compassion do I knock, Lord; send aid to my scattered impulses which are intoxicated with the multitude of the passions and the power of darkness. You can see my sores hidden within me: stir up contrition—though not corresponding to the weight of my sins, for if I receive full awareness of the extent of my sins, Lord, my soul would be consumed by the bitter pain from them. Assist my feeble stirrings on the path to true repentance, and may I find alleviation from the vehemence of sins through the contrition that comes of Your gift, for without the power of Your grace I am quite unable to enter within myself, become aware of my stains, and so, at the sight of them be able to be still from great distraction.

—The Prayers of St. Isaac the Syrian, 7th century Bishop of Nineveh

IN GOD'S PRESENCE, CONSIDER . . .

Even if I stumble again and again, if I feel bruised and discouraged and utterly repentant, I will not think myself incurable. I will turn to the Healer with a contrite heart and trust in His mercy.

CLOSING PRAYER

O Lord, better bruised than dead. Thank You for the wit of saints and the inexhaustible nature of Your mercy. While I have life to stumble, I have life to turn again to You. Give me a truly repentant heart, and one that rests in You with gratitude.

The Rent Heart

It was in his 40's, according to Dr. Robert Stackpole, that St. John Eudes began to write of the merciful love flowing from the Sacred Heart of Jesus. Pope Pius XI identified Eudes as foremost in guiding us to the hearts of Jesus and Mary.

The first cause of those most painful wounds in the Sacred Heart of our Redeemer is our sins. We read in the life of St. Catherine of Genoa that one day God let her see the horror of one tiny venial sin. She assures us that, although this vision lasted but a moment, she saw nevertheless an object so frightening that the blood froze in her veins and she swooned away in an agony that would have killed her if God had not preserved her to relate to others what she had seen. . . . If the sight of the smallest venial sin brought this saint to such a pass, what must we think of the state to which our Savior was reduced by seeing all the sins of the universe? He had them continually before His eyes, and His vision being infinitely more powerful than that of St. Catherine, He could behold infinitely more horror. . . .

As He had infinite love for His Father and His creatures, the sight of all those sins rent His Heart with countless wounds, such that if we were able to count all the sins of men, which are more numerous than the drops of water in the sea, we would then be able to count the wounds of the loving Heart of Jesus.

The second cause of His wounds is the infinite love of His Sacred Heart for all of His children, and his constant vision of all the afflictions and sufferings that are to happen to them, . . . Our Savior's love for us is so tremendous that if the love of all parents were centered in a single heart, it would not represent even a spark of the love for us that burns in His Heart. Our pains and sorrows, ever present to His vision and seen most clearly and distinctly, were so many wounds bleeding in His paternal Heart.

—St. John Eudes, *The Sacred Heart of Jesus*

IN GOD'S PRESENCE, CONSIDER . . .

Could my heart begin to look a little more like Jesus's wounded heart? Could I begin to recognize the depth of love Jesus has for me and the world? Could I begin to grieve the wounds that sin has caused?

CLOSING PRAYER

Jesus, loving Savior, You do not draw away from me or my distress. Thank you for pressing close to my pain, thank you for not letting me go. I never want to grieve You again by my sin.

Let Yourself Be Healed . . .

We don't go to confession just to be forgiven. Forgiveness is just the start of a process. We go to be healed. As the Catechism *explains, "God's forgiveness initiates the healing (1502). . . . He is the physician the sick have need of" (1503)*

When we sin, we wound ourselves; we disfigure ourselves, so that, though we were created to be like God, we don't resemble Him anymore. We don't *look* like Him, we don't *think* like Him, we don't *act* like Him.

Jesus wants to restore us in the Father's likeness. How? Through the sacrament of Reconciliation. He told St. Faustina that the greatest miracles take place in the confessional, and that there is no sinner who cannot be restored: "Were a soul like a decaying corpse so that from a human standpoint there would be no [hope of] restoration and everything would already be lost, it is not so with God. The miracle of Divine Mercy restores that soul in full" (*Diary*,1448).

As I mentioned in Secret 1, God's focus is not on our sin, but on our *relationship* with Him. He's focused on our pain—on our woundedness. He knows what sin is! He knows that sin is misery, that it's sickness. He knows that we're aching, and He wants to heal us, to restore all that has been lost.

As the *Catechism* simply expresses it: "In confession, we let ourselves be healed by Christ "(1458).

If we go into the confessional simply to confess our sins and receive forgiveness, we limit the experience that God wants for us. But if we go in confessing everything—yes, our sins, but also our misery: our sickness, our brokenness, our woundedness—then we not only receive forgiveness but also initiate a process of deep healing that will restore us as children of the Father.

No image of confession is as powerful for me as the image of the prodigal son wrapped in the arms of his father. Confession is when our misery meets His mercy, and all is restored in the Father's embrace.

—Vinny Flynn, *7 Secrets of Confession*

IN GOD'S PRESENCE, CONSIDER . . .

How sanitized is my presentation of myself to my loving Father in the confessional? Do I reveal my misery to the Living God, or do I believe the lie that He despises my frailty? Today can I bring my wounds to the One wounded for me?

CLOSING PRAYER

Lord Jesus Christ, wounded Savior, permit Your gentle light to reveal again to my eyes my vulnerability and brokenness, and stir up my soul in wholehearted confidence in Your healing balm of mercy.

The Tribunal of Mercy

The greatest miracles take place in the confessional—a tribunal not of judgment but of mercy.

Write, speak of My mercy. Tell souls where they are to look for solace; that is, in the Tribunal of Mercy [the Sacrament of Reconciliation]. There the greatest miracles take place [and] are incessantly repeated. To avail oneself of this miracle, it is not necessary to go on a great pilgrimage or to carry out some external ceremony; it suffices to come with faith to the feet of My representative and to reveal to him one's misery, and the miracle of Divine Mercy will be fully demonstrated. Were a soul like a decaying corpse so that from a human standpoint, there would be no [hope of] restoration and everything would already be lost, it is not so with God. The miracle of Divine Mercy restores that soul in full.

. . . When you go to confession, to this fountain of My mercy, the Blood and Water which came forth from My Heart always flows down upon your soul and ennobles it. Every time you go to confession, immerse yourself entirely in My mercy, with great trust, so that I may pour the bounty of My grace upon your soul. When you approach the confessional, know this, that I Myself am waiting there for you. I am only hidden by the priest, but I myself act in your soul. Here the misery of the soul meets the God of mercy. . . . Just as you prepare in My presence, so also you make your confession before Me. The person of the priest is, for Me, only a screen. Never analyze what sort of a priest it is that I am making use of; open your soul in confession as you would to Me, and I will fill it with My light.

. . . Come, then, with trust to draw graces from this fountain. I never reject a contrite heart . . . Sooner would heaven and earth turn into nothingness than would My mercy not embrace a trusting soul.

—St. Faustina, *Diary*, 1602, 1448, 1485, 1777

IN GOD'S PRESENCE, CONSIDER . . .

Do I view confession as something I "have" to do in order to receive Communion, or do I look forward to it as a healing encounter with Jesus Himself?

CLOSING PRAYER

Lord Jesus, help me to immerse myself completely in Your mercy each time I go to confession, trusting that Your mercy is greater than my misery.

If You Fall, Rise! . . .

From the east, St. John of Kronstadt calls us to rise like the dawning sun. The Christian isn't great because he has no sins; he is great because each morning God forgives him again. In fact, monks and married people alike have imperfections that are made manifest often many times a day; and the divine remedy is to learn to humbly ask for mercy.

"If you fall, rise and you shall be saved." You are a sinner, you continually fall, learn also how to rise; be careful to acquire this wisdom. This is what the wisdom consists in: learning by heart the psalm, "Have mercy upon me, O God, after Thy great goodness," inspired by the Holy Spirit to the king and prophet David, and say it with sincere faith and trust, with a contrite and humble heart. After your sincere repentance, expressed in the words of King David, the forgiveness of your sins shall immediately shine upon you from the Lord, and your spiritual powers will be at peace. The most important thing in life is to be zealous for mutual love, and not to judge anyone. Everybody shall answer for himself to God, and you must look to yourself.

—St. John of Kronstadt, *My Life in Christ*

IN GOD'S PRESENCE, CONSIDER . . .

Confession at least once a month is a great gift on my path to holiness. Yet, the closer I get to the Light, the more I see my little imperfections, each moment that I do not resemble the God of love. Have I learned the language of God, the language of love, the language of freedom? Mercy. It is a freeing thing to see myself in truth, but rise in mercy; to stop judging others and let them answer to God alone, loving them as He loves me. Do I rejoice to be forgiven each day; do I rejoice in forgiving others?

CLOSING PRAYER

Father of Mercy, Father of Love, You teach my heart where to find freedom, where to find peace. Release me from false perfectionism, and allow me to rest in Your mercy and forgiveness. Have mercy on me, O God, according to thy steadfast love; according to thy abundant mercy blot out my transgressions.

Love Your Enemies . . .

In the beautiful reversal that is Christianity, St. Augustine reveals our superpower—that we are now established in such authority as to liberate others of their offenses. God truly brings us into His dominion when we share in bringing His mercy to others.

Now because by reason of those daily sins of which I have spoken, it is necessary for you to say, in that daily prayer of cleansing as it were, Forgive us our debts, as we also forgive our debtors; what will you do? You have enemies. For who can live on this earth without them? Take heed to yourselves, love them. In no way can your enemy so hurt you by his violence, as you hurt yourself if you love him not. . . .

But still you are saying, Who can do, who has ever done this? May God bring it to effect in your hearts! I know as well as you, there are but few who do it; great men are they and spiritual who do so. Are all the faithful in the Church who approach the altar, and take the Body and Blood of Christ, are they all such? And yet they all say, Forgive us our debts, as we also forgive our debtors. What, if God should answer them, Why do you ask me to do what I have promised, when you do not what I have commanded? What have I promised? To forgive your debts. What have I commanded? That you also forgive your debtors. How can you do this, if you do not love your enemies?

—Saint Augustine *NEW ADVENT SERMONS Sermon 6 on the New Testament - On the Lord's Prayer in* Matthew 6:9

IN GOD'S PRESENCE, CONSIDER . . .

Do I still live in a servile state, clinging to others' faults because I don't recognize my own dignity as a beloved member of God's family? Or do I abide already in the Kingdom of Heaven, freely absolving others' offenses since I am myself freed through the Mercy of God?

CLOSING PRAYER

Father of Mercy, Father of Love, You call us into Your image and likeness. Allow me to truly mirror Your Love and Mercy in this darkened world, that Your radiance may break forth like the dawn.

Cry to Him Who Is Mighty to Save

In this foundational text for monastic life, seventh century St. John Climacus draws us to his monastery of St. Catherine at the foot of Mount Sinai where, like Moses removing his shoes in the presence of the Holy, we are called to physically move toward Mercy.

Those who have not yet obtained true prayer of the heart, can find help in violence in bodily prayer—I mean stretching out the hands, beating the breast, sincere raising of the eyes to heaven, deep sighing, frequent prostrations. But often they cannot do this owing to the presence of other people, and so the demons especially choose to attack them just at this very time. And as we have not yet the strength to resist them by firmness of mind and the invisible power of prayer, we yield to our enemies. If possible, go apart for a brief space. Hide for a while in some secret place. Raise on high the eyes of your soul, if you can; but if not, your bodily eyes. Hold your arms motionless in the form of a cross, in order to shame and conquer your Amalek (footnote: i.e. the unclean spirit) by this sign. Cry to Him who is mighty to save, using no subtle expressions but humble speech, preferably making this your prelude: Have mercy on me, for I am weak. Then you will know by experience the power of the Most High, and with invisible help you will invisibly drive away the invisible ones. He who accustoms himself to wage war in this way will soon be able to put his enemies to flight solely by spiritual means.

—St. John Climacus, *The Ladder of Divine Ascent*

IN GOD'S PRESENCE, CONSIDER . . .

How much is my flinging of myself into God muted and diminished by my self-conscious assessment of my surroundings? How do I conform to a secular and deadened world and withdraw from the surging tide of God's love?

CLOSING PRAYER

Sovereign Creator, You formed man from the dust and breathed into him Your life-giving Spirit. Draw me back to my true self that in both soul and body I may rejoice in Your freedom.

Confession—The Place of Mercy

Here St. Isidore of Seville, early doctor of the Church, provides a compelling introduction to the Catechism of the Catholic Church revealing the heart of the Sacrament of Confession: the Father of Mercies working through Son and Spirit.

"Confession heals, confession justifies, confession grants pardon of sin. All hope consists in confession. In confession is found the place of mercy. Believe, therefore, most certainly, and in no way hesitate, in no way doubt, and by no means despair of the mercy of God. Have hope in confession, have faith in it. Do not despair of this remedy of spiritual health. And do not despair in your healing, so long as you desire to turn to better things."

—*Catechism of the Catholic Church*

The formula of absolution used in the Latin Church expresses the essential elements of this sacrament: the Father of mercies is the source of all forgiveness. He effects the reconciliation of sinners through the Passover of his Son and the gift of his Spirit, through the prayer and ministry of the Church:

God, the Father of mercies,
through the death and the resurrection of his Son
has reconciled the world to himself
and sent the Holy Spirit among us
for the forgiveness of sins;
through the ministry of the Church
may God give you pardon and peace,
and I absolve you from your sins
in the name of the Father, and of the Son and of the Holy Spirit.

—*CCC* 1449; St. Isidore of Seville: *Synonyma*
(*On the Lamentations of a Sinful Soul*)

IN GOD'S PRESENCE, CONSIDER . . .

"And do not despair in your healing, so long as you desire to turn to better things." Can I experience the reawakening of hope through the ministry of my mother, the Church in the Sacrament of Confession? I resolve to go often to this place of mercy and to meditate often on this good Father and how He wants to transform my life.

CLOSING PRAYER

Father, who You are shines through Your gifts. Thank You for confession, this hopeful place of mercy, for the Church, for Your priests, for Your pardon and peace.

The Promise of Restoration

In Rich in Mercy *(4), St. Pope John Paul II wrote that mercy manifests itself when it "restores to value" and "overcomes evil with good." In this prophetic passage from Joel, we find the Lord's merciful promise to restore all that has been lost.*

Fear not, O land;
be glad and rejoice,
for the Lord has done great things!
Fear not, you beasts of the field,
for the pastures of the wilderness are green;
the tree bears its fruit,
the fig tree and vine give their full yield.
Be glad, O sons of Zion,
and rejoice in the Lord, your God;
for he has given the early rain for your vindication,
he has poured down for you abundant rain,
the early and the latter rain, as before.
The threshing floors shall be full of grain,
the vats shall overflow with wine and oil.
I will restore to you the years
which the swarming locust has eaten,
the hopper, the destroyer, and the cutter,
my great army, which I sent among you.
You shall eat in plenty and be satisfied,
and praise the name of the Lord your God,
who has dealt wondrously with you.
And my people shall never again be put to shame.
You shall know that I am in the midst of Israel,
and that I, the Lord, am your God
and there is none else.
And my people shall never again
be put to shame.

—Joel 2:21– 27

IN GOD'S PRESENCE, CONSIDER . . .

How often do I allow fear to compress my vision? Why is God's instruction from Genesis to Revelation, "Be not Afraid"? Am I ready to open my heart to trust in God and experience His light and joy breaking into my soul?

CLOSING PRAYER

Heavenly Father, Your Divine Spirit brings the gifts of joy, freedom and peace. Cast out from my heart the shadows of a malicious accuser, and open my soul to the joy that comes from trust in You.

Mercy Restores

Drawing us to the words of the prophet Joel, the author reveals that mercy is miraculous; with our human eyes we may see devastation and loss in our lives, but the mercy of the Lord transforms our story.

The person who is the object of mercy does not feel humiliated. God forgive me for any times I may have thought I was being merciful to someone, but did it in such a way that they felt shame or humiliation as I "bestowed" my generosity upon them. God never extends mercy like that. When God extends mercy, the one who receives it does not feel humiliated but "found again and restored to value" (*Rich in Mercy*, #5). This is the function of mercy. *Mercy restores!*

There's a beautiful promise of this in the Book of Joel. For four years in a row, all the fields have been devastated by a great army of locusts, destroying the crops and ruining the entire harvest. And then the Lord promises mercy: "I will restore to you the years which the swarming locust has eaten" (Joel 2:25).

God the Father wants to come into our lives. He wants to break through any way that He can, so that we will open ourselves to Him and allow Him to do what He longs to do—to restore all those "fields" in our lives that the locusts have eaten.

I don't know about you, but I have fields in my life that have been pretty devastated. I think we all do. God wants to restore everything that has been lost, because . . . all He wants to do is father us. . . . He wants to restore us in His image and likeness, restore us as His children. He wants to bring us back to Him. *He wants to bring us home.*

—Vinny Flynn, *7 Secrets of Divine Mercy*

IN GOD'S PRESENCE, CONSIDER . . .

I consider for a moment a deep place in me that longs to be restored. What have I sealed off as inaccessible to God's healing? What have I determined is lost to me and to my Savior? Where might I discover God surprising me today with His relentless renewal?

CLOSING PRAYER

God my Father, You have accompanied me all the days of my life. Reveal to me the fullness of Your plan, and free me from my self-imposed confinement. Help me to trust that Your mercy really can "turn all things to good" (Rom. 8:28) for those who love You.

Trials and Peace

St. Padre Pio joins St. Ignatius of Loyola in teaching us discernment of spirits: Knowing that all peace comes from God, we can learn to repudiate the agitation of the adversary.

When you are exposed to any trial, be it physical or moral, bodily or spiritual, the best remedy is the thought of Him who is our life, and not to think of the one without joining to it the thought of the other.

Jesus continues to love me and to draw me closer to Himself. He has forgotten my sins, and I would say that He remembers only His own mercy . . . Each morning He comes into my heart and pours out all the effusions of His goodness.

The Spirit of God is a spirit of peace. Even in the most serious faults He makes us feel a sorrow that is tranquil, humble, and confident. This is precisely because of His mercy. The spirit of the devil, instead, excites, exasperates, and makes us feel, in that very sorrow, anger against ourselves. We should, on the contrary, be charitable with ourselves first and foremost. Therefore if any thought agitates you, this agitation never comes from God, who gives you peace, being the Spirit of Peace, but from the devil.

—St. Padre Pio

IN GOD'S PRESENCE, CONSIDER . . .

Why do I remember my flaws and failures while Jesus remembers only His mercy? Today I welcome the Spirit of God, the spirit of peace into my soul.

CLOSING PRAYER

Come Holy Spirit, fill my heart with You, and remind me when I become agitated that this is never Your work. You alone, God, are my refuge and my home. Immerse me in Your peace.

Confidence in Confession

With gentle direction, de Caussade tells us that confession is not something we should have anxiety about, but instead, after contrition, we should have total peace and confidence in God's mercy.

With regard to confession, be firmly convinced that you need not trouble about it, either on account of your miseries or of your sins. St. Francis of Sales says that after sorrow for sin there should be peace. This then is what you ought to aim at, and above all you should be full of great confidence in the infinite goodness of God, remembering that His mercy is greater than any of His works, that He glories in forgiving us, but cannot prove His generosity if we are wanting in confidence. He loves simplicity, candour, and uprightness, go to Him therefore with perfect confidence, in spite of all your weakness, misery and unfaithfulness. That will win His heart, and He will forgive everything to those who trust in His goodness and love. . . . .

As regards the declaration of your sins; tell those that you recollect simply and in as few words as possible, leaving the rest to the unbounded mercy of God without troubling about what you do not remember, or do not know. . . .

The following is an easy way of practicing frequent confession. To prevent more certainly all anxiety about the past and as a help for the future here is a counsel in a few words. Leave the past to the infinite mercy of God—the future to His sweet providence, and the present give up entirely to the love of God . . .

—Rev. Jean-Pierre de Caussade SJ, *Abandonment to Divine Providence*

IN GOD'S PRESENCE, CONSIDER . . .

Where in my life do I tend to listen to the condemning voice of the accuser, instead of trusting in God's desire to love and to heal? What lies have I agreed with that keep me from truly leaving my past to the infinite mercy of God, and from running to Him in the Sacrament of Confession whenever I fall?

CLOSING PRAYER

God, thank you for your generosity and the abundance of Your mercy. I reject all the voices in my head that speak lies about who I am and who You are, and I recognize that anything that feels like condemnation is not from You. I want only Your Holy Spirit, only Your voice, and I open myself now to receive all the mercy You have for me.

Eyes of Mercy

Fr. Cantalamessa reflects on the importance of Christ's gaze—and ours.

One thing that clearly emerges in reading the Gospels is the importance of Jesus's eyes, his gaze. Many encounters with him are initiated and determined by a look of love and mercy on his part. This is the case with the rich young man (see Mark 10:21), with Zacchaeus (see Luke 19:5), and with Peter after his betrayal (see Luke 22:61). His gaze was not a hasty gaze; at times the Gospel says, "He looked around" (see Mark 3:34). Neither was it a superficial gaze but one that reached people in their innermost beings. He "sees the heart" (see Luke 16:15). His gaze is always one of mercy and acceptance when he is with people who are open or searching, but when he is with hypocrites or hostile people, it can be terrible: "He looked around at them with anger" (Mark 3:5).

. . . The language of the eyes has not changed: a smile, tears, fear, wonder, and trust are the same everywhere. Jesus said, "The eye is the lamp of the body. So, if your eye is sound, your whole body will be full of light" (Matthew 6:22). The eyes are the mirror of the soul. . . .

The eyes of insecure people never look directly at someone and never sustain the gaze of another person for long; the eyes of arrogant and presumptuous people always create a distance between themselves and others; the eyes of vain people only see themselves even when they are looking at others; the eyes of egotists see others from the perspective of possible advantages to themselves; the eyes of deceivers try to find the weak point of other people to "sell their wares"; the eyes of sensual people never see other people as human beings but only as objects to gratify their desires. . . .

We all have a valuable means at our disposal to exercise mercy: our gaze. It can be like balm for a wound or, unfortunately, like vinegar on a sore. What St. James says about the tongue (3:5–10) can also be said about eyes. We can kill with our eyes or bring life, spew venom or comfort someone's heart.

—Raniero Cantalamessa, *The Gaze of Mercy*

IN GOD'S PRESENCE, CONSIDER . . .

What is a situation where I think my gaze is typically one of kindness and mercy? And, if I'm honest, what does my gaze often convey to those around me that I need to work on?

CLOSING PRAYER

Oh Lord, show me where my gaze wounds. And show me where I am that person gazing from a place of insecurity, arrogance, presumption, vanity, ego, deception, or sensuality; and help me become an other-focused balm instead.

Heart "Wrenched Open"

A man, robbed and beaten, lies helpless on the side of the road. Unlike the priest and the Levite, who see him, but pass by on the other side of the road, a Samaritan has compassion on him, binds his wounds, and takes care of him. Pope Benedict writes that today's translations of this passage are not true to the original; to say that the Samaritan has "compassion" is just not strong enough.

And now the Samaritan enters the stage. What will he do? [Unlike the expert in the Law who had just been questioning Jesus] he does not ask how far his obligations of solidarity extend. Nor does he ask about the merits required for eternal life. Something else happens: His heart is wrenched open. The Gospel uses the word that in Hebrew had originally referred to the mother's womb and maternal care. Seeing this man in such a state is a blow that strikes him "viscerally," touching his soul.

"He had compassion"—that is how we translate the text today, diminishing its original vitality. Struck in his soul by the lightning flash of mercy, he himself now becomes a neighbor, heedless of any question or danger. The burden of the question thus shifts here. The issue is no longer which other person is a neighbor to me or not. The question is about me. I have to become the neighbor, and when I do, the other person counts for me "as myself."

—Pope Benedict XVI, *Jesus of Nazareth*

IN GOD'S PRESENCE, CONSIDER . . .

How am I serving the Lord's plan of mercy? Am I asking Him to fill me so full of mercy that I can radiate it to others? Am I allowing myself to become a neighbor to all?

CLOSING PRAYER

Lord, fill me with Your mercy and let it flow through me to those in need. Let my heart be so wrenched open by the suffering of others that I will be compelled to do whatever I can to help them.

Have You Been Mercified?

Sometimes combining words to form new ones can bring new ways of looking at things. Here it leads to a reflection that takes a fresh look at the relationships between Christ's death on the Cross, redemptive suffering, and the scriptural command to be merciful.

Mercified. The word just popped into my head again. Yeah, I know, it's not really a word—at least I've never seen it in a dictionary or heard it used on the street. But it's a word to me, a word that has intrigued and fed me since the day I first heard it.

It was several years ago, at a week-long retreat we were presenting at the National Shrine of Divine Mercy. After one of the talks, my son Tim came up to me and asked, "Dad, is *mercified* a word? I've never heard it, and I don't really know what it means, but I like it."

I don't really know what it means either, but I like it, too, and I've enjoyed musing about it over the years. Today my focus was on Jesus as He hung on the cross. When He was crucified—He who is Mercy itself—His whole being flowed from His pierced heart as a fountain of mercy for us. On the cross, He was the wounded lover; He was Mercy crucified for us.

As our hearts are pierced by His love, by His gaze from the cross, we are drawn to take up our own crosses, our own sufferings, and join them to His eternal offering to the Father for souls. We become "mercified"—consecrated to mercy, transformed *into* mercy. Our lives are now consecrated, set apart as, with Him, we become wounded lovers, wounded healers, sharing His love, His pain, and His thirst for souls.

Christ doesn't give us His mercy so that we can keep it for ourselves. He expects us to pass it on. Mercified from the cross, we are filled to overflowing, empowered to respond fully to His "new command" to love one another just as He has loved us. He gives us His mercy so that we can become mercy for others.

—Vinny Flynn, *Divine Mercy Reflections*

IN GOD'S PRESENCE, CONSIDER . . .

What does this meditation tell me about myself? Can I use this as an examination of conscience? How am I doing with taking up my cross and following Christ? With being merciful to others as a way of life?

CLOSING PRAYER

Lord Jesus, thank you for letting Your heart be pierced for me—and for all. Open my heart and draw me to follow Your way of mercy.

An Open Book

The "book of God's mercy," says Pope Francis, is not a closed book. We are all called to be witnesses to mercy in the context of our own lives as "living writers of the Gospel."

The Gospel is the book of God's mercy, to be read and reread, because everything that Jesus said and did is an expression of the Father's mercy. Not everything, however, was written down; the Gospel of mercy remains an open book, in which the signs of Christ's disciples—concrete acts of love and the best witness to mercy—continue to be written. We are all called to become living writers of the Gospel, heralds of the Good News to all men and women of today. We do this by practicing the corporal and spiritual works of mercy, which are the hallmarks of the Christian life. By means of these simple yet powerful gestures, even when unseen, we can accompany the needy, bringing God's tenderness and consolation. . . .

The story we have just heard presents an evident contrast: there is the fear of the disciples, who gathered behind closed doors; and then there is the mission of Jesus, who sends them into the world to proclaim the message of forgiveness. This contrast may also be present in us, experienced as an interior struggle between a closed heart and the call of love to open doors closed by sin. It is a call that frees us to go out of ourselves. Christ . . . wants to enter into each one of us to break open the locked doors of our hearts. . . . We see before us a humanity that is often wounded and fearful, a humanity that bears the scars of pain and uncertainty. Before the anguished cry for mercy and peace, we hear Jesus' inspiring invitation: "As the Father has sent me, even so I send you" (Jn 20:21).

—Pope Francis, Mercy Sunday Homily, April 3, 2016

IN GOD'S PRESENCE, CONSIDER . . .

It's so easy to get lulled into a superficial reading of the Gospel, viewing the Acts of the Apostles as simply inspiring but ancient history, over and done, with little if any relevance to us today. But what if we try to change that mindset and view it as a guidebook for becoming Christ's disciples and evangelists now?

CLOSING PRAYER

Lord, help me to hear and respond to the ways you call me each day to continue writing your Gospel of mercy with my life.

The Fast That I Choose

A familiar Lenten passage, Isaiah 58 brings about a pivot in our understanding of priorities. More important than the privations we impose on ourselves, God here looks for a heart open to our brothers and sisters in need.

Is not this the fast that I choose:
to loose the bonds of injustice,
to undo the thongs of the yoke,
to let the oppressed go free,
and to break every yoke?
Is it not to share your bread with the hungry,
and bring the homeless poor into your house;
when you see the naked, to cover them,
and not to hide yourself from your own kin?
Then your light shall break forth like the dawn,
and your healing shall spring up quickly;
your vindicator shall go before you,
the glory of the Lord shall be your rear guard.

—Isaiah 58:6–8 (NRSVCE)

IN GOD'S PRESENCE, CONSIDER . . .

Do I believe that the Lord will satisfy my needs, or do I wander in search of satisfaction? Can I open my heart to the abundance of the Lord—and let it overflow to each brother and sister that God places before me?

CLOSING PRAYER

Jesus, when You spoke of fasting, You spoke of Your absence as the bridegroom. Allow me to experience the desperate hunger I have for Your presence, and in entering into bodily fasts, let me be so filled with You that I long to give Your care to others. Most especially, through the Sacred Bread of Your Eucharistic Presence, change me into a vessel of mercy for the world.

A Watered Garden

Isaiah towers above the prophets of the Old Testament, giving us the richest insight into the coming Messiah and the blessings He floods into our lives when we call out to Him, becoming partners in mercy.

Then you shall call, and the Lord will answer;
you shall cry, and he will say, Here I am.
"If you take away from the midst of you the yoke,
the pointing of the finger, and speaking wickedness,
if you pour yourself out for the hungry
and satisfy the desire of the afflicted,
then shall your light rise in the darkness
and your gloom be as the noonday.
And the Lord will guide you continually,
and satisfy your desire with good things,
and make your bones strong;
and you shall be like a watered garden,
like a spring of water,
whose waters fail not.
And your ancient ruins shall be rebuilt;
you shall raise up the foundations of many generations;
you shall be called the repairer of the breach,
the restorer of streets to dwell in.

—Isaiah 58:9–12

IN GOD'S PRESENCE, CONSIDER . . .

If I call upon my Creator, he will restore communion in my soul, not only with my brother and sister before me, but also with my earliest longings. The God who in omniscience knows the path he has set every creature upon will draw me into the deepest purpose he has for me. A watered garden, an ever-flowing spring: both are images of rich fulfillment, all is well, there is abundance to offer.

CLOSING PRAYER

Father, sovereign and good, You satisfy my needs in the parched places of my soul. As I empty myself out for others, You pour forth Your mercy, that I might flourish in Your radiant light and join Your Son in sharing Your bounty in this world.

Blessed Are the Poor in Spirit

James will not allow us to keep our faith trapped in pious vagaries. He drives home the reality that true mercy shows no partiality, but is offered equally to all.

My brethren, show no partiality as you hold the faith of our Lord Jesus Christ, the Lord of glory. For if a man with gold rings and in fine clothing comes into your assembly, and a poor man in shabby clothing also comes in, and you pay attention to the one who wears the fine clothing and say, "Have a seat here, please," while you say to the poor man, "Stand there," or, "Sit at my feet," have you not made distinctions among yourselves, and become judges with evil thoughts? Listen, my beloved brethren. Has not God chosen those who are poor in the world to be rich in faith and heirs of the kingdom which he has promised to those who love him? But you have dishonored the poor man. . . .

If you really fulfil the royal law, according to the scripture, "You shall love your neighbor as yourself," you do well. But if you show partiality, you commit sin. . . . So speak and so act as those who are to be judged under the law of liberty. For judgment is without mercy to one who has shown no mercy; yet mercy triumphs over judgment.

—James 2:1–6, 8–9, 12–13

IN GOD'S PRESENCE, CONSIDER . . .

"Love your neighbor as yourself." It is often shame and self-hatred that lie underneath harsh judgment of others. How have I shunned or disparaged aspects of my life or of my neighbor's? How have I allowed a judgmental spirit to condemn myself or another, rather than allowing the triumph of mercy to find a home in my heart?

CLOSING PRAYER

Lord of glory, all who love You are called to be joint heirs of the kingdom. Grant me the grace to see as You see, to love as You love, to show others the mercy I hope for in the end.

Judge Not . . .

Fr. Cantalamessa clarifies the concept of judgment, showing us exactly what actions and attitudes the Lord calls us to avoid.

Jesus says, "Judge not, that you be not judged. . . . Why do you see the speck that is in your brother's eye, but do not notice the log that is in your own eye?" (Matthew 7:1, 3). Jesus does not mean, "Do not judge people and they will not judge you," because we know from experience that things do not always work this way. Instead, he means, "Do not judge your brother or sister so that God will not judge you." Or, even better, "Do not judge your brother or sister because God has not judged you." . . .

How can we actually live our lives without judging? Our judgment is implicit even in a look. We cannot observe, listen, and live without evaluating things, without judging things. It is not so much judgment that we need to remove from our hearts as it is the venom, the malice, the condemnation in our judgment! In Luke's compilation of Jesus' sayings, Jesus' command "Judge not, and you will not be judged" is immediately clarified in the very same verse by the command that comes next: "Condemn not, and you will not be condemned" (Luke 6:37).

In itself, judging is a neutral action; a judgment can end in condemnation or in acquittal and justification. Negative judgments are the ones being referred to and banned by the word of God, the ones that condemn the sinner as well as the sin. A mother and an outsider can judge the imperfection a baby objectively has, but how different their two judgments are! The mother actually suffers over this imperfection as if it were hers; she feels herself jointly responsible and is determined to help get it corrected. She does not go around shouting from the rooftops that her baby has an imperfection. Well, our judgment of a brother or a sister should be similar to that of the mother because "we, though many, are . . . individually members one of another" (Romans 12:5). These others are part of "our own family."

—Raniero Cantalamessa, *The Gaze of Mercy*

IN GOD'S PRESENCE, CONSIDER . . .

How often does my judgment, in the form of a natural evaluation of things, become harsh judgment, judgment with venom, malice, or condemnation? I wonder how many times I in condescension have judged or belittled someone in my mind, if not with my actions?

CLOSING PRAYER

God, You have judged me with mercy. Thank you. Rid me of anything within that causes me to fall into negative judgment of others.

Living Icons of Mercy

Catherine Doherty, founder of Madonna House, echoes the call to not just gaze on Jesus in the Divine Mercy Image, but to become His image-bearers in the world.

To be a witness . . . simply means to live in such a way that one's life would not make sense if God did not exist. This is the time. This is the hour when every Christian must reflect Christ in his life—be the icon of Christ. We must live the gospel. In order to do so we must pray for faith which is the cradle of charity and hope! We must pray and ask God to make us realize that he, the Triune God, lives within us. . . .

To love God with one's whole heart and to love one's neighbor as we love ourselves means also to love ourselves the way God wants us to. It means to follow his words, "By this shall all men know that you are my disciples, that you love one another as I have loved you." It means that we must straighten the paths of the Lord in ourselves so that he can come through, so that all men will know him through us.

Love means to approach our enemies with deep tenderness, compassion and understanding, which are the fruits of true love. Love does not mean the destruction of structures, but participating in restoring them to their original purity. Love means that the time has come to lay down our lives for our friends.

This is the time to realize the mystery of God's touching us, enveloping us, loving us. It is the time to understand that love is the key to the mystery of man, and that in love lies the answer to all our problems.

—Catherine de Hueck Doherty, *The Gospel Without Compromise*

IN GOD'S PRESENCE, CONSIDER . . .

Am I an icon of Christ in the world? Do I look like Him when I interact with others? Do I reflect His tenderness, understanding, and love to those around me—even my enemies?

CLOSING PRAYER

St. John the Baptist, make straight the paths of the Lord in me so that He can come through, so that all those I encounter will know Him through me. Jesus, let me be Your icon of mercy to the world.

Divine Mercy on the Cross . . .

What does it take to face the depths of our depravity, to take an honest look at the ugliness of our sin and the ramifications of our choices? Bishop Barron assures us that as we gaze at Jesus on the cross, we necessarily encounter our sin there, but it is also the place where we encounter the mercy that transforms.

LUKE 9:43B–45

Friends, in today's Gospel, Jesus predicts his being handed over to men—that is, his Crucifixion. Here is the point I want to make: we are meant to see on that cross our own ugliness. What brings Jesus to the cross? Stupidity, anger, mistrust, institutional injustice, betrayal, denial, unspeakable cruelty, fear. St. Peter puts it with disquieting laconicism: the Author of life came and you killed him. In the light of the cross, all of the vermin are revealed. This is why we speak of the cross as God's judgment on the world.

So far, so awful. But we can't stop telling the story at this point. Dante and every other spiritual master know that the only way up is down. When we live unaware of our sins, we will never make spiritual progress. So we need the light, however painful it is. Then we can begin to rise. Once Dante makes it all the way to the center of hell, he suddenly finds himself climbing out.

On the cross of Jesus, we meet our own sin. But we also meet the divine mercy, which has taken that sin upon himself in order to swallow it up.

—Bishop Robert Barron, *Daily Reflections on the Gospel*, September 25, 2021

IN GOD'S PRESENCE, CONSIDER . . .

How often do I reflect on Your Passion, Jesus, and on the sins I have committed that added to Your suffering? Are there any places where I am putting up barriers that keep me from seeing certain areas of sinfulness in my life? Are there patterns of sin that I have gotten comfortable allowing?

CLOSING PRAYER

Give me fervor and courage, Lord, to honestly face all of my sin, to weed out the very roots of it, and to turn from even the smallest instances where I am not who You call me to be. Let me spend more time with my eyes fixed on the cross and on the pain my sins—even those I haven't committed yet—caused You to suffer, thus convicting me to sin no more. Help me to do all of this with deep trust in Your love for me, and with the consolation that when I lay bare my misery, You meet me with mercy.

Mercy, an Aspect of God's Goodness

Reflecting on the teachings of St. Thomas Aquinas, Fr. Moloney presents a clear picture of Divine mercy as God's restorative response to our needs.

Saint Thomas Aquinas defined mercy as God's goodness in removing defects and suffering in his creatures (*Summa Theologiae*, I, q. 21, a. 3). Aquinas's argument also has a strong logic behind it:

1. Mercy includes the idea of responding to some suffering or defect in another;
2. The merciful person wants to remove the suffering or defect in the other;
3. To remove defects is to make something better;
4. To make something better is to make it more good;
5. Therefore, mercy is related to goodness.

Built into the very language of mercy is an idea of responding to some suffering or misery, which Aquinas defines generally as a deficiency of some sort. We can see what he means by noticing that the traditional list of the works of mercy mentions several types of deficiencies: nakedness is a deficiency of clothes, hunger comes from a lack of food, ignorance from a lack of instruction, and so on. Having a merciful heart makes one want to remove the deficiency in the other. . . .

Aquinas concludes that mercy is just the name for a specific aspect of God's goodness, the part of God's goodness that remedies deficiencies, that rights wrongs. Divine mercy is enacted whenever God adds goodness to someone who is missing it in some way or—what amounts to the same thing—takes away a badness. Mercy is restorative. . . .

Aquinas teaches that mercy is a response to a privation of whatever sort. It would not be mercy to give a man something he did not need, say, a blade of grass. . . . It would, however, be mercy to give him a meal when he is hungry, to give him knowledge when he is ignorant, and to help him go to Confession if he is in a state of sin. Any privation can be a wrong to be righted by mercy.

—Fr. Daniel Moloney, *Mercy: What Every Catholic Should Know*

IN GOD'S PRESENCE, CONSIDER . . .

As I struggle through daily life, I sometimes don't notice God's restorative work. But looking back, how many problems have been resolved, how many needs taken care of, how many blessings of mercy can I now recognize?

CLOSING PRAYER

Thank you, God, for your continual goodness, for all the countless ways you've been a loving Father to me. Thank you for meeting my misery with Your mercy.

C.S. Lewis on Forgiveness . . .

With his classic brilliance, C.S. Lewis cuts to the heart of the matter, elucidating for us what it really means to forgive—and what it means for us when we don't.

As regards my own sins it is a safe bet (though not a certainty) that the excuses are not really so good as I think; as regards other men's sins against me it is a safe bet (though not a certainty) that the excuses are better than I think. One must therefore begin by attending to everything which may show that the other man was not so much to blame as we thought.

But even if he is absolutely fully to blame we still have to forgive him; and even if ninety-nine percent of his apparent guilt can be explained away by really good excuses, the problem of forgiveness begins with the one percent of guilt which is left over. To excuse what can really produce good excuses is not Christian charity; it is only fairness. To be Christian means to forgive the inexcusable, because God has forgiven the inexcusable in you.

This is hard. It is perhaps not so hard to forgive a single great injury. But to forgive the incessant provocations of daily life . . . how can we do it? Only, I think, by remembering where we stand, by meaning our words when we say in our prayers each night "forgive us our trespasses as we forgive those that trespass against us." We are offered forgiveness on no other terms. To refuse it is to refuse God's mercy for ourselves. There is no hint of exceptions and God means what He says.

—C.S. Lewis, *The Weight of Glory*, pp. 135–136

IN GOD'S PRESENCE, CONSIDER . . .

What person/persons have I had a difficult time forgiving or even wanting to forgive? What wrongs have I seen as inexcusable and therefore unforgivable?

CLOSING PRAYER

Father of Mercy, Father of Love, thank you for extending so much mercy to me. Grant me the grace to let go of the unforgiveness I hold in my heart toward __________.

Indwelling Mercy

Fr. Eugene McCaffrey shares the insights of Elizabeth of the Trinity on the presence of God within us.

The message of Elizabeth of the Trinity *is spreading today*, John Paul II has declared, *with a prophetic force*. She is a prophet in the sense of someone who reminds us of a forgotten truth, sheds new light on old mysteries and stands out as a sure and steady guide in a world of uncertainty and ambiguity. Her life has become a beacon of light for us, a call to discover once again the truth that God not only loves each one of us personally but is also intimately and uniquely present to us.

The presence of which Elizabeth speaks is not a vague, indiscriminate power but something personal and individual. God is not the *ground of our being* in some dry, remote sort of way. We are not *surrounded* by God as by air, light or energy: he is a *personal* God who knows each of us individually and cares for us uniquely. Yet God is not just present *to* us, no matter how personal and immediate that may be; he is also present *within* us.

This is the great truth of which Jesus spoke at the Last Supper: *those who love me will . . . win my Father's love and we will come and make our home in them* (Jn 14:23). It is an indwelling presence; a homing presence, through which God is at home in the human heart; a presence based on choice, love and friendship. . . .

The doctrine of the indwelling became the key to her own spiritual life and is central to her teaching. She wished to *live through love in his presence* (Eph 1:4); her life was essentially a response to this presence, an awareness of the One dwelling in the depths of her heart. She wanted more than anything else to retire within herself and live in the little *cell*—the *little Bethany*, she called it (IN 5)—which God had built in her heart. *I have found my Heaven on earth, she wrote, since Heaven is God, and God is [in] my soul* (L 122).

—Eugene McCaffrey OCD, *Let Yourself Be Loved*

IN GOD'S PRESENCE, CONSIDER . . .

God does not surround me as an abstract or impersonal energy source, but He is intimately and uniquely a part of me as an "indwelling presence." I want to desire this communion with Him above all else.

CLOSING PRAYER

God, You choose to be at home in my heart in a very real union of love. Draw me into this deep mystery that You are not just present to me, but within me.

The Great "Yes" to Love

If our life here and now is a continuing "yes" to God, eternal life is not a different kind of living that comes after we die, but rather the fulfillment of the way we've been learning to live all along.

We are sent into this world for a short time to say—through the joys and pains of our clock-time—the great "Yes" to the love that has been given to us and in so doing return to the One who sent us with that "Yes" engraved on our hearts. Our death thus becomes the moment of return. But our death can be this only if our whole life has been a journey back to the One from whom we come and who calls us the Beloved. There is such confusion about the idea of a life "hereafter," or "the eternal life." Personally, I do believe deeply in the eternal life, but not simply as a life after our physical death. It is only when we have claimed for ourselves the life of God's Spirit during the many moments of our "chronology" that we expect death to be the door to the fullness of life. Eternal life is not some great surprise that comes unannounced at the end of our existence in time; it is, rather, the full revelation of what we have been and have lived all along. The evangelist John expresses this succinctly when he says: "My dear people, what we are to be in the future has not yet been recorded; all we know is that, when it is recorded, we shall be like him because we shall see him as he really is."

With this vision, death is no longer the ultimate defeat. To the contrary, it becomes the final "Yes" and the great return to where we can most fully become children of God. . . . Dying is the greatest act of love, the act that leads me into the eternal embrace of my God whose love is everlasting.

—Henri Nouwen, *Life of the Beloved*

IN GOD'S PRESENCE, CONSIDER . . .

Is my daily life a continuing and growing "yes" to God? Am I gradually becoming more like God now, or am I expecting it just to happen after I die?

CLOSING PRAYER

Lord, help me to say a full "yes" to You through all the ups and downs of my life so that each day will be another step of my journey back to You.

Startling Revelations

The passage below was written after an interview with Fr. Seraphim Michalenko, MIC, one of the world's leading experts on St. Faustina and the message of Divine Mercy. Michalenko gives insight into Faustina's confessor and spiritual director, Fr. Michael Sopocko.

Among his duties was serving as confessor to the Sisters of Our Lady of Mercy, who had a house in Vilnius. It was there where he first met St. Faustina, who shared with him her startling revelations. "At first, he wanted to quit," says Fr. Seraphim. "He didn't want to be the confessor there because of what she was saying. Then the Mother Superior said, 'Well, what are we supposed to do?' And he said, 'Well, have her checked out by a psychiatrist.'" She was tested, and she was deemed mentally stable.

"Father Sopocko found out from the nuns that she was one of the best nuns in the convent," says Fr. Seraphim. "But she told him things in confession that nobody could possibly have known. Nobody. And that scared him." Saint Faustina had less than three years of formal schooling, and yet here she was shedding light on the progress of the mystical life of the soul and giving an unparalleled understanding into the mystery of Divine Mercy. Father Sopocko had to turn to the writings of St. Thomas Aquinas and St. Augustine, among others, to help him to confirm the authenticity of St. Faustina's revelations that God's greatest attribute is mercy.

Divine Mercy has since become what Fr. Seraphim calls "the greatest grass-roots movement in the history of the Church." None of this would have been possible if it weren't for Fr. Sopocko, the priest who believed St. Faustina.

—The Divine Mercy, "The Priest Who First Believed Faustina"

IN GOD'S PRESENCE, CONSIDER . . .

This story fills me with gratitude and conviction! The Lord encountered many human obstacles to get His message of mercy out to the world, from the initial disbelief of Faustina's assertions to the temporary ban of the *Diary*. Yet, with St. Faustina's trust and the tireless effort of many in the years following, every hindrance was overcome one by one.

CLOSING PRAYER

Merciful God, You revealed so much of who You are—and who You are for us—to St. Faustina. What I know and believe is all brushed now with the strokes of mercy. Thank You for all those who brought this revelation of Your mercy to me. Let me be a bearer of it now for all those I encounter.

Forever New

From the thousands of years of Christian teaching and devotion, Father Carlo draws us toward a radiance that brings everything into focus: the Mercy of God.

. . . Faustina's message proposes a worship to us which can rightly be called "new." It is new in the sense that we call a day new very early in the morning, and in the sense that we call a season new when it returns. These things have been new since the world was created, and we greet them every time as if they were created anew every day. In this same sense, a rainbow which appeared today over the roofs of my little city was also very new, immediately following a series of violent thunderstorms. The newness of Maria Faustina's message is not different from the newness of this dazzling rainbow today. I thank you, little lay sister Faustina. I thank you, not for having revealed the rainbow of life, but for having opened my eyes to my culpable ignorance. I thank you, humble convent gatekeeper for opening a gate for me at which I had not thought to knock before. Thank you, sister, and thanks to God "rich in mercy" Who wanted me to meet you on my path. The content of the message is ancient, but I find it all new only now from your words and from the suffering it cost you. The ages sing the mercy of my God, but I begin only now to bind myself to His mercy with a "new dedication." Through your merit, Faustina, I have discovered the focal point of a vast plurality of dogmas and mysteries and devotions and prayers. "I have known and believed the mercy of God toward us" (1 John 4:16).

—From "Rainbow," *On Discovering Mercy*

IN GOD'S PRESENCE, CONSIDER . . .

Am I one who is jaded and cynical, chafed by life's afflictions into aloofness from God's kindness? Perhaps, like a little child, I can be drawn into wonder and delight, with a new vision of Divine Mercy as an umbrella over all the world, everything seen in this new light of mercy.

CLOSING PRAYER

Loving Jesus, You spoke the world into being, and You desire to speak to me today. Surprise me with the gifts that flow from Your hands. Open my heart to the blessing that You pronounce over me, and give me a new dedication to Your way of mercy.

God Is Happy!

In his General Audience, June 19, 1991, St. Pope John Paul II exclaimed that the human person is a being made for joy. And here we read that there is no such thing as a "sad saint." Fr. Cantalamessa shows us why, echoing the message that we are made for joy. Through the mercy of God we are brought into the joy of Trinitarian love.

It is time to shout to the world that the Trinity is first and foremost joy and happiness. The trinity is "our resting place," "the flood of delight" in whom our thirst will one day be quenched. . . .

God is happy! Augustine says that God is happy and makes people happy. Happiness is part of the very mystery of his being. Being the highest good, he is also the highest and infinite happiness. St Francis of Assisi exclaims, "You are joy; You are . . . joy" in his "Praises of God."

God is happiness for the very same reason that the Trinity is happy; because he is love. Happiness, in fact, is to love and be loved, God, from all eternity, loves his Son with an infinite love. The Father finds "all his pleasure," that is, his happiness, in him. Since God is happy, he does everything that he does with joy: he creates with joy (see Job 38:7), he saves with joy, and . . . he even suffers with joy.

The Holy Spirit, pouring the love of God into hearts (see Romans 5:5), at the same time pours into them the happiness of God that is inseparable from this love. Because of that, one of the first fruits that is produced in our souls is joy (see Galatians 5:22). The happiness of God is like an overflowing river "whose streams make glad the city of God" (Psalm 46:4), i.e., the church. . . .

We carry the desire to be happy engraved on our hearts, because God has created us in "his image and likeness," and since he is perfect happiness, he made us for happiness too.

—Fr. Raniero Cantalamessa, *Contemplating the Trinity*

IN GOD'S PRESENCE, CONSIDER . . .

How do I respond to the "Good News" of the Gospel? Do I give thanks more than I gripe? Is my glass half full or half empty? I am attentive to what comes up in my heart when I meditate on this message that I am made for joy.

CLOSING PRAYER

Thank you, Lord, for allowing me to enter into Your joy. What a gift of Your mercy! It is so easy to get weighed down by the trials of daily life. Help me to experience and embrace Your joy in all I do and radiate that joy to others.

The Joy of Being Found

We know how to draw close to God through penance . . . but joy? How do we celebrate and enter into the joy of Easter, and remain there day in and day out? In his Mercy Sunday homily during the extraordinary Jubilee Year of Mercy, Pope Francis gave us a meditation that can guide us to joy every day of the year.

This is a time for the Church to rediscover the meaning of the mission entrusted to her by the Lord on the day of Easter: to be a sign and an instrument of the Father's mercy (cf. Jn 20:21–23).

For this reason, the Holy Year must keep alive the desire to know how to welcome the numerous signs of the tenderness which God offers to the whole world and, above all, to those who suffer, who are alone and abandoned, without hope of being pardoned or feeling the Father's love. A Holy Year to experience strongly within ourselves the joy of having been found by Jesus, the Good Shepherd who has come in search of us because we were lost. A Jubilee to receive the warmth of his love when he bears us upon his shoulders and brings us back to the Father's house. A year in which to be touched by the Lord Jesus and to be transformed by his mercy, so that we may become witnesses to mercy.

Here, then, is the reason for the Jubilee: because this is the time for mercy. It is the favourable time to heal wounds, a time not to be weary of meeting all those who are waiting to see and to touch with their hands the signs of the closeness of God, a time to offer everyone, everyone, the way of forgiveness and reconciliation.

—Pope Francis, Homily at first Vespers for Divine Mercy Sunday

IN GOD'S PRESENCE, CONSIDER . . .

There are so many who do not know the joy of being found. So many who do not have the "hope of being pardoned or feeling the Father's love." Do I have that joy? Have I allowed my heart to be transformed by His love and mercy? And do I have the desire to share with everyone the joy and hope of this message?

CLOSING PRAYER

You have carried me, Jesus my Shepherd. You have carried me from sin and places of darkness into the light of Your mercy. Reveal to me each day concrete ways I can share the joy and hope of this reality with those who need it most.

Mission to Distribute Grace

Years before her beatification, Faustina had a prophetic vision of her difficult pathway to sainthood and her ultimate commission as an instrument of grace for others.

Once I saw a big crowd of people in our chapel, in front of the chapel and in the street, because there was no room for them inside. The chapel was decorated for a feast. There were a lot of clergy near the altar, and then our sisters and those of many other congregations. They were all waiting for the person who was to take a place on the altar. Suddenly I heard a voice saying that I was to take the place on the altar. But as soon as I left the corridor to go across the yard and enter the chapel, following the voice that was calling me, all the people began to throw at me whatever they had to hand: mud, stones, sand, brooms, to such an extent that I at first hesitated to go forward. But the voice kept on calling me even more earnestly, so I walked on bravely. When I entered the chapel, the superiors, the sisters, the students, and even my parents started to hit me with whatever they could, and so whether I wanted to or not, I quickly took my place on the altar. As soon as I was there, the very same people, the students, the sisters, the superiors and my parents all began to hold their arms out to me asking for graces; and as for me, I did not bear any grudge against them for having thrown all sorts of things at me, and I was surprised that I felt a very special love precisely for those persons who had forced me to go more quickly to my appointed place. At the same time my soul was filled with ineffable happiness, and I heard these words, Do whatever you wish, distribute graces as you will, to whom you will and when you will. Then, instantly, the vision disappeared.

—St. Faustina, *Diary*, 31

IN GOD'S PRESENCE, CONSIDER . . .

How do I tend to react when hurt by others? Do I hold a grudge, or choose to respond with love?

CLOSING PRAYER

Lord help me to become an instrument of grace for others, even those who have hurt me.

A Most Unexpected Love

The holiness we seek can only come through a radical change in how we see ourselves and God.

God's love for us is unconditional. It's not dependent on how we perform. It's not based on how many prayers we recite, how well we keep our Lenten resolutions, how well our kids behave at Mass, and how often we avoid falling into sexual sin. God loves us, as we are, with all our messiness. He longs for us. He thirsts for us. As we are. Not as we'd like to be.

Yes, Jesus calls us to repent when we sin. And he calls us to the highest standard of holiness. . . . To do that, he needs to forgive us, heal us, change us, and sanctify us. . . . But none of that can happen in a deep, lasting way until we embrace two fundamental truths: the truth about ourselves and the truth about how God sees us. We must face the truth about all our tragic weaknesses and wounds. And then we must see ourselves, even with those failures, in the way God sees us: with a surprising gentleness, patience, and mercy and with a total, unconditional love that we don't think we deserve.

And that's the whole point. It's not about winning God's approval or earning his love by doing enough good Catholic things. When we meet God in the valley of humility, we encounter a most unexpected love, a totally free gift that is completely different from our ordinary human experience . . .

We're not talking here about merely recognizing the truth that "God loves me" in the abstract, on a catechism quiz. . . . No, we're talking about God loving you in a unique and unrepeatable way, for he longs for you personally, individually. We're talking about having your world turned upside down and your view of yourself completely changed, for you begin to see yourself, perhaps for the first time in your life, not in terms of what you do for others nor in terms of your many faults and wounds, but in the way God sees you. . . . You are a beloved son or daughter of God, and nothing you've done or may do can change that. Your heavenly Father delights in and embraces you.

—Edward Sri, *Into His Likeness*

IN GOD'S PRESENCE, CONSIDER . . .

Do I strive for holiness as if it's based on how many good Catholic things I can check off daily? I realize more and more that the reason everything from God is mercy, is that I can't possibly do anything to deserve His gifts. How freeing! My faults do not cancel His love, nor do my good actions bring it about.

CLOSING PRAYER

Father, I want to encounter this "most unexpected love" of Yours more deeply. Remind me that I am not defined by my failings nor by my good deeds—but by Your love.

The Face of the Father's Mercy

On April 11, 2015, the vigil of Divine Mercy Sunday, Pope Francis issued Misericordia Vultus, a papal bull of indiction proclaiming an Extraordinary Jubilee of Mercy from December 8, 2015, The Feast of the Immaculate Conception, to November 20, 2016, the Feast of Christ the King.

Jesus Christ is the face of the Father's mercy. These words might well sum up the mystery of the Christian faith. Mercy has become living and visible in Jesus of Nazareth, reaching its culmination in him. The Father, "rich in mercy" (*Eph* 2:4), after having revealed his name to Moses as "a God merciful and gracious, slow to anger, and abounding in steadfast love and faithfulness" (*Ex* 34:6), has never ceased to show, in various ways throughout history, his divine nature. In the "fullness of time" (*Gal* 4:4), when everything had been arranged according to his plan of salvation, he sent his only Son into the world, born of the Virgin Mary, to reveal his love for us in a definitive way. Whoever sees Jesus sees the Father (cf. *Jn* 14:9). Jesus of Nazareth, by his words, his actions, and his entire person reveals the mercy of God [See *Dei Verbum*, 4].

We need constantly to contemplate the mystery of mercy. It is a wellspring of joy, serenity, and peace. Our salvation depends on it. Mercy: the word reveals the very mystery of the Most Holy Trinity. Mercy: the ultimate and supreme act by which God comes to meet us. Mercy: the fundamental law that dwells in the heart of every person who looks sincerely into the eyes of his brothers and sisters on the path of life. Mercy: the bridge that connects God and man, opening our hearts to the hope of being loved forever despite our sinfulness.

—Pope Francis, *Misericordiae Vultus (The Face of Mercy)*, 1–3

IN GOD'S PRESENCE, CONSIDER . . .

How often do I contemplate the mystery of the Father's mercy reflected in Jesus, so that I may better understand and bear witness to it by my life?

CLOSING PRAYER

Father God, help me to "gaze more attentively" on Your face of mercy, and let the fruit of this contemplation become visible in me, blessing all those I meet.

The Heart of God

Von Balthasar describes how the Heart of Jesus is the source of all giving, His love the source of all loving.

But you are always the fullness and we are the void, always . . . when you go through the world poor and gray, cloaked in the garments of the lowly and the disinherited, concealing yourself behind sinners and tax-collectors, and we absent-mindedly perform on you the eight works of mercy, even then you alone are the giver who has made love possible for us . . . You alone remain. You are all in all. Even if your love desires us in order to delight in twoness and in order to celebrate with us the mystery of begetting and conceiving, nevertheless it is always YOUR love in both instances, your love which both gives and is given, at once seed and womb. . . . If love needs two feet in order to walk, still the walker is but one person, and that one is you. And if love needs two lovers, a lover and a beloved, still the love is only one, and that one is you.

Everything hearkens back to your throbbing Heart. Time and the seasons still hammer away and create, and your Heart drives the world and all its happenings forward with great painful blows. It is the unrest of the clock, and your Heart is restless until it rests in me. Your Heart is restless until we rest in you, once time and eternity have become interfused. But: Be at peace! I have overcome the world. The torment of sin has already been submerged in the stillness of love. The experience of what the world is has made love darker, more fiery, more ardent. The shallower abyss of rebellion has been swallowed up in unfathomable mercy, and throbbing majestically reigns serene the Heart of God.

—Hans Urs von Balthasar, *Heart of the World*

IN GOD'S PRESENCE, CONSIDER . . .

The Heart of Jesus is throbbing, beating out a steady call of love to the children of God. I want to allow any rebellion in me to be swallowed up in His unfathomable mercy, so that I can participate in His mission. What would it be like to live my life in communion with the serene Heart of God?

CLOSING PRAYER

Divine Lover, Divine Giver, let me rest in the stillness of love. Fill the void in me with Your fullness.

Let Us Become Good

In one of his famous sermons, St. Gregory reminds us that we receive mercy by giving mercy—especially to those in most need; and that our acts of mercy should be continuous and joyful, with no excuses, no procrastination.

Blessed are the merciful, says Scripture, for they shall obtain mercy. Again: Blessed is he who is considerate to the needy and the poor. Once more: Generous is the man who is merciful and lends. In another place: All day the just man is merciful and lends. Let us appropriate the beatitude; let us earn a name for thoughtfulness; let us become good. Not even night should interrupt your mission of mercy. Do not say: Come back and I will give you something tomorrow. Do not let anything come between your impulse to do good and its execution: compassion is the one thing that cannot be put off. Share your bread with the hungry, and bring the needy and the homeless into your house, with a joyful and eager heart. He who does acts of mercy should do so with cheerfulness. The grace of a good deed is doubled when it is done with promptness and speed. . . .

Doing good is cause for celebration, not complaint. If you take away the yoke, says Scripture, that is, if you do away with miserliness and counting the cost, with hesitation and grumbling, what will be the result? Something great and wonderful! What a magnificent reward there will be: Your light shall break forth like the dawn . . .

While we may, let us visit Christ; let us care for him, feed him, clothe him, welcome him, honor him. Let us show him mercy in the persons of the poor.

—St. Gregory Nazianzen, Bishop and Doctor of the Church

IN GOD'S PRESENCE, CONSIDER . . .

Do I pray and go to church, but fail to show mercy to Christ in the "persons of the poor," the people around me in need of love and support? Scripture and the teachings of the saints are filled with the necessity of caring for the poor, helping the needy, serving Christ by serving those around me. Have I shied away from that? Is it easier and more comfortable for me give money or pray? Am I overwhelmed by the need and don't know where to start? Perhaps this week I can consider a new way in which I can love Christ by personally caring for my neighbor.

CLOSING PRAYER

Gracious God, help me become good, truly good. Show me how to empty myself and take on Your goodness. Let me show mercy promptly and with a cheerful heart.

Paint an Image

On February 22, 1931, the young Polish nun Faustina was granted an extraordinary vision of Jesus, which led to the painting of the now famous Divine Mercy Image.

+February 22, 1931

In the evening, when I was in my cell, I saw the Lord Jesus clothed in a white garment. One hand [was] raised in the gesture of blessing, the other was touching the garment at the breast. From beneath the garment, slightly drawn aside at the breast, there were emanating two large rays, one red, the other pale. In silence I kept my gaze fixed on the Lord; my soul was struck with awe, but also with great joy. After a while, Jesus said to me, Paint an image according to the pattern you see, with the signature: Jesus, I trust in You. I desire that this image be venerated, first in your chapel, and [then] throughout the world.

I promise that the soul that will venerate this image will not perish. I also promise victory over [its] enemies already here on earth, especially at the hour of death. I Myself will defend it as My own glory.

When I told this to my confessor, I received this "When I came out of the confessional, I again heard words such as these: My image already is in your soul. I desire that there be a Feast of Mercy. I want this image, which you will paint with a brush, to be solemnly blessed on the first Sunday after Easter; that Sunday is to be the Feast of Mercy.

—St. Faustina, *Diary*, 47–49

IN GOD'S PRESENCE, CONSIDER . . .

Since Jesus clearly wants us all to see Him as He appeared to Faustina through the image that portrays this vision, how can I better venerate the image and reflect on what it shows us about the Lord?

CLOSING PRAYER

Jesus, Merciful Savior, help me, like Faustina, to keep my gaze fixed on You with awe and joy.

Become What You Behold . . .

The Divine Mercy Image is not just a picture. It's an invitation to really see who God is and become like Him—a fulfillment of St. Paul's prophetic teaching: "All of us, gazing with unveiled face on the glory of the Lord, are being transformed into the same image (2 Cor 3:18, NAB)."

St. Faustina didn't see a vision of a *painting*. She saw *Jesus, Himself*, the visible "image of the invisible God" (Col 1:15). (And whenever she looked at the painting, she saw beyond it to the real Image.) Like the disciples at the Transfiguration, she beheld the glory of God. . . .

Want to know how to use the Divine Mercy Image most effectively? Look at it. *Gaze* at it. Keep your gaze fixed upon the Lord until you are struck with awe and joy, contemplating the incredible goodness of God, who is always loving you, always blessing you, always inviting you into His Heart. . . .

As we gaze upon the Image, *we come to see who God really is and who we are called to be*. Moment by moment, we are transformed into the image and likeness of what we see. We *become what we behold* until we, ourselves, are living reflections of God.

We're not supposed to just hang this Image on a wall; *we're supposed to become it*. . . . Jesus is Mercy Incarnate and we are each called to become like Him, *transfigured into living images of Divine Mercy*, reflecting and radiating the Father's mercy in the world. . . .

Our vocation is to make God visible *by the way we live*. . . . The Divine Mercy Image is what you and I should see every time we look in the mirror. *It's an examination of conscience*. Am I a mirror reflection of Christ? . . . Do I reflect His tenderness, His gentleness, His patience, His loving gaze from the Cross? When I look in the mirror, do I see someone with one hand always blessing, the other always inviting everyone into my heart?

—Vinny Flynn, *7 Secrets of Divine Mercy*

IN GOD'S PRESENCE, CONSIDER . . .

What do I see when I look in the mirror, when I honestly take stock of who and how I am to others? In what situations do I struggle to reflect Jesus?

CLOSING PRAYER

Lord Jesus Christ, Son of the Living God, Your glory radiates into the depths of my soul. Transform me so that I become transparent to You, revealing to all around me Your love, Your splendor, Your goodness.

The Fire of (God's) Mercy . . .

Prior to St. Faustina's sharing the message of Divine Mercy with the world, St. Margaret Mary Alacoque drew God's children to the tenderness of Jesus's Sacred Heart. Here, her confessor illustrates for us total confidence in God's love.

[I]t is a great consolation to me: at death, when my sins known and unknown trouble me, I will take them all and cast them at Our Lord's feet to be consumed in the fire of his mercy. The greater they are, the worse they seem to me, the more willingly will I give them to him because the offering will be all the more worthy of his mercy. It seems to me that I could do nothing more reasonable nor more glorious to God, and because of the idea I have of his goodness, this will not be difficult. I feel greatly drawn to act in this way. As for purgatory, I do not fear it. I am sorry to have deserved it because it has only been by offending God; but since I do deserve it, I am glad to go there to satisfy his justice as rigorously as possible even to the day of judgment. . . .

God sought me out when I fled from him; he will not abandon me now that I seek him, or at least do not flee from him any more. Cultivate thoughts of confidence as long as it pleases God to give them to you; they honor God far more than contrary thoughts. The more wretched we are, the more is God honored by the confidence we have in him. It seems to me that if your confidence were as great as it ought to be, you would not worry about what may happen to you; you would place it all in God's hands, hoping that when he wants something of you he will let you know what it is.

—*The Spiritual Direction of Saint Claude de la Colombière*

IN GOD'S PRESENCE, CONSIDER . . .

What is the great shadow, the immovable burden within, the one thing that impedes me from knowing the flood of God's mercy? It is God who has been pursuing me; can I believe that He knows what He's doing and is able to handle all I bear?

CLOSING PRAYER

Jesus, I trust in you. You insisted that the prayer of trust be inscribed on every image of You, The Divine Mercy. I make this prayer my own: Jesus, I trust in you!

The Steady Rhythm of the Sacred Heart

Faustina is such an amazing saint. Not simply because she accomplished great things here on earth, but because she was an incredible example of living and witnessing to trust and mercy in her daily life.

Trust and mercy: the great message that comes to us from St. Faustina, the great remedy for times when we find ourselves inevitably distracted, harried, strung-out, or just tired and in need of grace. *Refocus on God's mercy. . . . Accept our need. . . . Make an act of trust.*

A friend of mine said something to me a few weeks ago that I haven't been able to get out of my mind; and it's the perfect way to refocus, accept, and trust. I was sharing some of the little frustrations of everyday life and he said, "Just take a second to be still and listen *to the steady rhythm of the Sacred Heart* beating underneath all your activities, all your thoughts, all your stress."

The steady rhythm of the Sacred Heart! I caught my breath and said, "Can you repeat that, please?!" As he said it again, it was like breathing peace deep into my soul: "Be still and listen to the beating of His Heart . . . it's always there, you just need to tune in."

This simple phrase has made such a difference! Almost every day, I catch myself getting caught up in something silly or about to react poorly to a situation, and then I remember, *"Wait, . . . His Heart is still beating, still keeping that steady rhythm under all of this. I don't need to be anxious, annoyed, fearful, or anything else, because He is here with me."*

Whether we use words or not, when we simply refocus on God, humbly accepting our spiritual dependence, we can live trust, as Faustina did. And there's something so calming and hopeful in this, just letting go and allowing God to be in control.

Even if all you do is pray, "Jesus, I trust in You" over and over again; even if you only "tune in" a few times to listen to His Sacred Heart beating in the stillness underneath it all, it will fill you with peace and help you to grow in trust, living day-by-day in the unfathomable mercy of God.

—Mary Flynn, *Musings*

IN GOD'S PRESENCE, CONSIDER . . .

In the busyness of my days, can I make time to pause and refocus on God, taking a moment to rest in His Heart, recognize my total dependence on Him, and make an act of trust?

CLOSING PRAYER

Lord, help me to rely totally on You, and in the ups and downs of my life, let me find peace in the "steady rhythm" of your merciful Heart.

Merciful Love

One of our best loved saints and Doctor of the Church, St. Therese of Lisieux distinguishes love from mercy: while love abounds within the Holy Trinity, mercy is love that draws toward weakness and frailty. The greater our sins, the greater our claim on mercy.

After so many graces which I have received, may I not sing with the Psalmist: "The Lord is good; His mercy endures for ever." It seems to me that if everyone received such graces, no one would dread God but all would love Him with an unbounded love. Through sheer love, without any thought of fear, no one would ever willfully commit the least fault. But then I realize that all souls cannot be alike; they must differ so as to honor the different perfections of God.

To me He has given His Infinite Mercy, and it is in this resplendent mirror that I gaze upon all His other attributes. There all appear radiant with love; even justice, perhaps more than the others, seems to me clothed with love. . . . What sweet joy to think that the Lord is just, that He takes into account our weakness and knows so fully well the frailty of our nature. What then need I fear? Surely the good God of infinite justice who deigns to pardon with such mercy the sins of the prodigal son, will also be just towards me who am always with Him. . . .

It is not because I have been preserved from mortal sin that I go to God with confidence and love. Even if I had on my conscience all the crimes that one could commit, I am sure I would lose nothing of my confidence; I would throw myself, my heart broken with sorrow, into the arms of my Savior. I know how much He loves the prodigal son; I have heard His words to Mary Magdalene, to the woman taken in adultery, to the Samaritan woman. No, there is no one who could frighten me, for I know too well what to believe about His mercy, about His love. I know that in the twinkling of an eye, all those thousands of sins would be consumed as a drop of water cast into a blazing fire.

—St. Therese of Lisieux, *Derniers entretiens*, p. 70

IN GOD'S PRESENCE, CONSIDER . . .

Today I can throw myself into limitless love. Today the fire of God's mercy can consume my entire being, fears, failures. Today I look into my Father's eyes and see His limitless love for me.

CLOSING PRAYER

Father of Mercy, Father of Love, You astound me. You disconcert me, because Your ways are so far from my ways. I am in awe of Your all-consuming love. I release my fears and renew my trust.

Today Is the Day of Salvation

This passage is prophetic of Christ as the Word of mercy from the Father—and in a real sense, each of us is a unique word from the Father meant to accomplish His purpose. We have only a brief moment in this life, and Isaiah shares with us the priceless opportunity of seizing the chance to fling ourselves into God's eternal mercy, and become who He created us to be.

Seek the Lord while he may be found,
call upon him while he is near;
let the wicked forsake his way,
and the unrighteous man his thoughts;
let him return to the Lord, that he may have mercy on him,
and to our God, for he will abundantly pardon.
For my thoughts are not your thoughts,
neither are your ways my ways, says the Lord.
For as the heavens are higher than the earth,
so are my ways higher than your ways
and my thoughts than your thoughts.
For as the rain and the snow come down from heaven,
and return not thither but water the earth,
making it bring forth and sprout,
giving seed to the sower and bread to the eater,
so shall my word be that goes forth from my mouth;
it shall not return to me empty,
but it shall accomplish that which I purpose,
and prosper in the thing for which I sent it.

—Isaiah 55:6–11

IN GOD'S PRESENCE, CONSIDER . . .

While every day I breathe the air of a fallen and collapsed world, can I permit the Divine to invade my mind with the Word from heaven? Today I will repudiate my earthly ways of thinking, and turn to the Word of God to illuminate my heart. I want to seek His ways, His thoughts. And I ponder today what word the Father wishes to speak with my life.

CLOSING PRAYER

God my Father, speak Your words of deliverance over me that I may be freed from bondage to yesterday's lies, and prosper through Your heavenly mercy. Reveal to me what word You want to speak to the world through me. I want only Your will. Let me come to life and bear fruit in the ways You desire.

Sea of Mercy

The Papal Preacher tells us that Divine Mercy is endlessly flowing and inviting us to immerse ourselves. How will we respond?

A great fourteenth-century Flemish mystic wrote, "God is a flowing and ebbing sea which ceaselessly flows out into all his beloved according to their needs and merits and which flows back with all those upon whom he has bestowed his gifts in heaven and on earth." (13) This suggests the image of a sea that flows onto the beach at high tide and draws info itself whatever is on the beach with its receding waves. Some boats, however, are bounded on all sides or tied to a post in the ground. The sea surrounds them and caresses them, as though inviting them to follow. For a little while, the boats are lifted up and float, but since they are tied, they do not follow the sea as it recedes. They stay on the shore, while other boats that are not tied put out into the deep under the sun on the tranquil sea.

This is what happens with the Trinity. The Trinity sends out its word and its grace like a beneficial wave that envelops people and invites them to follow into its immensity. Some souls are "untied," ready, and they follow with joy. Others, instead, are tied by the ropes of old habits, by worldly attachments, or by fear of the unknown. For a moment they let themselves be lifted up and gently rocked, but when it comes time to decide to go forward, they do not feel like going, and they stay on land. What will happen to them? Will they one day know the intoxication of the open sea, or will they be like the boats that stay on the shore and become corroded by sea salt?

The cry of Christ that the pope [St. Pope John Paul II] has echoed in the letter with which he opened the new millennium resounds here more than ever: "*Duc in altum*, put out into the deep!" Hoist the sails, lift the anchors! Do not be afraid of venturing forth into the open sea of holiness.

—Fr. Raniero Cantalamessa, *Contemplating the Trinity*

IN GOD'S PRESENCE, CONSIDER . . .

What are the ties that bind me and keep me from making a full commitment to follow Christ?

CLOSING PRAYER

Lord, deliver me from any complacency or fear holding me back from letting You draw me deeper.

The Peace of Mercy

Blessed Sopocko found and hired the artist who painted the original Divine Mercy Image. Here, he speaks of the Image in relation to the peace Jesus wants to give us.

"Peace be to you... He therefore said to them again . . . peace be to you." (Jn 20:21) How gracious sound those words of Christ in our hearts. . . . The Most Merciful Savior proclaimed the manifesto of His peace as He was instituting the Sacrament of Penance, that Sacrament of God's Mercy, which alone gives true peace. This is not a voice from the earth! This is a voice from Heaven! This is the consummation of the angelic proclamation over Bethlehem's manger —"Peace to men of good will." With those words, "Peace be to you," the King of Mercy greeted His followers on the day of His Resurrection as He appeared to them in the Cenacle. This moment in the glorious life of Christ is depicted in that well known picture of the Most Merciful Savior, which is now venerated all over the world. Let us ponder briefly its meaning. . . .

With His right hand He slightly draws aside the garment in the vicinity of is Heart, from Which spring forth two rays . . . These rays signify the Blood and Water which flowed from the opened side of Jesus on the cross. From that time on they gush forth from the Divine Heart of the Savior in the form of graces purifying the soul from the stains of sin (in the Sacraments of Baptism and Penance) and of life-giving graces (in the Sacrament of the Altar . . .). . . . This picture . . . explains the anthem sung by the Church during Eastertime as the priest sprinkles the congregation with holy water . . . : "Vidi aquam—I saw water coming forth from the right side of the temple, alleluia: and all to whom it came were saved . . . Give praise to the Lord, for He is good: for His Mercy endureth for ever." This temple is Christ from Whose open side flows the water of inexhaustible graces purifying the soul from sins in the Sacraments of Baptism and Penance.

—Blessed Michael Sopocko

IN GOD'S PRESENCE, CONSIDER . . .

Sometimes interior peace feels impossible in our chaotic world, but I will call on the graces of my baptism, and open myself more to the River of Life flowing from the Savior's Heart, coming to me through the Eucharist and confession.

CLOSING PRAYER

King of Mercy, You desire Your peace to reign in my heart at all times. Remind me that Your life in me and a soul free of sin is what gives me true peace.

The Ray that Flashes Forth

One can't help but imagine the rays from the Divine Mercy Image while reading this quote from Von Balthasar—and how we are not just meant to gaze on the Image, but to become it.

"I am the light of the world," says God, "and without me you can do nothing. And, beside me, there is no light and no god. But you are the light of the world, a borrowed but not a false light; burning with my flame you are to enkindle the world with my fire. Go out into the furthest darkness! Take my love like lambs into the midst of wolves! Take my gospel to those who cower in the dark and in the shadow of death! Go out; venture beyond the well-guarded fold! I once brought you home when you were lost lambs and were bleeding among the thorns. Then did I bring you home on my good shepherd's shoulders. But now the flock is scattered and the gate of the pen gapes wide: this is the hour of mission! Out! Separate yourselves from me, for I am with you until the end of the world. For I myself went out from the Father and, by going out from him, I became obedient unto death, and by obeying I became the perfect image of his love for me. The going out itself is love; the going out itself is the return. Just as the Father has sent me, so do I send you. Going out from me as a ray from the sun, as a stream from its source, you remain in me, for I myself am the ray that flashes forth, the stream that is poured out from the Father. To give is more blessed than to receive. Just as I radiate the Father, so also are you to radiate me. So turn your face to me that I can turn it out into the world. You are to be so separated from your own ways that I can place you on the way that I am.

—Hans Urs von Balthasar, *Heart of the World*

IN GOD'S PRESENCE, CONSIDER . . .

Yes! The love of God so fills me, so illuminates me, that I become light in this world! Even when I go out on mission from my intimate time with Him in prayer, I do not depart from Him, but become more united to Him by becoming His image, by emptying myself so as to be filled more and more with His light and presence!

CLOSING PRAYER

Lord, God of Hosts, Heaven is Your throne and earth is Your footstool; You look upon all that You have made, and Your deep desire is oneness. Set me on fire and grant me zeal for the Gospel; fill me with Your light, so that I may flash and gleam with the radiance of Your love.

Transformed

Drawn from the Divine Mercy message and Ezekiel 47, this prayer poem speaks of the dichotomy of needing the mercy of transformation ourselves, and yet answering God's call to be a vessel for the transformation of the world. We need the water, and we also become part of the living stream flowing to others. We need healing, and we then bring the healing. How? Through the Holy Spirit; through the Eucharist. Our calling is to be transformed.

Like streams Your Blood
reaches me
Torrents rushing in,
As the fresh water,
To the salty sea.

Even the vast sea
cannot change
that fresh water.
Even the vast sea.

Wherever the river from the
temple flows,
The salty water shall be made fresh,
The trees shall bear fruit,
Their leaves serve for medicine.

And I am salt water,
And barren tree.
Yet I . . . I am Your temple,
Flow through me.

Cast out the worldly things
on the table of my heart.
Change me into You,
Oh Blood . . . Oh Water . . .
Oh Love!

—Erin Flynn

IN GOD'S PRESENCE, CONSIDER . . .

I must be nourished by His Presence before I can nourish the world. I am meant to be a holy temple (*Cor. 3:9c–11,16–17*), and through His kenosis—his outpouring—new life flows into me, and I am immersed in the river of Divine Life. O Blood and Water, which gushed forth . . . All my darkness, and the darkness of the world, cannot taint that life-giving stream of mercy. That's amazing! I am the dead sea brought to life. I am a tree that will bear fruit for the world and medicine for its wounds through His Life in me.

CLOSING PRAYER

No darkness can affect me unless I let it by removing myself from You, my Source.

Lord, Your power is so great that a drop of Your love can transform—and You in Your mercy give me a flood! Transform me. Make me into fresh water to quench the thirsty world with Your Presence in me.

Joy! Even in Our Faults

St. Claude de la Colombière tells us that, because of God's mercy, we can live in joy even in our weaknesses and sins.

By God's infinite mercy I feel a liberty of spirit which fills me with great joy. It seems as though nothing could now make me unhappy. The thought that I am serving God fills me with this joy, and I feel that it is of far greater value than all the favor of kings would be. The occupations of the worldly seem very despicable in comparison with work done for God.

I know no greater joy than to discover some weakness in myself that I did not realize before. I often taste this joy and shall always have it when God gives me his light when I am examining my conscience. I firmly believe, and in this I find joy, that God guides those who give themselves up to his leading and that he takes care of the least things that concern them.

We must serve God with our whole heart and do all in our power to prevent ourselves from sinning, but all this is to be done with joy, liberty of heart, and entire confidence, in spite of all the weakness that we feel and the faults we commit.

—*The Spiritual Direction of Saint Claude de la Colombière*

IN GOD'S PRESENCE, CONSIDER . . .

Do I scrutinize and inspect my sins and shortcomings with far greater intensity than I study the things of God? Am I in fact collapsing into egotism by focusing on my failures instead of fixing my vision on the infinite mercy of my Father? I will do all I can to keep from sinning, but receive with gratitude and peace the light that reveals my faults.

CLOSING PRAYER

Lord of Wisdom, Lord of Love, Your glance pierces the heavens and unravels the mysteries of all realms; *break the trance of the whispering accuser and draw me into Your enduring love. Help me to give myself up to Your leading, to have total confidence in Your care, and so enter in the freedom and joy You offer.*

Set Aside Your "Water Jar"

Pope Francis invites us to let go of anything that distracts or internally binds us from seeking the "living water" of mercy that Christ offers us.

Today's Gospel presents Jesus' encounter with the Samaritan woman . . . [Jn 4:6–30]. He immediately says to her: "Give me a drink" (v. 7). In this way he overcomes the barriers of hostility that existed between Jews and Samaritans and breaks the mould of prejudice against women. This simple request from Jesus is the start of a frank dialogue, through which he enters with great delicacy into the interior world of a person to whom, according to social norms, he should not have spoken. But Jesus does! Jesus is not afraid. . . . He never hesitates before a person out of prejudice. . . .

Jesus' thirst was not so much for water, but for the encounter with a parched soul. Jesus needed to encounter the Samaritan woman in order to open her heart: he asks for a drink so as to bring to light her own thirst. . . . The disciples marvelled that their Master was speaking to this woman. But the Lord is greater than prejudice, which is why he was not afraid to address the Samaritan woman: mercy is greater than prejudice. The outcome of that encounter by the well was the woman's transformation: "the woman left her water jar" (v. 28) . . . and ran to the city to tell people about her extraordinary experience. . . . She had gone to draw water from the well, but she found another kind of water, the living water of mercy from which gushes forth eternal life. . . . In this Gospel passage we likewise find the impetus to "leave behind our water jar," the symbol of everything that is seemingly important, but loses all its value before the "love of God." We all have one, or more than one! I ask you, and myself: "What is your interior water jar, the one that weighs you down, that distances you from God?" Let us set it aside a little and . . . let us hear the voice of Jesus offering us another kind of water.

—Pope Francis, Angelus, March 23, 2014

IN GOD'S PRESENCE, CONSIDER . . .

I take some time to wonder about my interior water jar. What things in my life insert any kind of distance between me and God? Are there big or little things that I've made more important than my relationship with Him? Perhaps there are even good things I've become attached to that I need to loosen my grip on because they are not the Life-giving water.

CLOSING PRAYER

Lord, reveal to me my true thirst, and fill me with the living water of Your mercy. Then help me to let go of any fears or prejudices that prevent me from seeing the thirst of others and loving them as You do.

The Father's Love Letter

Scripture makes it clear that the Father's mercy is not some general concern for humanity, but is the most personal, individual love imaginable. He doesn't just love "mankind." He loves each of us personally and forever as only a perfect father can love his children.

Fear not, for I have redeemed you; I have called you by name, you are mine. Is 43:1

Before I formed you in the womb I knew you. Jer 1:5

See, upon the palms of my hands I have written your name. Is 49:16 (NAB)

I have loved you with an everlasting love. Jer 31:3

You are precious in my eyes. Is 43:4

Even the hairs of your head are all numbered. Mt 10:30

Can a mother forget her infant, be without tenderness for the child of her womb? Even should she forget, I will never forget you. Is 49:15 (NABRE)

Though the mountains leave their place and the hills be shaken, My love shall never leave you. Is 54:10 (NAB)

I will be a father to you, and you shall be my sons and daughters. 2 Cor 6:18

For I know well the plans I have in mind for you . . . plans for your welfare, not for woe! Plans to give you a future full of hope. When you call me, when you go to pray to me, I will listen to you. . . . When you seek me with all your heart, you will find me with you. Jer 29:11–14 (NAB)

IN GOD'S PRESENCE, CONSIDER . . .

Do I really understand how precious I am to the Father, how deeply and personally He loves me? How can I respond to His love more completely?

CLOSING PRAYER

God, help me to understand that I'm not just a creature, but a child whom You love. Help me to receive that love and let it fill me with complete trust in You.

The Bliss of Mercy's Gentleness

Carmelite priest Fr. Iain Matthew writes that St. John of the Cross learned to live in the gentleness of the Father's embrace.

Addressing the Father, the "gentle hand," John comments: "But you, O life divine, you never slay except to give life; you never wound except to heal. When you chastise, you touch lightly, and this itself could burn up the world. But when it comes to showing kindness, you lay your hand most firmly, and so the bliss of your gentleness knows no bounds" (LF 2:16). . . .

When Jesus said, "Father," he could "rejoice" because he was allowing the fulfillment of all his Father's longing to love. The Father "rests," indeed "fits," only in the Son (cf SCB 1:5). Jesus could "rejoice" because the infinite force of his love was being received in the "limitless embrace" of the Father's "kindness" (LF 1:15). That is where John came to live, in the love uniting Son and Father.

All the baptized belong there, rising from the font to hear: "You are my beloved child; with you I am well pleased" (cf Lk 3:22). In a brittle world, there is a need for people who have learned to live in the Father's embrace.

—Iain Matthew OCD, *John of the Cross: Seasons of Prayer*

IN GOD'S PRESENCE, CONSIDER . . .

Everything that comes to us from the Father is mercy——mercy that comes from the depths of His tenderness. The Father longs to love, not just Jesus, but me. Trusting in His mercy means learning to rest in His embrace, which is kind and safe.

CLOSING PRAYER

Father, help me to trust that everything that comes to me is from Your mercy, even when I don't understand how. Teach me to rest in the depths of Your kindness and love, and to live in and from Your embrace.

The Old Testament God of Mercy

We often equate the Old Testament with God's wrath. But, in these passages from Hosea, you can feel the tenderness of God and His intense desire to have mercy on His people, even as He laments how they turn from Him.

God's Compassion Despite Israel's Ingratitude

When Israel was a child, I loved him,
and out of Egypt I called my son.
The more I called them,
the more they went from me;
they kept sacrificing to the Ba′als,
and burning incense to idols.

Yet it was I who taught E′phraim to walk,
I took them up in my arms;
but they did not know that I healed them.
I led them with cords of compassion,
with the bands of love,
and I became to them as one
who eases the yoke on their jaws,
and I bent down to them and fed them.

They shall return to the land of Egypt,
and Assyria shall be their king,
because they have refused to return to me.
My people are bent on turning away from me;
so they are appointed to the yoke,
and none shall remove it.

How can I give you up, O E′phraim!
How can I hand you over, O Israel!
My heart recoils within me,
my compassion grows warm and tender.
I will not execute my fierce anger,
for I am God and not man,
the Holy One in your midst,
and I will not come to destroy.

—Hosea 11:1–5, 7–9

IN GOD'S PRESENCE, CONSIDER . . .

This is God the Father speaking over my life. I am Israel, His beloved child. And throughout my life, He has been the one pouring out all of the goodness I have ever received. And despite every act of unfaithfulness to Him, He promises His mercy until the very end—because He loves me with the affection of a perfect Father.

CLOSING PRAYER

Father, You have loved me from the beginning; You have loved me through all my childishness and falls and wayward turns. Let me never refuse You, never turn away from You. Lead me by bands of love. I want nothing more.

Beloved of God

What a dichotomy of grace! The more I see my own misery, the more I attract God's mercy and rest in being the beloved. He is the merciful Lord and King of Psalm 145, and the God of Hosea 11, who bends down to feed us, takes us up in His arms, and heals us. Brother Lawrence tells us here what it is like to abandon ourselves to this kind King.

I regard myself as the most wretched of men, stinking and covered with sores, and as one who has committed all sorts of crimes against his King. Overcome by remorse, I confess all my wickedness to him, ask his pardon and abandon myself entirely to him to do with as he will.

But this King, filled with goodness and mercy, far from chastising me, lovingly embraces me, makes me eat at His table, serves me with His own hands, gives me the keys of His treasures, and treats me as His favorite. He talks with me and is delighted with me in a thousand and one ways; He forgives me and relieves me of my principle bad habits without talking about them. I beg Him to make me according to His heart, and the more weak and despicable I see myself to be, the more beloved I am of God.

—Brother Lawrence, *The Practice of the Presence of God*

IN GOD'S PRESENCE, CONSIDER . . .

When I think of my sins, faults, failures, what occurs in me when I think of coming before the Lord to reveal them all? Do I tend to fall into self-condemnation and discouragement? Do I make a list and resolve to fix myself, tending towards self-reliance? I consider now that God is this King who delights in me, even and especially when I come vulnerably before Him. I see how allowing Him to do *His* work in me counters both self-condemnation and self-reliance.

CLOSING PRAYER

Jesus, King of Mercy, I want to live in this truth, that even when I am faced with my weakness and misery and filled with remorse, You are "delighted with me in a thousand and one ways." Thank you for your tender mercies. I surrender myself to You; change me as You will.

Mercy Has A Face

In his homily at the Beatification of Fr. Sopocko (St. Faustina's confessor), Cardinal Stanisław Dziwisz, the faithful personal secretary to St. Pope John Paul II and early promoter of the Divine Mercy message, explains that mercy has a face—and a name.

Divine Mercy has its own face, this face is Jesus Christ, Son of God stooping over sinful man and feeding him with the word of truth and life and with the Sacrament of His Body and Blood, . . . It is the face of the One who leads us out of the dark world of sin and evil and leads us to the freedom of the children of God. It is the face of the One who became our Brother, and who said that we can recognize Him in the face of the hungry, the thirsty, the weary stranger, the naked, the sick and those in prisons. "Whatever you have done to the least of my brothers, you have done to me" (Mt 25:40). . . .

Mercy has its own name. To this name, every knee shall bow. This name is Jesus and expresses the truth, that "God saves." He saves every human person. That is why He waits upon all, even those who are lost the most, about whom today's Gospel speaks. "Truly I say to you, tax collectors and prostitutes are entering the Kingdom of God before you" (Mt 21:31). For God, it is never too late. He always waits for our conversion. He waits for our hearts, He waits for our [extended] hands. He waits for us, that we may partake of His work of salvation. He waits, that when in need, we would remember and, like the second son of today's Gospel, go to His vineyard. This is the message of mercy! This is our hope.

—Cardinal Stanisław Dziwisz, Homily at Beatification of Blessed Sopocko

IN GOD'S PRESENCE, CONSIDER . . .

The image of Jesus, the Divine Mercy, "stooping over sinful man and feeding him," conjures up the poignant passage from Hosea 11: "I led them with cords of compassion, with the bands of love, and I became to them as one who eases the yoke on their jaws, and I bent down to them and fed them." Just as He proved His love for Israel again and again, so now He feeds me with His very life and waits for my heart to be converted, waits for me to turn to Him in everything.

CLOSING PRAYER

Jesus, You are mercy's face, mercy's name, You are my Food, and the One who feeds me. You wait for me—in the Blessed Sacrament, in the poor, in the place of Divine union within. Always waiting for me to come. Draw me with bands of love and help me share this message of mercy and hope with the world.

Entering into Communion

Divine Mercy is not just a concept. Divine Mercy is a person—Jesus, Himself—the one who gives Himself to us as Eucharist, inviting us to enter into an active, and personal, relationship with Him.

Just as the phrase "the Body of Christ" can suggest merely the human nature of Christ or the image of His dead body on the cross, so the phrase "receiving Communion" can suggest a passive reality. It can reinforce the concept that we're not really "doing" anything. God is the one who is doing; we are simply receiving. . . . Yes, Christ is doing something. But part of what He's doing is calling to us, inviting us to respond to His initiative in an active way. . . .

"Receiving Communion," writes Pope Benedict XVI, "means entering into communion with Jesus Christ. . . . What is given us here is not a piece of a body, not a thing, but Him, the Resurrected one himself—the person who shares himself with us in his love. . . . This means that receiving Communion is always a personal act.

When I receive Communion properly, I am not merely receiving something into me; I am actively involved in the process, fully present to the One who is present within me, uniting my whole being with Him, becoming "one flesh" with Christ, and through Him entering into a uniquely personal encounter with the Father and the Holy Spirit as well.

This "entering into" communion, this personal encounter with Christ and, through Him, with the other persons of the Trinity, doesn't simply involve God dwelling in us. It involves relationship. The indwelling of God is a gift demanding a reciprocal response. We must give ourselves to Christ as He gives Himself to us. Christ's plan is not merely to live in us, but also to enable us to live in Him: "Whoever eats my flesh and drinks my blood remains in me and I in him" (Jn. 6:56).

—Vinny Flynn, *7 Secrets of the Eucharist*

IN GOD'S PRESENCE, CONSIDER . . .

The Eucharist is *alive.* If a stranger who knew nothing about the Eucharist were to watch the way we receive, would he know this? When I approach the Eucharist, does it look like I'm receiving the *living person*, Jesus Christ?

CLOSING PRAYER

Forgive me, Lord, for the times I've mindlessly received You as if You were just a thing instead of the living, loving Person of God. Help me to enter into communion more faithfully, keeping my focus on You in awe and gratitude for this miraculous, living gift of Yourself.

The Eucharist Reveals the Truth About Love

Christ's gift of Himself in the Eucharist, Pope Benedict explains, is also a revelation and manifestation of His infinite love.

. . . The Holy Eucharist is the gift that Jesus Christ makes of himself, thus revealing to us God's infinite love for every man and woman. This wondrous sacrament makes manifest that "greater" love which led him to "lay down his life for his friends" (Jn 15:13). Jesus did indeed love them "to the end" (Jn 13:1). In those words the Evangelist introduces Christ's act of immense humility: before dying for us on the Cross, he tied a towel around himself and washed the feet of his disciples. In the same way, Jesus continues, in the sacrament of the Eucharist, to love us "to the end," even to offering us his body and his blood. What amazement must the Apostles have felt in witnessing what the Lord did and said during that Supper! What wonder must the eucharistic mystery also awaken in our own hearts!

. . . In the sacrament of the Eucharist, Jesus shows us in particular the truth about the love which is the very essence of God. It is this evangelical truth which challenges each of us and our whole being. For this reason, the Church, which finds in the Eucharist the very centre of her life, is constantly concerned to proclaim to all . . . that God is love.

—Pope Benedict XVI, *Sacramentum Caritatis (Sacrament of Charity)*, 1–2

IN GOD'S PRESENCE, CONSIDER . . .

How often do I take the time to prepare for Holy Communion by reflecting on the great mystery of Christ's love?

CLOSING PRAYER

Lord, awaken wonder in me at this Eucharistic mystery. Help me to never receive mindlessly, but to be continually amazed at the gift and challenge of Your love.

The Eucharist as the Mercy of God

In her fervent hymn to God's mercy, St. Catherine of Siena speaks of the greatest gift of His mercy here and now, the Holy Eucharist.

You temper your justice with mercy. In mercy you cleansed us in the blood; in mercy you kept company with your creatures. O mad lover! It was not enough for you to take on our humanity: you had to die as well! Nor was death enough: You descended to the depths to summon our holy ancestors and fulfill your truth and mercy in them. Your goodness promises good to those who serve you in truth, so you went to call these servants of yours from their suffering to reward them for their labours!

I see your mercy pressing us to give you even more when you leave yourself with us as food to strengthen our weakness, so that we, forgetful fools should be ever reminded of your goodness. Every day you give us this food, showing us yourself in the sacrament of the altar within the mystic body of the Holy Church. And what has done this? Your mercy.

O Mercy! My heart is engulfed with the thought of you! For wherever I turn my thoughts I find nothing but mercy! O eternal Father, forgive my foolish presumption in babbling on so before you but your merciful love is my excuse in the presence of your kindness.

—Catherine of Siena, *The Dialogue*, D 30, 72

IN GOD'S PRESENCE, CONSIDER . . .

My God isn't far from me: he races toward me in His mercy and undertakes everything necessary for me to flourish in Him. He gives Himself totally to me in the Blessed Sacrament, a constant reminder of His goodness. Today I let go of my frailties and failures: I see only His radiance and love. He is eternal Truth: I lose myself in Him.

CLOSING PRAYER

O Mad Lover! My heart is engulfed with the thought of You! For wherever I turn my thoughts, I find nothing but mercy. I unite myself now to Your Eucharistic Presence. You are my life, my breath, my joy!

Mother of Divine Mercy

In his encyclical Rich in Mercy, St. Pope John Paul II includes a powerful teaching on Mary and her unique role in the revelation of mercy.

Mary is . . . the one who obtained mercy in a particular and exceptional way, as no other person has. At the same time, still in an exceptional way, she made possible with the sacrifice of her heart her own sharing in revealing God's mercy. This sacrifice is intimately linked with the cross of her Son, at the foot of which she was to stand on Calvary. Her sacrifice is a unique sharing in the revelation of mercy; that is, a sharing in the absolute fidelity of God to His own love, to the covenant that He willed from eternity and that He entered into in time with man, with the people, with humanity. . . .

No one has experienced, to the same degree as the Mother of the crucified One, the mystery of the cross, the overwhelming encounter of divine transcendent justice with love: that "kiss" given by mercy to justice. No one has received into his heart, as much as Mary did, that mystery, that truly divine dimension of the redemption effected on Calvary by means of the death of the Son, together with the sacrifice of her maternal heart, together with her definitive "fiat."

Mary, then, is the one who has the deepest knowledge of the mystery of God's mercy. She knows its price, she knows how great it is. In this sense, we call her the Mother of Mercy: our Lady of Mercy, or Mother of Divine Mercy; in each one of these titles there is a deep theological meaning, for they express the special preparation of her soul, of her whole personality. . . .

The above titles . . . speak of her principally, however, as the Mother of the crucified and risen One; as the one who, having obtained mercy in an exceptional way, in an equally exceptional way "merits" that mercy throughout her earthly life and, particularly, at the foot of the cross of her Son; and finally as the one who . . . was called in a special way to bring close to people that love which He had come to reveal.

—St. Pope John Paul II, *Dives in Misericordia (Rich in Mercy)*, 9

IN GOD'S PRESENCE, CONSIDER . . .

How strong is my devotion to Mary? Do I appreciate and reflect upon her exceptional union with Christ in the mystery of mercy and the power of her intercession for me?

CLOSING PRAYER

Mary, Mother of Mercy, be my mother, too, and draw me closer to the merciful heart of Jesus.

Gentle Rain from Heaven . . .

From Shakespeare, the great "Bard of Avon," comes a beautiful expression of the supreme power and gentleness of Divine Mercy.

The quality of mercy is not strain'd,
It droppeth as the gentle rain from heaven
Upon the place beneath: it is twice blest;
It blesseth him that gives and him that takes:
'Tis mightiest in the mightiest: it becomes
The throned monarch better than his crown;
His sceptre shows the force of temporal power,
The attribute to awe and majesty,
Wherein doth sit the dread and fear of kings;
But mercy is above this sceptred sway;
It is enthroned in the hearts of kings,
It is an attribute to God himself;
And earthly power doth then show likest God's
When mercy seasons justice. Therefore, Jew,
Though justice be thy plea, consider this,
That, in the course of justice, none of us
Should see salvation: we do pray for mercy;
And that same prayer doth teach us all to render
The deeds of mercy.

—William Shakespeare, *The Merchant of Venice*

IN GOD'S PRESENCE, CONSIDER . . .

Is justice my plea—do I strive to build a case for myself by my works and efforts, or am I ready to reach for a mightier and more majestic identity: being held in God's mercy?

CLOSING PRAYER

Father of mercy, Father of Love, You are King of kings and Lord of lords, yet Your greatness is revealed in Your mercy. Teach me gentleness, that I may rest in Your truest self, and cease from striving apart from You.

The Origin of the Chaplet

In an extraordinary sequence of dramatic revelations, the Lord gave St. Faustina the words of the prayer now known as the Chaplet of Divine Mercy, making it clear to her that this prayer, when prayed from the heart with trust, would have great power—even to draw mercy over justice.

In the evening, when I was in my cell, I saw an Angel, the executor of divine wrath. He was clothed in a dazzling robe, his face gloriously bright, a cloud beneath his feet. From the cloud, bolts of thunder and flashes of lightning were springing into his hands; and from his hand they were going forth, and only then were they striking the earth. When I saw this sign of divine wrath which was about to strike the earth, and in particular a certain place, which for good reasons I cannot name, I began to implore the Angel to hold off for a few moments, and the world would do penance. But my plea was a mere nothing in the face of the divine anger. Just then I saw the Most Holy Trinity. The greatness of Its majesty pierced me deeply, and I did not dare to repeat my entreaties. At that very moment I felt in my soul the power of Jesus' grace, which dwells in my soul. When I became conscious of this grace, I was instantly snatched up before the Throne of God. . . . I found myself pleading with God for the world with words heard interiorly. As I was praying in this manner, I saw the Angel's helplessness: he could not carry out the just punishment which was rightly due for sins. Never before had I prayed with such inner power as I did then.

The words with which I entreated God are these: Eternal Father, I offer You the Body and Blood, Soul and Divinity of Your dearly beloved Son, Our Lord Jesus Christ for our sins and those of the whole world; for the sake of His sorrowful Passion, have mercy on us.

The next morning, when I entered chapel, I heard these words interiorly: Every time you enter the chapel, immediately recite the prayer which I taught you yesterday. . . . The souls that say this chaplet will be embraced by My mercy during their lifetime and especially at the hour of their death.

—St. Faustina, *Diary*, 474–476, 754

IN GOD'S PRESENCE, CONSIDER . . .

Since the Lord clearly wants us to pray the Chaplet to implore His mercy for sinners, how can I incorporate it as a regular part of my prayer life?

CLOSING PRAYER

Thank you, Most Holy Trinity, for this prayer and for Your desire to have mercy on us all, even when our sins deserve strict justice. The power of this chaplet and the goodness of Your promises fill my heart with gratitude.

Deliverance from On High

Today we join Sirach (his full name is Jesus Eleazar ben Sira, so you can say we join Jesus) in praising the Father for His deliverance and His mercy. There is a beautiful parallel later in the New Testament, as we are asked to join the Son of God in His ultimate submissiom to the Father's plan.

I give you thanks, O Lord and King,
and praise you, O God my Savior.
I give thanks to your name,
for you have been my protector and helper
and have delivered me from destruction
and from the trap laid by a slanderous tongue,
from lips that fabricate lies.
In the face of my adversaries
you have been my helper and delivered me,
in the greatness of your mercy and of your name,
from grinding teeth about to devour me,
from the hand of those seeking my life,
from the many troubles I endured,
from choking fire on every side,
and from the midst of fire that I had not kindled,
from the deep belly of Hades,
from an unclean tongue and lying words—
the slander of an unrighteous tongue to the king.
My soul drew near to death,
and my life was on the brink of Hades below.
They surrounded me on every side,
and there was no one to help me;
I looked for human assistance,
and there was none.
Then I remembered your mercy, O Lord,
and your kindness from of old,
for you rescue those who wait for you
and save them from the hand of their enemies.

—Sirach 51:1–8 (NRSVCE)

IN GOD'S PRESENCE, CONSIDER . . .

In the Gospels, Jesus invites me, requires me to take up my cross with Him. This is not harshness, but a beautiful invitation to discover that I'm with Jesus, and that I receive the rescue of my Father. Instead of trying to save myself, I'm joining Jesus.

CLOSING PRAYER

God my Father, You delivered Your Son from the shadow of death and raised Him to glory on the third day. Give me the grace to commend myself entirely to Your mercy, and never to rely on my own ability.

Always Held by My Father

Today Isaiah shares with us one of the greatest words of the Old Testament: "Hesed," here translated steadfast love. This covenant loyalty of God is His unwavering mercy, everlasting and not dependent on our merits, but redeeming us into union with Him.

I will recount the steadfast love of the Lord,
 the praises of the Lord,
according to all that the Lord has granted us,
 and the great goodness to the house of Israel
which he has granted them according to his mercy,
 according to the abundance of his steadfast love.
For he said, Surely they are my people,
 sons who will not deal falsely;
 and he became their Savior.
In all their affliction he was afflicted,
 and the angel of his presence saved them;
in his love and in his pity he redeemed them;
 he lifted them up and carried them all the days of old.

—Isaiah 63:7–9

IN GOD'S PRESENCE, CONSIDER . . .

Do I determine my identity by my failings and weakness? Jesus plunges into the darkness of my sin and affliction to lift me up into the radiance of Divine life. Is there anything preventing me from truly receiving His steadfast love?

CLOSING PRAYER

Heavenly Father, sometimes I need my Abba to pick me up and carry me. There are times when I've lived the lie that I have to provide for myself, and sustain myself. Expel this whisper coming from the serpent, and hold me in Your fatherly care.

Prayers for Divine Mercy

Often recited after the Chaplet of Divine Mercy, these two prayers by St. Faustina have become, for many, a source of great comfort and hope in God's boundless and unending mercy.

Eternal God, in whom mercy is endless and the treasury of compassion inexhaustible, look kindly upon us and increase Your mercy in us, that in difficult moments we might not despair nor become despondent, but with great confidence submit ourselves to Your holy will, which is Love and Mercy itself. . . .

O Greatly Merciful God, Infinite Goodness, today all mankind calls out from the abyss of its misery to Your mercy—to Your compassion, O God; and it is with its mighty voice of misery that it cries out. Gracious God, do not reject the prayer of this earth's exiles! O Lord, Goodness beyond our understanding, Who are acquainted with our misery through and through, and know that by our own power we cannot ascend to You, we implore You: anticipate us with Your grace and keep on increasing Your mercy in us, that we may faithfully do Your holy will all through our life and at death's hour. Let the omnipotence of Your mercy shield us from the darts of our salvation's enemies, that we may with confidence, as Your children, await Your final coming—that day known to You alone. And we expect to obtain everything promised us by Jesus in spite of all our wretchedness. For Jesus is our Hope: Through His merciful Heart, as through an open gate, we pass through to heaven.

—St. Faustina, *Diary*, 950, 1570

IN GOD'S PRESENCE, CONSIDER . . .

Sometimes it's easy to pray the words and not allow a prayer to take root in my heart, to not allow time or space for the Lord to awaken areas in me where He wants to bring light and grace. I consider reading this entry again, stopping wherever I feel a movement of grace (often either a disquiet or consolation of the soul), and allowing God to speak.

CLOSING PRAYER

God of mercy, Your will is everything, and I trust that it is inseparably linked to Your mercy. Thank you for Your kindness, Your "treasury of compassion," Your promises. Thank you for being my hope.

"Begin Again"

The Venerable Bruno Lanteri, founder of the Oblates of the Blessed Virgin Mary, explains here one of his most beloved phrases. Only two words, it is a theological powerhouse that can absolutely transform your spiritual life.

"I urge you to begin each day, leaving the past to the mercy of the Lord, and the future to his Divine Providence. Do not let yourself be troubled by anything, not even by your own failings, taking care to overcome them immediately by an act of love of God."

. . . "If I should fall a thousand times a day, a thousand times a day I will begin again, with new awareness of my weakness, promising God, with a peaceful heart, to amend my life. I will never think of God as if he were of our condition and grows weary of our wavering, weakness, and negligence. Rather, I will think of what is truly characteristic of him and what he prizes most highly, that is, his goodness and mercy, knowing that he is a loving Father who understands our weakness, is patient with us, and forgives us." . . .

"Above all, I recommend with all my heart that you guard against discouragement, disturbance, and sadness. Seek always to keep your poor heart in peace, and encourage it, and always to serve God with holy joy."

—Venerable Bruno Lanteri, *Counsels of Mercy*

IN GOD'S PRESENCE, CONSIDER . . .

I wonder what would happen if, when I fall, when I see my utter inability to be consistent in certain areas, when I want to condemn myself for not being able to overcome an area of sin, I simply turn toward God and make an act of love. I could thank Him for His mercy, for being a loving and attentive Father who wishes to pick up His child after a fall and help him/her to walk again. And then I just begin again, step by step.

CLOSING PRAYER

Right now, Lord, I leave my past to Your mercy. I leave my future to Your Divine Providence. Thank you for never growing weary of me. Please help me to love You well, to serve You joyfully, and to always begin again, and again, and again.

The Initiative of Mercy

St. Bernard assures us that, although the initiative is always from God and that everything depends on His mercy, nevertheless, our free choice is not negated.

"Listen," I replied. "He saves us not because of deeds by us done in righteousness but in virtue of His own mercy. What? Did you imagine that you can create your own merits, that you can be saved by your own righteousness, you who cannot even say 'Jesus is Lord' without the Holy Spirit? Or have you forgotten the words: 'Without Me you can do nothing,' and 'It depends not on the one running, nor the one willing, but on God who has mercy'?"

You ask: "What part, then, does free choice play?" I shall answer you in a word: it is saved. Take away free choice and there is nothing to be saved. Take away grace and there is no means of saving. Without the two combined the work cannot be done . . . What, therefore, is given by God alone and to free choice alone, cannot any more happen without the recipient's consent than without the Bestower's grace. Consequently, free choice is said to cooperate with operating grace in its act of consent or, in other words, in its process of being saved. . . .

There can be no doubt, therefore, that the beginning action rests with God and is enacted neither through us nor with us. The consent and the work, however, though not originating from us nevertheless are not without us. . . . It is this grace which arouses free choice when it sows the seed of the good thought, which heals free choice by changing its disposition, which strengthens it so as to lead it to action, and which saves it from experiencing a fall. Grace so cooperates with free choice, however, that only in the first movement does it go a step ahead of it. In the others it accompanies it. Indeed, grace's whole aim in taking a step ahead is that from then on, free choice may co-operate with it. What was begun by grace alone is completed by grace and free choice together.

—St. Bernard of Clairvaux, "On Grace and Free Will," 1f; 46ff

IN GOD'S PRESENCE, CONSIDER . . .

I can do nothing without the giver of my breath, the holder of my existence. Yet He still desires me to have free will, which can cooperate with His grace toward my ultimate end. But in that freedom, I can also refuse to be saved.

CLOSING PRAYER

Father of mercy, in order to allow for the freedom and authenticity of love, You have given us such dignity. What an awesome and fearful prospect, that the initiative is Yours, but the rest depends on that cooperation of my will with Your grace. Everything is by virtue of Your mercy, but where my cooperation is then necessary, let me never part from You.

He Sees Me, He Loves Me

It only ever gets better with Jesus: He keeps far surpassing our wildest expectations. Thanks to the friends of the paralytic (we need the support of those who bring us to Jesus), he experiences miraculous transformation at every level of his being.

And behold, they brought to him a paralytic, lying on his bed; and when Jesus saw their faith he said to the paralytic, "Take heart, my son; your sins are forgiven." And behold, some of the scribes said to themselves, "This man is blaspheming." But Jesus, knowing their thoughts, said, "Why do you think evil in your hearts? For which is easier, to say, 'Your sins are forgiven,' or to say, 'Rise and walk'? But that you may know that the Son of man has authority on earth to forgive sins"—he then said to the paralytic—"Rise, take up your bed and go home." And he rose and went home. When the crowds saw it, they were afraid, and they glorified God, who had given such authority to men.

—Matthew 9:2–8

IN GOD'S PRESENCE, CONSIDER . . .

If I frequently resist or reject the hope for rescue, can today be the day I admit that I am powerless, that there are parts of me that are paralyzed in my woundedness, sins, and failures? God never expected me to save myself, but only waits for me to recognize my total need of Him in every aspect of my being.

CLOSING PRAYER

Heavenly Father, You have given all authority to Jesus; break the lie in me that I have to manage on my own, the blasphemy of believing I can save myself. Raise me up to experience healing and salvation flooding into me through the precious blood of Your Son.

Dependent on His Mercy

St. John of Kronstadt of the Russian Orthodox Church frees us from apprehension of our failures and sins, as he reveals we are helpless without Jesus's mercy.

God is love, a most-gracious, all-wise and omnipotent Being. Therefore, those who pray must believe that the Lord will give all things needful, bountifully, as He is loving, and bountiful . . . Be simple, trustful, undoubting as a child in godly matters. Cast all your care upon the Lord, and be entirely free from sorrow. . . . It ought to be easy for us to pray. Only the enemy troubles us. But what matters his troubling if our heart is firmly established in the Lord! It is only a misfortune if we do not rest in God.

Be as kind, meek, humble, and simple as possible. . . . Say to yourself, "Of all sinners I am the first." From pride proceeds self-sufficiency, coldness, and insincerity in our behaviour. . . . I wish to be patient, but before I have strengthened my heart in patience, I become irritable, impatient; I wish to be humble, but Satan's pride has already found ample room in my heart; I wish to be gracious, meanwhile, when it is necessary to show graciousness, I show myself rough; . . . I wish to be grave, concentrated, and reverent in my service to the Almighty, but light-mindedness and inattention of the heart prevent my becoming so; I wish to detach myself from earthly things, to be abstinent in food and drink, but when I see pleasant food and drink and sit down to table, I, like a slave, am taken a willing captive by my belly, I easily allow myself to eat and drink more than my nature requires . . . Who will heal me then? Jesus Christ alone. When He sees my sincere and firm desire to be healed of my spiritual infirmity, when He hears my fervent prayer, then He will say to me: "Take up thy bed and walk," and I shall rise from the bed of spiritual infirmity and walk; that is, by His grace I shall easily vanquish all my passions and fulfil every virtue.

—St. John of Kronstadt (Archpriest John Iliytch Sergieff), *My Life in Christ*

IN GOD'S PRESENCE, CONSIDER . . .

Have I created an alternate reality where God is looking to me to be virtuous on my own power, or do I recognize that I am nothing without the constant inflow of His love and mercy?

CLOSING PRAYER

Father of Mercy, Father of Love, let my heart rest in You. In Your mercy help me to vanquish all my passions and fulfill every virtue.

To Mary, Mother of Mercy

St. John Eudes entrusts everything and everyone into the merciful hands of Mary.

O sweetest and holy virgin, look down with the eyes of your mercy on all the afflictions and all the afflicted that fill the earth. Behold the many poor people, the many widows and orphans, the sick troubled with so many diseases, the captives and the prisoners, the thousands who are cursed and persecuted by the malice of men, the defenseless persons oppressed by the strong and the mighty, the seafarers and pilgrims struggling against perils on sea and land, the missionaries exposed to countless dangers in their task of saving endangered souls.

Look down upon the number of afflicted minds, of anguished hearts, of souls tormented by manifold temptations, and of souls suffering the frightful penalties of Purgatory. But above all, have pity on the countless souls that are in the state of sin and perdition and are groaning under the tyranny and the bondage of hell. . . .

Mother of Mercy, take pity on such great misery. You see, alas that the earth is crowded with miserable hearts enslaved by Satan, hearts that do not feel the extreme misfortune in which they are plunged!

Mother of Grace, . . . by your most compassionate heart, I beg you to take pity on them. Break their chains asunder; implore your beloved son, who came into the world to enlighten all men, that He deign to give sight to the blind, and to remove from sinners their hearts of stone, replacing them with hearts obedient to the inspirations of the Holy Spirit.

Mother of Fair Love, I also offer you the hearts of those of your children who are faithful, who love and honor you as their cherished Mother. Preserve and increase the precious treasure which is theirs, that they may love you more and more, and become more worthy to be the true children of your heart.

—St. John Eudes, *The Admirable Heart of Mary*

IN GOD'S PRESENCE, CONSIDER . . .

Now, just as then, there are so many afflictions and so many afflicted. Jesus invites us all to take Mary as our Mother and have recourse to her heart. What person, what affliction, what problem do I most want to entrust to her today?

CLOSING PRAYER

Mother of Mercy, I entrust to you this intention, knowing that you will look upon it with merciful eyes and a mother's heart. Thank you for your compassion and powerful intercession.

To Heal My Tongue

St James refers to the tongue as "a restless evil, full of deadly poison" (3:8), and in Matthew's gospel we read that on the day of judgment we will have to give an account for every careless word we utter (see 12:36). St. Faustina knew this well and shows us how to guard against sins of the tongue.

At those times when I suffer much, I try to remain silent, as I do not trust my tongue which, at such moments, is inclined to talk for itself, while its duty is to help me praise God for all the blessings and gifts which He has given me. When I receive Jesus in Holy Communion, I ask Him fervently to deign to heal my tongue so that I would offend neither God nor neighbor by it. I want my tongue to praise God without cease. Great are the faults committed by the tongue. The soul will not attain sanctity if it does not keep watch over its tongue.

. . . The tongue is a small member, but it does big things. A religious who does not keep silence will never attain holiness; that is, she will never become a saint. Let her not delude herself- unless it is the Spirit of God who is speaking through her, for then she must not keep silent. But, in order to hear the voice of God, one has to have silence in one's soul and to keep silence; not a gloomy silence, but an interior silence; that is to say, recollection in God. One can speak a great deal without breaking silence and, on the contrary, one can speak little and be constantly breaking silence. Oh, what irreparable damage is done by the breach of silence! We cause a lot of harm to our neighbor, but even more to our own selves.

. . . I tremble to think that I have to give an account of my tongue. There is life, but there is also death in the tongue. Sometimes we kill with the tongue: we commit real murders. And we are still to regard that as a small thing?

—St. Faustina, *Diary*, 92, 118, 119

IN GOD'S PRESENCE, CONSIDER . . .

Am I careful to "keep watch" over my tongue so that I will not hurt or offend anyone? When I receive Communion can I follow Faustina's example and ask Jesus to heal my tongue?

CLOSING PRAYER

Lord Jesus, bless and heal my tongue so that my words will affirm and encourage others and never hurt or offend.

United with His Eucharistic Heart

St. Margaret Mary Alacoque called the Sacred Heart an "ocean of mercy" and encouraged everyone to live a life of love, united to Jesus in the Blessed Sacrament.

The Divine Heart is an ocean full of all good things, wherein poor souls can cast all their needs; it is an ocean full of joy to drown all our sadness, an ocean of humility to drown our folly, an ocean of mercy to those in distress, an ocean of love in which to submerge our poverty.

You will do nothing unless you ask Him for the help of His grace. And this I am sure He will give you to the measure in which you trust Him. Moreover, we must live the life of love. By our humble submission and complete self-effacement it will unite us with Him and make us altogether like Him in His life of Sacrifice, abandonment and love in the Blessed Sacrament. Love keeps Him there as a victim completely and perpetually delivered over to sacrifice for the glory of the Father and for our salvation. Unite yourself with Him, then, in all that you do. Refer everything to His glory. Set up your abode in this loving Heart of Jesus and you will there find lasting peace and the strength both to bring to fruition all the good desires He inspires in you, and to avoid every deliberate fault. Place in this Heart all your sufferings and difficulties. Everything that comes from the Sacred Heart is sweet. He changes everything into love.

—*The Autobiography of St. Margaret Mary* and
The Letters of St. Margaret Mary Alacoque

IN GOD'S PRESENCE, CONSIDER . . .

If I learn to immerse all my needs in the merciful Heart of Jesus, and find that no matter what I present, I am met by an ocean of love; If I set myself up to live in and from His Eucharistic Heart, and gather all the strength and peace I need; . . . then, I will become like Him and become a place of refuge and mercy for others.

CLOSING PRAYER

Merciful Heart of Jesus, I unite myself to You now, especially with Your Eucharistic Presence in all the tabernacles of the world. I place all my cares, sufferings, and difficulties there, to be transformed in Your love.

Prayer, Fasting, and Almsgiving Inseparable

St. Peter Chyrsologus, whose name means "of golden speech," was one of the great preachers of the early Church. He teaches here that the three practices we associate most with the Lenten Season—prayer, fasting, and almsgiving (mercy)—should be a continual part of our lives and are inseparably linked to one another.

There are three things, my brethren, by which faith stands firm, devotion remains constant, and virtue endures. They are prayer, fasting and almsgiving. Prayer knocks at the door, fasting obtains, mercy receives. Prayer, mercy and fasting: these three are one, and they give life to each other.

Fasting is the soul of prayer, almsgiving is the lifeblood of fasting. Let no one try to separate them; they cannot be separated. If you have only one of them or not all together, you have nothing. So if you pray, fast; if you fast, show mercy; if you want your petition to be heard, hear the petition of others. If you do not close your ear to others you open God's ear to yourself.

When you fast, see the fasting of others. If you want God to know that you are hungry, know that another is hungry. If you hope for mercy, show mercy. If you look for kindness, show kindness. If you want to receive, give. If you ask for yourself what you deny to others, your asking is a mockery.

Let this be the pattern for all men when they practice mercy: show mercy to others in the same way, with the same generosity, with the same promptness, as you want others to show mercy to you. Therefore, let prayer, mercy and fasting be one single plea to God on our behalf, one speech in our defense, a threefold united prayer in our favor.

—St. Peter Chrysologus, excerpt from his Sermon 43: PL 52, 320, 322

IN GOD'S PRESENCE, CONSIDER . . .

Have I ever realized how important and intertwined all three of these are? Is there one that I struggle with more than the others? I could consider choosing that one to focus on right now. Or perhaps there is some small practice I could choose for each of the tenets that would help me grow deeper in all three.

CLOSING PRAYER

Mercy is Your language, Father of limitless life. Make me fluent in the kindness, generosity and openness that are of Your Divine nature. Today I open myself to Your Holy Spirit to be formed in Your love.

Watered by Mercy

St. Peter Chrysologus is a Doctor of the Church and was known not only for his preaching, but for his brevity. Taken from his discourse on the three tenets of Lent, this passage focuses on fasting and almsgiving, the latter of which he calls mercy.

Let us use fasting to make up for what we have lost by despising others. Let us offer our souls in sacrifice by means of fasting. There is nothing more pleasing that we can offer to God, as the psalmist said in prophecy: A sacrifice to God is a broken spirit; God does not despise a bruised and humbled heart.

Offer your soul to God, make him an oblation of your fasting, so that your soul may be a pure offering, a holy sacrifice, a living victim, remaining your own and at the same time made over to God. Whoever fails to give this to God will not be excused, for if you are to give him yourself you are never without the means of giving.

To make these acceptable, almsgiving must be added. Fasting bears no fruit unless it is watered by mercy. Fasting dries up when mercy dries up. Mercy is to fasting as rain is to earth. However much you may cultivate your heart, clear the soil of your nature, root out vices, sow virtues, if you do not release the springs of mercy, your fasting will bear no fruit.

When you fast, if your mercy is thin your harvest will be thin; when you fast, what you pour out in almsgiving overflows into your barn. Therefore, do not lose by saving, but gather in by scattering. Give to the poor, and you give to yourself. You will not be allowed to keep what you have refused to give to others.

—St. Peter Chrysologus, excerpt from his Sermon 43: PL 52, 320, 322

IN GOD'S PRESENCE, CONSIDER . . .

It is a mystery of personhood and the spiritual life that when I give, I receive; when I empty myself, I become full. I do not want to cultivate the heart, root out vices, etc., without releasing the "springs of mercy." I want the natural companion of my fasting to be an overflow of mercy.

CLOSING PRAYER

God of infinite mercy, help me to never think of my sacrifices as: "I'm doing enough and need not do anything more." Let my self-denial go hand in hand with my self-gift, transforming me to be more like You.

Fountain of Mercy

Thomas Aquinas, the Angelic Doctor whose writings have formed the cornerstone of Catholic theology for almost a thousand years, sees that everything is contained in the Eucharist, our life and our hope.

Almighty eternal God, behold, I come to the Sacrament of Your Only Begotten Son, our Lord Jesus Christ, as one sick to the physician of life, as one unclean to the fountain of mercy, as one blind to the light of eternal brightness, as one poor and needy to the Lord of heaven and earth.

I ask, therefore, for the abundance of Your immense generosity, that You may graciously heal my infirmity, wash away my defilement, give light to my blindness, enrich my poverty, clothe my nakedness, so that I may receive the bread of Angels, the King of kings and Lord of lords, with such reverence and humility, such contrition and devotion, such purity and faith, such purpose and intention as are conducive to the salvation of my soul.

Grant, I pray, that I may receive not only the Sacrament of the Lord's Body and Blood, but also its full grace and power.

Oh most gentle God, grant that I may so receive the Body of Your Only Begotten Son our Lord Jesus Christ, which He took from the Virgin Mary, that I may merit to be incorporated into His Mystical Body and counted among its members.

Oh most loving Father, grant that I may at last gaze for ever upon the unveiled face of Your beloved Son, whom I, a wayfarer, propose to receive now under the veil of this Sacrament.

—St. Thomas Aquinas, "Prayer before Communion,"
Vinny Flynn, *Mass & Adoration Companion*, p.38

IN GOD'S PRESENCE, CONSIDER . . .

At every Eucharist I come to the fount of mercy; I am healed and transformed by my encounter with love; the King of kings comes to me in littleness yet with full grace and power. And the more I dispose myself, the more I am capable of receiving! Everything I need is contained in this Sacred Host.

CLOSING PRAYER

Heavenly Father, Lord of Heaven and Earth, You sustain the universe with your Eternal Word, Jesus the King, hidden in the Holy Eucharist. Open my heart to this treasure of grace and let me approach the gift of each reception with profound reverence and awe.

Eucharist—the Living God

"Communion" means "union with." To be fruitful, our Sacramental Communion must include Spiritual Communion: a deep longing to be in union with the living God who comes to us.

After Communion today, Jesus told me how much He desires to come to human hearts. I desire to unite Myself with human souls; My great delight is to unite Myself with souls. Know, My daughter, that when I come to a human heart in Holy Communion, My hands are full of all kinds of graces which I want to give to the soul. But souls do not even pay any attention to Me; they leave Me to Myself and busy themselves with other things. Oh, how sad I am that souls do not recognize Love! They treat Me as a dead object.

. . . Oh, how painful it is to Me that souls so seldom unite themselves to Me in Holy Communion. I wait for souls, and they are indifferent toward Me. I love them tenderly and sincerely, and they distrust Me. I want to lavish My graces on them, and they do not want to accept them. They treat Me as a dead object, whereas My Heart is full of love and mercy. In order that you may know at least some of My pain, imagine the most tender of mothers who has great love for her children, while those children spurn her love. Consider her pain. No one is in a position to console her. This is but a feeble image and likeness of My love.

—St. Faustina, *Diary*, 1385, 1447

IN GOD'S PRESENCE, CONSIDER . . .

Do I sometimes receive Communion with my mind on other things, or do I consciously try to unite myself with Jesus and keep my focus on Him?

CLOSING PRAYER

Lord Jesus, forgive me for any times I have treated You as a "dead object," failing to recognize You as the living God who loves me.

Rescue of Mercy

God speaks to Moses about His plan of rescue, a plan of mercy and freedom.

God also said to Moses, "I am the Lord. As God the Almighty I appeared to Abraham, Isaac and Jacob, but my name, Lord, I did not make known to them. I also established my covenant with them, to give them the land of Canaan, the land in which they were living as aliens. And now that I have heard the groaning of the Israelites, whom the Egyptians are treating as slaves, I am mindful of my covenant.

"Therefore, say to the Israelites: I am the Lord. I will free you from the forced labor of the Egyptians and will deliver you from their slavery. I will rescue you by my outstretched arm and with mighty acts of judgment. I will take you as my own people, and you shall have me as your God. You will know that I, the Lord, am your God when I free you from the labor of the Egyptians and bring you into the land which I swore to give to Abraham, Isaac and Jacob. I will give it to you as your own possession—I, the Lord!"

But when Moses told this to the Israelites, they would not listen to him because of their dejection and hard slavery.

—Exodus 6:2–13 (NABRE)

IN GOD'S PRESENCE, CONSIDER . . .

There are times when part of me would prefer for God to stay out of things, to leave me be. Sometimes it's more comfortable to live with the suffering I know, rather than step out into the unknown. And sometimes it's hard to hope when things have been so hard. Is there any area in my life right now where I am resisting the Holy Spirit's nudge? Is there any place where I am comfortable in my chains?

CLOSING PRAYER

God of our fathers, You are a God of rescue, and yet part of me has trouble trusting completely in Your plan—and even at times in Your goodness to me. Help me to let go of anything I am clinging to that prevents me from reaching for Your outstretched hand.

Mercy Moves the Heart to Act . . .

Archbishop Emeritus of Philadelphia, Charles Chaput shares his familiar depth of insight, revealing the heart, remembrance . . . and love.

Mercy derives from the Latin word merces, "reward" or "gratuity." We see this meaning in the French expression merci. It's a courtesy that graces our social interactions with a touch of kindness. In English, however, mercy can take on a theological sense, even in secular contexts. God's grace comes to us as an unmerited gift. To be merciful, then, is to freely offer clemency to someone worthy of punishment, or to release someone from a debt he or she owes.

Mercy also has a meaning that involves more than gift, merit, grace, and the forgiveness of debts. It's often used as the word to translate misericordia, the Latin word for compassion, or, literally, having a "merciful heart." Here we speak of an emotional state of entering into someone else's plight and sharing in his burdens. As Chaucer put it, mercy is a "virtue by which a man's heart is stirred by the misery of those in distress." In Jesus Christ, God doesn't offer us grace from afar. He walks with us in our daily sufferings.

The Book of Exodus gives us a first model of God's mercy. It prefigures the life of the Church. Israel suffers in Egyptian slavery, and God hears the cries of his people. He remembers his covenant with the patriarchs. He turns his face toward them and, as Scripture says, using one of its terms for intimacy, the Lord knows their affliction. He comes to Moses in the burning bush. He states his purpose, which is to bring his people out of captivity and into the land he promised to Abraham. He gives Moses his name as a keepsake, a sharing of the divine with the human that foreshadows the Incarnation.

From that point in Exodus, God binds himself to his people. He seeks their freedom, not because they deserve it, but because they are his beloved ones.

—Archbishop Charles J. Chaput, OFM, "A Jubilee Year of Mercy"

IN GOD'S PRESENCE, CONSIDER . . .

Has my encounter with mercy remained exclusively in my head, under my rational control? God in His mercy wants to enter my plight, wants to enter the realm of the heart. He seeks my freedom because I am His beloved one, and He desires to release me from whatever captivity I am in. Will I let Him?

CLOSING PRAYER

Father of Mercy, Father of Love, from before the dawn of the universe You have existed in delight, pouring yourself out into the Son through the Holy Spirit. In an overflow of love You created this world, and that tide of mercy reaches me. Flood all the places in me where I need rescue and healing and wholeness.

The God Who Is Always There

God speaks to Moses from the burning bush, telling him to go to Egypt to free the people of Israel. When Moses asks who he should say sent him, God replies, "Say this to the people of Israel, 'I am has sent me to you.' . . . This is my name for ever, and thus I am to be remembered throughout all generations."

In revealing his mysterious name, YHWH ("I AM HE WHO IS", "I AM WHO AM" or "I AM WHO I AM"), God says who he is and by what name he is to be called. This divine name is mysterious just as God is mystery. It is at once a name revealed and something like the refusal of a name, and hence it better expresses God as what he is —infinitely above everything that we can understand or say: he is the "hidden God," his name is ineffable, and he is the God who makes himself close to men (cf. Isa 45:15; Judg 13:18). . . .

By revealing his name, God at the same time reveals his faithfulness which is from everlasting to everlasting. . . . God, who reveals his name as "I AM," reveals himself as the God who is always there, present to his people in order to save them. . . .

The divine name, "I Am" or "He Is," expresses God's faithfulness: despite the faithlessness of men's sin and the punishment it deserves, he keeps "steadfast love for thousands" (Ex 34:7). By going so far as to give up his own Son for us, God reveals that he is "rich in mercy" (Eph 2:4). By giving his life to free us from sin, Jesus reveals that he himself bears the divine name: "When you have lifted up the Son of man, then you will realize that "I AM" (Jn 8:28).

—*Catechism of the Catholic Church*, 206, 207, 211

IN GOD'S PRESENCE, CONSIDER . . .

We often pray, "As it was in the beginning is now and ever shall be . . . " But do I live in the reality that, no matter what, God is always there, always "rich in mercy" for me? Infinitely above everything in majesty and mystery . . . and yet, He desires to be close to this little being He created.

CLOSING PRAYER

Lord God, help me to remember, especially in difficult moments, that you are "the same, yesterday, today, and forever" (Heb 13:8), always close to me, always offering me Your steadfast love.

Chosen by the Creator

Moses speaks to the covenant people in the desert, delivered from Pharaoh's hand through the waters of the Red Sea, brought into the discovery that God will do everything needed to deliver us into mercy.

The Lord, your God, has chosen you from all the nations on the face of the earth to be a people peculiarly his own. It was because the Lord loved you and because of his fidelity to the oath he had sworn to your fathers, that he brought you out with his strong hand from the place of slavery, and ransomed you from the hand of Pharaoh, king of Egypt. Understand, then, that the Lord, your God, is God indeed, the faithful God who keeps his merciful covenant to the thousandth generation toward those who love him and keep his commandments.

—Deuteronomy 7:6, 8–9, *Liturgy of the Hours*

IN GOD'S PRESENCE, CONSIDER . . .

My God is faithful: He sees me where I am and does whatever is needed to draw me into life. Not my works, not my deeds—or my failures—but His unending love brings me into the blessing He pours forth. I truly belong to the family of God.

CLOSING PRAYER

O Lord, God of Hosts, Ruler over heaven and earth, You sustain all things in being and have called a people to Yourself in the blood of Your Son. Establish me in Your faithful covenant and reveal to me Your undying mercy.

Poured Out for You and for Many

The Ark of the Covenant received the name of the Mercy Seat in the tabernacle of Moses. Now Jesus reveals limitless mercy as he reveals Himself as the fulfillment of all we have longed for.

But when Christ appeared as a high priest of the good things that have come, then through the greater and more perfect tent (not made with hands, that is, not of this creation) he entered once for all into the Holy Place, taking not the blood of goats and calves but his own blood, thus securing an eternal redemption. For if the sprinkling of defiled persons with the blood of goats and bulls and with the ashes of a heifer sanctifies for the purification of the flesh, how much more shall the blood of Christ, who through the eternal Spirit offered himself without blemish to God, purify your conscience from dead works to serve the living God.

Therefore he is the mediator of a new covenant, so that those who are called may receive the promised eternal inheritance, since a death has occurred which redeems them from the transgressions under the first covenant. . . . For when every commandment of the law had been declared by Moses to all the people, he took the blood of calves and goats, with water and scarlet wool and hyssop, and sprinkled both the book itself and all the people, saying, "This is the blood of the covenant which God commanded you." And in the same way he sprinkled with the blood both the tent and all the vessels used in worship. Indeed, under the law almost everything is purified with blood, and without the shedding of blood there is no forgiveness of sins.

—Hebrews 9:11–15, 19–22

IN GOD'S PRESENCE, CONSIDER . . .

Jesus offered Himself as a sacrifice so that I could be purified to dwell in an eternity of love. I do not need to labor to gain acceptance and worth once I understand that He has come in mercy to free my soul and bring rest to my heart. The Precious Blood of Jesus is a purifying stream of solace, strength, and victory.

CLOSING PRAYER

Lord Jesus Christ, priest of the New Covenant, I place myself before the Blood and Water gushing forth from Your pierced Heart, rays of mercy flowing out upon me and upon the whole world. Purify me and strengthen me in Your service, O Living God.

Listen to the Wounds

All of our afflictions were borne by the Heart of our Redeemer in His bitter Passion. The seventeenth-century treasured preacher and confessor, St. John Eudes, poetically conveys how this knowledge can shape the way we view our sins, walk through suffering, and hear the divine wounds calling us home.

Therefore we have the greatest obligation to honor the gracious Heart that sustained so many wounds of love for us. . . . With what affection should we embrace, and endure all our afflictions, out of love for Jesus, our Savior, since He first bore them for love of us! Should they not be most sweet to us, since they have already passed through His most gentle and loving Heart? What a horror we should have of our sins that have caused so many wounds and such intense grief to the divine Heart of our Redeemer!

Let us learn from the foregoing example that it is not our Redeemer's fault if we are lost. There are hearts so hard that, even if Jesus Himself were to come down from heaven to preach to them and they were to see Him covered with wounds and bathed in His blood, they would still not be converted. O my God, let us not be one of them, but give us the grace to open our ears to the voice of all the sacred wounds of Thy body and Thy heart, which are so many mouths through which Thou dost call us unceasingly: Redite, praevaricatores, ad cor. "Return, ye transgressors, to the heart," which means to My Heart that is all yours, since I have given it entirely to you. Return to that most loving Heart of your Father, which is full of love and mercy for you, which will receive you home, heaping upon you blessings

—St. John Eudes, *The Sacred Heart of Jesus*

IN GOD'S PRESENCE, CONSIDER . . .

Oh that I would listen to the sacred wounds of Jesus! Have I ever thought of these wounds of love as themselves having something to say; as having voices that continually beckon me to believe and come to His Heart? I resolve to be one who listens.

CLOSING PRAYER

Most Sacred Heart of Jesus, thank you for enduring all of that pain for me. Soften my heart that it may never grow immune to this great price of love. Help me listen with my heart to the cry of each wound, "Redite, praevaricatores, ad cor."

Sharing in God's Pain

Protestants wonder at the Catholic centrality of the crucifix: in every church, in every home, Jesus is revealed to us in His broken, wounded state. Jesus's pain reveals His love in the greatest eloquence.

By exposing sin in us, the Spirit also reveals something of God's being. He is the one who "searches everything, even the depths of God" (1 Cor 2:10). What he reveals is God's *suffering*. There has been much discussion about whether one can speak of suffering in God. Pope John Paul II says very cautiously that the Bible, *in its anthropomorphic representation of God*, seems to hint at a suffering in God, yes, even in the heart of the Trinity itself. [See *Dominum et vivificantem*, #39].

Traditional theology has always described sin as an offense against God. The offense consists in the fact that love has been rejected. Is there anything more painful than the pain of love that is disdained? The Old Testament attempts to hint at this pain of God by pointing out that God regrets he has made man on earth (Gen 6:6–7). God feels deeply hurt, he is disappointed in man.

In the New Testament we get a deeper insight into God's pain. There we see how God cries, not because he feels hurt himself, but for man's sake. His suffering is *compassion* (suffering with). "O Jerusalem, Jerusalem. . . . How often would I have gathered your children together as a hen gathers her brood under her wings, and you would not!" (Mt 23:37).

But God's compassion is different from man's. It is not limited to suffering with us; instead, it results always in new "saving actions."

When the Holy Spirit works in man and makes him conscious of sin, he gives him the possibility of sharing in God's pain. He then regrets his sin, not only because he has lost his peace through sin or because sin has other negative consequences, but also because he has wounded God's love and prevented him from fulfilling his plan of love. A regret of this kind is especially painful, but it also has great power to create anew.

—Fr. Wilfrid Stinissen, OCD, *The Holy Spirit, Fire of Divine Love*

IN GOD'S PRESENCE, CONSIDER . . .

Do I shy away from my pain? Am I willing to draw it forward and unite it with the anguished love of God's compassion? Can I cast my cares on God, trusting in His care for me?

CLOSING PRAYER

God my Father, plunge into my misery to call me into communion. Touch my heart that I may unite myself to the wounded heart of the Savior.

Jesus's Desire for Mercy

Often our most seemingly pious thoughts are the most opposed to God's Will. Jesus directly confronts what masquerades as righteousness but is symptomatic of our hardness of heart. And it makes us impervious to His mercy.

Then said Jesus to the crowds and to his disciples, "The scribes and the Pharisees sit on Moses' seat; so practice and observe whatever they tell you, but not what they do; for they preach, but do not practice. They bind heavy burdens, hard to bear, and lay them on men's shoulders; but they themselves will not move them with their finger. They do all their deeds to be seen by men; for they make their phylacteries broad and their fringes long, and they love the place of honor at feasts and the best seats in the synagogues, and salutations in the market places, and being called rabbi by men. . . . "Woe to you, scribes and Pharisees, hypocrites! for you are like whitewashed tombs, which outwardly appear beautiful, but within they are full of dead men's bones and all uncleanness. So you also outwardly appear righteous to men, but within you are full of hypocrisy and iniquity.

"O Jerusalem, Jerusalem, killing the prophets and stoning those who are sent to you! How often would I have gathered your children together as a hen gathers her brood under her wings, and you would not! Behold, your house is forsaken and desolate. For I tell you, you will not see me again, until you say, 'Blessed is he who comes in the name of the Lord.'"

—Matthew 23:1–7, 27–28, 37–39

IN GOD'S PRESENCE, CONSIDER . . .

Have I agreed with lies of how things should be or bought into inauthentic religiosity because it seemed to be devout, holy, safe? Do I bind heavy burdens and lay them on others' shoulders—even if only in interior judgments? Where is Jesus calling my self-righteousness to be broken on the cornerstone of His mercy?

CLOSING PRAYER

Lord, Jesus Christ, where I find myself most agitated over something, or straining the hardest is often where I am furthest from You. Allow me to cast off the lies of the Accuser and come to rest in Your Heart that ceaselessly calls out to gather Your children. Jesus, Meek and Humble of Heart, make my heart like unto Thine.

Confession: Healing, Strength, and Mercy . . .

Each confession opens up a new future for the penitent. This is the power of God's mercy—that He continually makes all things new and allows us, at any moment, to begin again. All it takes is for us to open up our wounded and sinful hearts to Him, and we are not only progressively healed, but we become His mercy for others.

The reception of this sacrament ought to be prepared for by an examination of conscience made in the light of the Word of God. The passages best suited to this can be found in the moral catechesis of the Gospels and the apostolic Letters, such as the Sermon on the Mount and the apostolic teachings.[53]. . . Confession to a priest is an essential part of the sacrament of Penance: "All mortal sins of which penitents after a diligent self-examination are conscious must be recounted by them in confession, even if they are most secret . . . "[54]

When Christ's faithful strive to confess all the sins that they can remember, they undoubtedly place all of them before the divine mercy for pardon. But those who fail to do so and knowingly withhold some, place nothing before the divine goodness for remission through the mediation of the priest, "for if the sick person is too ashamed to show his wound to the doctor, the medicine cannot heal what it does not know."[55] . . .

Without being strictly necessary, confession of everyday faults (venial sins) is nevertheless strongly recommended by the Church.[59] Indeed the regular confession of our venial sins helps us form our conscience, fight against evil tendencies, let ourselves be healed by Christ and progress in the life of the Spirit. By receiving more frequently through this sacrament the gift of the Father's mercy, we are spurred to be merciful as he is merciful.[60]

—*Catechism of the Catholic Church*, 1455–1458

IN GOD'S PRESENCE, CONSIDER . . .

Confession is meant to be a healing encounter with God's mercy. Have I made confession a regular part of my life? Do I take responsibility for the ways I have turned from God, and do I take the time to prepare for a sincere revealing of my heart to Him?

CLOSING PRAYER

Lord, help me to take a sincere and thorough inventory of my heart and actions, so that my next confession will be a powerful experience of healing and transformation. Trusting in Your mercy I want to withhold nothing from You, so that I can experience deeper union with You and be a witness of Your mercy for others.

The Odds Are God's

God's mercy is such that even in our darkest sin and our most resistant patterns of succumbing to temptation, there is truly nothing hopeless, nothing impossible, nothing that cannot be transformed. There are only two things we must do as many times as necessary: trust in His mercy and return to the fight.

When the odds are against us and the battle seems lost, we need never give up hope, because confession can accomplish in us what we cannot, and God's grace in the sacrament is stronger than anything the devil can work against us. God's power to save, and heal, and create anew is infinitely stronger than our power to sin and to destroy. "I have swept away your transgressions like a cloud, and your sins like mist; return to me, for I have redeemed you" (Is 44:22). Jesus is the Lamb of God Who "takes away the sin of the world" (Jn 1:29). He *takes sin away*, at its source. He doesn't just forgive sin; He uproots it by removing our sinful heart. But then He goes one better still. He creates in you and me a new heart, a clean heart, as if we hadn't soiled the first one He gave us. "A new heart I will give you, and a new spirit I will put within you; and I will take out of your flesh the heart of stone and give you a heart of flesh" (Ezek 36:26).

Christ is invincible. We, too, will be, if only we return to fight by His side.

—Scott Hahn, *Lord Have Mercy*

IN GOD'S PRESENCE, CONSIDER . . .

Where in my life do I feel like the odds are against me; where I am tempted to just give up trying? With God's power and mercy I now renew my commitment to holiness in all areas and claim Jesus as Lord of every aspect of my life.

CLOSING PRAYER

Jesus, You are the Lamb of God who takes away the sins of the world, and You never tire of showing me mercy. Give me the strength and hope to turn to You with trust in that mercy, especially in those times when I want to give in and give up. I surrender to You and give you permission to uproot the most stubborn sins in my life. Jesus, give me the fortitude to continue the work of fighting with You for a heart of purity and a life of virtue.

Mercy Draws Good From Everything

Fr. Jacques Philippe offers a powerful, and perhaps surprising lesson in the measure of spiritual progress.

Our confidence in God must go at least that far: to believe that He is good enough and powerful enough to draw good from everything, including our faults and our infidelities. When he cites the phrase of Saint Paul, *Everything works together for the good of those who love God*, Saint Augustine adds: *Etiam peccata*—"even sins"! . . .

When we have been the cause of some evil, we must also try to rectify it to the extent that this is possible. But we must not distress ourselves excessively regarding our faults because God, once we return to Him with a contrite heart, is able to cause good to spring forth.

Accordingly, after committing a fault of whatever kind, rather than withdrawing into ourselves indefinitely in discouragement and dwelling on the memory, we must immediately return to God with confidence and even thank Him for the good that His mercy will be able to draw out of this fault!

We must know that one of the weapons that the devil uses most commonly to prevent souls from advancing toward God is precisely to try to make them lose their peace and discourage them by the sight of their faults. . . . Let us understand this: For the person of goodwill, that which is serious in sin is not so much the fault in itself as the despondency into which it places him. He who falls but immediately gets up has not lost much. He has rather gained in humility and in the experience of mercy. He who remains sad and defeated loses much more. The sign of spiritual progress is not so much never falling as it is being able to lift oneself up quickly after one falls.

—Fr. Jacques Philippe, *Searching for and Maintaining Peace*, pp. 61–64

IN GOD'S PRESENCE, CONSIDER . . .

A common pitfall in the spiritual life is to either become too focused on our faults and fall into despondency or an unhelpful preoccupation with how bad we are, or to diminish our faults and fall into presumption. Does either spiritual dead end characterize my moral life?

CLOSING PRAYER

God, You are so generous that You will even use the effects of my sins to work all things together for my good. All You require is that I get back up and turn to You with a humble and contrite heart, trusting in Your mercy.

The "Spacious Dome of Mercy"

Fr. Romano Guardini, a distinguished pre-conciliar theologian who has been praised by both Pope Benedict XVI and Pope Francis, reflects here on the Parable of the Prodigal Son, on justice and mercy, and on the Father's response to the older brother.

But what if the father had agreed with him? If he had said to the homecomer: Go your way! You've had what you wanted! Then justice would have been restored. The older brother would have been satisfied. Or would he? Completely? If he was a good man, certainly not. The sight of his brother would have robbed his peace. Contrary to all feeling of "justice" a not to be stilled small voice would have insisted that somehow he had missed a sacred opportunity.

Justice is good. It is the foundation of existence. But there is something higher than justice, the bountiful widening of the heart to mercy. Justice is clear, but one step further and it becomes cold. Mercy is genuine, heartfelt; when backed by character, it warms and redeems. Justice regulates, orders existence; mercy creates. Justice satisfies the mind that all is as it should be, but from mercy leaps the joy of creative life. That is why it is written that heaven rejoices more over one sinner who does penance than over a hundred just who have no need of it. High above all the stupidity and evil of mankind arches the spacious dome of mercy. When justice enters here insisting on its narrow rights it becomes repugnant. . . .

Does the person stiff with justice really want the sinner converted? Doesn't he somehow feel that he is thus escaping his just deserts, endangering the existent order? Wouldn't he prefer to see him remain locked in sin and forced to bear the consequences? Perhaps he considers the return to grace a more or less underhanded trick played at the expense of justice. What would things come to if everyone like that scamp there, after wasting half a fortune, extricated himself from the affair by turning virtuous! And actually, the true conversion does break the bounds of mere justice. It is a creative new beginning—in God.

—Romano Guardini, *The Lord*

IN GOD'S PRESENCE, CONSIDER . . .

Do I find myself caught in this kind of "repugnant" justice in my outlook toward others, repudiating the creative new beginning God desires to offer them?

CLOSING PRAYER

Creator God, I too am under Your "spacious dome of mercy" and there is nothing I have done or can ever do to deserve it. That, I know, is the nature of mercy. And You desire to give it. Make my heart like Yours.

In the Garden of God

Almost our contemporary, St. Nectarios of the Greek Orthodox Church died in 1920. Here he recognizes what it means to flourish: abundant life flows from abundant mercy.

The merciful does not shut his ears before the supplication of the poor, but rather rushes to help them. When he gives to the one in need, he does that with great love and compassion, and when he offers to the poor, his face is bright, because his heart rejoices for the act of mercy, for having helped the poor. And the merciful is beloved by God and will be saved in the day of doom, because God loves the one who gives with joy. The merciful gives charity in secret because his heart is guided by the love for the neighbor and not by the desire for glory. . . . Because he lives for the love of his neighbor and confesses his love for God through the love for his neighbor.

The merciful accepts the sad one, doesn't turn his eyes from the one in need, nor hides his face from the poor, doesn't abhor from lending a hand to the one who asks for it. He gives his bread to the hungry, gives water to the thirsty, covers the poor, clothes the undressed, helps the suffering, visits the prisoners, and hosts the strangers. Gives abundantly, placing all his hopes in God, and in such way attains treasure in heaven. The merciful is like a fertile olive in the Garden of God, never gives up his hope in God, but rather . . . so he resembles a forever blooming tree and being zealous for his great fruitfulness, he abundantly gives charity to everyone and in every time. Blessed is the merciful, for he would inherit the Heavenly Kingdom, prepared for us from the beginning of time. God tells the merciful: *Then shall the King say unto them on his right hand, Come, ye blessed of my Father, inherit the kingdom prepared for you from the foundation of the world* . . . (Mathew 25, 34).

—St. Nectarios of Aegina

IN GOD'S PRESENCE, CONSIDER . . .

Have I moved from my cramped vision to an open embrace of others because I am held in the infinite mercy of God? I would like to be a fertile olive tree in the garden of God, fruitful in generosity and abundant in charity.

CLOSING PRAYER

Heavenly Father, Creator of all that is good, You formed man in Your image and likeness. Expand my heart to love in fullness, and to recognize You in each brother and sister.

Turn to My Mercy Now

The mercy of God is available to all, but it doesn't come to us automatically. We have to actively seek it, ask for it, and receive it, in a spirit of "humility, repentance, and trust."

"Behold, I stand at the door and knock; if anyone hears my voice and opens the door, I will come in to him and eat with him, and he with me (Rev 3:20)."

We live in a troubled world. Turning with trust to God, who is mercy itself, and imploring his mercy is the only answer to our troubles and the only source of peace for mankind.

It's especially important for the world today to hear the message of God's mercy, because we've turned away from that mercy. We have lost that sense of sin that leads us to seek the mercy of God. We like to think we are independent; we don't like to admit that we are powerless without his mercy.

God wants to have mercy on everybody, but he won't force it on us; we have to ask for it freely. And, sometimes, if we don't know enough to ask, he allows events to shake us up until we cry out, "God have mercy!" And he says to us, "Hey, look, you've abused your freedom, but no matter what your sin, no matter how dark, if you turn to my mercy, mercy is available."

Turning to God's mercy means repenting, trusting, and changing your life. God's love is conditional in this way: it's always available on the condition that we receive it. And the only way we can receive it is through humility, repentance, and trust. God wants to be merciful; he's simply waiting for us—knocking at the door of our hearts and asking, "Will you please open the door? If you open it even a crack, I'll do the rest."

—Fr. George Kosicki, CSB, *New Covenant*, July–August 1991, pp. 15–16

IN GOD'S PRESENCE, CONSIDER . . .

In what ways have I closed the door to God's mercy? What do I need to repent of? What changes can I resolve to make with his grace?

CLOSING PRAYER

Lord, help me to turn with trust to your mercy more and more each day, repenting of anything that blocks me from receiving your love.

Always More

In a timely meditation, the author contrasts the vastness of each person's need for mercy in their own spiritual journey—along with the immense need in the world—with the encouraging realization that "there is enough mercy to turn everything around."

There are days when my sin and weakness seem overwhelming. Days when all the trials, inner growth, and striving for holiness seem like they have borne no fruit. My spirit is weak and I want to throw in the metaphorical towel and be done. It seems ridiculous, unfathomable even, that I can be so much the same after all this time, and the distance between where I am and holiness seems like a gaping chasm. His mercy is more.

There are days when the weary world seems wearier still. Days when I wonder how God can continue to allow us to exist when we have fallen so far. I fear for the future, for the souls of my loved ones, for the persecution of the just. And my heart breaks for the heart of Christ weeping over Jerusalem. The hardened hearts, the level of depravity, the slavery of addictions that seem unbreakable—even among those who love Him. His mercy is more. Always more.

Lamentations 3:22–23 says, "His mercies never come to an end; they are new every morning." And Jesus said to Faustina, "Now is the time for mercy." While I am here, there is time for mercy. While I draw breath, there is time for mercy. Here, I am never without hope. In the garden, Jesus experienced the horror of all the sin and depravity that had ever or would ever exist. I don't need to take it all on; He did. He took the weight of it upon Himself, and when His body was killed on the cross, the power of all that darkness was obliterated. Mercy flowed out from His pierced side and continues to flow out upon the world as much as we ask for it, as much as we trust Him that He longs to pour it out upon us. There is enough mercy to turn everything around. Each day I will depend on it, drawing it down upon myself, my family, the world by unceasingly asking for it, trusting in it, bearing it. The need is great. His mercy is more.

—Erin Flynn

IN GOD'S PRESENCE, CONSIDER . . .

No matter what my level of involvement is in the message of Divine Mercy or how much I practice the devotions, I recognize that I have not taken full advantage of how generous God wants to be—if only I call on His mercy, open my heart more fully, and trust even more. I resolve to do all of these things.

CLOSING PRAYER

Thank you, God, for the hope of Your mercy. Thank you that no matter how discouraging things are, within or without, Your mercy is more.

The Emptied Space Where All May Enter

One of our most poetic modern theologians, von Balthasar here draws on Old and New Testaments to reveal the incarnational presence of God's mercy in the torn-open heart of Jesus.

In the Old Testament, the heart is still largely understood as the seat of spiritual energy and of thought, while the bosom or "bowels" (as in "bowels of mercy": rachamim, splanchna) are rather taken to be the seat of the affections.

In the New Testament, however, both aspects coincide with the concept of "heart." Having one's "whole heart" turned to God means the opening of the whole man towards him (Acts 8, 37; Mt. 22, 37). . . .

The narrative of the piercing with the spear and of the outpouring of blood and water should be read as being continuous with the Johannine symbolism of water, spirit and blood, to which also belong the references to "thirst."

Earthly water again makes thirsty, but Jesus' water quenches thirst forever (4, 13f). . . . Related to this is the extraordinary promise that, in him who drinks it, Jesus' water would become a fountain leaping up to life eternal (4, 14) . . . It is at the moment when Jesus suffers the most absolute thirst that he dissolves, to become an eternal fountain. That verse may refer to the ever-present analogy between water and word/spirit (Jesus' words are "spirit and life"). Even better, it may be related to the "fountain" in Ezechiel's new temple (Ez. 47; cf Zach. 13, 1), with which Jesus compared his own body (2, 2t).

In the context of John's general symbolism, there can be no doubt that in the outpouring of blood and water the evangelist saw the institution of the sacraments of eucharist and baptism . . . The opening of the Heart is the handing over of what is most intimate and personal for the use of all. All may enter the open, emptied space.

—Hans Urs von Balthasar, *Heart of the World*, pp. 14–15

IN GOD'S PRESENCE, CONSIDER . . .

In the beating of my own heart, in the breathing of my own lungs, can I today sense the closeness of Jesus's heart, of His Mercy? Today in my own heart and core can I commune with the Heart of Jesus?

CLOSING PRAYER

Most Holy Spirit, breath of God, breathe into my lungs, fill my body and soul with the renewed life of my Creator. Wash me in the cleansing tide of Christ's mercy. Jesus, let me quench Your thirst with my love.

Self-Emptying Love

The most striking feature of the Divine Mercy Image and the feature that most sets it apart from all the other images of Christ is the rays of mercy streaming from Christ's Heart on the Cross. The pale rays are usually interpreted as representing the gift of the Holy Spirit and the Sacrament of Baptism. The red rays represent the Eucharist, "the new covenant" in His Blood (see Lk 22:20). But there's more these rays can tell us . . .

The rays also speak to us of God's self-emptying love. Nowhere is this love more completely expressed and manifested than at the piercing of Christ's Heart on the Cross.

Jesus has been bleeding for hours—from the thorns cutting into His head, from the open wounds where the scourges tore His flesh, from the nail holes in His hands and feet.

Now, with the piercing of His Heart, He is not just bleeding; He is bled out. The blood and water gushing from that tender Heart [see Jn 19:34] represents the complete outpouring of Christ's life blood. He has held nothing back; He has given all.

This is mercy! This is the self-emptying of God, the complete self-giving of the Father to His children. As Pope Benedict XVI expresses it, this is "the turning of God against himself" for love of us.

> For God so loved the world that he gave his only-begotten Son, that whoever believes in him should not perish but have eternal life (Jn 3:16).

That's what you're worth to God. That's how much He loves you. That's the story of mercy that these rays tell us.

—Vinny Flynn, *7 Secrets of Divine Mercy*

IN GOD'S PRESENCE, CONSIDER . . .

The Divine Mercy Image can be just a picture I look at occasionally, or it can be the stimulus for regular meditation on the Passion of Christ. Can I resolve today to gaze on it often and prayerfully, letting it lead me deeper into the story of God's mercy?

CLOSING PRAYER

*Lord Jesus, thank you for allowing Your Heart to be opened wide for us on the Cross so that You could "empty Yourself out upon us" (*Diary, *1319).*

Transformed into Mercy

To fulfill the Father's plan of mercy, Christ longs to pour Himself into our hearts so completely that we share in His divine life and become living images of His mercy, radiating His very being to others. Recognizing this, Faustina took on His longing and prayed fervently for this transformation.

O Most Holy Trinity! As many times as I breathe, as many times as my heart beats, as many times as my blood pulsates through my body, so many thousand times do I want to glorify Your mercy.

I want to be completely transformed into Your mercy and to be Your living reflection, O Lord. May the greatest of all divine attributes, that of Your unfathomable mercy, pass through my heart and soul to my neighbor. . . .

O Jesus, continue to grant me Your divine life. Let Your pure and noble Blood throb with all its might in my heart. I give You my whole being. Transform me into Yourself and make me capable of doing Your holy will in all things and of returning Your love. . . .

Most sweet Jesus, set on fire my love for You and transform me into Yourself. Divinize me that my deeds may be pleasing to You. May this be accomplished by the power of the Holy Communion which I receive daily. Oh, how greatly I desire to be wholly transformed into You, O Lord! . . .

I expose my heart to the action of Your grace like a crystal exposed to the rays of the sun. May Your image be reflected in it, O my God, to the extent that it is possible to be reflected in the heart of a creature. Let Your divinity radiate through me, O You who dwell in my soul.

—St. Faustina, *Diary*, 163, 822, 1289, 1336

IN GOD'S PRESENCE, CONSIDER . . .

The goal of the spiritual life is nothing short of transformation and union. I have "arrived" when I become holy like God, merciful like God, when His attributes radiate through me to others. Impossible, if not for God infusing His very life in me, through each encounter with grace and especially through receiving Him in Holy Communion.

CLOSING PRAYER

Most Holy Trinity, inspire a deeper longing in my heart for total transformation! I want to open myself without reserve to Your work in me, allowing You to change anything and everything as You wish. Transform me into a testament of Your mercy.

Gushed Forth

Dr. Stackpole discusses the historical and scriptural accuracy of Christ's revelations to St. Faustina about His mercy "gushing forth" from the piercing of His Heart, first referenced in John 19:34.

These two rays issued forth from the very depths of My tender mercy when my agonized Heart was opened by a lance on the Cross. (*Diary*, 299).

The historical reference that Jesus made here is significant ("when my agonized Heart was opened by a lance on the Cross") because it corresponds to what New Testament scholars tell us about this event. . . . Jesus was crucified by Roman soldiers, and Roman soldiers were trained to know exactly where to stick their enemies with a lance so that the lance would pass between the ribs and pierce the heart, thereby guaranteeing instant death.

In the Gospel story, the Roman soldiers were trying to make sure that Jesus was dead before they took Him down from the cross (Roman soldiers were subject to the death penalty themselves if they failed to successfully execute a criminal condemned under Roman law). So the lance passed into His side between the ribs, but went right up into His Heart (remember that they were thrusting the lance upward, from beneath the Cross). . . .

The phrase that Jesus taught St. Faustina to use in her prayer ("O Blood and Water, which gushed forth from the Heart of Jesus") is also precisely accurate. It corresponds to the word that St. John used in his gospel for the flow of blood and water: it "gushed out." The Roman spear evidently pierced the pericardial sack around the heart where relatively clear plasma would have collected after Jesus' death, and also probably pierced the Heart itself, where blood had settled.

The result would have been similar to the piercing of a water balloon: the blood and water "gushed forth" from His Heart. In short, the side of Christ was pierced, according to the Bible, but everything about this incident suggests that the wound in His side entered right into His Heart.

—Robert Stackpole

IN GOD'S PRESENCE, CONSIDER . . .

Sacred Heart of Jesus, beating out a steady rhythm of love for a broken world; pierced and gushing forth a fount of mercy; streams of blood and water for our salvation.

CLOSING PRAYER

Jesus, meek and humble of heart, Your radiant light shines to all corners of the earth through the piercing of Your side. Just as Adam's side was opened to draw forth a beautiful bride, reveal my transformation into life through Your Divine Mercy.

Love Is a Verb

God is not sitting idly on a throne in heaven. He is always active, always doing; and what He's doing is love.

St. John of the Cross gives us a wonderful little analogy, in which he compares God to the sun: "The sun is up early and shining on your house, ready to shine in if you open the curtains. So God, who never sleeps nor slumbers, . . . is like the sun, shining over souls" (*Living Flame*, 46–7).

Science tells us that the sun never sets, never "goes down." It's the earth that moves, turning away from the sun. The sun is still doing its thing. The sun is always shining. It gives light, it gives heat, it irradiates everything. That's what it does, all the time. You can't change that.

God is love and, in God, love is not a noun; it's a verb. Love is what God does, all the time. Just like the sun that is always shining, God is always loving you, always pouring His love upon you. You can't change that; your sin doesn't change that. He is always loving you, even when you sin. Nothing has the power to change God! He is always loving. That's simply what He does.

One of the greatest reminders of this for me is the Divine Mercy Image, the picture of Christ with His right hand raised in blessing, His left hand inviting you into His heart, and the red and pale rays gushing forth from His pierced heart as a fountain of mercy for the world.

No matter how much you stare at that picture, you can't change it. You can't turn that right hand into a clenched fist. You can't turn it into an angry finger pointing at you. It's always blessing you. All you can do is either receive the blessing or reject it. You can't turn that inviting left hand into a hand that pushes you away. You can't dry up that outpouring stream of mercy.

Christ is *Divine Mercy in Person*, the God who is always loving, always blessing, always inviting you deeper into His heart, always pouring His mercy upon you.

—Vinny Flynn, adapted from *21 Ways to Worship*

IN GOD'S PRESENCE, CONSIDER . . .

Do I think my behavior—good or bad—changes God, or do I realize that nothing changes Him? He is always the same, always loving.

CLOSING PRAYER

Lord, thank you for loving me no matter what. To have that kind of love is so unexpected and such a pure gift. Help me to live under Your blessing, to receive all You desire to give me.

The Great Mother of Mercy

Here Venerable Bruno Lanteri invites us into prayer to our loving mother: "Show yourself to be our mother, we fly to your protection, Mary, mother of grace." Knowing mothers, Lanteri teaches us to have unlimited confidence in the most compassionate Mother of God.

I desire to have a tender love for the Virgin Mary, and a confidence in her as a son toward his mother, to such a degree that it appears impossible to me that she could permit me to be overcome and that I be lost in the battle; I will have recourse to her, therefore, as the chick takes refuge under the wings of its mother when it hears the cries of the preying hawk, and, after the act of the love of God, I shall say, Monstra te esse matrem, Sub tuum praesidium, Maria mater gratiae, etc., and I will do this with the confidence that a child has toward its mother, asking of her what it needs with great surety, as if she were bound to grant it to him, and turning to her in all his troubles, such that the mother is, as it were, obliged to come to his aid, and draws from this a motive to love her son yet more deeply. And if earthly mothers, though at times they may not be good, do not refuse the requests of their children, what shall be said of the great Mother of God?

—Timothy M. Gallagher, *Overcoming Spiritual Discouragement: The Wisdom and Spiritual Power of Venerable Bruno Lanteri*

IN GOD'S PRESENCE, CONSIDER . . .

How often have I forgotten that I'm not here on my own, but am loved by a tender mother? Can I today learn to be unhesitating in calling upon her? Can I share with her my fears and failures, and experience her loving embrace?

CLOSING PRAYER

Merciful Mother, you know my wounded heart. Bring your pierced heart close to mine to reveal tenderness from heaven that refreshes my weary spirit. I'm tired of struggling on my own; let today and each day be lived in your warmth and loving presence.

Believing in Merciful Love

In his personal retreat based on the teaching of St. Therese of Lisieux, Fr. Jean D'Elbee tells us of a way to acknowledge the full weight of our wretchedness, while having total confidence and peace.

It is true that instinctively we seek to climb the rough stairway of perfection instead of taking the gentle elevator of the arms of Jesus. This is because we have been told so often of our miseries. We have been told, and rightly, that we are miserable; and then, we have been told about Jesus that He is good, yes, but not enough that He is wondrously good, infinitely good, infinite charity. No one has told us at the same time that He is Savior before He is Judge and that, in the Heart of God, 'justice and peace have embraced.'

We have been trained in the habit of looking at our dark side, our ugliness, and not at the purifying Sun, Light of Light, which He is, who changes the dust that we are into pure gold. We think about examining ourselves, yet we do not think, before the examination, during the examination, and after the examination, to plunge ourselves, with all our miseries, into the consuming and transforming furnace of His Heart, which is open to us through a humble act of confidence.

I am not telling you, "You believe too much in your own wretchedness." We are much more wretched than we ever realize. But I am telling you, "You do not believe enough in merciful love." We must have confidence, not in spite of our miseries, but because of them, since it is misery which attracts mercy.

—Jean C.J. d'Elbee, *I Believe in Love*, pp. 28–29

IN GOD'S PRESENCE, CONSIDER . . .

In those times when I veer toward the rough stairway of perfection, is it self-reliance, fear, doubt, or something else that's driving me there?

CLOSING PRAYER

Father of Mercy, whenever I examine myself and find all sorts of imperfections, let me do so always in the safety of Your Heart, and with the confidence of a child who is cherished.

Go in Peace, and Be Healed

Jesus insisted to St. Faustina that the Divine Mercy image must always include the invocation, "Jesus, I trust in you." The one key necessary for miracles of mercy is a faith that leads to complete trust.

And a great crowd followed him and thronged about him. And there was a woman who had had a flow of blood for twelve years, and who had suffered much under many physicians, and had spent all that she had, and was no better but rather grew worse. She had heard the reports about Jesus, and came up behind him in the crowd and touched his garment. For she said, "If I touch even his garments, I shall be made well." And immediately the hemorrhage ceased; and she felt in her body that she was healed of her disease. And Jesus, perceiving in himself that power had gone forth from him, immediately turned about in the crowd, and said, "Who touched my garments?" And his disciples said to him, "You see the crowd pressing around you, and yet you say, 'Who touched me?'" And he looked around to see who had done it. But the woman, knowing what had been done to her, came in fear and trembling and fell down before him, and told him the whole truth. And he said to her, "Daughter, your faith has made you well; go in peace, and be healed of your disease."

—Mark 5:24–34

IN GOD'S PRESENCE, CONSIDER . . .

Do I have the faith to press through the crowds, through doubt and opposition, and fling myself entirely upon God's mercy? In my present day, can I pierce through the veil to perceive Jesus present to me here in the Eucharist, and receive his healing power? When I encounter Him, I wonder what it would be like to tell Him the whole truth.

CLOSING PRAYER

Lord Jesus, I want to touch You, to receive You, to know Your love. Help me to trust entirely in You. Give me the courage to tell You everything: my brokenness, fears, desires, doubts, dreams, and the ways I feel unworthy of Your love. To relate anything and everything to You, knowing that You are trustworthy and that You want to know my heart.

Love Is the Only Law in the Father's House

Fr. Chevrot, a simple but brilliant curate in Paris, lived during two World Wars, refused all honorary titles out of humility, was Lenten preacher at the Cathedral of Notre-Dame, and retreat master throughout France. He writes here of love, freedom, and our true Father.

This father who asks instead of ordering, who gives in and cannot say No, who forgives instead of punishing . . . this father has no equal here on earth. It is our Father in Heaven, and St. John has told us his name: "God is love."

We recognize him by the traits shown in the parable: this God who keeps silent and stays in the background, this God who gives and forgives. He has given us just one law: "Thou shalt love." In the Father's house the children do not work for a salary; they are happy to share their father's labors, and their father is happy to share his wealth with them. Their one ambition is to love each other more and more, forever.

This household, which has no equivalent among families here on earth, nevertheless does exist on earth. We belong to it: it is the Church, which, by incorporating us into Jesus Christ, has made us God's children. In the Church and through it, we share everything with our brothers and sisters and share everything with our Father in Heaven.

This happy state, begun in us by Baptism, strengthened by Confirmation, increased by the Eucharist, is what we call the state of grace.

Love is the only law in the Father's house.

But love has one condition: freedom. No living being can be forced to love, as no one can be loved by force. Freedom is the condition for love, and love is the endless renewing of freedom. God, who loves us—because he loves us and because he expects love from us and wants nothing but love—has run the great risk of love, and the great risk of giving us freedom.

We are able—alas, we have the power, amazing and woeful as it is—to refuse him or haggle with him over our love. That is the story of the two sons in the parable, the story of sin, our own story.

—Georges Chevrot, *The Prodigal Son*

IN GOD'S PRESENCE, CONSIDER . . .

I don't want to refuse God or "haggle with Him" over whether I give Him my love or not. He has run the great risk of giving me freedom. What will I do with it?

CLOSING PRAYER

Father, let my one ambition be to love You—and my brothers and sisters—"more and more, forever."

Real Love Is Not Easy

In order to allow Christ to love through us, says Catherine Doherty, we must first "make room within ourselves."

Love eludes . . . intellectual approaches because love is not a thing, love is not a state. Love is a person. Love is God.

It may help us if we re-read what Jesus Christ has said about love. It might help if we meditated on his words and made them our own, made them both the way and the goal of our lives. For he told us first to love God with all our hearts, with all our being, and then to love our neighbor as ourselves, which implies that we must first learn to love ourselves well. He also said that "by this shall all men know that you are my disciples, that you love one another as I love you." Finally, he said, "Love your enemies."

Yes, he defined all the ways of loving. He not only defined them, he lived them. He was Love incarnate, and he showed us in truth that "greater love has no man than that he lay down his life for his friends." Love has no limits.

Perhaps that is why there is so much talk about love, so much experimenting, and so much disappointment too with what we imagine love to be. Because deep down in our hearts we know that his way of loving is the way of the cross, that it is painful, and that it demands an emptying of ourselves. Without his loving us, none of us could love the way he wants us to.

Christian love is allowing Christ to love with our own hearts. But in order to do this we must make room within ourselves to allow him to grow to his full stature. That means emptying ourselves from our self-centeredness, our egoism, from the desire to have all our needs fulfilled. It means that we must get busy filling the needs of others.

—Catherine de Hueck Doherty, *The Gospel Without Compromise*

IN GOD'S PRESENCE, CONSIDER . . .

So much to meditate on here. What resonates with me most right now? Recognizing that I haven't learned to love myself well? Or perhaps I see that there is fear involved when I think about loving as God loves, because I know it will involve sacrifice and I want to avoid suffering.

CLOSING PRAYER

Lord, I know that there is a very natural human aversion to suffering, but I do not want to be afraid of this emptying of self, this way of loving that calls me to die to my own self-focus and desires. Grant me a deep heart knowledge that more of You is all I need; that if I make space for You, I will never be depleted, no matter how much I give to others.

Field Hospital

It's so easy for all of us in the Church—priests and laity alike—to get caught up in the beauty of our devotions, the routine of our own spiritual life, our reception of the Sacraments, that we lose our focus on one of the primary purposes of them, and fail to see and attend to the woundedness around us. All of these things are meant to make us holy as He is holy; merciful as He is merciful.

Today we can think of the Church as a "field hospital". Excuse me but I repeat it, because this is how I see it, how I feel it is: a "field hospital." Wounds need to be treated, so many wounds! So many wounds!

There are so many people who are wounded by material problems, by scandals, also in the Church. . . . People wounded by the world's illusions. . . . We priests must be there, close to these people.

Mercy first means treating the wounds. When someone is wounded, he needs this immediately, not tests such as the level of cholesterol and one's glycemic index. . . . But there's a wound! Treat the wound, and then we can look at the results of the tests. Then specialized treatments can be done, but first we need to treat the open wounds. I think this is what is most important at this time.

And there are also hidden wounds, because there are people who distance themselves in order to avoid showing their wounds closer. . . . The custom comes to mind, in the Mosaic Law, of the lepers in Jesus' time, who were always kept at a distance in order not to spread the contagion. . . .

There are people who distance themselves through shame, through shame, so as not to let their wounds be seen. . . . And perhaps they distance themselves with some bitterness against the Church, but deep down inside there is a wound. . . . They want a caress! And you, dear brothers—I ask you—do you know the wounds of your parishioners? Do you perceive them? Are you close to them?

—Pope Francis to the Parish Priests of Rome, March 6, 2014

IN GOD'S PRESENCE, CONSIDER . . .

How can I help the Church be a place of mercy in today's world? What can I do to become more aware of the needs of those around me and to find ways to help?

CLOSING PRAYER

Lord, let Your mercy flow upon Your Church, so that it will become everywhere a place of refuge and healing.

The Medicine of Mercy

Pope St. John XXIII reassures us that the truth of the Lord will remain forever; the errors of men have to be guarded against and dissipated, but also met with mercy.

We see, in fact, as one age succeeds another, that the opinions of men follow one another and exclude each other. . . . The Church has always opposed these errors. Frequently she has condemned them with the greatest severity. Nowadays, however, the Spouse of Christ prefers to make use of the medicine of mercy rather than that of severity. She considers that she meets the needs of the present day by demonstrating the validity of her teaching rather than by condemnations. . . .

That being so, the Catholic Church, raising the torch of religious truth by means of this Ecumenical Council, desires to show herself to be the loving mother of all, benign, patient, full of mercy and goodness toward the brethren who are separated from her. To mankind, oppressed by so many difficulties, the Church says, as Peter said to the poor who begged alms from him: "I have neither gold nor silver, but what I have I give you: in the name of Jesus Christ the Nazorean, rise and walk (Acts 3:6). In other words, the Church does not offer to the men of today riches that pass, nor does she promise them a merely earthly happiness. But she distributes to them the goods of divine grace which, raising men to the dignity of sons of God, are the most efficacious safeguards . . . She opens the fountain of her life-giving doctrine which allows men, enlightened by the light of Christ, to understand well what they really are, what their lofty dignity and their purpose are, and, finally, through her children, she spreads everywhere the fullness of Christian charity.

—Pope St. John XXIII, Opening speech to The Second Vatican Council

IN GOD'S PRESENCE, CONSIDER . . .

Am I hesitant to share the richness of the Church's teachings? Or perhaps I "share" the truth with a sledgehammer? If a common sentence in my head before a discussion is a severe, "Well, there is no love without truth," I resolve to first consider whether my disposition is "patient, full of mercy and goodness" toward the person.

CLOSING PRAYER

Jesus, Your Church truly has a fountain of life-giving doctrine, which will help all people discover who they really are and convince them of "their lofty dignity and their purpose." I want to be a vessel to bring Your light of truth to the world, but let me always do so with a deep and humble recognition of how great Your mercy has been to me.

The Spiritual Strength We Need

Confession is not just for forgiveness of sin: it's a remedy for our weakness and selfishness, a "true meeting" with Jesus that renews the graces of our baptism and restores our relationship with the Father.

The Gospel is a message of reconciliation—that by Christ's passion and resurrection God has forgiven all our trespasses and set us free from sin and death.

Few of us are egregious, wicked sinners. But all of us are sinners. This is the testimony of sacred Scripture. "All have sinned," St. Paul said simply (Rom. 3:23).

We know this about ourselves. We want to do good but we find it hard to do the right thing all the time. We can be so weak at times, so selfish. How often we fall short in our devotion to God, in the little duties of love we owe to our families, loved ones, and neighbors.

Our Lord understood this about us, too. He knew all about human nature (John 2:25). He came among us to save his people from sin (Matt. 1:21). He poured out his blood on the cross for the forgiveness of sins, to take away the sin of the world (Matt. 26:28; John 1:29).

Each of us experiences this forgiveness in baptism, which cleanses us from the original sin of our first human parents and reconciles us to God, making it possible for us to live as his sons and daughters.

But our human nature remains weak and subject to temptation. For this reason, our Lord established the Sacrament of Penance, giving his apostles the Holy Spirit and the power to forgive sins in his name (Matt. 16:19; John 20:23).

He left us this sacrament as a remedy—to restore us to the innocence of our baptism, to give us the spiritual strength we need to struggle against our sinful tendencies and temptations, and to continue our conversion toward the Lord and his ways.

—Archbishop José H. Gomez, Pastoral Letter: *The Tender Mercy of God*

IN GOD'S PRESENCE, CONSIDER . . .

Do I look forward to confession as a "true meeting" with Jesus and a renewal of baptismal grace? Or do I see it as simply a requirement for forgiveness of sin?

CLOSING PRAYER

Lord, help me to seek more than forgiveness in the confessional. Help me to long for the remedy You want to provide for my weakness, the graces of deeper conversion You want to give me.

Mercy Is Always Linked to Truth . . .

It is an unfathomable mystery that when we were estranged from God, He entered Himself into that estrangement and freed us. This act of pure love, and the mercy that flows from it, demands a response from us—but the response to mercy has to be one of truth. The spiritual master Archbishop Chaput gives us much to meditate on here.

To save us, God assumes our human condition "from within" and becomes the most human of us all. In his crucifixion Jesus offers his life to the Father on our behalf out of love, in perfect innocence and justice. In doing so, he renders us "just," refashioning a right relationship between human beings and God. Precisely for this reason, the Cross is the greatest sign of divine mercy. Nailed to it, God enters into our estrangement from himself—and bridges the gap with an act of love that frees us.

Having said that, we are wise to remember that God does not owe us forgiveness or redemption—or anything else. Nor does God's mercy license us to continue in sin. It demands a response to "go, and do not sin again." To borrow a thought from Augustine: We must not despair, one of the thieves was saved; we must not presume, one of the thieves was damned. . . . true mercy is always intimately linked to truth.

In a truthful act of confession, an honest admission of our sins, we find consolation and peace. The sacrament of reconciliation, received and acted upon truthfully, is a steady path to transformation and holiness. Through it, we're given the grace to make an exodus, a going out from our destructive situations and patterns of behavior, and to attach ourselves more deeply to God. The mercy of God is meant to render us increasingly more honest, more just, and so also more loving and peaceful.

—Archbishop Charles J. Chaput, "A Jubilee Year of Mercy"

IN GOD'S PRESENCE, CONSIDER . . .

Do I lean towards despair or presumption in regards to my sin and God's mercy? What is a more truthful perspective? And is there a part of me that at times takes confession for granted, not truly renouncing sin and changing my life?

CLOSING PRAYER

God, give me the courage to be truthful, to look with open eyes at my sin, my patterns of choosing things other than what I ought to choose; the courage to honestly look at the underlying roots of these behaviors. The thought of You, Jesus, entering our estrangement from God, and freeing us with such an act of love, makes me want to be truly free, to not take that for granted, and to never be estranged from You again.

Let Us Make Up for Lost Time

In this letter to a Mother Superior with whom Brother Lawrence corresponded, we find the encouragement to see whatever time we have left in this life as a mercy granted by God. Each moment is an opportunity to begin again and use all the graces God gives us to live the life He calls us to and give ourselves more fully to Him.

Let us often consider . . . that our only concern in this life is to please God: What can anything else be but folly and vanity? You and I have been in the monastic life more than forty years. Have we used them to love and to serve God who in His mercy has called us to that state for that purpose? I am filled with shame and embarrassment when I reflect, on the one hand, on the great graces which God has granted me and which He continues to grant me and, on the other hand, how poorly I have used them and how little I have profited from them on the way to perfection.

Since in His mercy He still gives us a little time, let us begin in earnest; let us make up for lost time; let us return with complete confidence to that Father of goodness who is always ready to receive us lovingly. Let us renounce fully for His love everything that is not of Himself; He deserves infinitely more; let us think of Him continually, let us put all of our confidence in Him. I have no doubt but that we will soon experience the effects of so doing, and that we will receive His graces in abundance, with which we can do all, and without which we can do nothing but sin.

—Brother Lawrence, *The Practice of the Presence of God*

IN GOD'S PRESENCE, CONSIDER . . .

What are some of the significant graces God has granted me in my life, and what are some current graces I can think on with gratitude today? Are there graces I tend to take for granted? Recalling the goodness of God to me, I notice where my response to Him is lacking and resolve to begin again.

CLOSING PRAYER

Father, everything from Your hand is one vast divine blessing. I live and breathe because You hold me in existence with Your gaze of love. Help me to, without self-condemnation, see the truth of how I have failed to respond to You with generous love. Holy Spirit, convict me to restructure my priorities and strive to make up for the time I have wasted with things that were not of You.

Ready to Embrace Us

St. Proclus introduced into the Divine Liturgy the Trisagion (Holy God, Holy Mighty, Holy Immortal One), which concludes every Divine Mercy Chaplet, and here the Patriarch of Constantinople calls us to delight in the mercy of this thrice-holy God.

If we know ourselves, we shall be persuaded that no one is weaker and frailer than we are. Can any creature be more unworthy of the divine mercy than we who have repaid the greatest graces and favours with continual sloth and the basest infidelities? When, therefore, we read of the fall or sins of others, we ought to turn our eyes upon ourselves; to adore the divine mercy which has still borne with us, and is yet ready with stretched-forth arms to embrace us: to shake off our sloth in the practice of virtue, enter upon a fervent penitential life, and without ceasing, call upon God in fear and humility. He is our strength and support, who is almighty and most willing and desirous to save us, if our wilful wretchedness and pride stand not in the way. He alone can effectually remove these obstacles: humble prayer and compunction will not fail to obtain this constant grace.

—St. Proclus, Archbishop of Constantinople (1711–73)

IN GOD'S PRESENCE, CONSIDER . . .

The eternal God adored by the angels, enthroned in majesty, sees me and loves me. If the one worshiped by Seraphim looks on me with kindness, what do I have to fear? Turning my vision to where the angels gaze with unveiled sight, I discover the mercy that holds me in being and love.

CLOSING PRAYER

Father of Mercy, Father of Love, I am so small before you, yet You raise me up in the triumph of Your Son. I have no boast but the blood of my Savior; sustain me always in this gift.

Set Ajar the Door

God wants none of his children to be lost, so no matter how bad our sins, His mercy pursues us to the very last moment, seeking to draw us back to Him. But since He created us free, He can't save us without our cooperation.

The last hour abounds with mercy for us. Let no one doubt concerning the goodness of God; even if a person's sins were as dark as night, God's mercy is stronger than our misery. One thing alone is necessary: that the sinner set ajar the door of his heart, be it ever so little, to let in a ray of God's merciful grace, and then God will do the rest.

. . . God's mercy sometimes touches the sinner at the last moment in a wondrous and mysterious way. Outwardly, it seems as if everything were lost, but it is not so. The soul, illumined by a ray of God's powerful final grace, turns to God in the last moment with such a power of love that, in an instant, it receives from God forgiveness of sin and punishment, while outwardly it shows no sign either of repentance or of contrition, because souls [at that stage] no longer react to external things. Oh, how beyond comprehension is God's mercy! But—horror!—there are also souls who voluntarily and consciously reject and scorn this grace! Although a person is at the point of death, the merciful God gives the soul that interior vivid moment, so that if the soul is willing, it has the possibility of returning to God. But sometimes, the obduracy in souls is so great that consciously they choose hell; they [thus] make useless all the prayers that other souls offer to God for them and even the efforts of God Himself.

—St. Faustina, *Diary*, 1507, 1698

IN GOD'S PRESENCE, CONSIDER . . .

Psalm 23 promises that God's "goodness and mercy will follow me all the days of my life." I want to stay open to Him at every moment and remember to pray for those whose hearts are hardened to His grace.

CLOSING PRAYER

Lord, help me to open my heart more every day so that I will be able to continuously respond to You, especially in that final moment of grace.

The Most Loved Psalm

Almost everyone recognizes David's Good Shepherd. Jesus himself took David's name for him as His own, and the Gospels made sure we knew that Jesus's feeding of the five thousand took place on green grass so we could make the connection also.

The Lord is my shepherd, I shall not want;
  he makes me lie down in green pastures.
He leads me beside still waters;
  he restores my soul.
He leads me in paths of righteousness
  for his name's sake.
Even though I walk through the valley of the shadow of death,
  I fear no evil;
for thou art with me;
  thy rod and thy staff,
  they comfort me.
Thou preparest a table before me
  in the presence of my enemies;
thou anointest my head with oil,
  my cup overflows.
Surely goodness and mercy shall follow me
  all the days of my life;
and I shall dwell in the house of the Lord
  for ever.

—Psalm 23

IN GOD'S PRESENCE, CONSIDER . . .

It seems all God's best friends are shepherds: Abel, Abraham, Moses, David—Jesus wants me to know that he loves me tenderly, and I am in his care. Can I relinquish the world's insistence that this is a dog-eat-dog world and lay down my defenses to truly be shepherded by the Living God?

CLOSING PRAYER

Good Shepherd, You have sought me out and carried me as a lamb on Your shoulders. In You I find true rest and the restoration of my soul. When I am with You, Lord, there is nothing else I need. Thank you for loving me. Please keep me close.

A Force that Moves the World

Real prayer is not something we do to make ourselves feel good or obtain our wishes from God. It's the key to mercy, the key to opening the Father's heart.

Padre Pio used to say that prayer is a "force that moves the world. It spreads the smile and the blessing of God over every languor and weakness" (Second International Congress of Prayer Groups, 5 May 1966).

Prayer, then, is not a nice practice for finding a little peace of heart; nor is it a means of devotion for obtaining useful things from God. Were it so, then it would be an act of subtle selfishness: I pray in order to be well, just as if taking an aspirin. But this is just making a deal.

No, it's not like this. Prayer is something else; it is . . . *a spiritual work of mercy*, which means bringing everything to the heart of God. "You take it, you who are Father." It should be like this, speaking to him in a simple way . . . saying: "You, take it, you who are Father. Look at us, You who are Father." This is the relationship with the Father. . . .

In a word, it means *to entrust*: entrust the Church, entrust people, entrust situations to the Father—"I entrust this to you"—so that you will take care of it. That is why prayer, as Padre Pio liked to say, is "the greatest weapon we have, a key that opens the heart of God."

A key that opens God's heart: it is a simple key. The heart of God is not "heavily guarded" with many security measures. You can open it with a common key, with prayer. For his is a heart of love, a father's heart. And it is the Church's greatest strength, one which we must never let go of, for the Church bears fruit only if she does as did Our Lady and the Apostles, who "with one accord devoted themselves to prayer" (Acts 1:14), as they awaited the Holy Spirit. Dedicated and united in prayer. Otherwise we risk relying elsewhere for support: on means, on money, on power; then evangelization vanishes and joy is extinguished and the heart grows dull. . . .

Be always joyful Apostles of Prayer. Prayer does miracles.

—Pope Francis, Address to Padre Pio Prayer Groups, February 6, 2016

IN GOD'S PRESENCE, CONSIDER . . .

How do I pray? Have I become too reliant on recited prayers, or am I also comfortable just speaking to God simply and naturally as to someone who loves me?

CLOSING PRAYER

Father, help me to keep my prayers simple and real, a sincere and personal offering of everything to you, entrusting everything to Your mercy.

Prayer Outside of Time

God is not subject to time as we are. He sees everything—past, present, and future—now, so His mercy has no time limit. It's never too late to pray!

. . . One day in 2003, 10 years after my grandmother had died, I went to make a general confession . . . to a priest, and he told me all about Divine Mercy and the Divine Mercy Chaplet. I was intrigued by the Chaplet because he told me how powerful it is for the sick and the dying. So I told the priest, "I wish I had had this prayer for my grandmother 10 years ago."

And he looked at me and said, " . . . God is outside of time. In eternity, there is no past; there's no future. There's just one big, eternal now. Chris, God knew back in 1993 that you were going to be here today, 10 years later. So go home and pray the Chaplet for your grandmother. . . . All the graces from that prayer that you are going to do tonight will be showered upon your grandmother at the moment of her death, even at the moment of her judgment. The fact that it's 10 years ago to God means nothing. God is outside of time, there's no '10 years ago' to God."

. . . I asked him, "So you mean, Father, that praying right now for someone who died years ago can help them?" He said, "Not only can it help them—it will help them. Sometimes souls continue to suffer because no one is praying for them. So your grandmother may be suffering if no one is praying for her."

After our talk, I ran right home and prayed for her. After I had said the Chaplet, I felt this rush go through me. It was a sense of peace . . . that my grandmother was now at rest. . . . I just had this peace that the Divine Mercy Chaplet released my grandmother from suffering because of God's mercy—not merely because of what I did. But God's mercy allows us as the Body of Christ to pray for each other. I just feel that God accepted that prayer, and my grandmother . . . was released from Purgatory.

—Fr. Chris Alar, MIC, *After Suicide*

IN GOD'S PRESENCE, CONSIDER . . .

What past situation or person have I not lifted up in prayer because I thought it was too late?

CLOSING PRAYER

Lord, help me remember that I can pray now with the assurance that You will hear it then.

Loving the Person You Do Not Like

How refreshing to have a pope acknowledge that there are people we don't like. But he goes on to explain that liking or not liking others is not the point. The point is how to love them anyway.

Love of neighbour . . . consists in the very fact that, in God and with God, I love even the person whom I do not like or even know. This can only take place on the basis of an intimate encounter with God, an encounter which has become a communion of will, even affecting my feelings. Then I learn to look on this other person not simply with my eyes and my feelings, but from the perspective of Jesus Christ. His friend is my friend. . . . Seeing with the eyes of Christ, I can give to others much more than their outward necessities; I can give them the look of love which they crave.

. . . If I have no contact whatsoever with God in my life, then I cannot see in the other anything more than the other, and I am incapable of seeing in him the image of God. But if in my life I fail completely to heed others, solely out of a desire to be "devout" and to perform my "religious duties," then my relationship with God will also grow arid. It becomes merely "proper," but loveless. Only my readiness to encounter my neighbour and to show him love makes me sensitive to God as well. Only if I serve my neighbour can my eyes be opened to what God does for me and how much he loves me.

. . . Love of God and love of neighbour are thus inseparable, they form a single commandment. But both live from the love of God who has loved us first. No longer is it a question, then, of a "commandment" imposed from without and calling for the impossible, but rather of a freely-bestowed experience of love from within, a love which by its very nature must then be shared with others. Love grows through love. Love is "divine" because it comes from God and unites us to God; through this unifying process it makes us a "we" which transcends our divisions and makes us one, until in the end God is "all in all" (1 Cor 15:28).

—Pope Benedict XVI, *Deus Caritas Est (God is Love)*, 18

IN GOD'S PRESENCE, CONSIDER . . .

With people I don't know or have trouble liking, do I see just their outward appearances and behavior? Or do I try to "look inside" to see them as God sees them and love them as He loves them?

CLOSING PRAYER

Lord, draw me into a deeper personal relationship with You so that I can come to live from Your love, seeing others with Your eyes and sharing with them the love I receive from You.

Even As Your Father

Jesus's Magna Carta, found as the Sermon on the Mount in Matthew, is here presented in Luke's Gospel: the heart of His new, divine way of living while we are still on earth. Our new way of life is mercy.

But I say to you that hear, Love your enemies, do good to those who hate you, bless those who curse you, pray for those who mistreat you. To him who strikes you on the cheek, offer the other also; and from him who takes away your cloak do not withhold your coat as well. Give to every one who begs from you; and of him who takes away your goods do not ask them again. And as you wish that men would do to you, do so to them.

If you love those who love you, what credit is that to you? For even sinners love those who love them. And if you do good to those who do good to you, what credit is that to you? For even sinners do the same. And if you lend to those from whom you hope to receive, what credit is that to you? Even sinners lend to sinners, to receive as much again. But love your enemies, and do good, and lend, expecting nothing in return; and your reward will be great, and you will be sons of the Most High; for he is kind to the ungrateful and the selfish. Be merciful, even as your Father is merciful.

—Luke 6:27–36

IN GOD'S PRESENCE, CONSIDER . . .

It is a radical call—it was then and it is now: to love my enemy, do good even to those who hate me, lend while expecting nothing in return. But what is also radical is that God is kind and merciful "to the ungrateful and the selfish." That's me.

CLOSING PRAYER

Heavenly Father, You are a Father of love and goodness and radical mercy. Help me to trust that I can give to others, and You will give me my daily bread, providing me with all that I need. I can empty myself in mercy and will never lack love. Open my heart to the generosity of Your Son.

The Way Mercy Loves

Compared to the way we tend to love, "God loves backwards." We don't have to "do" anything to earn His love; we don't have to perform, look a certain way, accomplish specific goals, or reach a particular standard; He loves us. Full stop. That's mercy.

A wise soul once told me there are two ways you can choose to love. You can look for everything that is wrong with a person, judge behavior, and give love on that basis. Or, you can see and rejoice in all the good, and simply love without putting "shoulds" or expectations on the other. The first way is conditional and restrictive and does not allow the beloved to be herself, because she is always censored and almost forced to be someone she is not in order to be loved. But the second way accepts the beloved *as she is*, does not treat her as a problem to be solved, and thus frees her to be her truest and best self. In return, with a grateful heart, she then longs to return this unconditional love in any way she can.

This second way, *this* is how God loves us. And in the face of how painful human relationships can be, it is incredibly consoling. People will always love us imperfectly, betray us, abandon us, abuse us, neglect us, let us down in a million different ways—but God never will. His love, and His love alone, is perfect, steadfast, and endures *forever*.

This is how we are called to love others. But until we really allow the truth of how God loves us to fully enter into the core of our being, until we accept that we are loved in this way, we will not be able to embrace those around us with that same love. The old adage, "You cannot give what you do not possess" rings true here. We must each personally claim God's powerful love for us with faith and confidence, taking possession of it, so that in knowing how beloved we are, we will be enabled to love others as He has loved us.

—Mary Flynn, *A Study Guide for 7 Secrets of Divine Mercy*

IN GOD'S PRESENCE, CONSIDER . . .

We, of course, are the ones who really love "backwards." God has it right; we have it all wrong. Can I resolve today to make an act of faith in His love, to "claim" His love for me, live in it, and let it empower me to pass it forward to others?

CLOSING PRAYER

Lord, thank you that Your mercy is not contingent upon on any merit of mine, any behavior or performance, but is always pouring out for me, always available. Help me to receive it, Lord, to let myself believe, deep within, that You love me no matter what—and then let Your love free me to love as You love.

Son of David, Have Mercy on Me!

Why do the Gospels record so many accounts of the blind receiving their sight? Nothing opens our lives more fully to Jesus's mercy than His light shining into our darkness: we must fix our eyes on His radiant light.

As he drew near to Jericho, a blind man was sitting by the roadside begging; and hearing a multitude going by, he inquired what this meant. They told him, "Jesus of Nazareth is passing by." And he cried, "Jesus, Son of David, have mercy on me!" And those who were in front rebuked him, telling him to be silent; but he cried out all the more, "Son of David, have mercy on me!" And Jesus stopped, and commanded him to be brought to him; and when he came near, he asked him, "What do you want me to do for you?" He said, "Lord, let me receive my sight." And Jesus said to him, "Receive your sight; your faith has made you well." And immediately he received his sight and followed him, glorifying God; and all the people, when they saw it, gave praise to God.

—Luke 18:35–43

IN GOD'S PRESENCE, CONSIDER . . .

I imagine myself on the dusty roadside, an onlooker in the crowd. I watch this scene take place and notice what Jesus is like with the blind man, His eyes, His voice. I see how the man is transformed after he is healed and watch him glorifying God. And as the crowd is in awe and exclaiming to one another over the miracle, Jesus turns to me and I meet His gaze. The surrounding noise fades into the background and I hear Him say my name. Then He asks, "What do you want me to do for you?" And I tell Him.

CLOSING PRAYER

Lord Jesus Christ, Son of the Living God, You break into my darkness and cast out the lies that keep me from Your love. Help me to remain in the tender mercy of Your gaze and reveal the deepest places of my heart to You without fear.

Restoration

One of the earliest prophets, Amos speaks to us through the millennia, confirming that the eternal God has promised mercy and far surpasses our anticipation.

"In that day I will raise up
the booth of David that is fallen
and repair its breaches,
and raise up its ruins,
and rebuild it as in the days of old;
that they may possess the remnant of Edom
and all the nations who are called by my name,"
says the Lord who does this.
"Behold, the days are coming," says the Lord,
"when the plowman shall overtake the reaper
and the treader of grapes him who sows the seed;
the mountains shall drip sweet wine,
and all the hills shall flow with it.
I will restore the fortunes of my people Israel,
and they shall rebuild the ruined cities and inhabit them;
they shall plant vineyards and drink their wine,
and they shall make gardens and eat their fruit.
I will plant them upon their land,
and they shall never again be plucked up
out of the land which I have given them,"
says the Lord your God.

—Amos 9:11–15

IN GOD'S PRESENCE, CONSIDER . . .

How have I allowed my hopes to collapse in the headwinds of failure? Am I ready to relinquish my parameters for what the Living God is capable of and, looking into the face of my Father, recognize that He has a plan of abundant goodness for me rooted in His love?

CLOSING PRAYER

Lord God, God of Israel, God of David, You have been faithful, and You will be faithful to me. Rebuild the ruins of my life into something glorious; plant Your vineyard in the fertile soil of my trust and open wide my heart to Your abundance.

Praying the Chaplet for the Dying

Following St. Faustina's example and the request of Christ, the Chaplet of Divine Mercy has become widely used as a prayer for the dying; and in the year 2000 St. Pope John Paul II imparted an apostolic blessing for those who, during Eucharistic Adoration, would pray the Chaplet for the sick and dying.

My daughter, encourage souls to say the chaplet which I have given to you (1541). Whoever will recite it will receive great mercy at the hour of death (687) . . . When they say this chaplet in the presence of the dying, I will stand between My Father and the dying person, not as the just Judge but as the merciful Savior (1541). . . .

When I entered the chapel for a moment, the Lord said to me, My daughter, help Me to save a certain dying sinner. Say the chaplet that I have taught you for him. When I began to say the chaplet, I saw the man dying in the midst of terrible torment and struggle. His Guardian Angel was defending him, but he was, as it were, powerless against the enormity of the soul's misery. A multitude of devils was waiting for the soul. But while I was saying the chaplet, I saw Jesus just as He is depicted in the image. The rays which issued from Jesus' Heart enveloped the sick man, and the powers of darkness fled in panic. The sick man peacefully breathed his last. When I came to myself, I understood how very important the chaplet was for the dying (1565). . . .

Today, the Lord came to me and said, My daughter, help Me to save souls. You will go to a dying sinner, and you will continue to recite the chaplet, and in this way you will obtain for him trust in My mercy, for he is already in despair (1797).

Suddenly, I found myself in a strange cottage where an elderly man was dying amidst great torments. All about the bed was a multitude of demons and the family, who were crying. When I began to pray, the spirits of darkness fled, with hissing and threats directed at me. The soul became calm and, filled with trust, rested in the Lord. At the same moment, I found myself again in my own room. How this happens . . . I do not know (1798).

—St. Faustina, *Diary*

IN GOD'S PRESENCE, CONSIDER . . .

Is there someone I know who is sick or dying, or can I simply offer a Chaplet to the Lord for whoever needs it most as death approaches?

CLOSING PRAYER

Lord Jesus, give me the grace to help You save souls by praying the Chaplet regularly as a ministry of mercy for those who are sick or dying.

From St. Proclus to St. Faustina

"Holy God, Holy Mighty One, Holy Immortal One, have mercy on us." This ancient prayer, known as the Trisagion, dates back to the earliest days of the Church, if not to even earlier Jewish roots. We can thank Saint Proclus for bringing it into the Byzantine liturgy.

Finally, Proclus was elected bishop of Constantinople in 434 and remained in the see until 446. He was considered an exemplary prelate. It was said of him that few could equal him in holiness. He was good to all because he was convinced that goodness was of better use than severity in the service of truth. He courageously defended the truth against Nestorianism and other heresies of the time, such as that of Theodore of Mopsuestia, to which he replied in his remarkable work, "Tome to the Armenians." In it, he sets forth the true doctrine about the Incarnation, exhorting the Armenians to follow the doctrine of St. Basil and St. Gregory Nazianzen, whose works were highly esteemed among them. One of his most celebrated homilies was an exemplary tribute to the Virgin Mary and her Divine Maternity. Some of his letters and sermons have also been preserved.

During his episcopate, there was a violent earthquake in Constantinople. Terrified, men wandered through the ruins. Accompanied by his clergy, Proclus went out and helped his parishioners, comforted his people, and exhorted them to implore Divine Mercy. In his Menologion, Basil relates how as the people implored Divine Mercy praying the Kyrie Eleison, a boy was snatched up into the air until he was no longer seen. When he returned to earth, the boy declared that he had heard angelic choirs singing, "Holy God, Holy Mighty, Holy Immortal." The people repeated the words adding, "Have mercy on us." Then, the earthquakes ceased. From that moment, St. Proclus introduced the Trisagion Prayer into the liturgy.

—On St. Proclus

IN GOD'S PRESENCE, CONSIDER . . .

I may not remember the Cherubim, Seraphim, Thrones and Dominions assembled before the Lord, but I came from the glory and splendor of God. Do I permit the light of heaven to illuminate my path, keeping in my awareness the spiritual realm all around me?

CLOSING PRAYER

Holy God, Holy Mighty One, Holy Immortal One, have mercy on us, and on the whole world.

Mordecai's Prayer

We cannot enter into mercy unless we cry out for it wholeheartedly. With so many of his miracles, Jesus asks the supplicant, "Do you believe I can do this?" He calls forth petition from our hearts.

Then Mordecai prayed to the Lord, calling to remembrance all the works of the Lord. He said: "O Lord, Lord, King who rulest over all things, for the universe is in thy power and there is no one who can oppose thee if it is thy will to save Israel. For thou hast made heaven and earth and every wonderful thing under heaven, and thou art Lord of all, and there is no one who can resist thee, who art the Lord. Thou knowest all things; thou knowest, O Lord, that it was not in insolence or pride or for any love of glory that I did this, and refused to bow down to this proud Haman. For I would have been willing to kiss the soles of his feet, to save Israel! But I did this, that I might not set the glory of man above the glory of God, and I will not bow down to any one but to thee, who art my Lord; and I will not do these things in pride. And now, O Lord God and King, God of Abraham, spare thy people; for the eyes of our foes are upon us to annihilate us, and they desire to destroy the inheritance that has been thine from the beginning. Do not neglect thy portion, which thou didst redeem for thyself out of the land of Egypt. Hear my prayer, and have mercy upon thy inheritance; turn our mourning into feasting, that we may live and sing praise to thy name, O Lord; do not destroy the mouth of those who praise thee." And all Israel cried out mightily, for their death was before their eyes.

—Esther 13:8–18

IN GOD'S PRESENCE, CONSIDER . . .

Am I willing to reveal to God my true desperation, the pain I feel, the fear I experience? Like Mordecai, am I ready to admit I'm drained and empty, and violently in need of God's rescue? When I turn my eyes to God's glory, I discover that my emptiness is filled.

CLOSING PRAYER

Lord, King You rule over all and have guided Your children from creation to the present. Allow me to see that today is not the day You fail or fall short, but You again renew your mercies in my life and for my loved ones.

Jesus, Have Mercy On Us

The feared disease of leprosy caused the body to decay around the living soul of the afflicted person, cast out from society and synagogue. The mercy of God perceives our deepest shame and guilt, and brings miraculous healing.

On the way to Jerusalem he was passing along between Samaria and Galilee. And as he entered a village, he was met by ten lepers, who stood at a distance and lifted up their voices and said, "Jesus, Master, have mercy on us." When he saw them he said to them, "Go and show yourselves to the priests." And as they went they were cleansed. Then one of them, when he saw that he was healed, turned back, praising God with a loud voice; and he fell on his face at Jesus' feet, giving him thanks. Now he was a Samaritan. Then said Jesus, "Were not ten cleansed? Where are the nine? Was no one found to return and give praise to God except this foreigner?" And he said to him, "Rise and go your way; your faith has made you well."

—Luke 17:11–19

IN GOD'S PRESENCE, CONSIDER . . .

The Savior who does not break the bruised reed nor quench the smoldering wick (Is. 42:3) comes to me with that gentle power He has towards things that are fragile. He sees my troubled heart and stirs into flame the trust that will draw me into His Divine Mercy and healing.

CLOSING PRAYER

Lord Jesus Christ, Son of the Living God, have mercy on me. Help me to trust that You have true inner healing and transformation for me as miraculous as this healing of the lepers. And may I never miss an opportunity to see Your goodness and give You thanks.

And Their Eyes Were Opened

What is more powerful than calling out, "Have mercy on me," as these two role models do today? Here Jesus reveals what unlocks his limitless mercy: trust in Him through faith.

And as Jesus passed on from there, two blind men followed him, crying aloud, "Have mercy on us, Son of David." When he entered the house, the blind men came to him; and Jesus said to them, "Do you believe that I am able to do this?" They said to him, "Yes, Lord." Then he touched their eyes, saying, "According to your faith be it done to you." And their eyes were opened.

—Matthew 9:27–30

IN GOD'S PRESENCE, CONSIDER . . .

Am I hesitant to cry out to God in need and, if so, where does my hesitation spring from? I want to have faith strong enough to really trust in Him. I take a moment to make an honest internal assessment and consider what it is I most deeply long to ask Him. Where do I need His mercy to meet my misery, my poverty, my emptiness?

CLOSING PRAYER

Yes, Lord. I need Your love. I need You near me. Heavenly Father, draw forth from my deepest depths my greatest longing. Help me to trust that I can bring it to You, knowing that You will receive it with care. And no matter what I long for, help me to truly believe that the most fundamental and supreme gift would be for You to reveal the light of Divine Mercy to me, Jesus Himself, who is the Fulfillment of All Desire.

The Greatness of His Love

God doesn't just love, says Elizabeth of the Trinity—He loves "to excess."

For Elizabeth [of the Trinity], God was not some lonely celibate dwelling in outer space, an absentee landlord remote from his own creation. Her understanding of God was simple and direct: *God is love* (1 Jn 4:8.16). She quoted these words several times in her writings, sometimes placing them as a motto at the beginning of her letters.

Love, by definition, is relational; it is of the very nature of love to give and to share. This is how God has revealed himself in the Scriptures, especially in the luminous pages of the gospels: a God who *so loved the world that he gave his only Son . . . that we might have eternal life* (Jn 3:16). This is the only God Elizabeth knew: a passionate God, full of life, energy and love, personally and intimately involved in every aspect of our life and destiny.

Elizabeth was strongly drawn to Paul's words describing God as not just loving, but loving to excess (cf. Eph 2:4): *there is a phrase from Saint Paul that is like a summary of my life,* Elizabeth told her mother, *and could be written on every one of its moments: 'Because of His exceeding great love'* (cf. L 280). Elizabeth is a witness to the reality of this love; love is our true nature, it alone reveals who we are. We are called to live with God as with a friend, in the fellowship of love—a love that both gives and receives.

—Eugene McCaffrey OCD, *Let Yourself Be Loved*

IN GOD'S PRESENCE, CONSIDER . . .

Do I see God's excessive love through all the moments of my life—even the hard ones? Is my life with Him relational and reciprocal, a back and forth interchange of love?

CLOSING PRAYER

God of exceeding great love, sometimes I limit You, or don't see that You are "a passionate God, full of life, energy and love, personally and intimately involved" in every aspect of my life. When I am tempted to sideline You or doubt Your closeness, remind me that You are this dynamic Being who desires deep friendship with me.

All Occasions Invite His Mercies . . .

John Donne, the famous poet, scholar, and Anglican clergyman, invites us to ponder the goodness of God and His mercy, which is limitless in each present moment.

If I should declare what God hath done (done occasionally,) for my soul, where He instructed me for fear of falling, where He raised me when I was fallen, perchance you would rather fix your thoughts upon my illness, and wonder at that, than at God's goodness, and glorify Him in that; rather wonder at my sins than at His mercies, rather consider how ill a man I was, than how good a God He is. If I should enquire upon what occasion God elected me, and writ my name in the book of life, I should sooner be afraid that it were not so, than find a reason why it should be so. God made sun and moon to distinguish seasons, and day and night, and we cannot have the fruits of the earth but in their seasons; but God hath made no decree to distinguish the seasons of His mercies; in Paradise, the fruits were ripe the first minute, and in Heaven it is always autumn, His mercies are ever in their maturity. We ask our daily bread, and God never says you should have come yesterday. He never says you must again to-morrow, but to-day if ye will hear His voice, to-day He will hear you. If some king of the earth have so large an extent of dominion in north and south, as that he hath winter and summer together in his dominions, so large an extent east and west as that he hath day and night together in his dominions, much more hath God mercy and judgment together; He brought light out of darkness, not out of a lesser light; He can bring thy summer out of winter, though thou have no spring; though in the ways of fortune, or understanding, or conscience, thou have been benighted till now, wintred and frozen, clouded and eclipsed, damped and benumbed, smothered and stupified till now, now God comes to thee, not as in the dawning of the day, not as in the bud of the spring, but as the sun at noon, to illustrate all shadows, as the sheaves in harvest, to fill all penuries, all occasions invite His mercies, and all times are His seasons.

—John Donne, "Occasional Mercies"

IN GOD'S PRESENCE, CONSIDER . . .

How often do I focus on my own, or other's sins and failings more than on the goodness and mercy of God? Do I believe that His mercy can do all things in me—in the dark, cold, hard places within?

CLOSING PRAYER

Father, how good You are that You never say to me, "You should have come yesterday," or "Come instead tomorrow." Let me live my life in praise of Your mercy, and let it effect in me a continual restoration.

The Image of Consolation

Fr. Jason Lewis explains that simply contemplating the image of Jesus, The Divine Mercy, can bring great grace and consolation, especially in times of suffering and grief.

The visual image of Jesus, the Divine Mercy, can bring us tremendous grace and consolation without much effort on our part.

If you look at the Image of Divine Mercy, you will see that Jesus is emerging from thick darkness as a new light of hope in your life. Notice His left foot; Jesus is taking the first gentle step toward you, meeting you wherever you are in pain, suffering, and even despair. His step is not an aggressive one. He comes clothed as a gentle High Priest, with His right hand lifted to impart blessings to you. His eyes are full of compassion, looking at you with love; as He tells St. Faustina: "My gaze from this image is like My gaze from the cross" (*Diary*, 326).

As a tender, loving friend, He understands your heartache. . . . He is both priest and victim, able to sympathize with your every weakness because He has made Himself just like you in every way except sin (see Heb 4:14–16).

Jesus desires to hear every murmur of your very own heart in sorrow. He offers you an exchange of hearts as He pulls back the veil of His own Heart, revealing its infinite depths, saying, "Look into My Heart and see there the love and mercy which I have for humankind . . . look, and enter into My Passion" (*Diary*, 1663). In the Heart of Jesus, you will find every grace to help you in your time of need. . . .

> I am offering people a vessel with which they are to keep coming for graces to the fountain of mercy. That vessel is this image with the signature, "Jesus, I trust in You!" (*Diary*, 327).

—Jason Lewis, MIC, *After Suicide*

IN GOD'S PRESENCE, CONSIDER . . .

Where do I need the "new light of hope"? I give myself space in this moment to feel the sorrow and pain of my life and to experience Jesus's gaze of compassion and love as I share it all with Him.

CLOSING PRAYER

Jesus, thank You for loving me in my mess, for being so faithful to me no matter what. I know that You don't always fix things here on earth, that suffering is sometimes our path in this broken world. But You can turn all things to good, and there will come a time when there will be no more tears. You bear witness to my pain with kindness and compassion, and Your Presence begins to heal any isolation, loneliness, or abandonment attached to my sorrow. I rest now in Your gaze of mercy.

A Mother's Love

The Canaanite mother sees the profound harm her daughter is experiencing (here translated "severely possessed," the original Greek expresses great harm, cruel damage) and she persistently pleads for mercy. Your spiritual mother Mary sees the pain in your soul, and she also will not relent, but kneels before her Son, calling upon His mercy and insisting that He heal you.

And Jesus went away from there and withdrew to the district of Tyre and Sidon. And behold, a Canaanite woman from that region came out and cried, "Have mercy on me, O Lord, Son of David; my daughter is severely possessed by a demon." But he did not answer her a word. And his disciples came and begged him, saying, "Send her away, for she is crying after us." He answered, "I was sent only to the lost sheep of the house of Israel." But she came and knelt before him, saying, "Lord, help me." And he answered, "It is not fair to take the children's bread and throw it to the dogs." She said, "Yes, Lord, yet even the dogs eat the crumbs that fall from their master's table." Then Jesus answered her, "O woman, great is your faith! Be it done for you as you desire." And her daughter was healed instantly.

—Matthew 15:21–28

IN GOD'S PRESENCE, CONSIDER . . .

The Lord knows me better than I know myself. He knows what any given situation will bring about in me, strengthen in me, draw out of me. Do I trust in His goodness enough to persist in my petitions and in faith? And is my heart softened by seeing my mother's care for me? Can I allow her to bring me to the Father of mercies?

CLOSING PRAYER

Lord, sometimes You ask me to persist in faith and it feels like You are far off or uncaring. Thank You for sharing Your mother with me, for giving me a gentle and compassionate intercessor and comforter. Mother Mary, pray for the daily bread I need today and for the petitions of my heart.

Habitual Sin and God's Untiring Mercy

From his seminal book on holiness, Dietrich Von Hildebrand encourages those struggling with habitual sin, stressing that we all must have a firm "conviction of God's infinite mercy."

Habitual sin sorely tests our confidence in God - "Our trust in God is exposed to a particularly hard test if we have to wrestle with a habitual sin. When we again and again relapse into the same fault, when all our moral effort seems ineffective and all our religious zeal fruitless, we shall almost inevitably feel tempted to lose patience, to get discouraged and give up the struggle, or . . . to despair of God's help and believe ourselves abandoned by Him.

Yet we must believe in God's inexhaustible love and mercy. . . . We must stick unswervingly to the belief that God loves us with an infinite love and wills our sanctification, whatever our spiritual status may appear to our eyes. He who truly confides in God does not presume to decide himself, by experience, whether God is intent on saving him or has withdrawn from him. Once he has absorbed the message of the Gospels, his conviction of God's infinite mercy, of God's inexhaustible love . . . is so firm and unconditional as to preclude its dependence on any confirmation drawn from experience.

Nothing *can* come from God that is not a manifestation of His love. . . . Much as his ever-recurrent backslidings may depress him, he will seek their cause in himself alone, in his own weakness and lack of zeal; and at the same time thank God for the humiliation to which he owes a clear consciousness of his weakness. . . . Even in these disappointments, he will humbly look for the traces of God's love, and abide by the words of St. Paul: "For I know in whom I have believed" (2 Tim 1:12). Aware of the untiring mercy of God, full of confidence he will again and again begin anew.[3]

—Dietrich Von Hildebrand, *Transformation in Christ*

IN GOD'S PRESENCE, CONSIDER . . .

"Nothing can come from God that is not a manifestation of His love." I want to remember this and look for the traces of His love when I feel discouraged or abandoned.

CLOSING PRAYER

God of untiring mercy, I leave all judgment of my zeal, holiness, and the fruit of my efforts to You. I will focus on beginning anew again and again. Help me to never give up the struggle, but to trust fully in Your goodness and love.

Healing the Wounds of Sin

Do you go to confession just for forgiveness? If so, you're missing the most amazing things that are meant to happen!

There is no more profound encounter with God's mercy than in the Sacrament of Reconciliation. Let's consider the two amazing things that happen in Confession. First, we are freed. God wants to fee us of our sins and all the uneasiness, guilt, or shame we might experience over what we have done. When we are truly sorry for our sins, God sees our contrite hearts. He is not sitting back angry, pointing his finger, and condemning us for our sins. Rather, he's like the father racing out to meet his prodigal son. Love makes him want to remove whatever obstacles keep him from being reunited with his son. That's the God we meet in Confession. . . .

But that's not all. There's a second amazing thing Jesus wants to do in our souls through Confession. Jesus doesn't just want to forgive us. He wants to heal us. . . . He wants to get to the roots of our sins and cure us of our spiritual illnesses and wounds. He wants us to experience real change. In the Sacrament of Reconciliation, God gives us graces to avoid those sins in the future.

This is amazing! This is one of the main reasons to go to Confession regularly. If we want to grow as disciples—if we want to access Christ's power to heal our weaknesses, overcome bad habits, and avoid falling into the same sins in the future—we should go to Confession as much as possible. . . .

But our sins are not merely a stain on our soul that needs to be wiped away. Our sins leave us with a deep wound. They forge bad habits. They form patterns of living that make it difficult for us to love God fully. Jesus wants to get to the roots of our sins and heal those deeper wounds.

—Edward Sri, *Into His Likeness*

IN GOD'S PRESENCE, CONSIDER . . .

How do I prepare for confession? Do I pray about the root of my sins or do I just want to get the grace and forgiveness, and get back to life? And do I believe that Christ wants to heal my woundedness and empower me to change my habits and overcome patterns of sin?

CLOSING PRAYER

Father, I desire to come to You, to encounter You, and to find freedom and the grace necessary to change my life. Holy Spirit, reveal to me the roots of my sin. Jesus, grant me true conviction in Your power to heal.

Always Trusting

St. Padre Pio, with practical wisdom, shows us how to distinguish between certain reproaches and remorse we might feel and whether they come from God or the enemy.

Peace is simplicity of spirit, serenity of mind, tranquility of soul, the bond of love. Peace is order, it is harmony in each one of us. It is the continual rejoicing that is born from the testimony of a good conscience. It is the holy joyfulness of the heart in which God reigns. Peace is the way of perfection; or rather, in peace one finds perfection. And the devil, who knows all this very well, makes every effort to make us lose our peace (607). The soul need be saddened by only one thing: an offense against God. But even on this point, one must be very prudent. One must certainly regret one's failures, but with a peaceful sorrow and always trusting in Divine Mercy. One must beware of certain reproaches and remorse against oneself which most of the time come from our enemy who wants to disturb our peace in God. If such reproaches and remorse humble us and make us quick to do the right thing, without taking away our confidence in God, we may be assured that they come from God. However, if they confuse us and make us fearful, distrustful, lazy or slow to do the right thing, we may be sure that they come from the devil and we should consequently push them aside, finding our refuge in confidence in God.

—St. Padre Pio, Letter to Fr. Agostino, July 10, 1915

IN GOD'S PRESENCE, CONSIDER . . .

The devil makes every effort to make me lose my peace. Therefore, if I am disturbed, confused, discouraged, or falling into self-condemnation, I will remember that "in peace one finds perfection." And I will turn with total confidence to The Divine Mercy.

CLOSING PRAYER

Jesus, You are my peace. There is nothing I need to be sad about except offending You. And even if I fail, my sorrow, my remorse, must have an element of peace—knowing that all You desire is that I come back to You with trust in Your mercy. God, You are so good that even when I sin, Your will is that I turn to You like a child, with total abandonment to Your mercy and goodness. Let confidence in You be my refuge.

Sacraments and Peace

We've been looking for peace in all the wrong places. Blessed Sopocko wrote much on the peace God intends for us, and how it is especially connected to the Sacraments of mercy.

What is peace? Peace is tranquility of order which, according to St. Augustine, depends upon the order with oneself, with our neighbor, and with God. . . . Sin upset that order. It destroyed internal harmony within us so much so that in our present condition our intellect and will are beclouded and bound and dragged by our passions . . .

It is in that manner that every worldly man seeks peace and happiness. . . . However, instead of peace, they find disputes, family quarrels, competition and war of social classes and states. Why? Because they refuse to acknowledge God as their Father, and, consequently, they cannot see themselves as brothers. . . . True peace is given by Him alone who removes the cause of unrest which is sin. The Most Merciful Savior by His death on the Cross created an inexhaustible treasury of His merits. After His Resurrection He set up the Sacraments through which the Church applies those merits to individual souls. First of all, by the Sacrament of Baptism original sin is removed, and in the Sacrament of Penance . . . sins committed after Baptism are forgiven. Through these Sacraments the Divine Mercy pours down true peace unceasingly . . .

He who does not avail himself of those Sacraments finds his life a torture. . . . On the contrary, he who properly uses those Sacraments of God's Mercy has internal peace and happiness; . . . True peace, therefore, flows . . . from God's Mercy in the Sacraments of Baptism and Penance. This is the reason why Christ after His Resurrection greeted the Apostles with the words, "Peace be to you," and repeated His greeting twice while instituting the Sacrament of Penance.

—Fr. Sopocko, *Marian Helpers Bulletin*

IN GOD'S PRESENCE, CONSIDER . . .

Am I ready for unceasing peace? Am I ready to abandon the fruitless torture that my distance from God inflicts on me? Can I listen to my heart and my longing for peace, and give in to the tidal wave of mercy my Father draws over me?

CLOSING PRAYER

Father of Mercy, Father of Love, You are so good and so wise. You see the distress I find myself in, and do not hesitate to do whatever it takes to bring me back to You. Open my heart to Your peace and allow me to abide in Your Divine Mercy.

Heaven Revealed

Jesus is born of the Virgin to introduce something utterly new into this world. In place of the ancient curse, God introduces blessing into our lives. This Word of Blessing is fundamentally entering into the life of the Holy Trinity, the Kingdom of Heaven already revealed in our midst.

Seeing the crowds, he went up on the mountain, and when he sat down his disciples came to him. And he opened his mouth and taught them, saying:
"Blessed are the poor in spirit, for theirs is the kingdom of heaven.
"Blessed are those who mourn, for they shall be comforted.
"Blessed are the meek, for they shall inherit the earth.
"Blessed are those who hunger and thirst for righteousness, for they shall be satisfied.
"Blessed are the merciful, for they shall obtain mercy.
"Blessed are the pure in heart, for they shall see God.
"Blessed are the peacemakers, for they shall be called sons of God.
"Blessed are those who are persecuted for righteousness' sake, for theirs is the kingdom of heaven.
"Blessed are you when men revile you and persecute you and utter all kinds of evil against you falsely on my account. Rejoice and be glad, for your reward is great in heaven, for so men persecuted the prophets who were before you.

—Matthew 5:1–12

IN GOD'S PRESENCE, CONSIDER . . .

As Jesus blesses my hunger and poverty, can I also accept my emptiness, which can only be flooded by Him? Am I ready to reject the world's petty trinkets and baubles, which attempt to mask the deep void within me? Today can I receive the words of my maker, who knows the longings of my heart? I want to become who He's calling me to be.

CLOSING PRAYER

Lord, I have been so poor, so hungry, so thirsty, and nothing I have searched for reaches the ache within me. Reveal to me Your love, your Kingdom, Your mercy, which floods into my heart and stuns me with the experience of fulfillment.

And They Glorified the God of Israel

Healing, driving out demons, and proclaiming the arrival of God's Kingdom: these three distinctive acts confirmed the coming of the Messiah. Here Jesus's healing is followed by nourishment in His mercy.

And Jesus went on from there and passed along the Sea of Galilee. And he went up into the hills, and sat down there. And great crowds came to him, bringing with them the lame, the maimed, the blind, the dumb, and many others, and they put them at his feet, and he healed them, so that the throng wondered, when they saw the dumb speaking, the maimed whole, the lame walking, and the blind seeing; and they glorified the God of Israel.

Then Jesus called his disciples to him and said, "I have compassion on the crowd, because they have been with me now three days, and have nothing to eat; and I am unwilling to send them away hungry, lest they faint on the way." And the disciples said to him, "Where are we to get bread enough in the desert to feed so great a crowd?" And Jesus said to them, "How many loaves have you?" They said, "Seven, and a few small fish." And commanding the crowd to sit down on the ground, he took the seven loaves and the fish, and having given thanks he broke them and gave them to the disciples, and the disciples gave them to the crowds. And they all ate and were satisfied; and they took up seven baskets full of the broken pieces left over. Those who ate were four thousand men, besides women and children.

—Matthew 15:29–38

IN GOD'S PRESENCE, CONSIDER . . .

What healing do I need? What woundedness shows up in my relationships; what hunger is present in my life that I try to fill in various ways? Do I forge ahead on my own strength and effort, or have I brought my hunger and my need for healing to Jesus, opening myself to the outpouring of His mercy?

CLOSING PRAYER

Lord Jesus Christ, Son of the Father, You fulfill the words of promise which foretell Your radiant redemption of the human race. And on the journey, You not only provide enough, but in abundance. Draw my heart to trust fully in You.

The Presence of Mercy

In one of the early books written on the Divine Mercy message, Fr. Kosicki relates how integral the Eucharist is to Divine Mercy.

The Holy Eucharist is central to devotion to The Divine Mercy, so much so that Our Lord specifically asks, through St. Faustina, that we all receive Communion on the Feast of The Divine Mercy, after preparing for it through the Sacrament of Reconciliation. In the Eucharist, Jesus (Mercy Incarnate) is present Body and Blood, Soul and Divinity. The Eucharist is God's sacrificial gift of mercy, offered in atonement for our sins and those of the whole world; and in receiving it in Holy Communion, we are strengthened and consoled by the Lord who is Mercy itself.

In his last encyclical, Pope John Paul II called the Eucharist "a mystery of mercy" (see *Ecclesia de Eucharistia*. 2).

Through her life and writings, St. Faustina gives us a perfect model for responding to this mystery; the Eucharist was so central to her life that she referred to it in some way on most of the pages of her diary. . . . During Exposition of the Blessed Sacrament and during Mass itself, St. Faustina regularly saw our Lord. Most often she saw Him as a child; but at times, He appeared with rays of light as in the Image of The Divine Mercy; and at other times, she saw Him in His Passion and was able to participate in it with Him, sharing His pain:

"Today, from early morning, divine absorption penetrates my soul. During Mass, I thought I would see the little Jesus, as I often do; however, today during Holy Mass I saw the Crucified Jesus. Jesus was nailed to the cross and was in great agony. His suffering pierced me, soul and body, in a manner which was invisible, but nevertheless most painful" (*Diary*, 913, February 2, 1937).

—Fr. George Kosicki, *Now is the Time for Mercy*

IN GOD'S PRESENCE, CONSIDER . . .

How central is the Eucharist in my life? Whether I receive occasionally or daily, how can I enter more and more deeply into this "mystery of mercy."?

CLOSING PRAYER

Thank You, Jesus, for the immense gift of the Eucharist. May this "mystery of mercy" penetrate my soul, so that I will ceaselessly adore You, offer myself to You, and live in union with You, Mercy Incarnate.

Thanksgiving for Your Mercies

A prayer after Communion from an old and widely used Catholic prayer book extols the mercy of God.

Who am I, O God of infinite goodness, that You permit me to partake of this bread of angels? How am I the object of such unspeakable mercy?

Come, all you angels and saints of God, and I will recount to you what great things our Lord has done for my soul. He has raised me out of the dust, and delivered me from the bonds of sin; He has told me not to be dejected, because He Himself will be my support and my strength; and though I have forsaken Him by my repeated falls, yet behold He calls me once more, and invites me to receive the bread of life, that, as He made me, so I may ever live by Him.

What thanks can I give You, O merciful Jesus, Savior of the world? What return shall I make to You for all You have done for my soul? Were I to give all I have in acknowledgment of Your love, it would still be as nothing; for You, Lord, have poured forth Yourself upon me, and given me even all that You are. And if, in thanksgiving for Your mercies, I were to lay before You my body and soul, my life, liberty, and all I possess, what would they be, when compared to the blessings You have here bestowed on me?

What can I give You that could be equal to what I receive, O Infinite One? You have mercifully given Yourself to me for the food of my soul; and now behold I simply offer You all that I have, all that I am, all that I possess. To You I make a full surrender of them all, that, being wholly Yours, I may now no longer cling to my own will, but may live for You alone.

—*Key of Heaven* (Prayerbook)

IN GOD'S PRESENCE, CONSIDER . . .

I will spend the day remembering—calling to mind all of the ways God in His mercy has done great things for me. There is nothing I can ever do to make a return to the Lord for His goodness to me. I will offer Him "all that I have, all that I am," knowing that, unfathomably, this is all He desires.

CLOSING PRAYER

Lord, "I simply offer You all that I have, all that I am, all that I possess. To You I make a full surrender of them all, that, being wholly Yours, I may now no longer cling to my own will, but may live for You alone."

Faustina's Secret to Sanctity

The Eucharist is far more than just a ritual we observe at Mass. Its purpose is to sanctify us, to make us holy by enabling us to share in Christ's holiness. Faustina tells us that it's the "whole secret" of her sanctity.

O my merciful Lord, there are secrets in my heart which no one knows or will ever know except You because, even if I wanted to reveal them, no one would understand me. Your minister knows some because I confess to him, but he knows only the bit of these mysteries that I am capable of revealing; the rest remains between us for eternity, O My Lord! You have covered me with the cloak of Your mercy, pardoning my sins. Not once did You refuse Your pardon; You always had pity on me, giving me a new life of grace. To prevent doubts, You have entrusted me to the loving care of Your Church, that tender mother, who in Your name assures me of the truths of faith and watches lest I wander. Especially in the tribunal of Your mercy does my soul meet an ocean of favors. . . . O my Lord, you have provided saintly priests to show me the sure way. Jesus, there is one more secret in my life, the deepest and dearest to my heart: it is You yourself when You come to my heart under the appearance of bread. Herein lies the whole secret of my sanctity. Here my heart is so united with Yours as to be but one. There are no more secrets, because all that is Yours is mine, and all that is mine is Yours. Such is the omnipotence and the miracle of Your mercy. All the tongues of men and of angels united could not find words adequate to this mystery of Your love and mercy.

—St. Faustina, *Diary*, 1747

IN GOD'S PRESENCE, CONSIDER . . .

How often do I reflect on the mystery of the Eucharist as the "miracle" of Christ's mercy as He pours Himself into my heart to sanctify me?

CLOSING PRAYER

Lord Jesus, forgive me for anytime I have received You mindlessly. Help me to always seek to unite myself with You as I receive, and allow your presence within me to make me holy as You are holy.

Mercy-Made-Flesh

The Eucharist and the Divine Mercy Image are intrinsically connected, and neither is only about Jesus. Whenever we come before Jesus in Eucharistic Adoration or gaze on the Divine Mercy Image, we are drawn to the Father, from whom everything comes and to whom everything must return.

Lord Jesus, You are Mercy-Made-Flesh,
the visible "image of the invisible God" (Col 1:15).
You are the Father's love made present for us.
As I gaze upon You, I see the Father, "rich in mercy,"
raising His hand over me in blessing,
and pouring into me,
through Your pierced Heart,
the very life of the Trinity.
Immersing myself
in the living stream of blood and water
that flows endlessly from Your Heart
as a fountain of mercy for us,
I receive the Father's blessing
and recognize who I am as a child of His love.
In You, Lord Jesus, I see the reflection
of my own unique value and dignity
as a son (daughter) of the Father,
created in His image and likeness
and called to be holy as He is holy.
In You and with You,
I will forever call God my Father
and forever rejoice in the awesome reality
that He loves me even as He loves you (Jn 17:23).

—Vinny Flynn, *Mass & Adoration Companion*

IN GOD'S PRESENCE, CONSIDER . . .

What a gift this Image is! It can open up in me a whole new awareness of the Eucharist and what lies "beyond the veil' of Host and Chalice, a whole new awareness of who God is and who I can be in His love.

CLOSING PRAYER

Lord, Jesus, I come now to this endless fountain of Your mercy, and I say yes to You, yes to the Father so visible in You, yes to the Holy Spirit pouring Divine Life into me through Your pierced Heart.

To Live Eucharistically

The piercing of Christ's Heart shows us that he was not just bleeding; He was bled out. The blood and water gushing from his tender Heart represents the complete outpouring of his life-blood. He has held nothing back; He has given all. This is mercy! This is the self-emptying of God, the complete self-giving of the Son and of the Father to His children. And this self-giving finds its ultimate expression in the Eucharist.

"Greater love has no man than this, that a man lay down his life for his friends" (Jn 15:13). The definition Jesus gives of love is always the maximum love. He could have said: "Love is to give", or "Love is to give something of oneself." But no, he immediately points to the greatest possible love. He is not satisfied with mediocre solutions. For him, love is to give one's life, that is, all of oneself. And he does it. On the Cross, he shows a total outpouring. His hands and feet, yes, and even his heart are opened so that his blood, the symbol of life, pours out unhindered and flows over the whole world. He is given, poured out, literally.

The symbols that are used in the Eucharist, active symbols—that is, symbols that realize what they signify—are in some way still more clear and radical than the original reality that they express. There is surely no more drastic way to give oneself than to let oneself be eaten and drunk by those one loves.

The Eucharist shows that love means to go out of oneself. It points to the essential reason for which we were created. "Do not get fixed on yourself", says the Eucharist; "do not pity yourself. Leave yourself, think of others, live for others." To live Eucharistically is to live for others, given, poured out, to be food and drink. . . .

What is ingenious about the Eucharist is that it at once expresses God's self-giving love and awakens the same out-pouring love in us. It shows us that God is "offered", and it transforms us into "offered" people. We are allowed to be witnesses of Jesus' "ecstatic" love, and he transforms us himself into "ecstatic" people.

—Wilfred Stinissen, *Bread That Is Broken*, pp. 36–38

IN GOD'S PRESENCE, CONSIDER . . .

During Exposition, St. Faustina saw the same rays as depicted in the Image coming out of the Sacred Host. When I receive the Eucharist, do I realize that this is Christ's love, His whole being poured out for me? Do I accept the call to do likewise and pour myself out for others?

CLOSING PRAYER

Thank you, Lord, for pouring out Your lifeblood for me. Let it transform me and empower me to give myself for others as You have given yourself for me.

A New Capacity to Love

God's mercy to us, writes Fr. Cantalamessa, is a gift; the mercy we show to others is a duty. God's love is entrusted to us to share with others.

Mercy toward our neighbors, unlike God's mercy toward us, is not, however, a gift we give them but a duty we owe them: "Owe no one anything, except to love one another" (Romans 13:8). Why is it a debt? We have received an infinite measure of love to share with our brothers and sisters. However much we love a brother or sister, we can never match the measure of mercy for them that we have received from God and that is owed to them. God had infinite mercy toward us in giving us his Son Jesus, and he asks us not to keep him just for ourselves but to share him. He asks that the water he has given us become in us "a spring of water welling up to eternal life" (John 4:14). Brothers and sisters who knock at your door are thus creditors who are collecting their debt. Even if you cannot always give them what they ask you for, see that you do not send them away without what is owed to them.

We can see from all this that the essential reason for loving our neighbors is not extrinsic to us but intrinsic: it is not because God commands us to love them, nor is it because they are loved by God and therefore worthy of being loved by us. It is because God has placed in us, has entrusted to us, his own love for them. This is fundamentally the theological virtue of charity insofar as it is an infused virtue; it is a participation in the very love of God. It makes us become participants in the divine nature, which is love, and thus we have a new capacity to love like God loves.

—Raniero Cantalamessa, *The Gaze of Mercy*

IN GOD'S PRESENCE, CONSIDER . . .

Have I ever considered it a duty rather than a gift when I show mercy to another? Even if I know that the grace for me to do anything good comes from God, do I tend to think of acts of mercy as something that *I'm* giving, as opposed to simply an overflow of the love God has poured into me, which He desires for me to then share?

CLOSING PRAYER

Lord, help me to remember that I am not called to "drum up love" for anyone, but rather to recognize that I am participating in Your Divine love, the very life of the Trinity.

Faustina's Prayer for Sinners

Like Mother Teresa, St. Faustina came to understand the depth of Christ's thirst for souls and made it her own.

O Jesus, eternal Truth, our Life, I call upon You and I beg Your mercy for poor sinners. O sweetest Heart of my Lord, full of pity and unfathomable mercy, I plead with You for poor sinners. O Most Sacred Heart, Fount of Mercy from which gush forth rays of inconceivable graces upon the entire human race, I beg of You light for poor sinners. O Jesus, be mindful of Your own bitter Passion and do not permit the loss of souls redeemed at so dear a price of Your most precious Blood. O Jesus, when I consider the great price of Your Blood, I rejoice at its immensity, for one drop alone would have been enough for the salvation of all sinners. Although sin is an abyss of wickedness and ingratitude, the price paid for us can never be equalled. Therefore, let every soul trust in the Passion of the Lord, and place its hope in His mercy. God will not deny His mercy to anyone. Heaven and earth may change, but God's mercy will never be exhausted. Oh, what immense joy burns in my heart when I contemplate Your incomprehensible goodness, O Jesus! I desire to bring all sinners to Your feet that they may glorify Your mercy throughout endless ages.

—St. Faustina, *Diary*, 72

IN GOD'S PRESENCE, CONSIDER . . .

Do I tend to judge or look down upon people who seem lost in sin, or do I sincerely pray for them and implore God's mercy for them?

CLOSING PRAYER

Lord, help me to take on Your thirst for souls and continually lift others up to Your mercy.

Aglow with the Spirit

As St. Paul approaches the conclusion of his masterpiece, his longest letter in the New Testament, he confirms that our wholehearted trust in God frees us to live a life of abundance with others. The scarcity mindset of our past can be abandoned.

Let love be genuine; hate what is evil, hold fast to what is good; love one another with brotherly affection; outdo one another in showing honor. Never flag in zeal, be aglow with the Spirit, serve the Lord. Rejoice in your hope, be patient in tribulation, be constant in prayer. Contribute to the needs of the saints, practice hospitality.

Bless those who persecute you; bless and do not curse them. Rejoice with those who rejoice, weep with those who weep. Live in harmony with one another; do not be haughty, but associate with the lowly; never be conceited. Repay no one evil for evil, but take thought for what is noble in the sight of all. If possible, so far as it depends upon you, live peaceably with all. Beloved, never avenge yourselves, but leave it to the wrath of God; for it is written, "Vengeance is mine, I will repay, says the Lord." No, "if your enemy is hungry, feed him; if he is thirsty, give him drink; for by so doing you will heap burning coals upon his head." Do not be overcome by evil, but overcome evil with good.

—Romans 12:9–21

IN GOD'S PRESENCE, CONSIDER . . .

How restricted are the parameters of God's mercy in my life? Does God's radiance stop at the chapel door, or does Divine light shine into my every endeavor, into every encounter?

CLOSING PRAYER

Lord God, as long as I am with You, I have everything I need and can strive to live out this passage, as much as it demands. Grant me strong faith, deep trust, and a heart of mercy. Jesus, shine Your light through me wherever You would have me go.

Luminous Is the Light

Catherine Doherty, known for her deep devotion to the Eucharist and her radical service of the poor, shares a beautiful, poetic reflection on faith, hope, and love—and living in the light of Christ.

Soft pastel shades tint the evenings of spring and the early morning,
bringing new hope, new life, especially in the hearts of those who live close
to nature. So it is with the people of God. Hope is like sap rising in the trees.
Slowly the snow of doubts, confusion, and criticism is melting away.
More and more people are talking about love. More and more people begin
to realize all of us must begin with ourselves and must preach the Gospel
with our lives. Unless each one of us begins to love, and to serve both
brethren and enemies, there will be no real change in the world.

Luminous is the light of spring. Luminous is the light of Christ.
Let us enter into this light of the Lord, who brings us the spring of hope,
eternally renewed. He brings us the love that can change the whole world
if only we incarnate it as He wishes us to . . . Let us allow the
spring of faith, hope, and love to come to our hearts.

—Catherine Doherty, *Grace in Every Season*

IN GOD'S PRESENCE, CONSIDER . . .

How do I spiritually remain close to the Lord, celebrating the wonder of what He has done for me? My heart considers this from Catherine's words: Embody the luminous Christ. Become Joy. Become Mercy. And overflow.

CLOSING PRAYER

Lord, in a world rife with chaos and discord, help me to be Your light. Create in my life a new springtime, one rich with the virtues of faith, hope, and charity, so that I can incarnate Your love in the world.

The Eucharist Calls Us to Mutual Love

In his homily on the Eucharist at the 49th International Eucharistic Congress in Quebec City, Canada, June 21, 2008, Cardinal Arinze stressed that the Eucharist sends us forth into the world to live out Christ's command to love each other as He loved us.

The Eucharist is not only a mystery to be believed and celebrated, but also a mystery to be lived. . . . The Holy Eucharist sends us to show love and solidarity to our brothers and sisters who are in need. There are first the poor, the hungry, the sick, the prisoners, the handicapped, the old, and the homeless. Works of charity done in their favour are manifestations that we are living the message of our Eucharistic celebration. But we are also sent to console those who are in sorrow, to help to liberate those held in slavery, including the victims of sexual, racial or other forms of oppression, to give hope to street children, and to help underdeveloped peoples rise to an acceptable level of human existence.

Love for our neighbour must not stop here. It has to include the spiritually hungry and needy. People are hungry for the Word of God, for the liberating Gospel of Jesus Christ. Therefore missionary work, catechesis in its many forms and leading people to the Church and to the Sacraments are necessary manifestations of love of neighbour. . . . Pope John Paul II, told us that mutual love, especially solicitude for people in need, will show that we are true disciples of Christ and prove the authenticity of our Eucharistic celebration (cf. *Mane Nobiscum Domine*, 28). And Pope Benedict XVI reminds us that "A Eucharist which does not pass over into the concrete practice of love is intrinsically fragmented" (*Deus Caritas Est*, 14)

—Cardinal Francis Arinze, "A Mystery to be Lived"

IN GOD'S PRESENCE, CONSIDER . . .

Cardinal Arinze outlines various ways in which we can witness to the love of our Eucharistic Lord. Which of these can I incorporate into my life? What concrete steps can I resolve to take?

CLOSING PRAYER

Merciful Lord, give me the grace not merely to receive the Eucharist, but to take Your command of love seriously and find ways to live it out in the world as a witness of Your mercy.

To Radiate Mercy

Fr. Kosicki explains that we are all called to be "partners of mercy" with Jesus, allowing the Eucharist to transform us so completely that we become "living Eucharist," radiating his mercy to others.

The life of Jesus, from beginning to end, was a life of humble service and obedience to the Father's will: he came to do the Father's will (Heb. 10:7); he was born of a woman (Gal. 4:4), a man like us in all things but sin (Heb. 4:15); he emptied himself in humble submission to death on the cross (Phil. 2:7–8); he was buried in a tomb of stone (Jn. 19:42); and in all this he loved us to the utmost (Jn. 13:1), showing his humility by washing the feet of his disciples (Jn. 13:5) and then giving himself as food to remain with us.

Jesus gave us his body broken and blood poured out—now risen—as the seal of the new covenant of mercy. His complete and perfect act of humility cries out to us to receive it, and to follow in his footsteps, to be partners of Christ (cf. Heb. 3:14) in this work of mercy. The great mystery (the great plan of God for our salvation), is that he calls us to share with him in this work of mercy as his partners! Now he wants us to receive all and give all in humility. He wants us to be his body, bringing his mercy to a most needy world.

He wants us to be "Living Eucharist!"—totally given, broken and poured out for the salvation of souls. He wants us to "radiate mercy" like the Eucharist. That's what it's all about!

Without him, we can do nothing (cf. Jn. 15:5). Yet we can do all things in him who strengthens us (cf. Phil. 4:13)—strengthens us with the bread of life and the cup of eternal salvation, to do the work of salvation.

What a miracle of mercy we have in our midst! What a challenge to humbly receive humility itself, and be transformed into his body, to be his partners!

What a privilege we have to come into his humble, silent presence and be radiated with his mercy, so that we, in turn, might radiate mercy to others.

—Fr. George Kosicki, CSB, *What's It All About?*

IN GOD'S PRESENCE, CONSIDER . . .

Do I receive the Eucharist with the desire—and intention—to allow Jesus to transform me so I can become his body in the world, his "partner of mercy"?

CLOSING PRAYER

Lord Jesus, thank you for radiating your Eucaristic love into me. Help me to bring your radiance with me into the world.

Overflow

Receiving the Eucharist, named in the Catechism as one of the "Sacraments of Mercy," is not just for ourselves. It must change us and overflow to others. Here is a perfect prayer to pray when receiving Holy Communion—we take Mercy Incarnate in and then become mercy for the world.

What use is it if I receive You
and do not bear You to the world?
"Mary went in haste. . . .

What use is it if I join myself to You in love
and do not love my brother?
"They'll know you are my disciples" . . .

Is it even possible
to be truly united to Goodness
and not share that goodness?
What kind of union is it,
if I stay my same self thereafter?

Do not allow me to remain as I am, Jesus.
Help me to prepare my heart
for true union with You,
a union that will reveal You to the world
uniquely through me.

For what use is it if You come to me
and I refuse You to my neighbor?
What use is it, Lord, if You fill me
and I do not overflow?

—Erin Flynn, *Mass & Adoration Companion*

IN GOD'S PRESENCE, CONSIDER . . .

How often do I receive Holy Communion and treat Jesus in the way He lamented about to St. Faustina: "as a dead object"? What if I were to be more present to Him and allow Him to really transform me? And how can I more consciously bring Him into my daily life in the world?

CLOSING PRAYER

Jesus, let me be more aware of Your living Presence each time I receive You. And help me to be transformed, to bear Your mercy, to overflow.

Wisdom from Above

James holds nothing back, bulldozing our human interference to the free outpouring of God's mercy. He invites us to jettison self-reliance and to seek Wisdom and understanding from above, which necessarily negate selfishness and jealousy—and include the practice of mercy.

Who is wise and understanding among you? By his good life let him show his works in the meekness of wisdom. But if you have bitter jealousy and selfish ambition in your hearts, do not boast and be false to the truth. This wisdom is not such as comes down from above, but is earthly, unspiritual, devilish. For where jealousy and selfish ambition exist, there will be disorder and every vile practice. But the wisdom from above is first pure, then peaceable, gentle, open to reason, full of mercy and good fruits, without uncertainty or insincerity. And the harvest of righteousness is sown in peace by those who make peace.

—James 3:13–18

IN GOD'S PRESENCE, CONSIDER . . .

When I check my heart regarding my attitude toward others and my own desire to be seen as better than them (not just in earthly ambition, but even in spiritual matters), what do I find there?

CLOSING PRAYER

Jesus, Meek and Humble of Heart, I try to build my domain by my own effort, and fall miserably short of Your fullness. Grant me true Wisdom, understanding, and a heart full of mercy and sincerity.

She Will Teach You Everything

The wisest man in the Bible, Solomon the King, son of the great David the beloved, was cherished by God since he did not ask for riches, power, or honor, but requested the gift of God's own Wisdom. While Solomon tragically did not remain wise, we can be formed by the Blessed Mother, the "Seat of Wisdom," who relentlessly draws us to her Son.

O God of my ancestors and Lord of mercy,
who have made all things by your word,
and by your wisdom have formed humankind
to have dominion over the creatures you have made,
and rule the world in holiness and righteousness,
and pronounce judgment in uprightness of soul,
give me the wisdom that sits by your throne,
and do not reject me from among your servants.
For I am your servant the son of your serving girl,
a man who is weak and short-lived,
with little understanding of judgment and laws;
for even one who is perfect among human beings
will be regarded as nothing without the wisdom that comes from you.

—Wisdom 9:1–6 (NRSVCE)

IN GOD'S PRESENCE, CONSIDER . . .

Am I willing to relinquish my own understanding and be formed by my mother, conceived without sin? Can I recognize that Mary, Spouse of the Spirit, has so much to share with me through her holy mysteries, and accept her instruction?

CLOSING PRAYER

Oh Mary, Seat of Wisdom, I've tried to live by my own insight for far too long. Thank you for your patience with me, and reject me not from among your children. I am your child, and I am ready to be taught by you.

The Creator and the Creature

In His mercy, God consistently desires to abolish "the chasm which separates the Creator from the creature."—And most especially, through the Eucharist.

I adore You, Lord and Creator, hidden in the Blessed Sacrament. I adore You for all the works of Your hands, that reveal to me so much wisdom, goodness and mercy, O Lord. You have spread so much beauty over the earth, and it tells me about Your beauty, even though these beautiful things are but a faint reflection of You, Incomprehensible Beauty. And although You have hidden Yourself and concealed Your beauty, my eye, enlightened by faith, reaches You, and my soul recognizes its Creator, its Highest Good; and my heart is completely immersed in prayer of adoration. My Lord and Creator, Your goodness encourages me to converse with You. Your mercy abolishes the chasm which separates the Creator from the creature. To converse with You, O Lord, is the delight of my heart. In You I find everything that my heart could desire. Here Your light illumines my mind, enabling it to know You more and more deeply. Here streams of graces flow down upon my heart. Here my soul draws eternal life. O my Lord and Creator, You alone, beyond all these gifts, give Your own self to me and unite Yourself intimately with Your miserable creature. Here, without searching for words, our hearts understand each other. Here, no one is able to interrupt our conversation. What I talk to You about, Jesus, is our secret, which creatures shall not know and Angels dare not ask about. These are secret acts of forgiveness, known only to Jesus and me; this is the mystery of His mercy, which embraces each soul separately. For this incomprehensible goodness of Yours, I adore You, O Lord and Creator, with all my heart and all my soul. And, although my worship is so little and poor, I am at peace because I know that You know it is sincere, however inadequate . . .

—St. Faustina, *Diary*, 1692

IN GOD'S PRESENCE, CONSIDER . . .

I ponder all of the things that, each day, reflect to me God's wisdom, goodness, and beauty. I open my heart to the intimate union with Him that He longs for.

CLOSING PRAYER

This is what I want, Jesus: to be embraced by the mystery of Your mercy; to be immersed in intimate conversation and union with You; to find rest with You where "streams of graces flow down upon my heart." Help me to recognize You in all Your works, but especially in the great gift of Your Presence in the Eucharist.

Saint Francis and Divine Mercy

Like St. Faustina, St. Francis was devoted to imploring mercy for the whole world as he meditated on the sorrowful Passion of Christ.

We know from The Life of St. Francis written by St. Bonaventure (1217–1274) that one of the divine perfections Bonaventure saw most clearly reflected in St. Francis of Assisi was God's mercy. Saint Bonaventure writes the following lines in the "Prologue" to the biography:

> In these latter days the grace of God our Savior has appeared in his servant Francis to all who are truly humble and lovers of holy poverty. In him they can venerate God's superabundant mercy, and be taught by his example to live in conformity with Christ, and to thirst after blessed hope with unflagging desire (Paulist Press edition, 1978).

Later in the same work, St. Bonaventure tells us that one of the principal intentions of St. Francis's own prayers was pleading for mercy upon the world, on the basis of the sorrowful passion of Jesus Christ:

> When the man of God was left alone and at peace, he would fill the groves with sighs, sprinkle the ground with tears, striking his breast with his fist, and having found there a kind of secret hiding place, would converse with his Lord. There he would answer his Judge, there he would entreat his Father, there he would entertain his Friend; and there also on several occasions the friars who were devoutly observing him heard him groan aloud, imploring the divine mercy for sinners and weeping for the Lord's passion as if it were before his eyes (ch.10, no. 4).

—Dr. Robert Stackpole, *Divine Mercy: A Guide from Genesis to Benedict XVI*

IN GOD'S PRESENCE, CONSIDER . . .

How does God reveal His mercy to me today? Through whom have I witnessed God's love shining? I want, like St. Francis, to be absorbed by God's mercy and cry out for it for those who need it most.

CLOSING PRAYER

Alone with You, Heavenly Father, I see the depths of Your love. Draw my vision from the great need in this world to the superabundance of Your Divine Mercy—and instill in me an unfailing desire to meditate on the Passion of Your Son and implore Your mercy.

A Great River of Mercy

On February 6, 2016, Pope Francis, meeting with an international gathering of Padre Pio Prayer Groups who were in Rome to venerate the saint's relics, spoke of Padre Pio as a "servant of mercy," a "living caress of the Father."

I greet all of you who have come from many countries and regions, united in great love and gratitude to St Pio of Pietrelcina. You are very grateful, because he helped you to discover life's treasure, which is the love of God, and to experience the beauty of the Lord's forgiveness and mercy. And this is a science which we must learn day by day, for it is beautiful: the beauty of the Lord's forgiveness and mercy.

We can truly say that Padre Pio was *a servant of mercy*. He did so full-time, sometimes practicing "the apostleship of listening" to the point of exhaustion. Through the ministry of Confession, he became the living caress of the Father, who heals the wounds of sin and revives the heart with peace. St Pio never tired of welcoming people and listening to them, expending time and energy in order to spread the perfume of the Lord's forgiveness.

He could do this because he was always connected to the source: he ceaselessly quenched his thirst with Jesus Crucified, and thus became a channel of mercy. He bore in his heart many people and many sufferings, uniting all to the love of Christ who gave himself "to the end" (Jn 13:1). He lived the great mystery of sorrow offered up for love. In this way his little drop became a great river of mercy, which brought water to many deserted hearts and created oases of life in many parts of the world.

—Pope Francis

IN GOD'S PRESENCE, CONSIDER . . .

What little, daily things can I do to become, like Padre Pio, a "living caress of the Father" to those around me?

CLOSING PRAYER

Lord, help me to extend to others the "perfume" of your forgiveness, adding the drops of my love to the "great river" of your mercy.

A Mercy that Bleeds

Padre Pio, who bore the "stigmata," the wounds of Jesus, for more than 50 years, reflects on the Agony of Jesus in the Garden of Gethsemane and on the angel sent to console Him.

From now on Jesus responds to the loving cry of His Heart, to the cry of humanity, which, in order to be redeemed clamors for His death. At the sentence of death which His Father pronounces against Him heaven and earth demand His death. Jesus, resigned, bends His adorable head: "Father, if Thou dost not want that this chalice pass unless I drink it, not Mine but Thy Will be done." Behold He sends an Angel, an Angel-Messenger, to comfort Jesus. What motives of comfort, of relief does the Angel offer to the strong God, Lord of the Universe, the Invincible, the Omnipotent! . . . He has become subject to suffering, He has taken upon Himself our weakness; it is the man who suffers, and is in agony. It is the miracle of His infinite love which makes him sweat Blood and brings upon Him this agony. . . .

I believe that the Angel bows reverently before Jesus, before this Eternal beauty, now covered with blood and dust, and with deferential honor imparts that consolation of resignation of the human will to the Divine Will, beseeching Him for the glory of the Father and in the name of all sinners to drink that chalice which was offered to Him from Eternity for their salvation. He has prayed to teach us also that when our soul finds itself in desolation like His, we should seek consolation from Heaven only in prayer to sustain us in the sacrifice. He, our strength will be ready to assist us because He had willed to take upon Himself our miseries. . . .

Yes, O Jesus, it is for Thee to drink the chalice to the dregs, Thou art now vowed to the most terrible death. Jesus, may nothing be able to separate me from Thee, neither life nor death. . . .

—St. Padre Pio, "The Agony of Jesus"

IN GOD'S PRESENCE, CONSIDER . . .

I will meditate for a time on whatever part of this entry struck my heart, asking for a true desire to console the Heart of Christ and expressing gratitude for His infinite mercy.

CLOSING PRAYER

Oh Eternal beauty, my heart wants to comfort You in Your agony. I ask for the grace not only to avoid sin, but to follow You in the total resignation of my will to the will of the Father.

He Shows Mercy to You

When you least find yourself deserving of mercy, God surprises you and crosses over to lift you up, ministering to your soul and body. Then He commissions You to do the same.

And behold, a lawyer stood up to put him to the test, saying, "Teacher, what shall I do to inherit eternal life?" He said to him, "What is written in the law? How do you read?" And he answered, "You shall love the Lord your God with all your heart, and with all your soul, and with all your strength, and with all your mind; and your neighbor as yourself." And he said to him, "You have answered right; do this, and you will live."

But he, desiring to justify himself, said to Jesus, "And who is my neighbor?" Jesus replied, "A man was going down from Jerusalem to Jericho, and he fell among robbers, who stripped him and beat him, and departed, leaving him half dead. Now by chance a priest was going down that road; and when he saw him he passed by on the other side. So likewise a Levite, when he came to the place and saw him, passed by on the other side. But a Samaritan, as he journeyed, came to where he was; and when he saw him, he had compassion, and went to him and bound up his wounds, pouring on oil and wine; then he set him on his own beast and brought him to an inn, and took care of him. And the next day he took out two denarii and gave them to the innkeeper, saying, 'Take care of him; and whatever more you spend, I will repay you when I come back.' Which of these three, do you think, proved neighbor to the man who fell among the robbers?" He said, "The one who showed mercy on him." And Jesus said to him, "Go and do likewise."

—Luke 10:25–37

IN GOD'S PRESENCE, CONSIDER . . .

This is how the Savior is with me. Have I kept my wounds hidden where they fester, or do I trust Him enough to uncover the pain in my life, where He pours out His compassion? I want to be that compassion for others as well, to be "the one who showed mercy."

CLOSING PRAYER

Lord Jesus, I don't understand how and when I fell into the hands of brigands, but like all humankind, I find myself in a fallen world with deep wounds in my heart. Free me from the spirit of self-preservation, and allow me to cast my brokenness into Your Divine Intervention. Then make me a true neighbor, one whose heart is broken open at the suffering of others.

An Interior Act of Mercy

In a letter to her Spiritual Director Fr. Michael Sopocko (Dec. 20, 1936), St. Faustina shows us what it means to commit ourselves to being merciful.

. . . I have recently made an interior act of mercy which means that I am going to act in the same way as the merciful Heart of Jesus would in a given situation. If I cannot do it by deed, then I shall do so by word, and if I cannot do it by word, then I shall do so by ardent prayer, so that whoever comes in contact with me can experience God's mercy. Interiorly, I do not give any thought to all the hardships, adversities, and humiliations which I encounter or which may befall me, nor from whom they come, but I try to let a new flame of love burst from my heart towards God, the way it blazed forth from the merciful Heart of Jesus for the Heavenly Father and souls.

—*The Letters of Saint Faustina*

IN GOD'S PRESENCE, CONSIDER . . .

Would I consider making an interior act of mercy, committing myself to doing whatever is in my power in every situation to bring about for each person an encounter with God's mercy?

CLOSING PRAYER

St. Faustina, you desired to imitate the merciful Heart of Jesus. Pray for me that, in each circumstance, I will be able to act, speak, or pray so that those I encounter will experience God's mercy. Jesus, knowing that You want me to become like You, and that You want to flood the world with Your mercy, let this resolve be my primary aim.

The Face of God Reflected

Pope Francis teaches us that the greatest treasures are to be found in love of God and love of neighbor, and that these are not two separate virtues but simply two "faces" of the one, great commandment.

There is a hierarchy of virtues that bids us seek what is essential. The primacy belongs to the theological virtues, which have God as their object and motive. At the centre is charity.

Saint Paul says that what truly counts is "faith working through love" (*Gal* 5:6). We are called to make every effort to preserve charity: "The one who loves another has fulfilled the law . . . for love is the fulfilment of the law" (*Rom* 13:8.10). "For the whole law is summed up in a single commandment, 'You shall love your neighbour as yourself'" (*Gal* 5:14).

In other words, amid the thicket of precepts and prescriptions, Jesus clears a way to seeing two faces, that of the Father and that of our brother. He does not give us two more formulas or two more commands. He gives us two faces, or better yet, one alone: the face of God reflected in so many other faces. For in every one of our brothers and sisters, especially the least, the most vulnerable, the defenseless and those in need, God's very image is found. Indeed, with the scraps of this frail humanity, the Lord will shape his final work of art. For "what endures, what has value in life, what riches do not disappear? Surely these two: the Lord and our neighbour. These two riches do not disappear!"

—Pope Francis, *Gaudete et Exsultate (Rejoice and Be Glad),* 60, 61

IN GOD'S PRESENCE, CONSIDER . . .

In my daily life, do I separate my love for God from the love that's due my neighbor? Or is the love I show to others a natural extension and reflection of my love for God?

CLOSING PRAYER

Lord, help me to see the Father's face in the faces of all I meet and to respond to each with love.

All Generations Will Call Me Blessed

The Mother of Jesus is the Church's most beloved hymnist. Every evening at Vespers Mary's daughters and sons join her hymn of praise to the Father for His mercy, which he promised to Abraham and his children forever.

My soul magnifies the Lord,
and my spirit rejoices in God my Savior,
for he has regarded the low estate of his handmaiden.
For behold, henceforth all generations will call me blessed;
for he who is mighty has done great things for me,
and holy is his name.
And his mercy is on those who fear him
from generation to generation.
He has shown strength with his arm,
he has scattered the proud in the imagination of their hearts,
he has put down the mighty from their thrones,
and exalted those of low degree;
he has filled the hungry with good things,
and the rich he has sent empty away.
He has helped his servant Israel,
in remembrance of his mercy,
as he spoke to our fathers,
to Abraham and to his posterity for ever.

—Luke 1:46–55

IN GOD'S PRESENCE, CONSIDER . . .

Do I hear the sound of my mother's voice singing in joy and thanksgiving to the Father? The Blessed Mother teaches me how to pray and how to have complete trust in God's plan of mercy.

CLOSING PRAYER

O Blessed Mother, Queen of angels and saints, you teach my earthbound heart how to soar up into the heights. Teach me your hymn of praise, that I may always follow the Father's will and rejoice in His mercy.

The Merciful Mother as the New Eve

Saint Pope John Paul II, reflecting on the Assumption of the Blessed Virgin Mary, reminds us that, just as Christ forever continues His mission as Redeemer, so Mary continues to reveal to us His plan of mercy.

Both representations of Mary, the historical one described in the Gospel, and the one mentioned in the Book of Revelation symbolize the Church. The fact that the condition of pregnancy, like the impending birth, the perils of the dragon and the abduction of the newborn child "caught up to God and to his throne" (*Rv* 12:4–5) also belong to the "heavenly" Church contemplated in the Apostle John's vision, is very eloquent, and in today's solemnity becomes a reason for deep reflection.

Just as the risen Christ who has ascended into heaven forever bears the wounds of his redemptive death within his glorious body and his merciful heart, so his Mother brings to eternity "the pangs" and "anguish for delivery" (*Rv* 12:2). And as the Son, through his death, never stops redeeming all who have been begotten by God as his adopted children, thus the new Eve continues from generation to generation to give birth to the new man, "created after the likeness of God in true righteousness and holiness" (*Eph* 4:24). This is the Church's eschatological image, which is present and active in the Virgin. . . .

Taken up into heaven, Mary shows us the way to God, the way to heaven, the way to life. She shows it to her children baptized in Christ and to all people of good will. She opens this way especially to the little ones and to the poor, those who are dear to divine mercy. The Queen of the world reveals to individuals and to nations the power of the love of God whose plan upsets that of the proud, pulls down the mighty from their thrones and exalts the humble, fills the hungry with good things and sends the rich empty away (cf. *Lk* 1:51–53).

—Solemnity of the Assumption of the Blessed Virgin Mary,
August 15,1999

IN GOD'S PRESENCE, CONSIDER . . .

The plan of the powerful and loving God upsets the proud and mighty but exalts the humble and fills the hungry. I want to be the latter. I want to be one of the little ones, dear to Divine Mercy.

CLOSING PRAYER

Mary, you are the new Eve, the merciful Mother—Mother to me and Mother of the Church. Show me how to be continually recreated in God's likeness in whatever ways I need to be and illuminate the path to heaven for our struggling Church.

Held in Love

Martyred as the Church entered the Solemnity of his Queen's Assumption, St. Maximilian Kolbe lived in deep assurance that God would turn all things to good. His trust in God's mercy and Mary's care left him perfectly at peace and able to provide merciful care to all of his companions.

In August of 1939, when it was inescapably obvious that the second Great War was very close, Fr. Kolbe addressed the 837 or so friars of the City of the Immaculata on the edge of Warsaw specifically about the third stage: "Suffering". He reminded them that they could not know the hour nor the means of their death, but urged them all to shed their blood in the service of the Immaculata to seal a true love for her. He quoted the words of Our Saviour that: "There is no greater love than this, that a man give his life for his friend." For himself, this was indeed to be a prophetic statement. . . .

As when Fr. Kolbe had earlier been obliged to undergo confinement (at the sanatorium in Zakopane in June of 1920, and on that occasion for health reasons), he now busied himself by instructing fellow prisoners, organizing prayer groups and holding conferences in a similar manner, insofar as he could get away with it under the watchful eyes of the camp guards. His charitable generosity knew no bounds. For example, when an admirer managed to smuggle a portion of cheese from the camp kitchen and presented it to Fr. Kolbe, he did no more than share it out amongst the others near him. The rations were barely enough to live on, and yet he would share his portion with the others. On another occasion, a prisoner awoke in a fit of shivers from the cold to find that Fr. Kolbe was covering him with a blanket. These little acts of mercy may have had their origins in the privations that Fr. Kolbe had undergone earlier in his life, and also being buoyed up by his trust that the Immaculata would make up any shortfall for him.

—*St. Maximilian Maria Kolbe, His Life, Apostolate, and Spirituality*

IN GOD'S PRESENCE, CONSIDER . . .

Do I require a flawless life to feel able to present myself to God? Or do I recognize even in my wounds and suffering exquisite gifts that I can offer to the Lord?

CLOSING PRAYER

Dear Merciful Mother, soften my heart to recognize the healing hand of your Son. You are Queen of my life: I entrust myself into your gentle care.

Good News Your Friends Need to Hear

One of the greatest evangelists in Mark's Gospel we meet first as a raging demoniac, but the strength of his cries becomes the strength of his proclamation as he single-handedly preaches to the Decapolis region of 10 cities, centers of Greek and Roman culture, thus preparing the way for a fervent future response of faith from this area.

And when he had come out of the boat, there met him out of the tombs a man with an unclean spirit, . . . And when he saw Jesus from afar, he ran and worshiped him; and crying out with a loud voice, he said, "What have you to do with me, Jesus, Son of the Most High God? I adjure you by God, do not torment me." For he had said to him, "Come out of the man, you unclean spirit!" And Jesus asked him, "What is your name?" He replied, "My name is Legion; for we are many." And he begged him eagerly not to send them out of the country. Now a great herd of swine was feeding there on the hillside; and they begged him, "Send us to the swine, let us enter them." So he gave them leave. And the unclean spirits came out, and entered the swine; and the herd, numbering about two thousand, rushed down the steep bank into the sea, and were drowned in the sea. . . .

And as he was getting into the boat, the man who had been possessed with demons begged him that he might be with him. But he refused, and said to him, "Go home to your friends, and tell them how much the Lord has done for you, and how he has had mercy on you." And he went away and began to proclaim in the Decapolis how much Jesus had done for him; and all men marveled.

—Mark 5:2, 6–13, 18–20

IN GOD'S PRESENCE, CONSIDER . . .

Just as the Blessed Mother ponders God's mighty deeds in her heart, do I reflect on how much the Lord has done for me? Do I tell others about God's abundant mercy to me, allowing those I love to discover Jesus's handiwork?

CLOSING PRAYER

Lord, you have done all things well. I am in awe of Your goodness. Even if I have no externally transforming encounters to point to like this man who was possessed, I know that it is Your mercy alone that underscores my creation, continued existence, salvation, each moment I'm granted, and every experience of goodness, love, and blessing. Grant me the gratitude and courage to proclaim Your mercy to those I encounter.

The Lord Has Shown Great Mercy

One of the greatest signs of God's mercy freely operating in our lives is our hearts flooded with gratitude and praise. As Zechariah witnesses the mercy of God, he leads us in praise to our Father.

Now the time came for Elizabeth to be delivered, and she gave birth to a son. And her neighbors and kinsfolk heard that the Lord had shown great mercy to her, and they rejoiced with her. And on the eighth day they came to circumcise the child; and they would have named him Zechariah after his father, but his mother said, "Not so; he shall be called John." And they said to her, "None of your kindred is called by this name." And they made signs to his father, inquiring what he would have him called. And they made signs to his father, inquiring what he would have him called. And he asked for a writing tablet, and wrote, "His name is John." And they all marveled. And immediately his mouth was opened and his tongue loosed, and he spoke, blessing God. And fear came on all their neighbors. And all these things were talked about through all the hill country of Judea; and all who heard them laid them up in their hearts, saying, "What then will this child be?" For the hand of the Lord was with him.

—Luke 1:57–66

IN GOD'S PRESENCE, CONSIDER . . .

Where do I find myself mute and confined? Where in my life have I not yet permitted the dawn from on high to break into my shadows? As with Zechariah I obey God's command, can I open my heart to deliverance?

CLOSING PRAYER

Lord, God of our Fathers, Your mighty hand is upon me for restoration and deliverance. Break me out of the confines of my apprehension and permit me to trust in You alone.

The Lord Remembers His Holy Covenant

Three months after the Blessed Mother's jubilant hymn of praise, the mute Zechariah's tongue is loosed, and as priest of God he is able to proclaim God's mercy.

Blessed be the Lord, the God of Israel;
for he has come to his people and set them free.

He has raised up for us a mighty savior,
born of the house of his servant David.

Through his holy prophets he promised of old
that he would save us from our enemies,
and from the hands of all who hate us.

He promised to show mercy to our fathers
and to remember his holy covenant.

This was the oath he swore to our father Abraham:
to set us free from the hand of our enemies, free to worship him without fear,
holy and righteous in his sight
all the days of our life.

You, child, shall be called prophet of the Most High,
for you will go before the Lord to prepare his way,
to give his people knowledge of salvation
by forgiveness of their sins.

In the tender compassion of our God,
the dawn from on high shall break upon us,
to shine on those who dwell in darkness and the shadow of death,
and to guide our feet into the way of peace.

—Luke 1:68–79, Liturgy of the Hours

IN GOD'S PRESENCE, CONSIDER . . .

Zechariah and Mary sing of deliverance from our enemies: do I recognize that God's mercy is greater than all my foes, material and spiritual? Even as I catalog my fears and am aware of the shadows of this world, will I trust God to guide my feet into the way of peace?

CLOSING PRAYER

Blessed are you, God most high, creator of the heavens and the earth. You hold all things in your sovereign might, and you will safely lead me into righteousness.

In the Breaking

It's amazing what one word can encompass. Break, breaking, broken—when dark is transformed to light, when a heart feels the pain of loss, when a body goes from whole to harmed. So much meaning and nuance as we are invited here to meditate on the way Jesus experienced the supreme pain of this word and, in His mercy, how we experience the glory of it.

"The dawn from on high shall
break upon us (Lk. 1:78)."
You, Jesus, are this Dawn, radiant and
humble and broken.

In the flesh—breaching the infinite
chasm between God and man,
In Your giving, in Your preaching,
in the healing of Your hands . . .
Your Divine Life broke upon us.

In stunning words of forgiveness,
And the gift of your Mother to us who
sleep,
In the sweat and blood and misery . . .
Your Love broke upon us.

In the consummate kenosis of Your
Passion,
In the blood and water gushing from
Your heart,
Ocean of mercy for the world . . .
As You, Jesus, broke upon us.

In the surrendering of Your Spirit,
The mutilation of Your Body and our
sin,
Lying still in Mary's arms, damning
death defeated . . .
Your Salvation broke upon us.

In Your rising—brilliant light and
hope,
In the Pentecost of flames,
In the Sacred Bread that still remains
. . .
Your Presence breaks upon us.

"The Dawn from on high shall break
upon us,
To shine on those who dwell in darkness and the shadow of death,
And to guide our feet into the way of
peace."

You are our Peace.
Break us with your breaking—rend our
hearts wide open,
Restore us now with tears and grace . . .
Jesus, break upon us.

—Erin Flynn

IN GOD'S PRESENCE, CONSIDER . . .

Every aspect of the Lord's breaking is always a mercy—walls, resistance, and patterns of sin. Even when uncomfortable or painful, it is His patient and kind mercy.

CLOSING PRAYER

You are the God who was broken and the God who breaks upon me with light and life and love. Gently break down what needs to be restructured and restored in me, and fill me with Your glory.

Suffering as God's Mercy . . .

In his spiritual classic, Fr. Caussade speaks of the grace and motivation to suffer simply and well. It requires deep faith, but he reminds us that not only is there immense value in our suffering here, but that it is a sign of God's mercy.

ABANDONMENT IN SICKNESS. Your incurable complaints would affect me with a very great compassion did I not know that they form a great treasure for you in eternity. . . . I assure you that all this, borne as you are doing it, without complaint, or murmuring, is very likely to sanctify you. Even if you only practised the patience of ordinary good Christians you would gain a great deal of merit; but, from what you say I gather that you are doing more than this, and the involuntary rebellion of nature and occasional little signs of impatience which escape you in spite of yourself will not impede your union with God which remains in the centre of your heart. Your life may well be called a hard and laborious one, a life of pain and trial, it will, therefore be your purgatory in this world and deliver you from that of the next or at any rate shorten it considerably.

This is why I do not dare to ask God to deliver you from a trouble that must soon end, and for which you will have to thank Him for all eternity as a special sign of His mercy. The only request I could make Him for you is an increase of His love, and the virtues of submission, patience, and resignation . . . To feel no fear at the thought of death is a grace from God. As for your sufferings and the outward annoyances you have to endure, bear them as you do your physical ills. God does not require more; just a daily "fiat" applied to all your exterior sufferings ought to work your salvation as well as your perfection. All that books or directors can say may be reduced to this one word, "Fiat, fiat," at all times and for everything, but especially in the penitential and crucified life to which it has pleased Providence to reduce you. Tobias in his blindness, Job on his dung-hill, and so many other saints prostrate on beds of suffering did no more than this.

—Rev. Jean-Pierre de Caussade, SJ, *Abandonment to Divine Providence*

IN GOD'S PRESENCE, CONSIDER . . .

If I believe that union with God is my deepest joy, fulfillment, and peace, and the only thing that truly matters, then there is nothing to fear. Not suffering, not even death. I will consider praying regularly for this grace.

CLOSING PRAYER

Fiat, fiat, fiat, Lord! Let this be my response at all times and for everything.

All Shall Be Well . . .

The Catechism *and the saints remind us that everything God permits to happen will ultimately—if we are receptive to it—be transformed by His mercy and goodness, leading in the end to the best possible outcome: the definitive rest and fulfillment for which we long.*

"We know that in everything God works for good for those who love him." The constant witness of the saints confirms this truth:

We firmly believe that God is master of the world and of its history. But the ways of his providence are often unknown to us. Only at the end, when our partial knowledge ceases, when we see God "face to face", will we fully know the ways by which—even through the dramas of evil and sin—God has guided his creation to that definitive sabbath rest for which he created heaven and earth.

—*Catechism of the Catholic Church*, 313–314

IN GOD'S PRESENCE, CONSIDER . . .

Do I truly believe that everything that happens to me is somehow part of the mystery of God's providence, and that His mercy invites me to trustful surrender in all things?

CLOSING PRAYER

Father of Mercy, I recognize that Your ways are not my ways, that You are God and I am not. But, it can be difficult to see Your hand in the circumstances around me. Help me to trust more in Your mercy, that You really are working all things for good, and that I can trust You to lead me to that ultimate joy and peace I long for, which can only be found in You.

Pondering Salvation

St. Charles Borromeo received news by an express that his uncle Pope Pius IV lay dangerously ill; in his response, we see the beauty of helping the dying focus on the mercy of God and prepare for eternity.

He hastened to Rome, and being informed by the physicians that his uncle's life was despaired of, he went into his chamber, and showing him a crucifix which he held in his hand, said to him, "Most holy father, all your desires and thoughts ought to be turned towards heaven. Behold Jesus Christ crucified, who is the only foundation of our hope; he is our mediator and advocate; the victim and sacrifice for our sins. He is goodness and patience itself; his mercy is moved by the tears of sinners, and he never refuses pardon and grace to those who ask it with a truly contrite and humbled heart."

He then conjured his holiness to grant him one favour, as the greatest he had ever received from him. The pope said anything in his power should be granted him. "The favour which I most earnestly beg," said the saint, "is, that as you have but a very short time to live, you lay aside all worldly business and thoughts, and employ your strength and all your powers in thinking on your salvation, and in preparing yourself to the best of your power for your last passage." His holiness received this tender advice with great comfort, and the cardinal gave strict orders that no one should speak to the pope upon any other subject. He continued by his uncle's bedside to his last breath, never ceasing to dispose him for death by all the pious practices and sentiments which his charity could suggest; and administering himself the viaticum and extreme unction. Pope Pius IV was also assisted in his last moments by St. Philip Neri, and died on the 10th of December in 1565.

—Rev. Alban Butler, *The Lives of the Fathers, Martyrs and Other Principal Saints*

IN GOD'S PRESENCE, CONSIDER . . .

Not only do I want someone at my deathbed praying with me and encouraging me to turn to the mercy of God, but I want to go through life this way. Do I have people in my life like that, and if not, what steps can I take to change that? (Whether that means creating change in current relationships or finding spiritual companions.)

CLOSING PRAYER

Jesus Christ, crucified for me, help me to turn my thoughts toward heaven. May I live my life here with one foot in eternity, loving the world You created, but unattached to everything but You.

Confidence, Hope, and Peace

St. Claude de la Colombière knows well the spiritual jiu jitsu of our Father that later authors describe in the interior life: all trials and failures can be turned to our advantage. Where we have trust in God, everything is to our advantage.

I do not know what you mean by despair: one would think you had never heard of God or of his infinite mercy. Hold such sentiments in horror, and remember that all you have done is nothing in comparison with your want of confidence. Hope on to the end. Pray that my faults, however grave and frequent, may never make me despair of his goodness. That, in my opinion, would be the greatest evil that could befall anyone. When we can protect ourselves against that evil, there is no other which may not turn to our good and from which we cannot easily draw great advantage . . .

My God, I am so intimately convinced that thou dost watch over all those who hope in thee, and that we can want for nothing while we expect all from thee, that I am resolved to live without anxiety in the future, casting all my care on thee. "In peace I will sleep and I will rest for thou hast wonderfully established me in hope" (Ps 4:8). . . . Men may turn against me; sickness may take away my strength and the means of serving thee; I may even lose thy grace by sin, but I will never lose my hope. I will keep it even to the last moment of my life, and all the demons in hell shall try in vain to tear it from me. In peace I will sleep and I will rest.

—*The Spiritual Direction of Saint Claude de la Colombière*

IN GOD'S PRESENCE, CONSIDER . . .

God is smart and God is strong: do I include myself under the purview of God's omniscience and omnipotence? If He who is all loving finds nothing impossible, why do I hold myself in jeopardy? I can rely more on Him than on my own insight. Peace is possible no matter what.

CLOSING PRAYER

Lord of Heaven and Earth, You who hold all things in being, thank you for Your tenderness and the depth of insight into my lowliness and dependence—and my radiant destiny in Your love. Redouble my confidence in You, that faith and trust may anchor my every thought and deed.

Trust in Divine Providence

St. Francis de Sales exhorts us to make a continuing and firm resolution to belong entirely to God, entrusting everything to His merciful love.

Our Lord loves with a most tender love those who are so happy as to abandon themselves wholly to His fatherly care, letting themselves be governed by His Divine Providence, without any idle speculations as to whether the workings of this Providence will be useful to them to their profit, or painful to their loss. This is because they are well assured that nothing can be sent, nothing permitted by this paternal and most loving Heart, which will not be a source of good and profit to them. All that is required is that they should place all their confidence in Him, and say from their heart, "Into Thy blessed hands I commend my spirit, my soul, my body, and all that I have, to do with them as it shall please Thee." . . .

It is quite true that it takes a very great confidence thus to abandon ourselves without any reserve to Divine Providence; but then, when we abandon everything, our Lord takes care of everything and orders everything. On the other hand, if we reserve anything to ourselves, instead of confiding it to Him, He leaves it to us, saying as it were, "You think yourselves wise enough to manage this matter without me; well, I will leave you to do so. You will see how you will succeed." . . .

Our confidence in God must be founded on His infinite goodness and on the merits of the Passion and death of our Lord Jesus Christ, with this condition on our part: that we should preserve and recognize in ourselves an entire and firm resolution to belong wholly to God, and to abandon ourselves in all things and without any reserve to His Providence. Observe that I do not say that we must feel this resolution to belong wholly to God, but only that we must not concern ourselves with what we feel or do not feel, since the greater part of our feelings and satisfactions are only the movements of self-love.

—St. Francis de Sales, *The Art of Loving God*

IN GOD'S PRESENCE, CONSIDER . . .

Can I resolve to relinquish control today and entrust myself more fully into God's care? Can I trust that He knows what will profit me most and flood my life with blessing?

CLOSING PRAYER

Great and Loving God, You who called the angels into being, and guide the course of human affairs, open my heart to trust in Your presence, and to recognize Your handiwork in all things. Help me abandon myself in confidence that You will take care of everything.

Nothing Hinders Us

Saint Francis's simple joy has resonated throughout the centuries: 800 years after his exuberant freedom unleashed a torrent of God's love in the Church through his life and preaching, we receive in this passage inspiration to be wholehearted and to hold nothing back from the God of mercy.

Let us all love with all our heart, with all our soul, with all our mind, with all our strength and fortitude, with all our understanding and with all our powers, with our whole might and whole affection, with our innermost parts, our whole desires, and wills, the Lord God, who has given, and gives to us all, the whole body, the whole soul, and our life; who has created and redeemed us, and by His mercy alone will save us; who has done and does all good to us, miserable and wretched, vile, unclean, ungrateful, and evil.

Let us therefore desire nothing else, wish for nothing else, and let nothing please and delight us except our Creator and Redeemer, and Saviour, the only true God, who is full of good, all good, entire good, the true and supreme good, who alone is good, merciful and kind, gentle and sweet, who alone is holy, just, true, and upright, who alone is benign, pure, and clean, from whom, and through whom, and in whom is all mercy, . . . Let nothing therefore hinder us, let nothing separate us, let nothing come between us. Let us all, everywhere, in every place, at every hour, and at all times, daily and continually believe, truly and humbly, and let us hold in our hearts, and love, honor, adore, serve, praise and bless, glorify and exalt, magnify and give thanks to the most High and Supreme, Eternal God, in Trinity and Unity, to the Father, and Son, and Holy Ghost, to the Creator of all, to the Saviour of all who believe and hope in Him, and love Him, who, without beginning or end, is inmutable, invisible, unerring, ineffable, incomprehensible, unfathomable, blessed, praiseworthy, glorious, exalted, sublime, most high, sweet, amiable, lovable, and always wholly desirable above all forever and ever.

—St. Francis of Assisi, *The Writings of Saint Francis of Assisi*

IN GOD'S PRESENCE, CONSIDER . . .

St. Francis invites me into total freedom—can I let go of the flimsiness of my life to embrace the fullness of God's mercy poured out in abundance? Will I give Him everything?

CLOSING PRAYER

Jesus Healer of Hearts, Your wounded hands grasp mine, Your wounded heart meets mine; draw me into love, draw me into life, draw me into the gentleness of You. Let nothing come between us.

Know the Meek and Humble Jesus

Writing from the 1800's in Tsarist Russia, St. John of Kronstadt of the Orthodox Church reveals that merciful love is so abundant that it spontaneously spills over into compassion for our brother.

If, during service, your brother does anything irregularly, or somewhat negligently, do not become irritated, either inwardly or outwardly with him, but be generously indulgent to his fault, remembering that during your life you yourself commit many, many faults, that you yourself are a man with all infirmities, that God is long-suffering and most merciful, and that he forgives you and all of us our iniquities an innumerable multitude of times. Remember the words of the Lord's Prayer: "And forgive us our trespasses, as we forgive them that trespass against us." These words should always remind us that we ourselves at all times are great trespassers, great sinners before God, and that, remembering this, we should be humble in the depths of our hearts, and not be very severe to the faults of our brethren, weak like ourselves; that as we do not judge ourselves severely, we must not judge others severely, for our brethren are—our members, like ourselves. Irritability of temper proceeds from want of self-knowledge, from pride, and also from the fact that we do not consider the great corruption of our nature, and know but little the meek and humble Jesus.

—St. John of Kronstadt, *My Life in Christ*

IN GOD'S PRESENCE, CONSIDER . . .

Has St. John given me the clue into my lack of receiving God's mercy—that I am still abrupt and harsh toward others? Does my lack of doing unto others reveal what I have not yet permitted God to do unto me, flood me with love and kindness?

CLOSING PRAYER

Father of Mercy, Father of Love, Your ministry of love in my life is revealed in the communion You bring with those around me. Allow me to experience tenderness from my brothers and sisters, and break open my heart in compassion for them.

The Great High Priest

Jesus, the Son of God, has done everything to plunge down to our level, to enter into our weakness. We can turn to Him with confidence.

For the word of God is living and active, sharper than any two-edged sword, piercing to the division of soul and spirit . . . and discerning the thoughts and intentions of the heart. And before him no creature is hidden, but all are open and laid bare to the eyes of him . . . Since then we have a great high priest who has passed through the heavens, Jesus, the Son of God, let us hold fast our confession. For we have not a high priest who is unable to sympathize with our weaknesses, but one who in every respect has been tempted as we are, yet without sinning. Let us then with confidence draw near to the throne of grace, that we may receive mercy and find grace to help in time of need.

—Hebrews 4:12–16

IN GOD'S PRESENCE, CONSIDER . . .

Today can I turn my heart to the stunning gift Jesus makes of Himself to me in the Mass? In the liturgy, I truly come to the throne of grace, where His Word is proclaimed over me for the healing of my soul; and my body receives His Body for the outpouring of mercy.

CLOSING PRAYER

Lord Jesus Christ, Son of the Living God, You bring heaven to earth, You lift me to heaven, You enfold me in Your love. Open wide my arms to Your mercy.

Relying on His Mercy

In his famous prayer before Communion, St. Ambrose models for us the importance of trusting and relying on the mercy of God.

I draw near, loving Lord, Jesus Christ, to the table of Your most delectable banquet in fear and trembling; for I am a sinner, relying not on my own merit, but trusting rather in Your mercy and goodness. I come with a heart and body defiled by many offenses, and a mind and tongue I have not guarded well. Therefore, O loving God, O awesome Majesty, I, in my misery and caught in snares, turn to You the fount of mercy, hastening to You for healing, flying to You for protection; I would fear to draw near You as Judge, but long to have You as Savior. To You, O Lord, I display my wounds, to You I uncover my shame. I am aware of my many and great sins, and they fill me with fear, but I hope in Your mercies, for they cannot be numbered.

Look upon me, then, with eyes of mercy, Lord Jesus Christ, eternal King, God and Man, crucified for mankind. Hear me, for my hope is in You; have mercy on me, full of miseries and sins, You, who will never cease to let the fountain of compassion flow. Hail, O Saving Victim, offered for me and for all humanity on the wood of the Cross. Hail, O noble and precious Blood, flowing from the wounds of Jesus Christ, my crucified Lord, and washing away the sins of all the world.

Remember, Lord, Your creature, whom You redeemed by Your Blood. I repent of my sins, and I desire to put right what I have done. Take from me, therefore, most merciful Father, all my iniquities and sins, so that, purified in mind and body, I may worthily taste the Holy of Holies.

And grant that this sacred foretaste of Your Body and Blood which I, though unworthy, intend to receive, may be for the remission of my sins, the perfect cleansing of my faults, the banishment of shameful thoughts, and the rebirth of holy desires. May it bring about the accomplishment of works most pleasing to You; and may it be for me a firm defense of body and soul against the snares of my enemies.

—St. Ambrose, "As I Approach Your Banquet,"
Mass & Adoration Companion

IN GOD'S PRESENCE, CONSIDER . . .

To You, O Lord, I display my wounds, to You I uncover my shame.

CLOSING PRAYER

Lord, You are the Fountain of mercy. With each reception of the Eucharist, draw me deeper into union with you and help me to trust more fully that Your mercy is greater than my sins.

In Communion with These Three

The mystical experiences that St. Faustina shares in her diary show us that whenever we receive Communion, we are called to enter into communion with the Holy Trinity. We become a dwelling place for God, fulfilling Christ's promise: "If a man loves me, he will keep my word, and my Father will love him, and we will come to him and make our home with him" (Jn 14:23, RSVCE).

I often feel God's presence after Holy Communion in a special and tangible way. I know God is in my heart. And the fact that I feel Him in my heart does not interfere with my duties. Even when I am dealing with very important matters which require attention, I do not lose the presence of God in my soul, and I am closely united with Him. With Him I go to work, with Him I go for recreation, with Him I suffer, with Him I rejoice; I live in Him and He in me. I am never alone, because He is my constant companion. He is present to me at every moment.

Once after Holy Communion, I heard these words: You are Our dwelling place. At that moment, I felt in my soul the presence of the Holy Trinity, the Father, the Son and the Holy Spirit. . . . My soul is in communion with these Three; but I do not know how to express this in words; yet my soul understands it well. Whoever is united to One of the Three Persons is thereby united to the whole Blessed Trinity, for this Oneness is indivisible.

O Jesus! I sense keenly how Your divine Blood is circulating in my heart; I have not the least doubt that Your most pure love has entered my heart with Your most sacred Blood. I am aware that You are dwelling in me, together with the Father and the Holy Spirit, or rather I am aware that it is I who am living in You, O incomprehensible God! I am aware that I am dissolving in You like a drop in an ocean. I am aware that You are within me and all about me, that You are in all things that surround me, in all that happens to me.

—St. Faustina, *Diary*, 318, 451, 472, 478

IN GOD'S PRESENCE, CONSIDER . . .

Do I realize that the Eucharist is an invitation for me to become a dwelling place for the Trinity? Do I tend to receive as a habitual act, going through the motions and saying a few prayers, or do I consciously enter into a relationship and meaningful encounter with each of the persons in God?

CLOSING PRAYER

Most Holy Trinity, Father, Son, and Holy Spirit, help me make my heart a better dwelling place for You. Help me to recognize and welcome Your Presence within me.

What Is Impossible with Men, is Possible with God

Even when things are hard for us because we are weak and fearful, Jesus continues to have mercy on us. Looking upon us, He loves us, wanting to fill us with reassurance, peace, strength . . . but it has to be received. He has mercy on any who have the courage and love to leave homes and families and earthly treasure, promising He will give us so much more than anything we give up for the kingdom.

And as he was setting out on his journey, a man ran up and knelt before him, and asked him, "Good Teacher, what must I do to inherit eternal life?" And Jesus said to him, "Why do you call me good? No one is good but God alone. You know the commandments: 'Do not kill, Do not commit adultery, Do not steal, Do not bear false witness, Do not defraud, Honor your father and mother.'" And he said to him, "Teacher, all these I have observed from my youth." And Jesus looking upon him loved him, and said to him, "You lack one thing; go, sell what you have, and give to the poor, and you will have treasure in heaven; and come, follow me." At that saying his countenance fell, and he went away sorrowful; for he had great possessions.

And Jesus looked around and said to his disciples, "How hard it will be for those who have riches to enter the kingdom of God!" And the disciples were amazed at his words. But Jesus said to them again, "Children, how hard it is for those who trust in riches to enter the kingdom of God! It is easier for a camel to go through the eye of a needle than for a rich man to enter the kingdom of God." And they were exceedingly astonished, and said to him, "Then who can be saved?" Jesus looked at them and said, "With men it is impossible, but not with God; for all things are possible with God." Peter began to say to him, "Lo, we have left everything and followed you." Jesus said, "Truly, I say to you, there is no one who has left house or brothers or sisters or mother or father or children or lands, for my sake and for the gospel, who will not receive a hundredfold now in this time, houses and brothers and sisters and mothers and children and lands, with persecutions, and in the age to come eternal life.

—Mark 10:17–30

IN GOD'S PRESENCE, CONSIDER . . .

Do I trust Him? Jesus's look of love is not just Him feeling love for me. It is active and creative, and it has the power to transform. Will I allow His gaze of mercy to change me, or will I walk away disheartened and unwilling?

CLOSING PRAYER

Lord Jesus, one thing I still lack: Your love flooding into my heart, filling my being. I know that there are things in me still untouched, still hesitant. Your relentless love never ceases: open my heart to receive it fully and to follow You with courage.

The Yoke of Mercy . . .

Doctor of the Church St. Augustine provides extraordinary freedom by revealing that the humility of mercy releases us from defending ourselves, proving ourselves with lofty thoughts. We can be little in Christ's gentleness.

To this is added another form of temptation more manifoldly dangerous. For besides that concupiscence of the flesh which consists in the delight of all senses and pleasures, wherein its slaves, who go far from You, waste and perish, the soul has, through the same senses of the body, a certain vain and curious desire, veiled under the title of knowledge and learning, . . . it is in Divine language called The lust of the eyes. . . . since so many things of this kind buzz on all sides about our daily life . . . dare I say that nothing of this sort engages my attention, or causes in me an idle interest? . . . in how many most petty and contemptible things is our curiosity daily tempted, and how often we give way, who can recount? How often do we begin as if we were tolerating people telling vain stories, lest we offend the weak; then by degrees we take interest therein! . . . And of such things is my life full; and my one hope is Your wonderful great mercy. For when our heart becomes the receptacle of such things . . . then our prayers are also often interrupted and distracted, and while in Your presence we direct the voice of our heart to Your ears, this so great concern is broken off by the rushing in of I know not what idle thoughts. . . .

And You know how far You have already changed me, who first healed me of the lust of vindicating myself, that so You might forgive all the rest of my iniquities, and heal all my infirmities, and redeem life from corruption, and crown me with mercy and pity, and satisfy my desire with good things: You who curbed my pride with Your fear, and tame my neck to Your yoke. And now I bear it and it is light unto me, because so You have promised, and have made it; and verily so it was, and I knew it not, when I feared to take it.

—*The Confessions of Saint Augustine*

IN GOD'S PRESENCE, CONSIDER . . .

How do I subtly inflate myself by thinking big thoughts, pious thoughts, ambitious thoughts, when God wants my littleness? Am I willing to relinquish everything to meet the humble Savior?

CLOSING PRAYER

Glorious Lord of the Heavens, you stun me by Your littleness. The Living God, the Lion of Judah, has become the gentle lamb of sacrifice. Unite me with Your full Presence, found in the smallest Host.

Begin from Zero . . .

Fr. Jacques Philippe offers what may seem like a radical practice of beginning again from zero despite the past. We are often so used to getting bogged down with "if onlys" and dwelling on how much time we've wasted on our journey to holiness, that this concept seems almost too good to be true. But God desires us to simply believe in the power of His mercy and move forward with total trust.

Sometimes we feel we've wasted much time and missed all too many opportunities to love and grow. If the feeling leads to real repentance and to starting again courageously and trustingly, then it is something positive. But if the sense of time wasted gets us down and makes us feel we have ruined our lives, we must reject it. To lock ourselves in the past would only add another sin to those already committed. It would be a serious lack of trust in the infinite mercy and power of God, who loves us and wants always to offer us a new chance to become holy, despite the past. When the thought of how little progress we've made threatens to overwhelm us, we must make an act of faith and hope, such as: "Thank you, my God, for all my past. I firmly believe that you can draw good out of everything I have lived through. I want to have no regrets, and I resolve today to begin from zero, with exactly the same trust as if all my past history were made up of nothing but faithfulness and holiness." Nothing could please God more than that!

—Fr. Jacques Philippe, *Interior Freedom*

IN GOD'S PRESENCE, CONSIDER . . .

How often do I find myself ruminating on the past, or getting discouraged or down on myself for time I've wasted, or opportunities I've missed to love better? What would it be like to live in the freedom of mercy, always striving for holiness, but never becoming discouraged or despondent about my littleness or failures?

CLOSING PRAYER

"Thank you, my God, for all my past. I firmly believe that you can draw good out of everything I have lived through." I choose to trust in Your infinite mercy and to always courageously begin again.

Overflowing Grace

Paul the Apostle writes to Timothy, whom he established as bishop. Here St. Paul shows that mercy easily overcomes all sin. We can receive mercy today to experience Divine Life now.

I thank him who has given me strength for this, Christ Jesus our Lord, because he judged me faithful by appointing me to his service, though I formerly blasphemed and persecuted and insulted him; but I received mercy because I had acted ignorantly in unbelief, and the grace of our Lord overflowed for me with the faith and love that are in Christ Jesus. The saying is sure and worthy of full acceptance, that Christ Jesus came into the world to save sinners. And I am the foremost of sinners; but I received mercy for this reason, that in me, as the foremost, Jesus Christ might display his perfect patience for an example to those who were to believe in him for eternal life. To the King of ages, immortal, invisible, the only God, be honor and glory for ever and ever. Amen.

—1 Timothy 1:12–17

IN GOD'S PRESENCE, CONSIDER . . .

What are the sins that I reserve to myself, deciding that they cannot be entrusted to Jesus? Where have my failures eclipsed the light of mercy? Can I acknowledge today that God's mercy is greater than my weakness?

CLOSING PRAYER

Sovereign God, Your faithfulness endures through all ages, and You have created me at this moment in history to share in Your redeeming work. I glorify You for Your power, which overcomes my weakness.

A Face Streaming with Tears

Pope Francis reflects on the purest form of weeping—the weeping of a loving heart that has been moved to tears of repentance (see CCC, *1429).*

Blessed are those who mourn, for they shall be comforted. . . . In the Scriptures, this weeping, can have two aspects: the first is for the death or suffering of someone. The other aspect is the tears for the sin—for one's own sin—when the heart bleeds for the suffering of having offended God and neighbor. . . . This is crying for not having loved, that springs from caring about the life of others. Here one cries because one does not match the Lord who loves us so much, and the thought of the good not done makes one sad. . . . These people say: "*I have hurt the one I love*" and this causes them to suffer to the point of tears. May God be blessed if these tears arrive! . . .

Let us think about the weeping of Saint Peter which takes him to a new and much truer love. It is weeping that purifies, renews. Peter looked at Jesus and cried: his heart had been renewed. . . .

One of the first monks, Ephrem the Syrian said that a face streaming with tears is indescribably beautiful (cf. *Sermo Asceticus*). The beauty of repentance, the beauty of weeping, the beauty of contrition! As always, Christian life has its best expression in mercy. . . . God always forgives. Let us not forget this. God always forgives, even the worst of sins, always. . . .

If we always remember that God "does not deal with us according to our sins, nor requite us according to our iniquities" (Ps 103[102]:10), we will live in mercy and compassion, and love will appear within us. May the Lord grant us to love abundantly, to love with a smile, with closeness, with service, and also with tears.

—Pope Francis, General Audience, February, 12, 2020

IN GOD'S PRESENCE, CONSIDER . . .

I will remember the beauty of repentance. I will welcome these tears, this suffering that is bound to love. I will focus on His goodness and my desire to change. And I will receive the tenderness of God, which will comfort, forgive, and correct with gentleness.

CLOSING PRAYER

Lord, let me weep for the ways I have sinned against You and my neighbor. Move my heart with true repentance. I want to feel the full weight of my faults, without falling into self-condemnation, fixing my eyes on You and the promise of Your mercy. You always forgive. Thank You.

Dirty Faces

Commenting on a passage from Venerable Bruno Lanteri, Fr. Gallagher exhorts us to have an "invincible hope in divine mercy."

As you work, do your hands or face grow dirty? You are not surprised, and you do not lose peace. You simply wash them and go on with the day. "Have the patience to do the same in the things of the soul." God's Providence is at work in this cycle of resolution, constancy mixed with inconstancy, and peaceful, patient renewal. Each time you do renew your resolution, he infuses all the more grace in your soul. . . .

Remember that we do not acquire holiness in twenty-four hours nor without continual defects and failings. The awareness that we will commit many failings, very many, greatly helps us toward holiness because it roots us in self-knowledge and in humility, and this is one of the foundations of our sanctification, the other being an invincible hope in divine mercy. Be attentive, then, not to allow yourself to be discouraged by any defect, and be always ready to begin at every moment.

"Remember that we do not acquire holiness in twenty-four hours." Do not put this burden on yourself, and do not let the enemy put it on you. He will try to discourage you, saying: "Look at you. Look at the years of your spiritual life and how far from holiness you are. What is wrong with you? Who are you to think that you will ever become holy?" . . . As St. John of the Cross says, "On this road we must always keep walking if we are to arrive" (*Ascent of Mount Carmel*, I, 11, 6). Two things will help us to keep walking: humble self-knowledge and "an invincible hope in divine mercy." Invincible. This hope in God's ever-present and ever-loving mercy warms, encourages, and infuses energy for the journey. "Be attentive, then, not to allow yourself to be discouraged by any defect, and be always ready to begin."

—Timothy M. Gallagher, *Overcoming Spiritual Discouragement: The Wisdom and Spiritual Power of Venerable Bruno Lanteri*

IN GOD'S PRESENCE, CONSIDER . . .

In what areas of my life do I most often hear the voice of the enemy trying to discourage me with how far I am from holiness? I reject that voice of the accuser, remain aware in humility that I will fail many times on this journey, and continue to get up and walk forward with hope in God's invincible mercy.

CLOSING PRAYER

Father of mercy, You are the true and faithful Father, unbothered by my dirty hands and face as I journey with You. May I never be surprised or discouraged by my faults, but simply begin again with gratitude and trust in Your mercy.

Cling to God

It's often the times of greatest difficulty that God uses to bring us to a deeper awareness and experience of His mercy.

. . . It's only by coming to know how much my God loves me, as I am, with all my faults and shortcomings, that I can come to see reality properly—most particularly, the reality of my life properly. As Pope St. John Paul II says, "We are not the sum of our weaknesses and failures; we are the sum of our Father's love for us and our real capacity to become the image of his Son" (Homily, July 28, 2002). . . .

God often uses moments when we are broken down and stripped of all that we think supports us to bring us to a deeper experience of his love. Even many of us Christians go through life relying on our talent, hard work, popularity, success, looks, or ability to keep others pleased to give us the sense that our lives have meaning. We might know in our heads that there's more to life than all this, but we still turn to these supports as the foundation for our happiness. But when all is taken away—when we experience broken relationships, health problems, job problems, marriage problems, being overwhelmed by the demands of raising children, or other sufferings—and none of our normal supports are working, the only thing left to cling to is God. It's then that we come to know God's love as more than an abstract theory. We experience his love personally supporting us, holding us together, and helping us through.

—Edward Sri, *Into His Likeness*

IN GOD'S PRESENCE, CONSIDER . . .

What things do I tend to rely on in my day-to-day life more than on God? What situations in my life right now can I turn over more completely to Him, trusting in His support?

CLOSING PRAYER

Lord, help me to see the "problems" of my life as an invitation to cling to You more completely and trust more fully in Your Fatherly love.

He Sees You; Abide with Him

The predominance of action verbs in this passage from Sirach—verbs like "come forward, serve, prepare, cleave, accept, trust, hope, persevere, call upon"—provide us with a clear roadmap for how to receive the Lord's mercy.

My son, if you come forward to serve the Lord,
prepare yourself for temptation.
Set your heart right and be steadfast,
and do not be hasty in time of calamity.
Cleave to him and do not depart,
that you may be honored at the end of your life.
Accept whatever is brought upon you,
and in changes that humble you be patient.
For gold is tested in the fire,
and acceptable men in the furnace of humiliation.
Trust in him, and he will help you;
make your ways straight, and hope in him.
You who fear the Lord, wait for his mercy;
and turn not aside, lest you fall.
You who fear the Lord, trust in him,
and your reward will not fail;
you who fear the Lord, hope for good things,
for everlasting joy and mercy.
Consider the ancient generations and see:
who ever trusted in the Lord and was put to shame?
Or who ever persevered in the fear of the Lord and was forsaken?
Or who ever called upon him and was overlooked?
For the Lord is compassionate and merciful;
he forgives sins and saves in time of affliction.

—Sirach 2:1–11

IN GOD'S PRESENCE, CONSIDER . . .

So much of the unknown in serving the Lord, so much surrender—and yet so much promise, so much goodness. He is merciful and trustworthy.

CLOSING PRAYER

Heavenly Father, today I affirm that I am ready to serve You. I surrender my demands and insistence and resolve to receive every blessing and hardship from Your gentle hand with complete trust in You.

The Father's Plan of Mercy

Think about your life, your family, your work, your desires, your goals—all the things you worry about, fret about, dream about each day. According to St. Pope John Paul II, none of that will turn out to be important or necessary unless it relates to three things.

When he was a young man, Pope John Paul II wrote a poetic essay entitled "Reflections on Fatherhood," in which he expressed a central reality. . . . "Everything else," he wrote, "will turn out to be unimportant and inessential except for this: *Father, Child, Love.*" . . .

In one sense, of course, we can interpret the Pope's words as referring to the Trinity. . . . As the Pope explained . . . "God in his deepest mystery is not a solitude, but a *family*, since he has in himself *fatherhood, sonship*, and the essence of family, which is *love*." The Trinity is not just an idea, not just a theological concept. It's three *real* Persons in a Divine *Family* of love, and the Father's plan can only be understood in light of this Family. . . .

The *Catechism of the Catholic Church* [#257] reveals that, before the world was created, God the Father had conceived a plan of mercy:

> Such is the "plan of his loving kindness," conceived by the Father before the foundation of the world in his beloved Son. "He destined us in love to be his sons" and "to be conformed to the image of his Son" through "the Spirit of Sonship" (Eph 1:4–5, 9; Rom 8:15, 29).

So *Father, Child, Love* isn't just about the Trinity. It's about the Trinity *and us*! Before the creation of the world, God the *Father*, in His *Love*, planned for you and me to become His *children*—not just creatures, but *children*. St. John speaks with awe about this reality: "See what love the Father has given us that we should be called children of God; and so we are" (1 Jn 3:1).

—Vinny Flynn, *7 Secrets of Divine Mercy*

IN GOD'S PRESENCE, CONSIDER . . .

So much to think about here. How much could my life change if I could fully recognize the Trinity as a *Family* of Divine Persons—fully realize that I'm not just a *creation*, but a *child*, loved by the Father and invited to be embraced into that Family?

CLOSING PRAYER

Eternal God, thank you for Your plan of mercy, for Your loving plan for me, for "birthing" me into life as one of Your children. Help me to respond to You always with love and joy.

No Longer a Stranger . . .

St. Paul stunned the early Church, and he can stun us today, with his insistence that we no longer do things alone, but everything in Christ Jesus. Through Christ we are truly brought into a union of belonging and made members of a family. The Catechism *speaks of the entire plan of salvation as "one vast divine blessing" (1079), and so we can read each line of God's action below as a great gift of the Father's mercy.*

Remember that you were at that time separated from Christ, alienated from the commonwealth of Israel, and strangers to the covenants of promise, having no hope and without God in the world. But now in Christ Jesus you who once were far off have been brought near in the blood of Christ. . . . And he came and preached peace to you who were far off and peace to those who were near; for through him we both have access in one Spirit to the Father. So then you are no longer strangers and sojourners, but you are fellow citizens with the saints and members of the household of God, built upon the foundation of the apostles and prophets, Christ Jesus himself being the cornerstone, in whom the whole structure is joined together and grows into a holy temple in the Lord; in whom you also are built into it for a dwelling place of God in the Spirit.

—Ephesians 2:12–22

IN GOD'S PRESENCE, CONSIDER . . .

Can I accept an invitation from Jesus to join him—and the saints—in living in the fullness of God today? Am I ready to cease being a stranger and discover my true identity and place in God's plan?

CLOSING PRAYER

Lord Jesus Christ, You startle us with the discovery that You have come for us; You seek out Your lost sheep, and You draw us into Your fold. Let me never live in this world as one without God or without hope.

The Priestly Prayer of Mercy Incarnate

Hans Urs von Balthasar recognizes that Divine Mercy draws us up into the very mystery of the life of the Holy Trinity. To be loved by God is to enter the eternal outpouring of Father, Son and Spirit.

Father, the hour is here. Glorify your Son that your Son may glorify you! Let me descend into death and let my veins gush forth. Allow my Heart to grow wide, great as the world's bounds, by dying a death that is greater than life. Allow me to manifest in gestures of earthly suffering the glory of our love, a glory which you bestowed on me in the beginning, before the world came to be . . . Do not refuse me this request . . . so that you too may be glorified through me in these, my members and branches. For henceforth we—they and I—are one . . . I cover them like a hen protects her chicks. I take their place. . . . I forge the arrow of your justice into the scepter of your mercy. For, O my Father! . . . It is not I who am the lover: it is you, and all that is mine is yours. And so look: even your enemies here, my friends, are yours . . . I take them into my hand like the celebrant takes his paten and I raise them up to you. . . . They are yours; you have entrusted them to me and they have kept your Word. . . . And when I now go and sacrifice myself for them, to whom should I entrust them if not to you, Father, as my precious inheritance. . . . They are yours: protect them from the Evil One . . . that as rays of light, they may shed light as they go down into the darkness and, as they themselves are consumed, they may brighten the darkness. . . . Partaking in my mission from you . . . they will realize their unity with me and realize my unity with you. . . . For you, Father, are now going to let go of me. And before I no longer know it because of the night which will soon overtake me, I want to tell you this for the last time: in this night I recognize your highest love, and do not wish it to be otherwise (your will be done!).

—Hans Urs von Balthasar, *Heart of the World*

IN GOD'S PRESENCE, CONSIDER . . .

Jesus paid such a price of love for me. In my aspirations, do I still remain earthbound? Do I recognize that the infinite Father wants to raise me to the mystery of Triune love?

CLOSING PRAYER

Most Holy Trinity, Father, Son, and Holy Spirit, reveal Your love to me. Allow me to discover more deeply what you hold in store for me in heaven. Help me to never take Your sacrifice of love for granted and may my life never cease to glorify You.

The Hour Has Come

It all comes down to this: The consummate act of God's mercy is laid out in full in the striking High Priestly Prayer of Jesus at the Last Supper—and with it, the Divine purpose and intention, the kenosis of God, the battle for our hearts, and the outpouring of love.

After Jesus had spoken these words, he looked up to heaven and said, "Father, the hour has come; glorify your Son so that the Son may glorify you, . . . "I have made your name known to those whom you gave me from the world. They were yours, and you gave them to me, and they have kept your word. . . . But now I am coming to you, and I speak these things in the world so that they may have my joy made complete in themselves. I have given them your word, and the world has hated them because they do not belong to the world, just as I do not belong to the world. I am not asking you to take them out of the world, but I ask you to protect them from the evil one. . . . Sanctify them in the truth; your word is truth. As you have sent me into the world, so I have sent them into the world. And for their sakes I sanctify myself, so that they also may be sanctified in truth.

"I ask not only on behalf of these, but also on behalf of those who will believe in me through their word, . . . The glory that you have given me I have given them, so that they may be one, as we are one, I in them and you in me, that they may become completely one, so that the world may know that you have sent me and have loved them even as you have loved me. Father, I desire that those also, whom you have given me, may be with me where I am, to see my glory, which you have given me because you loved me before the foundation of the world.

"Righteous Father, the world does not know you, but I know you; and these know that you have sent me. I made your name known to them, and I will make it known, so that the love with which you have loved me may be in them, and I in them."

—John 17:1, 6, 13–15, 17–20, 22–26 (NRSVCE)

IN GOD'S PRESENCE, CONSIDER . . .

So much richness, so much love contained in mere paragraphs. The Divine intention for the world, for my life; the evoked awe that God would become one of His creatures, would suffer; that He desires joy for me, union with me, love from me. How will I respond?

CLOSING PRAYER

Father of mercy, sanctify me in the truth. I consecrate my life to You. Send me. And let me move and act only in union with You.

Invincible as a Lion in Battle

One of the greatest spiritual warriors of our era, Padre Pio, identifies where our power and weaponry come from: prayer immersing us in God's mercy.

But look! Jesus raises Himself from the ground, strong, invincible as a lion in battle; behold now that Jesus . . . shakes the disarray from His noble head, wipes the Bloody Sweat from His face, and resolutely goes towards the entrance of the Garden. Where art Thou going, Jesus? Art Thou not that Jesus I saw languishing in Thy soul, a prey to terror, fatigue, fear, discouragement, desolation? Whom I saw trembling, crushed under the immense weight of the evils which were about to overcome Thee? Where art Thou going now so ready, so resolute, so full of courage? To whom art Thou exposing Thyself? Oh! I hear it! The weapon of prayer has helped Me conquer, and the spirit has subjected the weakness of nature to itself. In prayer have I obtained strength and now I can face everything. Follow My example and deal with Heaven with the same confidence as I have done.

Jesus approaches the three Apostles. They are still sleeping. Strong emotion, the late hour of the night, that presentiment of something awful—irreparable—which seemed to be approaching, and fatigue, had put them to sleep, such a sleep that weighs down upon one and seems impossible to shake off, and trying to shake it off, one falls into it again without knowing how. Jesus has pity on them saying: "The spirit is willing but the flesh is weak."

Jesus beholds everything with His all-seeing glance. He seems to say: You who are My friends and disciples sleep, but My enemies are awake and are about to seize Me. . . . But be calm, I clothed Myself with weakness and I have prayed for you. . . . I will be your strength. . . . Rise, let us go, there is no more time to sleep, the enemy is at the gate; . . . My hour has come; the hour of great mercy for humanity. And, in fact, there is heard the sound of steps, a reddish light of torches penetrates the Garden and Jesus, followed by the three disciples, advances, intrepid and calm.

—St. Padre Pio, "The Agony of Jesus"

IN GOD'S PRESENCE, CONSIDER . . .

Today God the Son reveals where His power comes from: deep communion with His Father. Through prayer, I also can enter into that calm and peace, intrepid with my Savior.

CLOSING PRAYER

Lord Jesus Christ, Son of the Living God, have mercy on me, a sinner; Help me to rise from sleep and enter into prayer with You.

Radical Revelation of Mercy

Saint Pope John Paul II explains that the cross doesn't just remind us of Christ's suffering and death. It is above all a revelation of the Father and His plan of mercy for all.

The *cross* on Calvary, the cross upon which Christ conducts His final dialogue with the Father, *emerges from the very heart of the love* that man, created in the image and likeness of God, has been given as a gift, according to God's eternal plan. God, as Christ has revealed Him, does not merely remain closely linked with the world as the Creator and the ultimate source of existence. He is also Father: He is linked to man, whom He called to existence in the visible world, by a bond still more intimate than that of creation. It is love which not only creates the good but also grants participation in the very life of God: Father, Son and Holy Spirit. For he who loves desires to give himself. . . .

The cross . . . *speaks and never ceases to speak* of God the Father, who is absolutely faithful to His eternal love for man, since He "so loved the world"—therefore man in the world—that "he gave his only Son, that whoever believes in him should not perish but have eternal life" (Jn 3:16).

Believing in the crucified Son means "seeing the Father" (Cf Jn 14:9), means believing that love is present in the world and that this love is more powerful than any kind of evil in which individuals, humanity, or the world are involved. Believing in this love means *believing in mercy*. For mercy is an indispensable dimension of love; it is as it were love's second name. . . .

The cross of Christ, on which the Son, consubstantial with the Father, *renders full justice to God*, is also a *radical revelation of mercy*, . . . of the love that goes against what constitutes the very root of evil in the history of man: against sin and death.

—St. Pope John Paul II, *Rich in Mercy*, 7–8

IN GOD'S PRESENCE, CONSIDER . . .

When I look at the cross, do I see the Father and his love? Do I see and believe in the power of mercy over evil?

CLOSING PRAYER

Thank you, Father, for your faithful love. Help me to believe—and live—in the mystery of mercy you reveal through the cross.

According to Thy Steadfast Love

Trusting that God's mercy is greater than even his terrible sins of adultery and murder, King David acknowledges his sin, sincerely repents, and calls upon the Lord for forgiveness.

Have mercy on me, O God,
according to your steadfast love;
according to your abundant mercy
blot out my transgressions.
Wash me thoroughly from my iniquity,
and cleanse me from my sin.

For I know my transgressions,
and my sin is ever before me.
Against you, you alone, have I sinned,
and done what is evil in your sight,
so that you are justified in your sentence
and blameless when you pass judgment.
Indeed, I was born guilty,
a sinner when my mother conceived me.

You desire truth in the inward being;
therefore teach me wisdom in my secret heart.
Purge me with hyssop, and I shall be clean;
wash me, and I shall be whiter than snow.
Let me hear joy and gladness;
let the bones that you have crushed rejoice.
Hide your face from my sins,
and blot out all my iniquities.

Create in me a clean heart, O God,
and put a new and right spirit within me.
Do not cast me away from your presence,
and do not take your holy spirit from me.
Restore to me the joy of your salvation,
and sustain in me a willing spirit.

Then I will teach transgressors your ways,
and sinners will return to you.

—Psalm 51:1–13 (NRSVCE)

IN GOD'S PRESENCE, CONSIDER . . .

I have a savior who pours forth His blood for my salvation. Jesus says to us: "This is my blood, poured out for the forgiveness of sins." I bring my sins to Jesus, and He gives His joy to me.

CLOSING PRAYER

Jesus, Lamb that was slain, thank you for Your blood; for Your joy; for our restoration. As the High Priest sprinkled the blood of the lamb on the people with hyssop, purify my life through the blood and water which gushed forth from Your Heart.

The Hour of Mercy

In His revelations to St. Faustina, Christ made it clear that, every afternoon, when we hear the clock strike three, He wants us, at the very least, to pause in the midst of our day and focus on His Passion and Death.

Good Friday. At three o'clock, I saw the Lord Jesus, crucified, who looked at me and said, I thirst. Then I saw two rays issue from His side, just as they appear in the image. I then felt in my soul the desire to save souls and to empty myself for the sake of poor sinners. I offered myself, together with the dying Jesus, to the Eternal Father, for the salvation of the whole world (648). . . .

At three o'clock, implore My mercy, especially for sinners; and, if only for a brief moment, immerse yourself in My Passion, particularly in My abandonment at the moment of agony. This is the hour of great mercy for the whole world. I will allow you to enter into My mortal sorrow. In this hour, I will refuse nothing to the soul that makes a request of Me in virtue of My Passion (1320). . . .

As often as you hear the clock strike the third hour, immerse yourself completely in My mercy, adoring and glorifying it; invoke its omnipotence for the whole world, and particularly for poor sinners; for at that moment mercy was opened wide for every soul. In this hour you can obtain everything for yourself and for others for the asking; it was the hour of grace for the whole world—mercy triumphed over justice. . . . Try your best to make the Stations of the Cross in this hour, provided that your duties permit it; and if you are not able to make the Stations of the Cross, then at least step into the chapel for a moment and adore, in the Blessed Sacrament, My Heart, which is full of mercy; and should you be unable to step into the chapel, immerse yourself in prayer there where you happen to be, if only for a very brief instant (1572).

—St. Faustina, *Diary*, 648, 1320, 1572

IN GOD'S PRESENCE, CONSIDER . . .

What can I resolve to do to develop a "3 o'clock habit" of prayer every day, pausing for at least a "brief instant" to reflect on Christ's Passion and implore His mercy for myself and the whole world?

CLOSING PRAYER

Lord Jesus, help me to break out of my self-focus and make the Hour of Mercy a sacred part of my day.

The Descent

When we pray in the Apostles Creed that Jesus "descended into hell," this should not be confused with today's usage of the word as the "abode of the damned." Rather it refers to Christ's merciful visit to the "abode of the dead" to free the just who have been awaiting the redeemer (cf CCC, *635).*

Something strange is happening—there is a great silence on earth today, a great silence and stillness. The whole earth keeps silence because the King is asleep. The earth trembled and is still because God has fallen asleep in the flesh and he has raised up all who have slept ever since the world began. God has died in the flesh and Hell trembles with fear. He has gone to search for our first parent, as for a lost sheep. Greatly desiring to visit those who live in darkness and in the shadow of death, he has gone to free from sorrow the captives Adam and Eve, He who is both God and the Son of Eve.

The Lord approached them bearing the Cross, the weapon that had won him the victory. At the sight of him Adam, the first man he had created, struck his breast in terror and cried out to everyone, 'My Lord be with you all.' Christ answered him: 'And with your spirit.' He took him by the hand and raised him up, saying: 'Awake, O sleeper, and rise from the dead, and Christ will give you light.'

I am your God, who for your sake have become your son. Out of love for you and your descendants I now by my own authority command all who are held in bondage to come forth, all who are in darkness to be enlightened, all who are sleeping to arise. I order you, O sleeper, to awake. I did not create you to be held a prisoner in Hell. Rise from the dead, for I am the life of the dead. Rise up, work of my hands, you who were created in my image. Rise, let us leave this place, for you are in me and I in you; together we form one person and cannot be separated. . . .

—Ancient Homily for Holy Saturday
Liturgy of the Hours, 496–497

IN GOD'S PRESENCE, CONSIDER . . .

In what ways am I in bondage, a prisoner of my own sins, cravings, desires, habits? Into what areas of my life do I need the Risen Christ to come and free me?

CLOSING PRAYER

Lord, just as You descended to the abode of the dead to raise up those who were awaiting redemption, so descend into the dark regions of my heart, and in Your mercy raise me up from the death of sin.

The Resurrected Wound, Gate of Life and Mercy

Swiss theologian, priest, and author Hans Urs von Balthasar blends aesthetics and literature with theology. Here he sees the new life of redemption springing from the outpouring of Divine Mercy.

A nameless thing, more solitary than God, it emerges out of pure emptiness. . . . It is a beginning without parallel, as if Life were arising from Death . . . The magic of Holy Saturday. . . . Could this be the residue of the Son's love which, poured out to the last when every vessel cracked and the old world perished . . . the first seed of the New Heaven and the New Earth? The spring leaps up even more plenteously. To be sure, it flows out of a wound and is like the blossom and fruit of a wound; like a tree it sprouts up from this wound. But the wound no longer causes pain. The suffering has been left far behind as the past origin and previous source of today's wellspring. What is poured out here is no longer a present suffering, but a suffering that has been concluded–no longer now a sacrificing love, but a love sacrificed. Only the wound is there: gaping, the great open gate, the chaos, the nothingness out of which the wellspring leaps forth. Never again will this gate be shut. Just as the first creation arose ever anew out of sheer nothingness, so, too, this second world – still unborn, still caught up in its first rising – will have its sole origin in this wound, which is never to close again. In the future, all shape must arise out of this gaping void, all wholeness must draw its strength from the creating wound. High-vaulted triumphal Gate of Life! Armored in gold, armies of graces stream out of you with fiery lances. Deep-dug Fountain of Life! Wave upon wave gushes out of you inexhaustible, ever-flowing, billows of water and blood baptizing the heathen hearts, comforting the yearning souls, rushing over the deserts of guilt, enriching overabundantly, overflowing every heart that receives it, far surpassing every desire.

—Hans Urs von Balthasar, *Heart of the World*, p.152, 153

IN GOD'S PRESENCE, CONSIDER . . .

Jesus approaches me with an open side, with a pierced heart. Can I meet his life-giving wound with my own wounds? Do I feign to be unwounded and uninjured before the One whose wounds heal the world?

CLOSING PRAYER

Lord Jesus Christ, Son of the Living God, You were pierced that I may be made whole. Open my heart to the healing love flowing from Your wounded side.

Hymn to the Mercy of God . . .

St. Catherine of Siena's great "hymn" speaks of the immutability and pervasiveness of God's mercy, from the act of creation to His descent into the realm of the dead.

O eternal Mercy, you who cover over your creatures' faults! It does not surprise me that you say of those who leave deadly sin behind and return to you: "I will not remember that you had ever offended me." O unspeakable mercy! I am not surprised that you speak so to those who forsake sin, when you say of those who persecute you: "I want you to pray to me for them so that I can be merciful to them." What mercy comes forth from your Godhead, eternal Father, to rule the whole world with your power!

By your mercy we were created. And by your mercy we were created anew in your Son's blood. It is your mercy that preserves us. Your mercy made your Son play death against life and life against death on the wood of the cross. In him life confounded the death that is our sin, even while that same death of sin robbed the spotless Lamb of his bodily life. But who was conquered? Death! And how? By your mercy!

Your mercy is life giving. It is the light in which both the upright and the sinners discover your goodness. Your mercy shines forth in your saints in the height of heaven. And if I turn to the earth, your mercy is everywhere. Even in the darkness of hell your mercy shines, for you do not punish the damned as much as they deserve.

—St. Catherine of Siena, *The Dialogue*, D 30, 71–72.

IN GOD'S PRESENCE, CONSIDER . . .

God's mercy reaches all places and all time. Where are the areas in my life where I need His mercy most? And where in me am I most hesitant to really allow His mercy to enter, places where I may feel unworthiness, shame, resistance?

CLOSING PRAYER

Father of Mercy, Father of Love, I praise You for your mercy, which never changes, and I ask now for the balm of that mercy to come into the places inside of me—and into the circumstances in my life—where I need it most.

In the Womb of Mary

Born of the Virgin, Jesus is our brother, giving himself the title "Son of Man." Here Dr. Stackpole shows how intimately close Divine Mercy is to us in the Son of the Maiden of Nazareth.

Saint Thomas points to the significance of the fact that when our Lord speaks of His Second Coming as judge of the world, He refers to Himself as the "Son of Man." There are several reasons for this: (1) if He came only in divine form to be our judge, He could not be seen except by the blessed; (2) it is fitting that Christ comes again to judge the world in the same form in which He was judged and condemned by Pontius Pilate; (3) it is in accord with the mercy of God that mankind will be given final judgment by a man. In this regard, St. Thomas refers to Hebrews 4:15: "We have not a high priest who is unable to sympathize with our weaknesses." In other words, as it is in His human form that the Son of God ascends to the Father, so it is in the same compassionate human nature, both affectively and effectively merciful, that He comes again to judge the living and the dead.

Preaching on the Feast of the Purification of Mary, St. Thomas quotes a text from the letter to the Hebrews: "Let us therefore go with confidence to the temple of grace, that we may find mercy at the opportune time" (Heb. 4:16). St. Thomas applies this text to Mary and sees her womb as the temple of grace. In other words, by bringing the merciful Christ into the world, Mary shows mercy to us, her fellow creatures, a mercy that is feminine and motherly. For example, in the Summa Theologiae, St. Thomas writes: "At the Annunciation the Virgin's consent was besought in lieu of that of the entire human race" (ST II.30.1). Again, the thought here is that by her "fiat," by her consent in faith and love to the divine plan of the Incarnation, "Mary gave the Son of God in his human nature to the world, and so made possible the supreme revelation of God's mercy" (Saward, p. 94).

—Dr. Robert Stackpole, *Divine Mercy: A Guide from Genesis to Benedict XVI*

IN GOD'S PRESENCE, CONSIDER . . .

Mary gave her consent on my behalf, and in bringing Jesus into the world, made possible the supreme revelation of God's mercy. Her womb truly is a temple of grace, and she shows a mercy to me that is motherly. I reflect on this temple of grace: the outpouring of mercy, the safety, the quiet, the nurturing space of motherly attunement.

CLOSING PRAYER

Queen of Heaven, Radiant Mother, your tenderness allows my heart to soften. Let me rest in your motherly care.

With All Our Hearts

Azariah prays from the hell-like furnace, but the flames do not consume him, revealing we can trust the Redeemer in every trial.

For thy name's sake do not give us up utterly,
  and do not break thy covenant,
  and do not withdraw thy mercy from us,
for the sake of Abraham thy beloved
  and for the sake of Isaac thy servant
  and Israel thy holy one.
Yet with a contrite heart and a humble spirit may we be accepted,
  as though it were with burnt offerings of rams and bulls,
  and with tens of thousands of fat lambs;
  such may our sacrifice be in thy sight this day,
  and may we wholly follow thee,
  for there will be no shame for those who trust in thee.
And now with all our heart we follow thee,
  we fear thee and seek thy face. Do not put us to shame,
  but deal with us in thy forbearance
  and in thy abundant mercy.
Deliver us in accordance with thy marvelous works,
  and give glory to thy name, O Lord!
Let all who do harm to thy servants be put to shame;
let them be disgraced and deprived of all power and dominion,
  and let their strength be broken.
Let them know that thou art the Lord, the only God,
  glorious over the whole world.

—Daniel 3:11–12, 16–22

IN GOD'S PRESENCE, CONSIDER . . .

Do I recognize the presence of the angel of the Lord with me when I am struggling? Can I perceive that the Father's work in my life is not for my shame but for my glory? In this life, as I am struck down, each descent is for far greater ascent into the light of Divine Mercy.

CLOSING PRAYER

Lord Jesus Christ, You who are Divine Mercy, light shining into my darkness, never allow me to take my eyes from You. Keep my vision fixed on Your radiance, as I physically and spiritually experience the blows this life deals out—a sharing in Your death, which draws me into Your resurrection.

A Personal Encounter with the Risen One

Any repeated act or ritual can become simply a habit or duty. Fr. Raniero Cantalamessa, emphasizes that, for both confessor and penitent, the Sacrament of Reconciliation should be continually "renewed in the spirit" as a personal encounter with Christ.

Confession is the moment when the believer's dignity is affirmed most clearly, because . . . in confession he or she is unique. At that moment the Church exists only for him or her.

This way of freeing oneself from sin by confessing it to God through his minister corresponds to the natural need of the human psyche to be free from what oppresses the conscience, by manifesting it, bringing it out into the light, and expressing it verbally.

. . . [However,] if we want this sacrament to be really effective in the struggle against sin, the way it is administered and received must be renewed in the Spirit. To renew the sacrament in the Spirit, means not to live confession as a rite, a habit or a canonical obligation, but as a personal encounter with the Risen One who allows us, as he did Thomas, to touch his wounds, to feel in ourselves the healing force of his blood and taste the joy of being saved, . . . to experience in ourselves what the Church sings in the Exultet in the Easter Vigil: "O happy fault that merited such a Redeemer!" . . .

Jesus knows how to make all human faults, once acknowledged, "happy faults," faults that are no longer remembered save by the experience of divine mercy and tenderness that they have occasioned.

—Fr. Raniero Cantalamessa, *Lenten Meditation to the Papal Household*, April 2, 2004

IN GOD'S PRESENCE, CONSIDER . . .

Has confession become a "Catholic routine" for me, an obligatory habit; or do I go to experience Christ in person, to be freed by His love and "taste the joy of being saved"?

CLOSING PRAYER

Lord, renew me in Your Spirit and let me really experience Your love and Your presence in the confessional.

Mercy and Joy

Jean C.J. D'Elbee shares the wisdom of St. Therese of Liseux's Little Way.

You must believe in mercy to the point of believing that you are a joy for Jesus. I return to this thought which I have already touched upon, for it is essential. The life of the Christian is a life of love. Can people love one another without knowing that they are a joy for each other?

Ask yourself, "How does Jesus see me?" He sees me as His child since my baptism. He sees me, since my confirmation, filled with the superabundance of the gifts of His Spirit, marked with the indelible character of a soldier of His kingdom. He sees married people bathed in the grace of the sacrament of marriage. And, looking at husband and wife, He thinks of His union with the Church. He sees me as His lamb which has so often let itself be led back to the fold in His arms, purified by absolution. He sees my soul transformed into Himself by Mass and Communion—my soul, where His Father and He have made their dwelling place because, "if anyone loves me he will keep my word, and my Father will love him, and we will come to him and will make our abode with him" (Jn. 14:28). These are the actual realities of sacramental graces!

How many causes of joy for Him there are in us!

What more does He see? All you have done for Him: your prayers, your good impulses, all the acts which, in the course of your life, have been determined by your faith, your hope, and your love; your acts of generosity, your acts of charity, especially which you have forgotten in part but which Jesus has not forgotten, because they are engraved in His Heart. On the day of judgment, with what happiness and what approval He will remind you of all that, in detail, for His own glory, since He is the author of all that is good, but for yours, also, because you will have believed in His love. "Come, you blessed of my Father" (Mt 25:34).

—Jean C.J. d'Elbee, *I Believe in Love*, pp. 96–97

IN GOD'S PRESENCE, CONSIDER . . .

How does Jesus see me? Do I believe that I am a joy for Jesus? It's a wondrous thing that just by being a child of God, receiving His grace, uniting myself to Him in Holy Communion, letting my heart be filled with love for others (all the things that bring me peace and fulfillment anyway!) I bring Him joy.

CLOSING PRAYER

Lord Jesus, I love You. Help me have the heart of a child and bask in Your delight. You are so good, and I am happy that I bring Your heart joy.

Mother of Mercy

Pope Francis encourages us to turn to Mary, whose whole life was centered on mercy.

My thoughts now turn to the Mother of Mercy. May the sweetness of her countenance watch over us . . . so that all of us may rediscover the joy of God's tenderness. No one has penetrated the profound mystery of the incarnation like Mary. Her entire life was patterned after the presence of mercy made flesh. The Mother of the Crucified and Risen One has entered the sanctuary of divine mercy because she participated intimately in the mystery of His love.

Chosen to be the Mother of the Son of God, Mary, from the outset, was prepared by the love of God to be the Ark of the Covenant between God and man. She treasured divine mercy in her heart in perfect harmony with her Son Jesus. Her hymn of praise, sung at the threshold of the home of Elizabeth, was dedicated to the mercy of God which extends from "generation to generation" (Lk 1:50). We too were included in those prophetic words of the Virgin Mary. This will be a source of comfort and strength to us as we cross the threshold of the Holy Year to experience the fruits of divine mercy.

At the foot of the Cross, Mary, together with John, the disciple of love, witnessed the words of forgiveness spoken by Jesus. This supreme expression of mercy towards those who crucified him show us the point to which the mercy of God can reach. Mary attests that the mercy of the Son of God knows no bounds and extends to everyone, without exception. Let us address her in the words of the Salve Regina, a prayer ever ancient and ever new, so that she may never tire of turning her merciful eyes upon us, and make us worthy to contemplate the face of mercy, her Son Jesus.

—Pope Francis, *Misericordiae Vultus (The Face of Mercy)*, 24

IN GOD'S PRESENCE, CONSIDER . . .

In her unique relationship with Jesus, how much Mary must have experienced and understood. There's so much she has to share with us, her spiritual children. How can I draw closer to her and learn from her?

CLOSING PRAYER

Mary, Mother of Jesus, thank you for being my mother, too. Help me to more deeply experience and rejoice in the tenderness of God and be able to pass that tenderness on to others.

Beautiful Paradox

A prayer poem meditating on the paradox of Mary's role in the order of salvation. Our Mother of Mercy: Consecrated virgin, yet mother of all mothers; pondering and contemplative, yet an integral part of the most vibrant community of believers—and of our own lives as well, because God filled her with grace and then made her the vessel of grace flowing out to the world.

She is the Woman
of all women.

She is mother, who nurtured
and cared for her Son,
She is virgin, her entire being
dedicated to God,
She is hope of the future
for the broken.

She was the one who watched
her loved one suffer,
Who suffered herself
as her heart was pierced,
And who saw her child and Lord
killed before her eyes.

She was a housewife,
A contemplative,
Alone, as one set apart.
She was immersed
in a strong community,
She was immersed
in the garden of her thoughts,
Immersed in the heart of God,
pondering His mysteries.

She is the Grace-bearer,
And bearer of our burdens,
Tenderhearted towards our weakness,
Leading us to Christ.

She is Mary, the virtuous,
Comfort of the weary,
Refuge for the sinner,
Mother to the children of the vale.

—Erin Flynn

IN GOD'S PRESENCE, CONSIDER . . .

Mary is a model of true womanhood for me. Of all women, she was chosen to bear the Son of God, and in His mercy, He gave her to me as my mother too. Is there any barrier, any resistance I have to a close relationship with her?

CLOSING PRAYER

Jesus, if there is anything in me, in my experience with women in my life, that is keeping me from a closer relationship with Mary, I invite You into that place and ask for Your healing there. Mother of Mercy, pray for me.

To Save You

The Letter to the Hebrews gives us stunning Eucharistic theology—and a stunning glimpse into the power of Divine Mercy. The fruit of this letter is joy.

For Christ has entered, not into a sanctuary made with hands, a copy of the true one, but into heaven itself, now to appear in the presence of God on our behalf. Nor was it to offer himself repeatedly, as the high priest enters the Holy Place yearly with blood not his own; for then he would have had to suffer repeatedly since the foundation of the world. But as it is, he has appeared once for all at the end of the age to put away sin by the sacrifice of himself. And just as it is appointed for men to die once, and after that comes judgment, so Christ, having been offered once to bear the sins of many, will appear a second time, not to deal with sin but to save those who are eagerly waiting for him.

—Hebrews 9:24–28

IN GOD'S PRESENCE, CONSIDER . . .

Why did Jesus pour out His own blood for me? What is this Divine equation, where it makes sense for the infinite God of the Universe to exchange Himself for me?

CLOSING PRAYER

Lord Jesus Christ, open my heart to Your Holy Spirit, to begin to glimpse the torrent of love that draws You to sacrifice Yourself for me, to rescue me, to bring me home to Your Father.

Faustina's Daily Preparation for Communion

For St. Faustina, receiving Communion was the most solemn moment of her life—a time of recognizing who Christ is and running to meet Him, joining her heart to His.

Today I prepare for the coming of the King.

What am I, and who are You, O Lord, King of eternal glory? O my heart, are you aware of who is coming to you today? Yes, I know, but—strangely—I am not able to grasp it. Oh, if He were just a king, but He is the King of kings, the Lord of lords. Before Him, all power and dominion tremble. He is coming to my heart today. But I hear Him approaching (1810). . . .

I go out to meet Him, and I invite Him to the dwelling place of my heart, humbling myself profoundly before His majesty. But the Lord lifts me up from the dust and invites me . . . to sit next to Him and to tell Him everything that is on my heart (1806). . . .

Today, my soul is preparing for Holy Communion as for a wedding feast, wherein all the participants are resplendent with unspeakable beauty. And I, too, have been invited to this banquet, but I do not see that beauty within myself, only an abyss of misery. And, although I do not feel worthy of sitting down to table, I will however slip under the table, at the feet of Jesus, and will beg for the crumbs that fall from the table. Knowing Your mercy, I therefore approach You, Jesus, for sooner will I run out of misery than will the compassion of Your Heart exhaust itself. That is why during this day I will keep arousing trust in The Divine Mercy (1827).

—St. Faustina, *Diary*

IN GOD'S PRESENCE, CONSIDER . . .

Do I just receive Communion or do I make time before receiving (or even before Mass starts) to clear my mind and heart to receive the Lord more worthily?

CLOSING PRAYER

Lord, increase my awe at the amazing gift You offer me in Communion and help me to prepare my heart for union with You each time I receive.

To "Assimilate" Mercy

In the Father's plan of mercy, we are all called to holiness; but it doesn't happen all at once. It's a process, in which Christ shares His holiness with us more and more to lead us into a whole new way of living—the way God Himself lives.

Pope John Paul II defines the Eucharist as "a mode of being," a way of living that passes from Jesus into each of us and is meant to pass through us to others. But in order for us to be able to pass on this way of living, we ourselves first have to "assimilate" Christ's values, . . . Christ's whole way of existing (*Stay With Us Lord*, #25).

Assimilate. To "take in, to gradually absorb. . . . " Pope Benedict uses the same term: "This act of "eating" [he explains], "is actually a meeting between two persons; it is to allow myself to be penetrated by the life of the One who is Lord. . . . The purpose of this communion is the *assimilation* of my life with His" (May 30, 2005).

It's as if Christ, in the Eucharist, is saying to you and me: *"Here's my way of living, my way of being, my thoughts, my feelings, my attitudes, my values, my perceptions, my way of seeing the world, my way of loving. Take it all into yourself and then pass it on."*

Just as, by gazing at the Divine Mercy Image, we're supposed to become what we behold, so, as we receive the Eucharist (the real Divine Mercy Image), we are supposed to become who we receive, to become living Eucharist, living images of Divine Mercy..

This transformation doesn't happen with one reception of the Eucharist; it's a process. The more we long for this complete union with Christ, . . . the more we are able to "take on" Christ's whole way of being and allow it to permeate our entire life (see *The Sacrament of Charity*, #71–84). Gradually, through each reception of Communion, each moment spent in Eucharistic Adoration, we become more and more like Christ.

—Vinny Flynn, *7 Secrets of Divine Mercy*

IN GOD'S PRESENCE, CONSIDER . . .

Mode of being . . . assimilate . . . living Eucharist . . . living images of Divine Mercy. So much to think about! For a moment, I let my mind take it all in, and I consider my response to the Lord's plan of mercy.

CLOSING PRAYER

Lord Jesus, Help me to long for this complete union with You more and more and allow You to transform me to be holy as You are holy.

Trusting, I Come to You

St. Basil's famous prayer before Communion speaks of the great mercy of God that enables us to come forward with trust, despite our unworthiness.

Oh Lord, I know that I am unworthy to receive Your Holy Body and Precious Blood, and that if I do not first discern the Body and Blood of Christ my God, I eat and drink condemnation to myself. But trusting in Your loving kindness, I come to You who have said: "He that eats my Body and drinks my Blood shall dwell in me and I in him."

Therefore, O Lord, treat me, Your sinful servant, according to Your great mercy, and grant that these Holy Gifts may be for me healing, purification, enlightenment, protection, salvation, the sanctification of my soul and body, and that they may expel every disordered imagination, sinful deed, or work of the evil one.

May they move me to rely completely on You; to love You always; to firmly amend my life and stay true to this intention; and may they effect in me the increase of virtue, the continual indwelling of the Holy Spirit, and the defense against anything that would keep me from eternal life with You.

—St. Basil, *Mass & Adoration Companion*

IN GOD'S PRESENCE, CONSIDER . . .

It is such a great mercy that the Lord has not only saved me but offers me His entire Presence in Holy Communion. How do I prepare for such a gift?

CLOSING PRAYER

Lord, let me always discern before I receive You in the Eucharist, taking time to reflect, and, if needed, to go to the Sacrament of Mercy to confess my sins first. But then, Jesus, increase my trust in Your mercy. As sinful and unworthy as I am, You truly desire to unite Yourself with me, and through this union comes a multitude of gifts that lead to the transformation of my entire being.

Mercy through Eucharistic Adoration

When Francisco, the youngest of the Fatima sons, was asked why he was spending so much time in adoration, he answered "to console God." Dr. Stackpole leads us to explore this beautiful concept of consolation more fully.

Jesus makes it clear to St. Margaret Mary . . . that the Holy Eucharist is the principal means by which He applies His merciful love to her soul. Moreover, she is asked to keep a "Holy Hour" every Thursday night, and thereby, in some way, keep our Lord company in His agony in the Garden of Gethsemane long ago. Indeed, twice in this revelation Jesus assures her by doing these things she can bring comfort and consolation to His Sacred Heart, wounded as it is by the sins of thankless men and women. It appears that St. Margaret Mary is the first one in the history of Catholic spirituality fully to appreciate that in our relationship with Jesus not only is His "Heart" the source of His merciful love for us, but also that we can, in a sense, show mercy to Him and console Him in the Garden and on the Cross by returning His love today. Pope Pius XI wrote of this mystery in his encyclical *Miserentissimus Redemptor* (1928):

> . . . If because of our sins also which were as yet in the future, but were foreseen, the soul of Christ became sorrowful unto death, it cannot be doubted that then, too, already He derived somewhat of solace from our reparation, which was likewise foreseen, when "there appeared to Him an angel from heaven" (Luke XXII, 43) in order that His Heart, oppressed with weariness and anguish, might find consolation. And so even now, in a wondrous yet true manner, we can and ought to console that most Sacred Heart, which is continually wounded by the sins of thankless men.

—Dr. Robert Stackpole, *Divine Mercy: A Guide from Genesis to Benedict XVI*

IN GOD'S PRESENCE, CONSIDER . . .

What can I do—in and outside of adoration—to focus on pleasing and consoling the Heart of God?

CLOSING PRAYER

Lord, let my time spent with You and my focus throughout the day be rooted in this desire to console Your Heart, returning Your love as fully as I can.

Showing Mercy

St. Francis of Assisi gives us here a number of spiritual counsels, especially stressing the need to treat others with the mercy we would like to be shown.

We ought indeed to confess all our sins to a priest and receive from him the Body and Blood of our Lord Jesus Christ. He who does not eat His Flesh and does not drink His Blood cannot enter into the Kingdom of God. . . . And let us love our neighbors as ourselves, and, if any one does not wish to love them as himself or cannot, let him at least do them not harm, but let him do good to them.

Let those who have received the power of judging others, exercise judgment with mercy, as they hope to obtain mercy from the Lord . . . Let us then have charity and humility and let us give alms . . . For men lose all which they leave in this world; they carry with them, however, the reward of charity and alms which they have given . . .

We ought to love our enemies and do good to them that hate us. We ought to observe the precepts and counsels of our Lord Jesus Christ. We ought also to deny ourselves and to put our bodies beneath the yoke of servitude and holy obedience as each one has promised to the Lord. . . . But let him to whom obedience has been entrusted and who is considered greater become as the lesser and the servant of the other brothers, and let him show and have the mercy toward each of his brothers that he would wish to be shown to himself if he were in the like situation. And let him not be angry with a brother on account of his offence, but let him advise him kindly and encourage him with all patience and humility.

—St. Francis of Assisi, Letter to all the Faithful

IN GOD'S PRESENCE, CONSIDER . . .

Is there anyone in my life to whom I consistently have a hard time being merciful? Among other things, this may manifest in me being impatient, condescending, judgmental or easily annoyed. If so, is there something that needs to be communicated that I've been avoiding? Are there boundaries I'm responsible for and failing at setting, and taking that out on him/her? What is the root reason I am so bothered?

CLOSING PRAYER

Father of Mercy, You continually have mercy on my soul, though my offenses against You as the Creator are great. I want to follow Your command to be merciful. Show me what the root is of why I am having trouble doing that with this person and how to bring healing there, and then give me Your heart for him/her.

Tabernacle of Mercy

The Annunciation is Mary's first Holy Communion. She was the first one asked to believe that God Himself wanted to take flesh in her; and by her "Yes" (her Fiat), she became the first living tabernacle of Mercy. You and I are called to echo that "yes" every time we receive Communion. St. Pope John Paul II says that there's "a profound analogy" between the Fiat she said at the Annunciation and the "Amen" we say when we receive the Eucharist (see The Church of the Eucharist, *#55).*

Fiat/Amen

Amen! Yes, Lord, I believe that You are truly present here,
Body and Blood, Soul and Divinity,
hidden under what still looks like bread.
Yes, Lord, I believe that You actually want to live in me, flesh of my flesh.

Fiat, Lord! Let it be done to me according to Your will.
Live in me. Let Your whole "mode of being" pass into me —
Your thoughts, Your feelings, Your attitudes, Your values,
Your way of seeing and living and loving.
Keep me conscious of Your presence within me as I leave this church,
and let me bring You with me into the world.

Let me become living Eucharist,
a living tabernacle of Your love.
Let me be, like Mary, a living monstrance,
bringing Your love and the power of Your Spirit to all I meet,
so that they, like the babe in Elizabeth's womb,
may leap for joy at the tenderness of Your touch.

—Vinny Flynn, *Mass & Adoration Companion*

IN GOD'S PRESENCE, CONSIDER . . .

What an amazing thought that Jesus wants to take flesh in me, to live in me!— That, through His gift of Himself in Communion, Jesus invites and enables me to become a living tabernacle, a traveling monstrance, bringing His mercy with me wherever I go!

CLOSING PRAYER

Mary, help me, like you, say a full "Yes" to Jesus, receiving His very life, His very presence into my being and then sharing Him with others.

Koinonia: All is Revealed in Communion

St. Teresa of Calcutta insisted that her sisters always include in their chapels by the cross of the Lord the inscription of His words, "I thirst." Stinissen tells us here that the Holy Spirit both awakens this thirst within us and draws us out of ourselves to quench the thirst of the Lord. We are called into a perfect dynamism of love.

What is love? Philosophers, artists, and authors all wrestle with this question. We can say: Love is self-giving. The Greek word *agape* is translated in this way. Love is to give oneself to another. It is this love that Jesus shows us on the Cross: he gives his life for us. It is also this love that he shows us in the Eucharist, where he is given and poured out—the love that goes completely out of itself, that thinks only of what is best for the other. . . .

But love is not only self-giving; it is not only a desire to go out of myself. It is also a desire that the other should come into me. Love is not only *agape*; it is also *eros* (which should not necessarily be associated with eroticism). Love is also desire, thirst. "Come!" says eros, "I long for you, we must be together." In the Eucharist, there is *agape* as well as *eros*. The Eucharist is not only sacrifice; it is also presence. . . .

There is a word that expresses the fullness of love, both *agape* and *eros*, and that is koinonia, fellowship, the very word that is typical of the Holy Spirit and that expresses his being. In fellowship, one shares everything in common. Nothing is just yours. "All that is mine is yours," you say, "And all that is mine is yours," answers the other. You empty yourself of what is yours in order to fill the others, and that is *agape*. But by the fact that the other empties himself of what is his in order to fill you, *eros* is also satisfied. "I am yours," says *agape*. "You are mine," says eros. Is that not what love repeats for all eternity? "I am yours—you are mine," together, is the fullness of love: koinonia. Love is perfect in the Holy Trinity, and its name is koinonia.

—Fr. Wilfrid Stinissen, OCD, *The Holy Spirit, Fire of Divine Love*

IN GOD'S PRESENCE, CONSIDER . . .

Am I willing to lose control of my life in the dynamism of the Holy Trinity? Today, I will enter more deeply into this holy flow of reception and gift.

CLOSING PRAYER

Come Holy Spirit, fire of Divine Love. Draw me into a new communion of love, this koinonia, so far from the barrenness of my own forging.

Spirit of Mercy

Jesus continues His mission of mercy, explains Fr. Cantalamessa, through the Holy Spirit, who "opens the treasure of Jesus's mercy" for us.

Returning to his home in Nazareth after his baptism in the Jordan, Jesus solemnly applies the words of Isaiah to himself:

> The Spirit of the Lord is upon me, because he has anointed me to preach good news to the poor. He has sent me to proclaim release to the captives and recovering of sight to the blind, to set at liberty those who are oppressed, to proclaim the acceptable year of the Lord (Luke 4:18–19).

It was thanks to the anointing of the Holy Spirit that Jesus preached the good news, healed the sick, comforted the afflicted, and performed all his works of mercy. St. Basil writes that the Holy Spirit was "inseparably present" with Jesus so that his "every operation was wrought with the co-operation of the Spirit" (De Spiritu Sancto, #37).

The Holy Spirit, who is love personified in the Trinity, is also the mercy of God personified. He is the very "content" of divine mercy. Without the Holy Spirit, "mercy" would be an empty word.

The name "Paraclete" clearly indicates this. In announcing his coming, Jesus says, "And I will pray the Father, and he will give you another Counselor, to be with you for ever" (John 14:16). "Another" here implies "after having given me, Jesus, to you." The Holy Spirit is, therefore, the one through whom the risen Jesus now continues his work of "doing good and healing all" (Acts 10:38). The statement that the Paraclete "will take what is mine and declare it to you" (John 16:14) also applies to mercy: the Holy Spirit will open the treasures of Jesus' mercy to believers in every age. He will make Jesus' mercy not just be remembered but also experienced.

—Raniero Cantalamessa, *The Gaze of Mercy*

IN GOD'S PRESENCE, CONSIDER . . .

Fr. Cantalamessa has opened up a whole new understanding of how the Holy Spirit is involved in the message of mercy. Not just involved, but "mercy personified."

CLOSING PRAYER

Holy Spirit, I want to know You better, and there is so much I don't know. I invite You into my life in a deeper way, and ask too that You continue to "open the treasures of Jesus's mercy" to me and help me share it with others.

Unwavering Trust

Inspired by Christ's words to St. Faustina that the graces of His mercy are drawn by trust (see Diary, *1578), her spiritual director, Fr. Michael Sopocko, gives us a wonderful little litany.*

Holy Spirit, give me the grace
of unwavering trust
when I think of Our Lord's merits,
and of fearful trust
when I think of my own weakness.

When poverty comes knocking at my door,
Jesus, I Trust in You;
When sickness lays me low, or injury cripples me,
Jesus, I Trust in You;
When the world pushes me aside,
and pursues me with its hatred,
Jesus, I Trust in You;
When I am besmirched by calumny,
and pierced through by bitterness,
Jesus, I Trust in You;
When my friends abandon me,
and wound me by word and deed,
Jesus, I Trust in You.

Spirit of love and Mercy, be to me a refuge,
a sweet consolation, a blessed hope,
that in all the most trying circumstances of my life
I may never cease to trust in You.

—Blessed Fr. Michael Sopocko

IN GOD'S PRESENCE, CONSIDER . . .

Do I continually pray, "Jesus, I trust in you"? Or do I fail to trust when things aren't going well?

CLOSING PRAYER

Lord Jesus, help me to live in trust, consistently renewing my trust in you, no matter what happens in my life.

Loving the God Who Relieves Our Burdens

Fr. Jean writes that we are "bathed in love and mercy," but we so often settle for far less.

Is it not a matter of the most elementary logic that a father and his child should be a joy for one another? "Jesus, you are my joy, and I, too, am your joy." Is it not written that *his delight is to be with the children of men*" (Prv 8:31). There are persons who are baptized, who are confirmed, who receive Communion, who are in a state of grace, who are temples of the Holy Spirit, yet who pass their whole lives on earth without ever having experienced this heart-to-heart relationship with their Father in heaven, their Creator and Savior, in the happiness which comes from being a joy for one another. Is not the life of grace the beginning of eternal beatitude? People examine themselves in terms of what is forbidden them and not in terms of what is asked of them. People examine themselves on faults and failings, and not on their intimacy with Jesus . . . .

I assure you, we are bathed in love and mercy. We each have a Father, a Brother, a Friend, a Spouse of our soul, Center and King of our hearts, Redeemer and Savior, bent down over us, over our weakness and our impotence, like that of little children, with an inexpressible gentleness, watching over us like the apple of his eye, who said, *I will have mercy and not sacrifice, for I have not come to call the just, but sinners*; a Jesus haunted by the desire to save us by all means, who has opened heaven under our feet. And we live, too often, like orphans, abandoned children, as if it were hell which had opened under our feet. We are men of little faith!

Oh, how I would love it if at the end of this retreat you were able to cry out with the Psalmist: *Lord, you have opened my heart and I run in the way of your commandments* (Ps 119:32).

—Jean C.J. d'Elbee, *I Believe in Love*, pp. 22–24

IN GOD'S PRESENCE, CONSIDER . . .

Do I regularly experience this with God—being a joy, one to the other? If not, what prevents Him from truly being my joy or me from believing I am His joy? And how often do I get caught up in doing spiritual things and lose the sense of person-to-Person intimacy that He offers?

CLOSING PRAYER

Father of inexpressible gentleness, I am never abandoned by You, and I know that if I could live believing that You truly watch over me as the apple of Your eye, my whole life would change. This is where I want to be, living in Your gaze of love, with You as my joy, and me as Yours.

God—The Joy of My Life

If you haven't yet met St. Elizabeth of the Trinity, you're in for a real treat: as a contemporary of St. Therese of Lisieux, Elizabeth's gentle heart draws us into the radiance of the Holy Trinity.

The question is often asked: what is Elizabeth's most important message to the modern world? Many suggestions have been made: prophet of the presence of God, saint of the indwelling, lay contemplative, praise of glory. Perhaps John Paul II comes closest to providing an answer when, in his homily at her beatification in November 1984, he spoke of her as *a brilliant witness to the joy of being rooted and grounded in love* (cf. Eph 3:17). *Your Presence is my Joy* is how Conrad De Meester, in the title of one of his books, sums up the life and teaching of Elizabeth.

Her message is essentially one of joy—a joy that springs from knowing that I am loved, not in some vague, uncertain way but with a love that is personal and without limit. This is a love that does not depend on anything I have done or not done, it is not something I have to merit or earn: it is a gift. *God is love* (1 Jn 4:8.16): he loves us with an everlasting love, whether we are aware of it or not. If he did not love us, he would cease to be God! As God, he can only love with infinite tenderness and compassion: *I have called you by name, you are mine. . . . I have carved you on the palms of my hands!* (Is 43:1; 49:16).

—Eugene McCaffrey OCD, *Let Yourself Be Loved*

IN GOD'S PRESENCE, CONSIDER . . .

St. Elizabeth invites me into the true identity of God: love without limits. Do I live rooted and grounded in love? Have I opened my heart to being loved personally and without limit?

CLOSING PRAYER

Father, Son and Holy Spirit, Your presence is my joy. You love me, You call me: I am Yours.

Too Easily Pleased . . .

God's mercy has unimaginable joy and fulfillment in store for us, and yet, as C.S. Lewis writes, we settle for far less than what He is offering.

If you asked twenty good men today what they thought the highest of the virtues, nineteen of them would reply, Unselfishness. But if you had asked almost any of the great Christians of old, he would have replied, Love. You see what has happened? A negative term has been substituted for a positive, and this is of more than philological importance. The negative idea of Unselfishness carries with it the suggestion not primarily of securing good things for others, but of going without them ourselves, as if our abstinence and not their happiness was the important point. I do not think this is the Christian virtue of Love. The New Testament has lots to say about self-denial, but not about self-denial as an end in itself.

We are told to deny ourselves and to take up our crosses in order that we may follow Christ; and nearly every description of what we shall ultimately find if we do so contains an appeal to desire. If there lurks in most modern minds the notion that to desire our own good and earnestly to hope for the enjoyment of it is a bad thing, I submit that this notion has crept in from Kant and the Stoics, and is no part of Christian faith.

Indeed, if we consider the unblushing promises of reward and the staggering nature of the rewards promised in the Gospels, it would seem that Our Lord finds our desires not too strong, but too weak. We are half-hearted creatures, fooling about with drink and sex and ambition when infinite joy is offered us, like an ignorant child who wants to go on making mud pies in a slum because he cannot imagine what is meant by the offer of a holiday at the sea. We are far too easily pleased.

—C.S. Lewis, *The Weight of Glory*

IN GOD'S PRESENCE, CONSIDER . . .

God often speaks through the desires of our hearts. What are the deepest desires of my heart and, when I speak to God about them, relating them to Him, what does He have to say about them? Are there places where I settle for less than what God wants for my life out of fear, doubt, or something else?

CLOSING PRAYER

Father, Jesus, Holy Spirit, You offer me the staggering gift of infinite joy, eternal bliss, the most intimate union of love my heart could ever desire. Let me not stifle my desires, but rather relate them to You and allow them to be purified and directed to their true end.

Love Finds Joy in the Beloved

"Seek first the kingdom [of God]," Jesus tells us, "and all these things will be given you" (Mt 6:33, NABRE). True life in the Spirit is finding our joy in the Lord.

. . . We are comforted by the Spirit in yet another way. He teaches us to find our joy in God. Is that not what characterizes love more than anything else: that one finds joy in the beloved, that one is happy because of the beloved? "Thank you for existing" is an expression one often hears nowadays [In Scandinavia]. It has become almost a cliché. But the one who really means what he says gives expression to real love. It gives me joy that you exist. You are beautiful, you are wonderful, you are precious. In the Gloria at Mass, we sing: "We praise you for your glory." It is the Holy Spirit who gives our love this quality, and without this, it is not real love . . . .

The Spirit creates in us the joy that is characteristic of the kingdom of God. "For the kingdom does not mean food and drink but righteousness and peace and joy in the Holy Spirit" (Rom 14:17). His deepest and most important work in us is to make us become fascinated with God's beauty, so that we cease to find our joy in ourselves and instead find it in God. He brings about that Copernican revolution in our life, so that we no longer let God revolve around us (God for me), but, rather, we begin to revolve around God (me for God). . . . According to Saint Paul, it is the Holy Spirit who intoxicates us and causes us to sing and play before the Lord with all our hearts (Eph 5:18–19) . . . .

To love God is to find joy in him . . . . It is the Spirit who awakens this joy in us. He wants us to grow in it so that in the end the promise of Jesus will be fulfilled: "These things I have spoken to you, that my joy may be in you, and that your joy may be full" (Jn 15:11).

—Fr. Wilfrid Stinissen, OCD, *The Holy Spirit, Fire of Divine Love*

IN GOD'S PRESENCE, CONSIDER . . .

Me for God instead of God for me. It may be disconcerting to family and friends, but am I ready for my world to be turned upside down because of my love of God? Will I give permission for the Holy Spirit to awaken in me a fascination with the beauty of God that leads to finding my deepest joy in Him?

CLOSING PRAYER

I love You, God. Truly, I love You. It gives me joy that You exist. I praise You for Your glory and delight in Your goodness. You are beautiful in all Your ways. Awaken my heart to the fullness of You.

Entrustment

To St. John of the Cross, the scriptural story of the wedding at Cana is not just the occasion for the first of Christ's signs; it's a powerful "way of prayer."

This, then, is one of the seasons of prayer in John of the Cross. We have been led by him to Cana: the family wedding where the wine runs out. Mary sees the anxiety, and has a quiet word with her Son just pointing out what she has noticed.

This is a scene with cosmic scope: the wedding of the Lamb, espousing humanity, a humanity in peril. The mother of Jesus perceives what is lacking, and names it, without dictating a solution: "They have no wine" (Jn 2:3). Hers is a prayer of need; her perception of need is a prayer. She takes it, holds it, allows it to ache before him. And that precipitates glory. He "manifested his glory; and his disciples believed in him" (Jn 2:11).

This, then, is a way of prayer: to feel our way to the wound that is in us, to the place of our need. Go there, take it, name it; hold it before Christ.

To feel our way to the wounds of the world, to those people or situations in dire need of healing. Go there, take them, name them, and hold them before him.

Go there, not to dictate to Christ what the answer should be or what he should do about it; but to hold the wound before him.

'They have no wine. "John of the Cross sees wisdom here. A love which does not spell out "what it needs or wants, but holds out its need so that the Beloved might do what pleases him" is especially powerful . . .

This, then, is a way of prayer in John of the Cross: to go to the place of our need, and to hold that before God. "We have no wine"—a service to the world, a prayer that precipitates glory.

—Iain Matthew, OCD, *John of the Cross: Seasons of Prayer*

IN GOD'S PRESENCE, CONSIDER . . .

Do I try to tell God how to answer my prayers in specific ways? Or do I simply hold up the need to him with expectant trust?

CLOSING PRAYER

Lord, unless I feel prompted by the Holy Spirit to be persistent in asking for a specific intention, help me learn to pray without asking for a particular solution. Grant me the grace to surrender everything, so that I can simply feel my way to the wound, to the need, name it, and present it to You for You to resolve as you wish, trusting completely in Your mercy.

Awaited by Love

Our Holy Father Benedict shares with us one of the most moving stories of a modern saint, a slave girl of Sudan who discovers that she is not property, but beloved and awaited by God.

To come to know God—the true God—means to receive hope. . . . The example of a saint of our time can to some degree help us understand what it means to have a real encounter with this God. . . . I am thinking of the African Josephine Bakhita. . . . At the age of nine, she was kidnapped by slave-traders, beaten till she bled, and sold five times in the slave-markets of Sudan. Eventually she found herself working as a slave for the mother and the wife of a general, and there she was flogged every day till she bled; . . .

Finally, in 1882, she was bought by an Italian merchant. . . . Here, after the terrifying "masters" who had owned her up to that point, Bakhita came to know a totally different kind of "master"—in Venetian dialect, which she was now learning, she used the name "*paron*" for the living God, the God of Jesus Christ . . . a "*paron*" above all masters, the Lord of all lords, . . . goodness in person.

She came to know that this Lord even knew her, that he had created her. . . . She too was loved, and by none other than the supreme "*Paron*.". . . What is more, this master had himself accepted the destiny of being flogged and now he was waiting for her "at the Father's right hand." Now she had the great hope: "I am definitively loved and whatever happens to me—I am awaited by this Love. And so my life is good." . . .

On 8 December 1896, in Verona, she took her vows in the Congregation of the Canossian Sisters and . . . made several journeys round Italy in order to promote the missions: the liberation that she had received through her encounter with the God of Jesus Christ, she felt she had to extend. . . . The hope born in her which had "redeemed" her she could not keep to herself; this hope had to reach many, to reach everybody.

—Pope Benedict XVI, *Spe Salvi (Saved in Hope)*, 3

IN GOD'S PRESENCE, CONSIDER . . .

Do I see my Savior's love for me in His wounds? Like Bakhita, can I recognize that my life's sorrowful mysteries do not deny God's love but reveal it?

CLOSING PRAYER

St. Josephine Bakhita, open my heart to discover the Father's love for me, and the embrace of the Bridegroom, Jesus the King who gives his life for the world—and for me.

Eyes of Mercy . . .

St. Bede says here of the Apostle Matthew that Jesus saw him through the eyes of mercy and chose him. Matthew responded immediately and drew many with him on the road of salvation.

Jesus saw Matthew, not merely in the usual sense, but more significantly with his merciful understanding of men. He saw the tax collector and, because he saw him through the eyes of mercy and chose him, he said to him: *Follow me.* This following meant imitating the pattern of his life—not just walking after him. St. John tells us: *Whoever says he abides in Christ ought to walk in the same way in which he walked.*

And he rose and followed him. There is no reason for surprise that the tax collector abandoned earthly wealth as soon as the Lord commanded him. Nor should one be amazed that neglecting his wealth, he joined a band of men whose leader had, on Matthew's assessment, no riches at all. Our Lord summoned Matthew by speaking to him in words. By an invisible, interior impulse flooding his mind with the light of grace, he instructed him to walk in his footsteps. In this way Matthew could understand that Christ, who was summoning him away from earthly possessions, had incorruptible treasures of heaven in his gift.

As he sat at table in the house, behold many tax collectors and sinners came and sat down with Jesus and his disciples. This conversion of one tax collector gave many men, those from his own profession and other sinners, an example of repentance and pardon. Notice also the happy and true anticipation of his future status as apostle and teacher of the nations. No sooner was he converted than Matthew drew after him a whole crowd of sinners along the same road to salvation. He took up his appointed duties while still taking his first steps in the faith . . .

—St Bede the Venerable, Hom. 21: CCL 122, 149–151

IN GOD'S PRESENCE, CONSIDER . . .

Am I quick to follow when and where the Lord calls? Are there times I feel I have to be more *perfect*, more holy, more put together before I can evangelize and lead others to Jesus?

CLOSING PRAYER

Jesus, caller of the broken, the needy, the wayward . . . bid me come after You. I want to follow You in a new and more fervent way. Let me see Your gaze of mercy and know I have nothing to fear in leaving everything behind. I will do whatever You ask.

Conversion Is Discovering the Father

Conversion is much more than just turning away from sin.

A son who rejects his father, takes his family's inheritance early, leaves home for a distant land, and squanders the inheritance on immoral living comes to experience his father's love in a whole new way. Many people think the son's point of conversion comes when he is living as a slave, hungry and poor, and decides to return to his father . . . .

But another level of conversion happens when he arrives home and encounters something completely unexpected. The son admits his sin, is truly sorry, and turns back to the father—a good first step—but it isn't enough. He isn't turning back as a beloved son. . . . After all he has done to shame the family, how can he be called a son? The possibility of receiving his father's love isn't even on his radar screen. . . . the best he can hope for is that the father will pardon him and accept him as a hired worker. . . . That's why, as soon as he meets his father, he starts saying those words, "I am no longer worthy to be called your son. . . . "

But the father will have absolutely none of this. He cuts his son off and will not allow him to continue his self-effacing sentence. The father embraces him—nothing that the son has done can make the father turn away from him. The father declares the truth that the son can't see in himself. "This *my son* was dead, and is alive again; he was lost, and is found" (Lk 15:24, emphasis added). The parable of the prodigal son is about more than turning away from sin and finding forgiveness. It's also about turning away from the incorrect picture we have of God and of ourselves. At heart, the conversion in this story involves our very identity as beloved children of God ("This my son . . . ") and a most unexpected love that turns our world upside down. As Pope St. John Paul II explains, conversion is always the fruit of rediscovering the Father.

—Edward Sri, *Into His Likeness*

IN GOD'S PRESENCE, CONSIDER . . .

Do I find myself simply repenting and confessing my sins without reflecting on the truth of who God is and who I am to Him? Am I just "mea culpa-ing" my way to avoid punishment, without allowing the encounter with the Father of mercy to draw me into deep communion with Him?

CLOSING PRAYER

Abba, convert my heart truly, so that beyond repentance there can always be a recognition of You as a tender Father, and me as Your beloved son/daughter—in whom You delight.

Rediscovering the Father

To St. Pope John Paul II, conversion doesn't simply consist of a single, dramatic moment, but is a continual process—and it's always the fruit of discovering and rediscovering the Father, who is rich in mercy.

Mercy in itself, as a perfection of the infinite God, is also infinite. Also infinite therefore and inexhaustible is the Father's readiness to receive the prodigal children who return to His home. Infinite are the readiness and power of forgiveness which flow continually from the marvelous value of the sacrifice of the Son. No human sin can prevail over this power or even limit it. On the part of man only a lack of good will can limit it, a lack of readiness to be converted and to repent, in other words persistence in obstinacy, opposing grace and truth, especially in the face of the witness of the cross and resurrection of Christ.

Therefore, the Church professes and proclaims conversion. Conversion to God always consists in discovering His mercy, that is, in discovering that love which is patient and kind (cf 1 Cor 13:4) as only the Creator and Father can be; the love to which the "God and Father of our Lord Jesus Christ" (2 Cor 1:3) is faithful to the uttermost consequences in the history of His covenant with man; even to the cross and to the death and resurrection of the Son. Conversion to God is always the fruit of the "rediscovery" of this Father, who is rich in mercy.

Authentic knowledge of the God of mercy, the God of tender love, is a constant and inexhaustible source of conversion. . . . Those who come to know God in this way, who "see" Him in this way, can live only in a state of being continually converted to Him. . . . It is this state of conversion which marks out the most profound element of the pilgrimage of every man and woman on earth.

—St. Pope John Paul II, *Rich in Mercy*, 13

IN GOD'S PRESENCE, CONSIDER . . .

Sometimes the thing that keeps me from discovering the kindness of God, is the part of me that doesn't believe I deserve such kindness. This is why punishment can feel more comfortable than kindness and mercy. We make the prodigal son's line our own: "I no longer deserve to be called Your son/daughter." But that's either a lie from an earlier wound or a whisper of the enemy. I am the Father's delight.

CLOSING PRAYER

Father, help me to rediscover,—daily if necessary—the depths of your mercy and come to live in a continual state of conversion to you.

It's All About the Father . . .

*Confession is a "Tribunal of Mercy" (*Diary, *1448) where we encounter the Trinity Itself and are drawn back to the merciful love of the Father.*

In confession, through the ministry of the priest acting *in persona Christi*, we are brought into the presence of God's "awe-inspiring tribunal"—the Tribunal of Mercy: the Father, the Son, and the Holy Spirit. But they aren't there to sit in judgment. They're on our side.

We need to understand that we're not dealing with abstract concepts here. What we're dealing with is *persons*—divine, yes, but *real persons*, each distinct from the other, yet inseparable! Jesus is a person; the Holy Spirit is a person; the Father is a person. And together these three persons of God have one goal: to bring us back to the Father, the source of all life, all goodness, all blessing.

"Reconciliation," writes Pope John Paul II, "is principally a gift of the heavenly Father." This, to me, is the most important thing, and it's something I never knew:

Confession is all about the Father.

In the confessional, Christ, through the power of the Holy Spirit, leads us back to the Father so that, now that we have been "ransomed, healed, restored, and forgiven," we can enter into the fullness of our dignity as His children. Pope Benedict XVI points out that the role of priests in the confessional is "to make their penitents experience the Heavenly Father's merciful love," because what is central to confession is the "personal encounter with God, the Father of goodness and mercy" (Address, March 7, 2008).

The "call to conversion," he explains, is "an encouragement to return to the arms of God, the tender and merciful Father, to trust in him and . . . to entrust ourselves to him as his adopted children, regenerated by his love" (General Audience, February 6, 2008).

If only we could really understand the infinite love and tenderness of this Father who waits for us to come to Him in the confessional!

—Vinny Flynn, *7 Secrets of Confession*

IN GOD'S PRESENCE, CONSIDER . . .

How different it is to think of a tribunal of mercy rather than one of judgment! Confession is where I go to meet the three Persons who only have my good in mind, who want to restore and heal and love me.

CLOSING PRAYER

Father of infinite love, You are the source of all life, all goodness, all blessing. Draw me into the embrace of Your mercy.

The Voice of the Liar

Fr. Gallagher warns us not to listen to the voice of the enemy after a fall, but to turn immediately to God, where we will find mercy and healing.

23. Be aware that after a fall the evil spirit makes it seem difficult to return to ask God for forgiveness and almost impossible to correct the fault; . . . St. Ignatius writes that the enemy places obstacles, and the good spirit eases and takes away all obstacles (*Rules for the Discernment of Spirits*, Rule 2). When you have fallen into a defect or sin, you may feel a heavy sense that this will never change. You may hear insinuations like these: "You will just keep falling in this way. Here you are, yet again, with the same failing. You will always be the same. You will never change." This is the voice of the enemy! Recognize it as such, and reject it. Never believe this voice. It is the voice of the liar (John 8:44).

But when you have fallen, you will also hear another voice in your heart that says, "Do not hesitate to turn, now, to God. All you will find there is love, understanding, mercy, healing. It is easy to ask forgiveness of one who so loves you. He delights in pouring out upon you his healing love. And you can make progress in this failing. It is not so hard: God's grace will always be with you to strengthen you. Yes, you will struggle and will fall at times. This is the human condition. But these very falls can lead you to a blessed humility and to seek a forgiveness that makes you all the stronger." This is the voice of the good spirit! Recognize it as such, and accept it. Believe it, and be guided by it.

24 . . . Continue to reflect on the parable of the Prodigal Son, on the Good Shepherd, on the way Jesus dealt with sinners, . . . we place ourselves immediately in God's presence, . . . never for a moment doubting that we shall be well received by so good a heavenly Father, and that he will generously forgive us, and that, indeed, we will be filled with his blessings.

—Timothy M. Gallagher, *Overcoming Spiritual Discouragement: The Wisdom and Spiritual Power of Venerable Bruno Lanteri*

IN GOD'S PRESENCE, CONSIDER . . .

What are the common insinuations and lies the enemy uses with me when I have failed in some way? What accusations about myself do I hear? Even if they feel partially true, I will reject them as being parts of a false whole, a deceitful narrative the enemy is using to keep me from God. I will only accept correction and truth from the voice of God, which convicts without condemnation.

CLOSING PRAYER

God of truth and goodness, let me only and always follow Your voice. Help me to recognize it, believe it, and be guided by it.

The Healing Power of Mercy

Hahn explains here that the Sacrament of Confession is the way we come to truly see, "to get our stories straight" by seeing them through the lens of mercy. This illumination of our inner life isn't always comfortable, but it is the beautiful and ordinary way that allows for true healing and transformation.

Jesus is infinite mercy, and He shares His mercy infinitely through His Church, in the sacrament of confession. Confession is key to our spiritual growth, and it is the ordinary way that we believers come to a deeper knowledge of ourselves as we truly are—that is, as God sees us. Confession keeps us from living and laboring under delusions about the world, about our place in it, and about the story of our lives. It brings the dark corners of our soul into the clear morning light of eternal day, for ourselves to see in the sight of God. That can be difficult, and it can sometimes be painful, but in the end it heals with the all-powerful touch of Jesus Christ.

Through confession, we begin to heal. We begin to get our stories straight. We come home through the open door, to resume our place in God's family. We begin to know peace.

Again, none of this comes easily. Indeed, confession doesn't make change easy, but it does make it possible, supernatural, and salvific—not just for ourselves, but for every life we touch. Confession is not a quick fix, but it is a sure cure. We need to go to the sacrament, and go again, and keep going back, because life is a marathon, not a forty-yard dash. We'll often want to stop, but like a distance runner, we need to press on for our second wind, and our third, and our fourth. In this case, we can count on the wind coming, because it's the "wind" of the Holy Spirit.

—Scott Hahn, *Lord Have Mercy*

IN GOD'S PRESENCE, CONSIDER . . .

What is one way I tend to see myself that is actually based on lies whispered by the world, Satan, or voices within that come from my woundedness? (Hint: God's voice is never condemning.) Next time I go to confession, I will bring this dark corner of my heart into the light of God's mercy, and repent not only of my sins, but of any lies I have made agreements with.

CLOSING PRAYER

Father, Jesus, Holy Spirit, I invite You into this wounded place, this area in my life where I am prone to believe a lie about who I am. What word of truth do You want to speak to me here?

"My Own Will Does Not Exist."

During an eight-day retreat in February 1935, in response to specific directives from the Lord, St. Faustina completely canceled out her own will and resolved to entrust herself entirely to the will of God.

In the evening, after the conference, I heard these words: I am with you. During this retreat, I will strengthen you in peace and in courage so that your strength will not fail in carrying out My designs. Therefore you will cancel out your will absolutely in this retreat and, instead, My complete will shall be accomplished in you. Know that it will cost you much, so write these words on a clean sheet of paper: "From today on, my own will does not exist," and then cross out the page. And on the other side write these words: "From today on, I do the will of God everywhere, always, and in everything." Be afraid of nothing; love will give you strength and make the realization of this easy (372). . . .

From today on my will does not exist (374) . . . O Divine Will, You are the delight of my heart, the food of my soul, . . . for when I unite myself with Your will, O Lord, Your power works through me and takes the place of my feeble will (650). . . .

From today onward, Your will, Lord, is my food. . . . Whatever Your fatherly hand gives me, I will accept with submission, peace and joy. . . . Lead me, O God, along whatever roads You please; I have placed all my trust in Your will, which is, for me, love and mercy itself (1264). . . .

O my Jesus, You know that, in all my desires, I always want to see Your will. Of myself, I would not want to die one minute sooner, or to live one minute longer, or to suffer less, or to suffer more, but I only want to do Your holy will. Although I have great enthusiasm, and the desires burning in my heart are immense, they are never above Your will (1729).

—St. Faustina, *Diary*

IN GOD'S PRESENCE, CONSIDER . . .

Am I inspired or resistant when I think about Faustina's trust in God's will to the point of canceling out her own will? How often in my daily life am I able to cross out my own will in deference to the Lord's?

CLOSING PRAYER

Lord, help me always to accept whatever Your fatherly hand gives me with submission, peace, and joy. Grant me trust in Your goodness and mercy, so that I am not afraid to surrender to whatever You ask.

Living the Lord's Prayer

In giving us the "Our Father," Jesus gave us more than a way to pray. He gave us a teaching about how to live as He Himself lived, in trust and mercy.

He was praying in a certain place, and when he ceased, one of his disciples said to him, "Lord, teach us to pray, as John taught his disciples" (Lk 11:1).

Once, when Jesus was praying in a certain place (see Lk 11:1), the sight of what he was doing fascinated his disciples. "Lord, teach us to pray," one of them blurted out. And so, Jesus taught them, but he did more than give them words to say; he gave them a way to live, the way he himself lived—as Mercy Incarnate.

Jesus lived for his Father, pleasing him, doing his will, revealing him as the Father, who is "rich in mercy" (Eph 2:4). In revealing God as the Father, Jesus was proclaiming and establishing the kingdom of God; and in this way, he hallowed the name of the Father and did his will. He trusted in the Father to provide all his needs each day, and he forgave all who hurt Him. By his redemption on the Cross, he forgave us our sins (see Col 1:14); and by his daily living of trust and mercy, he destroyed the power of the Evil One. In a word, he lived and revealed *Mercy*.

And so for us, too, The Lord's Prayer is a way to live. We can look at this prayer and see two pivotal points: the Father and the *kingdom*. Our whole life is to be for the Father, who is "rich in mercy." His kingdom is established as we follow him and do his will. Prayer teaches us how to do his will—by totally trusting in him for our daily bread, which includes all our daily needs; and by being merciful as He is merciful, forgiving others' sins as we are forgiven ours. This way, we are not put to the test, but are delivered from the prince of this world, the Evil One.

—Fr. George Kosicki, CSB, *Faustina, Saint for Our Times*

IN GOD'S PRESENCE, CONSIDER . . .

Christ came to reveal the Father's mercy and to show us how to do His will. How can I respond more fully in living my whole life for the Father, trusting Him, trying to please Him and doing all I can to let His kingdom come?

CLOSING PRAYER

Merciful Father, help me to foster your kingdom here on earth by following Christ in doing Your will. Show me the places in my life where I need to trust in Your Providence more fully, and areas where I can be more forgiving and merciful.

This Is Daunting

Here the Catechism starts to tell us something important about God's mercy and the strict requirement to forgive as we've been forgiven (Mt 6:12). Then it interrupts itself in mid-sentence to warn us that what it's about to say is "daunting"—it's scary!

Now—and this is daunting—this outpouring of mercy cannot penetrate our hearts as long as we have not forgiven those who have trespassed against us. Love, like the Body of Christ, is indivisible; we cannot love the God we cannot see if we do not love the brother or sister we do see. [Cf. 1 Jn 4:20] In refusing to forgive our brothers and sisters, our hearts are closed and their hardness makes them impervious to the Father's merciful love; but in confessing our sins, our hearts are opened to his grace. [1864]

—*Catechism of the Catholic Church*, 2840

IN GOD'S PRESENCE, CONSIDER . . .

Wow! This is daunting! God is always pouring His mercy out upon me, but if there's any unforgiveness in my heart, His mercy can't get in; it's like water flowing over rock. So I can be going to Mass regularly, praying the Chaplet, the Rosary, etc., but God's mercy can't get into my closed, hard heart. That's definitely scary. Time for some serious "house cleaning" in my heart. (If there is deep pain from harm and I find serious resistance to forgiving someone, I will talk to the Lord about it—who is patient and infinitely kind and will let me be like a child taking baby steps—and I will simply start by asking for the grace to want to forgive.)

CLOSING PRAYER

Come, Holy Spirit, and help me search my heart. Who do I need to forgive? Family? . . . friends? . . . co-workers? . . . others? . . . myself? . . . Lord, open and soften my heart, and give me the courage to search for and dig out left-over resentments, grudges, bitterness—any unforgiveness—and release it all to You in the confessional.

And Your Heart Will Overflow

Christ's call for us to let go of anger, judgment, and vengeance, and show mercy and forgiveness to all, was not an abolishment of the law given in the Old Testament, but rather its fulfillment.

He that takes vengeance will suffer vengeance from the Lord,
  and he will firmly establish his sins.
Forgive your neighbor the wrong he has done,
  and then your sins will be pardoned when you pray.
Does a man harbor anger against another,
  and yet seek for healing from the Lord?
Does he have no mercy toward a man like himself,
  and yet pray for his own sins?
If he himself, being flesh, maintains wrath,
  who will make expiation for his sins?
Remember the end of your life, and cease from enmity,
  remember destruction and death, and be true to the commandments.
Remember the commandments, and do not be angry with your neighbor;
  remember the covenant of the Most High, and overlook ignorance.
Refrain from strife, and you will lessen sins;
  for a man given to anger will kindle strife,
and a sinful man will disturb friends
  and inject enmity among those who are at peace.

—Sirach 28:1–9

IN GOD'S PRESENCE, CONSIDER . . .

Have I truly received God's abundant mercy, or do I experience it so minimally that none brims over for my neighbor? Do I recognize that every place where I find it difficult to forgive those who have harmed me is a gentle invitation from my Savior to receive His love and mercy more deeply?

CLOSING PRAYER

Jesus, I trust in You. I believe in Your infinite grace and power. Today I accept Your healing of all my wounds, and wondrously discover that I can relinquish the grip that others hold over me and, in Your holy Name, forgive them.

Constant Mercy

Forgiveness is integral to the practice of mercy, and Jesus teaches us that we are to follow His example of constant mercy.

Then Peter came up and said to him, "Lord, how often shall my brother sin against me, and I forgive him? As many as seven times?" Jesus said to him, "I do not say to you seven times, but seventy times seven.

"Therefore the kingdom of heaven may be compared to a king who wished to settle accounts with his servants. When he began the reckoning, one was brought to him who owed him ten thousand talents; and as he could not pay, his lord ordered him to be sold . . . and payment to be made. So the servant fell on his knees, imploring him, 'Lord, have patience with me, and I will pay you everything.' And out of pity for him the lord of that servant released him and forgave him the debt. But that same servant . . . came upon one of his fellow servants who owed him a hundred denarii; and seizing him by the throat he said, 'Pay what you owe.' So his fellow servant fell down and besought him, 'Have patience with me, and I will pay you.' He refused and went and put him in prison till he should pay the debt. When his fellow servants saw what had taken place . . . they went and reported to their lord. . . . Then his lord summoned him and said to him, 'You wicked servant! I forgave you all that debt . . . and should not you have had mercy on your fellow servant, as I had mercy on you?' And in anger his lord delivered him to the jailers, till he should pay all his debt. So also my heavenly Father will do to every one of you, if you do not forgive your brother from your heart."

—Mt. 18:21–35

IN GOD'S PRESENCE, CONSIDER . . .

When I'm burdened by the awareness of my own sins, or hurt by those who have sinned against me, do I allow the influence of the evil one as he whispers that my sins are too much for God's mercy, or that others' sins are too much for me to forgive? Jesus wasn't telling Peter (and us) to forgive only 490 times, but rather, to be like God in His unlimited mercy. I know that if I gratefully receive this from Him, it will transform me.

CLOSING PRAYER

Father of Mercy, Father of Love, You reveal that all has been paid in the Blood of Christ; Help me to remember that everytime I fall, I can come back to You for forgiveness. Flood me with Mercy, so that the only language my heart understands is the language of freedom, the language of forgiveness, the eloquence of heavenly abundance, and help me to respond to others in this way.

As the Father Loves . . .

Pope Francis shows us that forgiving others is not just a duty—it's the measuring gauge for becoming "true children of the Father," and the pathway to real peace and joy.

In the parables devoted to mercy, Jesus reveals the nature of God as that of a Father who never gives up until he has forgiven the wrong and overcome rejection with compassion and mercy. We know these parables well, three in particular: the lost sheep, the lost coin, and the father with two sons (cf. Lk 15:1–32). In these parables, God is always presented as full of joy, especially when he pardons. In them . . . mercy is presented as a force that overcomes everything, filling the heart with love and bringing consolation through pardon. . . .

In reply to Peter's question about how many times it is necessary to forgive, Jesus says: "I do not say seven times, but seventy times seven times" (Mt 18:22). . . . Jesus affirms that mercy is not only an action of the Father, it becomes a criterion for ascertaining who his true children are. In short, we are called to show mercy because mercy has first been shown to us. Pardoning offenses becomes the clearest expression of merciful love, and . . . pardon is the instrument placed into our fragile hands to attain serenity of heart. To let go of anger, wrath, violence, and revenge are necessary conditions to living joyfully. Let us therefore . . . listen to the words of Jesus who made mercy an ideal of life and a criterion for the credibility of our faith: "Blessed are the merciful, for they shall obtain mercy" (Mt 5:7). . . .

The mercy of God is his loving concern for each one of us. He . . . desires our wellbeing and he wants to see us happy, full of joy, and peaceful. This is the path which the merciful love of Christians must also travel. As the Father loves, so do his children. Just as he is merciful, so we are called to be merciful to each other.

—Pope Francis, *Misericordiae Vultus (The Face of Mercy)*, 9

IN GOD'S PRESENCE, CONSIDER . . .

Do I thank God for adopting me as His own child? Do I seek to live my life according to my adoption as a child of God?

CLOSING PRAYER

Lord Jesus, You are the First-born of all creation, send us Your Holy Spirit. Let us live according to the dignity given to us in our adoption by the Father. Help us to live as faithful members of the divine family. Make us worthy sons and daughters of God. Teach us to love. For You are Lord forever and ever. Amen.

Forgiving but Not Forgetting . . .

"I can forgive, but I cannot forget." A pretty common experience. So, what can we do? At times people are told that they need to work harder at it, that they need to forgive AND forget. But the Catechism explains that we don't have the power to forget, or to stop feeling hurt. And forgetting isn't the point. It's what we do when the memories resurface that matters.

. . . as we forgive those who trespass against us

This "as" is not unique in Jesus' teaching: "You, therefore, must be perfect, as your heavenly Father is perfect"; "Be merciful, even as your Father is merciful"; "A new commandment I give to you, that you love one another, even as I have loved you, that you also love one another." [Mt 5:48; Lk 6:36; Jn 13:34] It is impossible to keep the Lord's commandment by imitating the divine model from outside; there has to be a vital participation, coming from the depths of the heart, in the holiness and the mercy and the love of our God. Only the Spirit by whom we live can make "ours" the same mind that was in Christ Jesus. [Cf. Gal 5:25; Phil 2:1, 5] Then the unity of forgiveness becomes possible and we find ourselves "forgiving one another, as God in Christ forgave" us. [Eph. 4:32] [521]

Thus the Lord's words on forgiveness, the love that loves to the end, [Cf. Jn 13:1] become a living reality.The parable of the merciless servant, . . . ends with these words: "So also my heavenly Father will do to every one of you, if you do not forgive your brother from your heart." [Cf. Mt 18:23–35] It is there, in fact, "in the depths of the heart," that everything is bound and loosed. It is not in our power not to feel or to forget an offense; but the heart that offers itself to the Holy Spirit turns injury into compassion and purifies the memory in transforming the hurt into intercession. [368]

—*Catechism of the Catholic Church*, 2842–2843

IN GOD'S PRESENCE, CONSIDER . . .

"The unity of forgiveness"—I can't forgive on my own. I need to ask the Holy Spirit to give me the "mind of Christ" so that I can forgive with Him and in Him, and learn to "turn injury into compassion."

CLOSING PRAYER

Lord, I forgive (or I want to forgive) all who have hurt me. But I know I won't be able to fully forget; so each time the memory of a past hurt comes back and re-wounds my heart, help me to offer it to the Holy Spirit as a prayer of intercession for the one who hurt me. If I'm not there yet, fill me with more of Your grace so that I can be truly free and love like You.

Love Rewrites Everything

We have lived in a fallen human world with our fallen human perspective for so long that we can't fathom there is another way to see things—another way to live. The Holy Spirit invites us into the freedom of love.

We are told that we must forgive one another, that we may not bear a grudge, that we should be meek and kind. . . . All of this is important. But if we regard it as a list of different commands to observe, it will look quite hopeless. . . .

Instead of thinking of rules and regulations, we can be conscious of reality. . . . If we *know*, if we existentially know, that together we make up *one* Body, we no longer *can* be angry or envious of one another. The ears are not envious of the eyes, nor are the eyes envious of the ears. When one part of the body suffers, the remaining part does not feel malicious pleasure, but, rather, the entire body mobilizes to help the suffering part. "If one member suffers, all suffer together; if one member is honored, all rejoice together" (1 Cor 12:26).

Everything becomes so simple when we live in the truth. To forgive is no longer something magnificent, making us feel proud of ourselves. To forgive is obvious. Or rather, there is hardly anything to forgive. The arm does not forgive the leg because it is broke. When the prodigal son returns to the Father, the Father does not say in a solemn way: "My son, I forgive you." He does not even give his son the chance to finish his repentant confession. "His father saw him and had compassion, and ran and embraced him and kissed him" (Lk 15:20). He immediately brings him back to the level where they are one with each other. Love makes sin invisible (1 Pet 4:8). Forgiveness is not necessary, since love hides the sins.

—Fr. Wilfrid Stinissen, OCD, *The Holy Spirit: Fire of Divine Love*

IN GOD'S PRESENCE, CONSIDER . . .

Do I believe in the Holy Spirit, the Lord, the giver of life? Do I believe that His infinite power can illuminate my being entirely with a love that transforms me completely? That with the blind who see and the lame who dance, I can experience the liberating mercy of God?

CLOSING PRAYER

Come Holy Spirit, breathe into me the love of the Father, that I may discover who I truly am—a delight to you, a delight to the Good Shepherd who seeks me.

First Forgiving

Catherine Doherty exhorts us that to love we must forgive—And not just extending mercy to others, but to ourselves.

The time is now to forgive. Begin with oneself, for one must always begin with one-self. Christians on the North American continent are guilt-ridden. Because of this we often attack the ones before whom perhaps we ought to feel especially guilty, if we're going to feel guilty at all! We do this to get out of the dead-end street to which we have come.

The Lord said, "Love your neighbor as yourself." Which means we must love ourselves first, for we are, in a manner of speaking, our first neighbor. In order to love, one must forgive. For one cannot love the object of hostility, anger, hatred and unforgiveness. Yes, we must begin with forgiving ourselves as our Father in heaven forgives us. Simply, most sincerely and with grave humility, we must acknowledge our sins. . . . This means that we have to go into the very depths of our souls and bring them, our faults, into the light. . . . Then, after having begged forgiveness for them from God, we must forgive ourselves.

How often have we gone to confession, been forgiven, but remained uneasy, tragically still feeling guilty of those very sins we have just confessed to God. We do not really trust either his love or his forgiveness. This is the hour in which we must begin to understand that we must love one another, and that means first forgiving ourselves and everybody else!

—Catherine de Hueck Doherty, *The Gospel Without Compromise*

IN GOD'S PRESENCE, CONSIDER . . .

Are there weaknesses I struggle with or sins in my past that I have not forgiven myself for, even though I have received God's mercy through the Sacrament of confession? Is there a part of me that cannot seem to receive love? Perhaps the good of sacrificing myself for others is partially tainted by lies I believe about my own worth. But Jesus makes it clear that I cannot truly love the "other" unless I love myself as beloved of God, deserving of care and kindness.

CLOSING PRAYER

Oh Lord, it is often easier to forgive others than it is to forgive myself. But how can I truly love my neighbor if I refuse to believe that I am Your beloved? I see that it is when I believe I am precious, unrepeatable, overflowing with Your mercy that I can authentically love those around me.

Be Merciful Before He Comes

How do you know you've learned a language well? When you can speak it fluently. Entering fully into God's mercy means we effortlessly share mercy with others. St. Augustine takes us from rookie to pro level.

All the trees of the forest will exult before the face of the Lord, for he has come, he has come to judge the earth. . . .

He will judge the world with equity and the peoples in his truth. What are equity and truth? He will gather together with him for the judgment of his chosen ones, but the others he will set apart; for he will place some on his right, others on his left. What is more equitable, what more true than that they should not themselves expect mercy from the judge, who themselves were unwilling to show mercy before the judge's coming. Those, however, who were willing to show mercy will be judged with mercy. For it will be said to those placed on his right: *Come, blessed of my Father, take possession of the kingdom which has been prepared for you from the beginning of the world.* And he reckons to their account their works of mercy: *For I was hungry and you gave me food to eat; I was thirsty and you gave me drink.*

What is imputed to those placed on his left side? That they refused to show mercy. And where will they go? *Depart into the everlasting fire. . . .* If you wish to receive mercy, be merciful before he comes; forgive whatever has been done against you; give of your abundance. Of whose possessions do you give, if not from his? If you were to give of your own, it would be largess; but since you give of his, it is restitution. *For what do you have, that you have not received?* These are the sacrifices most pleasing to God: mercy, humility, praise, peace, charity. Such as these, then, let us bring and, free from fear, we shall await the coming of the judge *who will judge the world in equity and the peoples in his truth.*"

—St. Augustine of Hippo, *Discourse on the Psalms*
(Ps 95, 14,15: CCL39, 1351–1353)

IN GOD'S PRESENCE, CONSIDER . . .

Do I find myself critical, judging others, quick to condemn? The fruit I bear springs from the heart—if I haven't truly received mercy, I won't be capable of sharing it with others.

CLOSING PRAYER

Lord Jesus Christ, You delight in showing mercy, You rejoice to bless. Make my heart like unto Thine, swift to love and console.

Seventy Times Seven

Being merciful, writes Fr. Kosicki, means "continuously forgiving," every time we're hurt or displeased by anything or anyone—no matter what the situation.

Then Peter came up and said to him, "Lord, how often shall my brother sin against me, and I forgive him? As many as seven times?" Jesus said to him, "I do not say to you seven times, but seventy times seven." (Mt 18:21–22)

We are merciful by being continuously forgiving—70 times seven times a day! This means forgiving in all the great and "little" things of our daily lives, forgiving ourselves, friends, family, co-workers—and even God—for situations that displease us. Every time we feel ourselves getting impatient, angry, or frustrated, we have an opportunity to forgive, an opportunity to cry, "I repent, I forgive." I repent for my part in this situation, and I forgive them for their part . . . "Jesus, mercy!"

A beautiful example of being merciful by forgiving comes out in an incident between two women at a bookshop. The owner came into the bookshop one day, and started directing the work of the manager, and this with her usual gusto. The manager started to fume inside while trying to keep her cool on the outside. Afterwards, she went to her parish priest and vented her feelings about the interference in her work. After she had vented her anger for a while, Father interrupted with the question, "Was the owner right or wrong?"

"She was wrong!" retorted the woman with no uncertainty in her voice.

"Wonderful," Father responded, "Now you are in the perfect situation to be a Christian and forgive her!"

To be merciful is to forgive without considering the rightness or the wrongness of the situation. This is the way Christ has forgiven us, and the way we are to forgive one another.

—Fr. George Kosicki, CSB, Faustina, *Saint for Our Times*

IN GOD'S PRESENCE, CONSIDER . . .

Do I get so caught up in responding to my own hurts, my own awareness of being wronged by others, that I miss the opportunities to forgive?

CLOSING PRAYER

Lord, help me develop an "attitude of forgiveness" as a way of life. Reveal to me any areas where I'm holding on to resentment or unforgiveness. And, during times when I feel I need to cling to an injustice, remind me of Your mercy to me, which is far greater than any mercy I could ever show to another.

Reciprocal Love

Mercy in its truest form, is where our misery meets the Heart of God. This meeting can be explained with different nuances: His Heart is moved by our misery and comes toward us; the love from the Heart of the Trinity overflows into our misery and transforms it; our misery is dissolved in the Heart of God; and so much more. But the important thing is that mercy involves both an opening and an outpouring of hearts. And even in human interactions where mercy is received but not returned, it is a creative love which benefits the giver.

Man attains to the merciful love of God, His mercy, to the extent that he himself is interiorly transformed in the spirit of that love towards his neighbor. This . . . is not just a spiritual transformation realized once and for all: it is a whole lifestyle, an essential and continuous characteristic of the Christian vocation. It consists in the constant discovery and persevering practice of love as a unifying and also elevating power despite all difficulties of a psychological or social nature: it is a question, in fact, of a merciful love which, by its essence, is a creative love.

In reciprocal relationships between persons, merciful love is never a unilateral act or process. Even in the cases in which everything would seem to indicate that only one party is giving and offering, and the other only receiving and taking . . . in reality the one who gives is always also a beneficiary.

—St. Pope John Paul II, *Rich in Mercy*, 14

IN GOD'S PRESENCE, CONSIDER . . .

My entire life with God is meant to be a dialogue of mercy. I want to open myself up to receiving His mercy through the beauty of trust. And, though it's often harder to desire, I do want to show love to those who won't necessarily return it. I know that when I am filled by You, God, I feel content and fulfilled no matter what happens around me.

CLOSING PRAYER

Your mercy, Lord, is a creative love, whether it comes to me from Your Heart, or goes out to others through me. Help me to remember that all I need is You, and that whenever I show love to others, it is simply me sharing what You have already given me in great abundance.

Good Measure, Running Over

Jesus upends our human structures with His Divine Vision: Divine Mercy. In these central verses of His teaching in Luke's Gospel, He invites us to trust fully in His mercy, and become merciful ourselves.

Judge not, and you will not be judged; condemn not, and you will not be condemned; forgive, and you will be forgiven; give, and it will be given to you; good measure, pressed down, shaken together, running over, will be put into your lap. For the measure you give will be the measure you get back.

He also told them a parable: "Can a blind man lead a blind man? Will they not both fall into a pit? A disciple is not above his teacher, but every one when he is fully taught will be like his teacher. Why do you see the speck that is in your brother's eye, but do not notice the log that is in your own eye? Or how can you say to your brother, 'Brother, let me take out the speck that is in your eye,' when you yourself do not see the log that is in your own eye? You hypocrite, first take the log out of your own eye, and then you will see clearly to take out the speck that is in your brother's eye.

—Luke 6:37–42

IN GOD'S PRESENCE, CONSIDER . . .

Do I believe that God pours out his gifts upon me in abundance? Or do I still live with a scarcity mindset, feeling the need to hoard my limited resources? Can I open my heart to God's fullness?

CLOSING PRAYER

Heavenly Father, Your mercies wash over me like an endless flood. Hold me always in Your goodness, that I may be radiant with Your love and overflow with Your mercy.

Becoming Paracletes

Christ promised to send the Holy Spirit as "another Paraclete." Fr. Cantalamessa explains that when the Holy Spirit fills us, he enables each of us to become paracletes as well.

The title "Paraclete" not only speaks about God's mercy toward us but also opens for us a whole new field of acts of mercy for one another. We need, in other words, to become paracletes ourselves! If it is true that the Christian needs to be an alter Christus, "another Christ," it is just as true that he or she needs to become "another paraclete." The love of God has been poured into our hearts through the Holy Spirit (see Romans 5:5), whether it be the love with which God loves us or the love that has made us in turn capable of loving God and our neighbor. When applied to mercy—which is the form love takes in the face of the suffering and sin of a person who is loved— . . . the Paraclete not only comforts us; he also comes to comfort others and makes us able to comfort them and be merciful. St. Paul writes, "Blessed be the God and Father of our Lord Jesus Christ, the Father of mercies and God of all comfort, who comforts us in all our affliction, so that we may be able to comfort those who are in any affliction, with the comfort with which we ourselves are comforted by God [italics added]" (2 Corinthians 1:3–4). . . .

In a certain sense, the Holy Spirit needs us in order for him to be the "Paraclete." He wants to comfort, defend, and exhort, but he has no mouth, hands, or eyes to "embody" his consolation. . . . Just as our soul acts, moves, and smiles through the members of our body, so the Holy Spirit does the same through the members of "his" body, the Church and us. St. Paul recommends to the early Christians, "Therefore encourage one another" (1 Thessalonians 5:11); translated literally the verb here means "make yourselves paracletes for one another." If the consolation and the mercy we receive from the Spirit do not flow from us to others, if we selfishly want to keep it for ourselves, then very soon it stagnates.

—Raniero Cantalamessa, *The Gaze of Mercy*

IN GOD'S PRESENCE, CONSIDER . . .

I know I'm called to receive and give mercy, but have I realized that it's the Holy Spirit who makes that possible, who pours the love of the Father and the Son out for me as mercy—not only to comfort and encourage me but to also enable me to extend that same mercy to others? Can I now turn to Him more earnestly and often for that grace?

CLOSING PRAYER

Come Holy Spirit and fill me with a longing to become "another paraclete," another comforter for those in need of mercy,

Love Is a Person

As the most neglected person of the Trinity, the Holy Spirit, whom we profess as the Lord, the giver of life, is the presence that lifts us up into love that is living, breathing—personal.

The Holy Spirit is love, and love is the Holy Spirit. Love is a person. Even this can become concrete for us. If love is the Holy Spirit, then you know that you are in contact with him when you live in love. *Ubi caritas et amor, Deus ibi est* (Where there is love, there is God). As soon as you begin to love, you are living in the atmosphere of God.

At the same time, you realize that it now becomes easier to love. You do not need to do it yourself. There is no need to strain or force yourself to have beautiful feelings. It is the Spirit who loves in you, and it is enough that you let him in.

In the end, love becomes more personal. It issues forth from a Person, a divine Person, and therefore it also makes the human being a person. Love is not a diffuse, impersonal force but, rather, a "personalizing" force. The love that is the Holy Spirit makes you who you are. And when you become an instrument of the Spirit and allow him to work in you, you in your turn help others to become real persons. . . .

Is this not the hallmark of Christian love, that it is extremely personal and gives rise to deep, personal bonds of friendship?

—Fr. Wilfrid Stinissen, OCD, *The Holy Spirit, Fire of Divine Love*

IN GOD'S PRESENCE, CONSIDER . . .

Am I ready to live in the Divine atmosphere—love overflowing? Today can I invite the Holy Spirit to fill me, and to awaken love and delight in my heart? Who is the Holy Spirit drawing into my life today for me to love and to reveal love to me?

CLOSING PRAYER

Come Holy Spirit, fill the hearts of Your faithful. Fill my heart with the fire of Your love. Inflame me with Your love from on high, that I may abide this entire day held in Your fire.

The Demands of Mercy . . .

Jesus made it clear to St. Faustina that faith in his mercy is not enough. If we wish to receive mercy, we must show mercy to others in whatever ways we can, through our actions, words, and prayers.

My daughter, if I demand through you that people revere My mercy, you should be the first to distinguish yourself by this confidence in My mercy. I demand from you deeds of mercy, which are to arise out of love for Me. You are to show mercy to your neighbors always and everywhere. You must not shrink from this or try to excuse or absolve yourself from it. I am giving you three ways of exercising mercy toward your neighbor: the first—by deed, the second—by word, the third—by prayer. In these three degrees is contained the fullness of mercy, and it is an unquestionable proof of love for Me. By this means a soul glorifies and pays reverence to My mercy. Yes, the first Sunday after Easter is the Feast of Mercy, but there must also be acts of mercy, and I demand the worship of My mercy through the solemn celebration of the Feast and through the veneration of the image which is painted. By means of this image I shall grant many graces to souls. It is to be a reminder of the demands of My mercy, because even the strongest faith is of no avail without works. . . .

Write this for the many souls who are often worried because they do not have the material means with which to carry out an act of mercy. Yet spiritual mercy, which requires neither permissions nor storehouses, is much more meritorious and is within the grasp of every soul. If a soul does not exercise mercy somehow or other, it will not obtain My mercy on the day of judgment. Oh, if only souls knew how to gather eternal treasure for themselves, they would not be judged, for they would forestall My judgment with their mercy.

—St. Faustina, *Diary*, 742, 1317 (Christ's words)

IN GOD'S PRESENCE, CONSIDER . . .

How seriously do I take the Lord's command to be merciful? And do my works of mercy come from a sense of social obligation, or do they "arise out of love" for Jesus?

CLOSING PRAYER

Lord, don't let me just hang the Divine Mercy Image on the wall and look at it occasionally. Let it be a constant reminder to me to be merciful in my daily life.

Draped in Beauty . . .

Fr. Iain Matthew tells us that the brothers who were difficult would be sent to live with St. John of the Cross, who would receive it as a mercy from God. In fact, he saw everything and everyone he encountered as coming from that powerful and merciful Hand—given its being, held in existence, and utterly dependent on the merciful gaze of the Father.

'Oh—send him to John of the Cross. He won't mind . . . ' There is evidence here of someone who sees beneath the gauche exterior; who reads creation in a different way. . . . For John, the created universe, from the slightest inflection of a thought to the course of a comet, is being given its being by Another. It exists, because Another is looking at it. The world is that childlike: total dependence on the sustaining breath of God. Constantly we are being held out of disintegration by the loving gaze of our Father.

Hence John's language: to love creation apart from God, outside of God, in opposition to God—with 'disordered longing'—is really to commit it to nothingness, to make it supremely ugly. To love creation in God is to be part of something supremely tender. Creation—the mountains round Granada; the night sky at Segovia; philosophy at Salamanca; gaolers, lice and nightmares in Toledo—is in fact bathed, held, in the gaze of John's Beloved, and cannot but be a motive for praise:

Mil gracias derramando
Pasó por estos sotos con presura,
y, yéndolos mirando,
con sola su figura
vestidos los dejó de hermosura.

Pouring out a thousand graces
He passed this way in haste;
He cast his gaze across the
  woodland
Bathed it with his face,
And left it draped in beauty. (SC, stanza 5)

—Fr. Iain Matthew OCD, *John of the Cross: Seasons of Prayer*

IN GOD'S PRESENCE, CONSIDER . . .

All things are utterly dependent on God holding them in existence—including me. How easy it is for me to think I have control over things, how easy it is to love creation apart from the Creator. How many things have I made supremely ugly with disordered longing, separating them from God?

CLOSING PRAYER

God of beauty, teach me to praise You for all things. May I never love anything apart from You, but rather love it in You, as a part of You.

Fixed on You

God is so supremely merciful, that not only did He take on our nature, but He knows we cannot even love Him, or turn from things that keep us from Him, without His grace.

My Lord, I believe, and know, and feel, that You are the Supreme Good. And, in saying so, I mean, not only supreme Goodness and Benevolence, but that You are the sovereign and transcendent Beautifulness. I believe that, beautiful as is Your creation, it is mere dust and ashes, and of no account, compared with You . . . I know well, that this is why the Angels and Saints have such perfect bliss, because they see You. To see even the glimpse of Your true glory, even in this world throws holy men into an ecstasy. And I feel the truth of all this, in my own degree, because You have mercifully taken our nature, and have come to me as man. "Et vidimus gloriam ejus, gloriam quasi Unigeniti a Patre"—"and we saw His glory, the glory as it were of the only begotten of the Father." The more, O my dear Lord, I meditate on Your words, works, actions, and sufferings in the Gospel, the more wonderfully glorious and beautiful I see You to be.

And therefore, O my dear Lord, since I perceive You to be so beautiful, I love You, and desire to love You more and more. Since You are the One Goodness, Beautifulness, Gloriousness, in the whole world of being, and there is nothing like You, but You are infinitely more glorious and good than even the most beautiful of creatures, therefore I love You with a singular love. . . . Everything, O my Lord, shall be dull and dim to me, after looking at You. There is nothing on earth, not even what is most naturally dear to me, that I can love in comparison to You. And I would rather lose everything than lose You. . . .

O my God, whatever is nearer to me than You, things of this earth, and things more naturally pleasing to me, will be sure to interrupt the sight of You, unless Your grace interfere. . . . Keep my whole being fixed on You. Let me never lose sight of You; and, while I gaze on You, let my love of You grow more and more every day.

—St. John Henry Newman, *Meditations on Christian Doctrine*, III, 3, 1–3

IN GOD'S PRESENCE, CONSIDER . . .

"Beauty will save the world." Dostoevsky saw what Newman shares today: God draws me to Himself by overwhelming attraction. What distracts me from that vision today? What impedes me from resting in God's delight?

CLOSING PRAYER

Most Loving Savior, You are radiance and beauty: smash the lies that drive my vision downward into grim responsibility and burden, and raise my eyes to the majesty of Your presence.

The Turning of God Against Himself

God's love for us, says Pope Benedict, is so strong that it actually turns God against Himself—against the strict norms of justice.

God's love for man goes far beyond the aspect of gratuity. Israel has committed "adultery" and has broken the covenant; God should judge and repudiate her. It is precisely at this point that God is revealed to be God and not man: "How can I give you up, O Ephraim! How can I hand you over, O Israel! . . . My heart recoils within me, my compassion grows warm and tender. I will not execute my fierce anger, I will not again destroy Ephraim; for I am God and not man, the Holy One in your midst" (Hos 11:8–9). God's passionate love for his people—for humanity—is at the same time a forgiving love. It is so great that it turns God against himself, his love against his justice. Here Christians can see a dim prefigurement of the mystery of the Cross: so great is God's love for man that by becoming man he follows him even into death, and so reconciles justice and love.

. . . In Jesus Christ, it is God himself who goes in search of the "stray sheep," a suffering and lost humanity. When Jesus speaks in his parables of the shepherd who goes after the lost sheep, of the woman who looks for the lost coin, of the father who goes to meet and embrace his prodigal son, these are no mere words: they constitute an explanation of his very being and activity. His death on the Cross is the culmination of that turning of God against himself in which he gives himself in order to raise man up and save him. This is love in its most radical form. By contemplating the pierced side of Christ (cf. 19:37), we can understand the starting-point of this Encyclical Letter: "God is love" (1 Jn 4:8). It is there that this truth can be contemplated. It is from there that our definition of love must begin. In this contemplation the Christian discovers the path along which his life and love must move.

—Pope Benedict XVI, *Deus Caritas Est (God is Love)*, 10, 12

IN GOD'S PRESENCE, CONSIDER . . .

In recognizing my own sinfulness, do I tend to see God as angry, judgmental, or condemning, or do I rejoice that His love is greater than my sin? I take a moment now to contemplate this mystery: the tenderness of a love that should smite, but instead suffers—all for love.

CLOSING PRAYER

Lord, help me to learn from You how to respond to others with a warm and forgiving love.

Justice and Mercy

Father Jean D'Elbee, in his book on the spirituality of St. Therese, presents here her insightful and comforting view of God's justice.

We can base our confidence, not only on the mercy of God, but also on His justice, always following the example of little Thérèse. "To me," she cries, "He has given His infinite mercy, and it is through this that I contemplate and adore the other divine perfections. Then they all appear to me radiant with love. Even justice itself, perhaps even more than anything else, appears to me clothed in love. What a sweet joy to think that God is just, that is to say, that He takes our weaknesses into account, that He knows perfectly the frailty of our nature! Of what, therefore, should I be afraid?" [*Manuscrits autobiograpiques*, 209]

And to her spiritual brother, Father Roulland: "I know that we must be very pure in order to appear before the God of all holiness., but I know also that the Lord is infinitely just and it is justice, which terrifies so many souls, which is the object of my joy and confidence. . . . I hope for as much from the justice of God as from His mercy. It is because He is just that He is compassionate and full of gentleness, slow to punish and abounding in mercy, for He knows our frailty. He remembers that we are nothing but dust." [Letter, May 9,1897]

And climbing higher: "since You have loved me to the point of giving Your only Son as my Savior and my Spouse, the infinite treasures of His merits are mine. I gladly offer them to You, begging You to look at me only through the face of Jesus and in His Heart burning with love. . . . In the evening of this life I shall appear before You with empty hands, for I do not ask You to count my works. All our justices are stained in Your eyes. I want therefore to clothe myself in Your own justice and receive from Your love the eternal possession of Yourself." [St. Therese's *Act of Offering*]

—Jean C.J. d'Elbee, *I Believe in Love*, pp. 75–76

IN GOD'S PRESENCE, CONSIDER . . .

Have I understood justice this way before, or do I see it more as something to fear? Do I think of it as the attribute that opposes God's mercy, instead of as integral to His mercy?

CLOSING PRAYER

God of justice, You know all my frailty and failings, and it is Your justice that takes my "weaknesses into account." You see in justice what I am due, and yet in justice You also see my utter weakness and failed attempts as mitigating factors. It is because You are perfectly just that Your mercy then overflows to my weak soul. Help me to have abounding joy and confidence in Your justice as well as Your mercy.

God's Justice *Is* His Mercy

Pope Francis shows us that mercy is "not opposed to justice," but goes beyond it.

It would not be out of place at this point to recall the relationship between *justice* and *mercy*. These are not two contradictory realities, but two dimensions of a single reality that unfolds progressively until it culminates in the fullness of love. Justice is a fundamental concept for civil society, which is meant to be governed by the rule of law. Justice is also understood as that which is rightly due to each individual. . . . The appeal to a faithful observance of the law must not prevent attention from being given to matters that touch upon the dignity of the person.

Jesus affirms that . . . the rule of life for his disciples must place mercy at the centre, as Jesus himself demonstrated by sharing meals with sinners. Mercy, once again, is revealed as a fundamental aspect of Jesus' mission. This is truly challenging to his hearers, who would draw the line at a formal respect for the law. Jesus, on the other hand, goes beyond the law; the company he keeps with those the law considers sinners makes us realize the depth of his mercy. . . .

God's justice is his mercy (cf. *Ps* 51:11–16). Mercy is not opposed to justice but rather expresses God's way of reaching out to the sinner, offering him a new chance to look at himself, convert, and believe. . . . If God limited himself to only justice, he would cease to be God, and would instead be like human beings who ask merely that the law be respected. But mere justice is not enough. . . . God goes beyond justice with his mercy and forgiveness. Yet this does not mean that justice should be devalued or rendered superfluous. On the contrary: anyone who makes a mistake must pay the price. However, this is just the beginning of conversion, not its end, because one begins to feel the tenderness and mercy of God. God does not deny justice. He rather envelopes it and surpasses it with an even greater event in which we experience love as the foundation of true justice.

—Pope Francis, *Misericordiae Vultus (The Face of Mercy)*, 20–21

IN GOD'S PRESENCE, CONSIDER . . .

Do I associate justice only in reference to following rules or do I also understand it as relating to the respect and dignity owed to each person?

CLOSING PRAYER

Lord, help me not to be so focused on the strict norms of justice that I fail to be forgiving and merciful.

Mercy, the Central Nucleus of the Gospel

Saint Pope John Paul II and Pope Benedict XVI both had hearts that compelled them to promulgate the message of Divine Mercy.

In one of his *Regina Caeli* Messages, Pope John Paul II said, "What is mercy if not the boundless love of God, who confronted with human sin, restrains the sentiment of severe justice and, allowing Himself to be moved by the wretchedness of His creatures, spurs Himself to the total gift of self, in the Son's cross . . . ? Who can say that he is free from sin and does not need God's mercy? As people of this restless time of ours, wavering between the emptiness of self-exaltation and the humiliation of despair, we have a greater need than ever for a regenerating experience of mercy."

Years later, in an *Angelus* Message, Pope Benedict XVI called John Paul "a great apostle of Divine Mercy" and echoed his predecessor's thoughts saying, "In our time, humanity needs a strong proclamation and witness of God's mercy. Beloved John Paul II, a great apostle of Divine Mercy, prophetically intuited this urgent pastoral need. He dedicated his second Encyclical to it and throughout his pontificate made himself a missionary of God's love to all peoples."

And in a *Regina Caeli* Address, Benedict expounded on this theme saying that, "Mercy is the central nucleus of the Gospel message; it is the very name of God, the Face with which he revealed himself in the Old Covenant and fully in Jesus Christ, the incarnation of creative and redemptive Love. May this merciful love also shine on the face of the Church and show itself through the sacraments, in particular that of Reconciliation, and in works of charity, both communitarian and individual. May all that the Church says and does manifest the mercy God feels for man."

—*Quotes from Pope Benedict XVI and Pope John Paul II*

IN GOD'S PRESENCE, CONSIDER . . .

Does my life witness to the "central nucleus of the Gospel message"? Do my thoughts, words, and actions "manifest the mercy God feels for man"?

CLOSING PRAYER

Father of mercy, I am in need, sometimes multiple times a day, of a "regenerating experience of mercy." And I want to be a part of bringing that to a world that so desperately needs Your mercy. Help me to manifest in my daily life, in my daily interactions, the mercy You feel for each person.

Turning Toward the Lord

Psalm 86 is from Book III of the Psalms, a very honest passage in which David shares his heart with us as he finds himself falling into grief—to be human is to need God, and neediness often feels like pain.

Turn your ear, O Lord, and give answer
for I am poor and needy.
Preserve my life, for I am faithful:
save the servant who trusts in you.

You are my God, have mercy on me, Lord,
for I cry to you all the day long.
Give joy to your servant, O Lord,
for to you I lift up my soul.

O Lord, you are good and forgiving,
full of love to all who call.
Give heed, O Lord, to my prayer
and attend to the sound of my voice.

In the day of distress I will call
and surely you will reply.
Among the gods there is none like you, O Lord;
nor work to compare with yours.

All the nations shall come to adore you
and glorify your name, O Lord:
for you are great and do marvelous deeds,
you who alone are God.

Show me, Lord, your way
so that I may walk in your truth.
Guide my heart to fear your name.

—Psalm 86:1–11 *Liturgy of the Hours*

IN GOD'S PRESENCE, CONSIDER . . .

When I'm hurting, do I try to repair myself? How much of my life have I lived trying to clean myself up before presenting myself to my Father? Can David help me discover that I have a Father filled with mercy, a Father whose love I desperately need?

CLOSING PRAYER

Father of Love, I am sorry for how often I try to pull myself together on my own. Thank you for inspiring Your beloved David to show me that I'm never alone—and that I should always call upon You in the instant I feel distress. You are here for me, Father—I love You.

Well-groomed

Fr. Jacques Philippe reminds us that true sanctity is not becoming good on our own but is, on the contrary, absolute dependence on God's mercy.

There is an important illusion that must be exposed: we would like to present ourselves before the Lord only when we are presentable, well-groomed and content with ourselves! But there is a lot of presumptuousness in that attitude! In effect, we would like to bypass the need for mercy. But what is the nature of this pseudo-sanctity . . . which would result in our thinking that we no longer have need of God? True sanctity is, on the contrary, to increasingly recognize how much we absolutely depend upon His mercy!

When you feel wounded . . . when you feel that you have committed some fault, whether it be from pure weakness or with reflection and malice, do not distress yourself . . . do not allow yourself to become chagrined and irritated; but address yourself immediately to God and tell Him, with humble confidence: "It is now, oh, my God, that I can see what I am. For what can one expect from a weak and blind creature like me but wrongdoing and failure?

Then without becoming troubled, turn all of your anger against the passions that dominate you, principally against those that were the cause of your sin. . . . Afterwards, render a thousand thanks to the Father of Mercies; love Him more than ever, seeing that far from resenting the hurt that you just caused Him He still extends His hand to you, for fear that you will fall again into a similar mess.

Finally, full of confidence, tell Him: "Show me oh, my God, that which you are; help a humiliated sinner to feel your divine mercy; forgive me all my offenses; do not permit me to separate or distance myself from you, however little; fortify me with your grace, so that I may never offend you again."

—Fr. Jacques Philippe, *Searching for and Maintaining Peace*

IN GOD'S PRESENCE, CONSIDER . . .

It is hard to accept that God really does want me to come to Him with my mess, my weakness, my imperfection. The world tells me to get my act together, put forward a good image, get it right . . . and all I need to do with Him is to say with confidence, "I love You, I need You, have mercy on me."

CLOSING PRAYER

Lord, sometimes I choose the wrong fight. When I fail, I turn my anger against You or against myself in condemnation. Help me to turn instead to You with contrition and confidence, and then bring the battle to my passions and to the enemy of my soul.

The Triumph of Mercy

God's plan of mercy cannot be defeated. There will be times of destruction and desolation, times when all seems lost, but mercy will triumph. All will be reclaimed, restored, rebuilt; all will be drawn back to the Lord.

Go to Media, my son, for I fully believe what Jonah the prophet said about Nineveh, that it will be overthrown. But in Media there will be peace for a time. Our brethren will be scattered over the earth from the good land, and Jerusalem will be desolate. The house of God in it will be burned down and will be in ruins for a time. But God will again have mercy on them, and bring them back into their land; and they will rebuild the house of God, though it will not be like the former one until the times of the age are completed. After this they will return from the places of their captivity, and will rebuild Jerusalem in splendor. And the house of God will be rebuilt there with a glorious building for all generations for ever, just as the prophets said of it. Then all the Gentiles will turn to fear the Lord God in truth, and will bury their idols.

—Tobit 14:4–6

IN GOD'S PRESENCE, CONSIDER . . .

As I listen to the gentle father Tobit send his brave son Tobiah on mission, can I hear God the Father speaking to me through the trials and setbacks of this life, which relentlessly drive forward to the fulfillment of God's merciful and providential plan?

CLOSING PRAYER

Father, You are so good, You are so faithful, You see my past, present and future; and You divinely script every affliction and blessing to draw me and all Your children into the divine remedy of Christ's blood and victory.

"Abba," the Tender Father

Through the indwelling of the Holy Spirit we come to discover the true face of the Father of Mercy.

An essential work of the Holy Spirit with respect to mercy is also that of changing the picture people have in their minds of God after they sin. One of the causes—perhaps the main one—for the alienation of people today from religion and faith is the distorted image they have of God. It is also the cause of a lifeless Christianity that has no enthusiasm or joy and is lived out more as a duty than as a gift, by constraint rather than by attraction. . . .

The first thing the Holy Spirit does when he comes to dwell in us is to reveal a different face of God to us. He shows him to us as an ally, as a friend, as the one who "did not spare his own Son but gave him up for us all" (Romans 8:32). In brief, the Holy Spirit shows us a very tender Father who has given us the law not to stifle our freedom but to protect it. A filial sentiment then arises that makes us spontaneously cry, "Abba, Father." It is like saying, "I did not know you, or I knew you only from hearing about you. Now I know you, I know who you are, and I know that you truly wish good for me and that you look upon me with favor!" A son or daughter has now replaced a servant; love has replaced fear. This is what happens on the subjective and existential level when a person is "born anew of the Spirit" (see John 3:5, 7–8).

—Raniero Cantalamessa, *The Gaze of Mercy*

IN GOD'S PRESENCE, CONSIDER . . .

There are many reasons people have a distorted image of who the Father is. Are there any ways I still view Him, especially after I sin, that are not compatible with this view of Him as a tender Father, who looks on me with delight and wants to give me good things?

CLOSING PRAYER

Abba, my friend, my good Father, the One who finds joy in my existence . . . I want to know You more. Holy Spirit, please continue to reveal to me the true face of the Father.

God Images & Mercy

In this fallen world, we all bear wounds that are linked to sin, or simply to others not being who we needed them to be, failing to reflect to us the tenderness of God and how He delights in us. These wounds often grow deeper because we then develop false images of who we are and who the Father is, and so keep Him at a distance. But mercy longs to heal . . .

One of the reasons the Image of Divine Mercy is so powerful, is that it came directly from Jesus revealing Himself and the Father. Jesus is "the image of the invisible God" (Col.1:15), the true and perfect image of the Father. Seeing Him, we see the Father and realize that there's no need to hide or run from Him. He is the One who comes to us with gentle mercy, one hand raised in blessing to counter all the times we have not been blessed by those around us, the other inviting us into His Heart of love. He is the One with kind eyes that do not lie, the One who speaks the truth over our lives: that we are created in His image, that we are good, and that the only way to keep His mercy from penetrating our lives is to harden our hearts to receiving it.

Learning Who God really is—His goodness, His character, His desire to heal our wounds—enables us to begin to truly trust Him. And as we gaze on the Divine Mercy Image, that trust is engendered in us as we come to see Him as He is, as we come to see that He is actually the only one who is fully trustworthy! Our false images of Him are destroyed by encountering Who He has revealed Himself to be. And the truth about God also reveals the truth about us. As we come to recognize Who He is and how He looks on us, the false images we have of ourselves fall away as well. Our hearts were made from Love and for Love. Nothing in this world matters more than discovering that we are each the precious lost sheep He comes to find, the child He longs to hold and protect, the beloved He wants to bless with His mercy.

—Erin Flynn

IN GOD'S PRESENCE, CONSIDER . . .

What false images do I have of God? Do I see Him as a taskmaster, a tyrant, a puppet master, a clockwinder who sets me up and expects me to function in this world on my own? Are there experiences I have had with people that have caused me to see God for something other than who He has revealed Himself to be?

CLOSING PRAYER

Father, Jesus, Holy Spirit, I want to know You as You truly are and trust in the revelation that You are a God of mercy and love. What do You want to say to me about who You are? Please eradicate any of my false beliefs and reveal Your Heart to me.

The Father's Love Made Visible

St. Paul refers to Christ as "the image of the invisible God" (Col 1:15). Who's the invisible God? The Father. Christ came to let us see the Father in Him and to show us that this Father is rich in mercy.

In Christ and through Christ, God . . . becomes especially visible in His mercy. . . . Not only does He speak of it and explain it by the use of comparisons and parables, but above all He Himself makes it incarnate and personifies it. He Himself, in a certain sense, is mercy. To the person who sees it in Him—and finds it in Him—God becomes "visible" in a particular way as the Father who is "rich in mercy. . . ."

Christ, then, reveals God who is Father, who is "love," as St. John will express it in his first letter; Christ reveals God as "rich in mercy," as we read in St. Paul. This truth is not just the subject of a teaching; it is a reality made present to us by Christ. Making the Father present as love and mercy is, in Christ's own consciousness, the fundamental touchstone of His mission as the Messiah. . . .

The truth, revealed in Christ, about God the "Father of mercies," enables us to "see" Him as particularly close to man especially when man is suffering. . . . In fact, revelation and faith teach us not only to meditate in the abstract upon the mystery of God as "Father of mercies," but also to have recourse to that mercy in the name of Christ and in union with Him. Did not Christ say that our Father, who "sees in secret," is always waiting for us to have recourse to Him in every need and always waiting for us to study His mystery: the mystery of the Father and His love?

—St. Pope John Paul II, *Rich in Mercy*, 2–3

IN GOD'S PRESENCE, CONSIDER . . .

What does it mean to "study the mystery of the Father and his love"? How can I begin to do that? How might it change my life to really take into my heart the awareness that God the Father is "always waiting" for me to turn to Him in every need?

CLOSING PRAYER

Thank you, Father, for sending Jesus to show us who you are. Help me to fully embrace you as my Father and turn to you with trust in every situation.

From Glory to Glory . . .

What did people see in Moses after his encounter with God on the mountain and in Jesus on the mountain of the Transfiguration? The Glory of God.

Glory. Another often-used Christian word. What *is* glory? What is it that they see? St. Paul speaks of "the glory of Christ, who is the *likeness* of God," and again, of "the glory of God in the *face* of Christ" (2 Cor 4:4, 6; emphasis added). So glory somehow involves being in the likeness of God. And that likeness can be reflected in the human body.

Ring any bells? There are some pretty clear echoes here of some of the *Catechism's* teachings we saw back in Secret 2. Our human bodies are created in such a way—in His image and likeness—that they can *reflect the divine form*. But then, "disfigured by sin" we are "deprived 'of the glory of God,' of his 'likeness.'" So Christ is sent to "assume that 'image' and restore it in the Father's 'likeness.'" How? "By giving it again its Glory, the Spirit who is 'the giver of life'" (#705).

So, the glory of God is manifested in us by His Holy Spirit, the radiating, transforming, life-giving Spirit of God.

What did the people see in Moses' face? What did the disciples see in Christ's face? They saw the manifestation of divinity, the reflected glory of God. Moses and Jesus were transfigured, meaning that they radiated God's glory. They had become transparent to God, and divinity was visible in their human bodies.

That's the goal of Divine Mercy, for each of us to become transparent to God, so restored in the Father's likeness, so filled with God's own life, His holiness, that we reflect His eternal glory.

—Vinny Flynn, *7 Secrets of Divine Mercy*

IN GOD'S PRESENCE, CONSIDER . . .

How often do I mistake human endeavor for what will lift me up, rather than recognize that my transformation flows from the radiant Glory of God? Where the angels veil their faces, can I open myself to encounter the transforming, life-giving Spirit of God, who alone can restore me?

CLOSING PRAYER

Lord God of Hosts, You have revealed Your Glory in the Eucharistic presence of the Lamb of God, Jesus my Merciful Savior. Raise my eyes to the Glory of Jesus's divine face. Help me to become so filled with His mercy that I become "transparent" to Him and radiate His Glory to others.

Miracles in Us

Receiving miracles in our lives involves believing what God wants to do—and allowing Him to do it.

Jesus doesn't just want to forgive us. He wants to change us. He doesn't merely want to pardon us for our trespasses, like a judge would do. He wants to heal us of the roots of sin, like a doctor, so we can live life to the fullest and not be weighed down by our many weaknesses.

But the problem today is that many of us don't really believe we can be healed. Yes, we say we believe in a God who hears our prayers and can work wonders in our souls. But deep down we're not convinced. We think we have too many problems. Our lives are too complex for God to fix. Some of our hurts and bad habits run so deep that, as Pope Francis says, we consider "our illness, our sins, to be incurable, things that cannot be healed or forgiven. . . . We don't believe that there is a chance for redemption; for a hand to raise you up; for an embrace to save you, forgive you, pick you up, flood you with infinite, patient, indulgent love; to put you back on your feet" (*The Name of God is Mercy*).

But the same Jesus who gave sight to the blind, cured the sick, and helped the lame to walk wants to work miracles in us—if we let him. He wants to cure us of whatever blindness keeps us from seeing our lives accurately. He wants to heal us of whatever sins hinder us from following him. And in the areas of our lives where we feel helpless, paralyzed, or completely unable to change, he wants to liberate us and empower us to pick up our mats and walk again.

—Edward Sri, *Into His Likeness*

IN GOD'S PRESENCE, CONSIDER . . .

Do I truly believe that God wants to pour His mercy on the areas in my life where I need healing? Do I sometimes feel unfixable, or get stuck in self-reliance, doubt, or even resentment because I still feel broken or in need, and trusting Him hasn't seemed to "work" to bring about healing?

CLOSING PRAYER

Increase my faith, Jesus, that there is a hand reaching out to me, that there is freedom and healing for me as I journey with You, and that You will bring it about in Your perfect time and way.

The Son Set

Confession is about forgiveness, right? Scott Hahn teaches here that while forgiveness is a good (and necessary) gift, it is actually meant to prepare us for something more. We are forgiven so that God can fulfill in us His plan of mercy, to restore us as children and heirs.

Forgiveness is a great gift, but it's a penultimate gift. It's intended to prepare us for something still greater. Christians are saved not only *from* sin, but *for* sonship—divine sonship in Christ. We are not just criminals who have been exonerated; we are sons and daughters who have been adopted. We are children of God, "sons in the Son," and we share the life of the Trinity.

We are indeed forgiven by God's grace, but not merely forgiven; we are adopted and divinized. That is, we "become partakers of the divine nature" (2 Pet 1:4). This is ultimately why God created man, to share in the life-giving love of the Trinity. Self-sacrificial love is the essential law of God's covenant, which man broke but Jesus kept. Through the incarnation, God transformed human nature into a perfect image—and instrument—of the Trinity's love, by offering it as a sacrificial gift-of-self to the Father on our behalf. The Son of God "took the form of a servant" (Phil 2:6) so that sinful servants may be restored as sons of God. As Saint Athanasius declared; "The Son of God became the son of Man so that sons of men could become sons of God."

The essential effect of confession, then, is enabling our forgiveness so that we can be restored to Trinitarian life. As adopted children, Christians can "call God 'Father,' in union with the only Son" (*CCC*, n. 1997).

—Scott Hahn, *Lord Have Mercy*

IN GOD'S PRESENCE, CONSIDER . . .

How many times do I treat confession as just a thing I have to do so that I can get forgiveness? What needs to happen in me and in my life so that I can more fully resemble God in whose image I was created—to look like my Dad the way Jesus does? And what is one thing I can do each day to foster the type of union I am called to have with God?

CLOSING PRAYER

Father, remind me that repentance and forgiveness are about me being transformed into the person I was created to be, and returning to my relationship with You as Your child. Draw me deeper into the reality of this gift and help me be a better vessel of the life-giving love of the Trinity to those around me.

A Tombstone Over Our Sins

Like his order's founder, St. Francis of Assisi, a fellow stigmatist, Padre Pio knew the transforming power of Christ's wounds. He writes here of the value of suffering and of the inexhaustible mercy Jesus won for us.

"One day when we are able to see the full midday light, we will know what value and what treasures our earthly sufferings have been that have made us gain our everlasting Homeland."

"I feel a great desire to abandon myself with greater trust to the Divine Mercy and to place my hope in God alone."

"When disturbed by passions and misfortunes, may the sweet hope of His inexhaustible mercy sustain us. Let us hasten confidently to the tribunal of penance where He awaits us at every instant with the anxiety of a father; and even though we are aware of our inability to repay Him, let us have no doubts about the solemn pardon pronounced over our errors. Let us place a tombstone over them, just as the Lord has done."

"My past, O Lord, to your Mercy; my present, to your Love; my future, to your Providence!"

—St. Padre Pio

IN GOD'S PRESENCE, CONSIDER . . .

I am truly transformed in the confessional by the Lord's mercy. What happens after that depends very much on whether I trust in that mercy and live in each present moment of grace. Do I have a tendency to ruminate on either the past or the future?

CLOSING PRAYER

Father, You wait for me always to return to You after a fall and, with astonishing mercy, You place *a tombstone over my sins. Grant me a "great desire to abandon myself with greater trust to the Divine Mercy" in all things and to place my hope in You alone.*

Returning to the Father

In the parable of the prodigal son, Jesus shows us that the various stages of our lives can be seen as parts of a "process of conversion" in our journey back to the Father and His mercy.

. . . [E]very sincere act of worship or devotion revives the spirit of conversion and repentance within us and contributes to the forgiveness of our sins.

The process of conversion and repentance was described by Jesus in the parable of the prodigal son, the center of which is the merciful father: the fascination of illusory freedom, the abandonment of the father's house; the extreme misery in which the son finds himself after squandering his fortune; his deep humiliation at finding himself obliged to feed swine, and still worse, at wanting to feed on the husks the pigs ate; his reflection on all he has lost; his repentance and decision to declare himself guilty before his father; the journey back; the father's generous welcome; the father's joy—all these are characteristic of the process of conversion. The beautiful robe, the ring, and the festive banquet are symbols of that new life—pure, worthy, and joyful—of anyone who returns to God and to the bosom of his family, which is the Church. Only the heart of Christ who knows the depths of his Father's love could reveal to us the abyss of his mercy in so simple and beautiful a way.

—*Catechism of the Catholic Church*, 1437, 1439

IN GOD'S PRESENCE, CONSIDER . . .

Do I get lost in focusing on and rehashing individual experiences and situations, or am I able to truly accept the Father's welcome and His desire to grant me new life?

CLOSING PRAYER

Father, let every sincere act of worship and devotion revive the spirit of repentance and conversion in me. Sometimes I stray from You many times a day and need to turn and come back to You with my whole heart. I love You, God. Help me to be fully open to Your grace at every junction of my path back to You.

(Nothing but) Our Miseries (and) His Mercy . . .

The French Catholic Jesuit Jean-Pierre de Caussade writes here in one of his letters about the necessity of abandoning all to the mercy of God, even our uncertainty about where we are in the spiritual life.

When, in the course of one's life one has made a general confession in good faith; all the ideas and anxieties that follow are so many idle scruples which the enemy makes use of to trouble the peace of the soul, to make one lose time, and to weaken and diminish one's confidence in God. Do not let us foolishly fall into this trap; let us abandon all the past to the infinite mercy of God, all the future to His fatherly Providence, and think only of profiting by the present. The "fiat" formed in the mind by repeated acts and gradually reduced to an habitual disposition, leads to all that perfection which ignorant and mistaken people seek far and wide in all sorts of ways.

For the rest, do not imagine that you tire me by speaking of your miseries. By dint of seeing nothing but poverty and misery in oneself, one is not surprised at finding the same in others. . . . May it sink deeply into your heart as well as this sentence . . . which I copy for you because I think it is exactly what will console and encourage you. "We are obliged to live and to die in the deepest uncertainty, not only as to the judgments of God about us, but also as to our own dispositions." "We must," says St. Augustine, "have nothing of our own to present to God but our own miseries, but then we have His very great mercy which is our only title to His love, through the merits of Jesus Christ." Often reflect on these beautiful sayings in which you will find peace for your mind, abandonment, confidence, and the greatest certainty in the very midst of doubt.

—Rev. Jean-Pierre de Caussade SJ, *Abandonment to Divine Providence*

IN GOD'S PRESENCE, CONSIDER . . .

Are there any sins in my life that I have confessed and yet am still troubled by? Even if I believe I am forgiven, is there shame that lingers or thoughts about myself that repeat in my head? I want to abandon all to God's infinite mercy and fatherly Providence.

CLOSING PRAYER

Lord, with my sins, once I have confessed them, and even with any uncertainty about my growth in holiness, help me to form within myself a perpetual fiat that simply seeks to say yes to You in all things and abandon everything to Your mercy.

The Sacrament of Healing . . .

Many do not know that confession is actually a sacrament of healing. And it is such a rich experience of relationship with God that, under the main title of healing, there are a list of other names as well.

The Lord Jesus Christ, physician of our souls and bodies, . . . has willed that his Church continue . . . his work of healing and salvation. . . . This is the purpose of the two sacraments of healing: the sacrament of Penance and the sacrament of Anointing of the Sick.

THE SACRAMENT OF PENANCE AND RECONCILIATION

It is called the sacrament of conversion because it makes sacramentally present Jesus' call to conversion, the first step in returning to the Father from whom one has strayed by sin. It is called the sacrament of Penance, since it consecrates the Christian sinner's personal and ecclesial steps of conversion, penance, and satisfaction. It is called the sacrament of confession, since the disclosure or confession of sins to a priest is an essential element of this sacrament. In a profound sense it is also a "confession"—acknowledgment and praise—of the holiness of God and of his mercy toward sinful man. It is called the sacrament of forgiveness, since by the priest's sacramental absolution God grants the penitent "pardon and peace." It is called the sacrament of Reconciliation, because it imparts to the sinner the love of God who reconciles.

This endeavor of conversion is not just a human work. It is the movement of a "contrite heart," drawn and moved by grace to respond to the merciful love of God who loved us first.[19] St. Peter's conversion after he had denied his master three times bears witness to this. Jesus' look of infinite mercy drew tears of repentance from Peter and, after the Lord's resurrection, a threefold affirmation of love for him.

—*Catechism of the Catholic Church*, 1421–1424, 1428–1429

IN GOD'S PRESENCE, CONSIDER . . .

I think of the grace-filled reality behind the names of this great Sacrament: confession, forgiveness, penance, reconciliation, conversion, healing. Which names resonate with me? Which ones am I disinclined towards?

CLOSING PRAYER

God of infinite mercy, no matter how I view this Sacrament, there is always more. Show me what aspect of it to focus on now that will help me most.

Coming Out of Ourselves

Pope Francis shows us what it means to follow Jesus in a life of mercy for others.

God does not wait for us to go to him but it is he who moves towards us. . . . . That is what God is like. He always takes the first step, he comes towards us.

Jesus lived the daily reality of the most ordinary people: he was moved as he faced the crowd that seemed like a flock without a shepherd; he wept before the sorrow that Martha and Mary felt at the death of their brother, Lazarus; he called a publican to be his disciple; he also suffered betrayal by a friend. In him God has given us the certitude that he is with us, he is among us.

"Foxes," Jesus, said, "have holes, and birds of the air have nests, but the Son of man has nowhere to lay his head" (Mt 8:20). Jesus has no house, because his house is the people; it is we who are his dwelling place. His mission is to open God's doors to all, to be the presence of God's love. . . .

What is the meaning of all this for us? It means that this is my, your, and our road too. . . . Following Jesus means learning to come out of ourselves . . . in order to go to meet others, to go towards the outskirts of existence, to be the first to take a step towards our brothers and our sisters, especially those who are the most distant, those who are forgotten, those who are most in need of understanding, comfort and help. There is such a great need to bring the living presence of Jesus, merciful and full of love!

Following and accompanying Christ, staying with him, demands "coming out of ourselves," . . . out of a dreary way of living faith that has become a habit, out of the temptation to withdraw into our own plans which end by shutting out God's creative action. . . .

Be sure to remember: coming out of ourselves, . . . just as God came out of himself in Jesus, and Jesus came out of himself for all of us.

—Pope Francis, General Audience, March 27, 2013

IN GOD'S PRESENCE, CONSIDER . . .

How seriously have I taken Christ's command to take up my cross and follow Him? What can I do to come out of myself more and "take a step" towards others in need?

CLOSING PRAYER

Lord Jesus, help me to make my heart a dwelling place for You and become a reflection of Your presence to all I meet.

Help Me, Lord . . .

St. Faustina's prayer reflects specific ways we can truly become the body of Christ in response to the scriptural command to "be merciful just as [also] your Father is merciful" (Lk 6:36, NABRE)

Help me, O Lord, that my eyes may be merciful, so that I may never suspect or judge from appearances, but look for what is beautiful in my neighbors' souls and come to their rescue.

Help me, that my ears may be merciful, so that I may give heed to my neighbors' needs and not be indifferent to their pains and moanings.

Help me, O Lord, that my tongue may be merciful, so that I should never speak negatively of my neighbor, but have a word of comfort and forgiveness for all.

Help me, O Lord, that my hands may be merciful and filled with good deeds, so that I may do only good to my neighbors and take upon myself the more difficult and toilsome tasks.

Help me, that my feet may be merciful, so that I may hurry to assist my neighbor, overcoming my own fatigue and weariness. My true rest is in the service of my neighbor.

Help me, O Lord, that my heart may be merciful so that I myself may feel all the sufferings of my neighbor.

I will refuse my heart to no one. I will be sincere even with those who, I know, will abuse my kindness. And I will lock myself up in the most merciful Heart of Jesus. I will bear my own suffering in silence. May Your mercy, O Lord, rest upon me.

—St. Faustina, *Diary*, 163, 692, 164

IN GOD'S PRESENCE, CONSIDER . . .

If I use Faustina's prayer as an examination of conscience, what can I learn about myself? How am I doing as a member of the mystical body of Christ? Eyes, ears, tongue, hands, feet, heart? Which of Faustina's petitions do I need to pray most fervently?

CLOSING PRAYER

Father of mercy, help me to focus more intentionally on the ways I can love as You love and become a more complete embodiment of Your mercy to others.

The Renewal of Your Mind

St. Paul in the letter widely considered to be his masterpiece reveals to us a life transformed in the merciful radiance of God, utterly transfused with Divine Life. Here, he extends to us an invitation to throw off the confines of the former selves, and to live in an entirely new realm of the Spirit in communion with one another.

I appeal to you therefore, brethren, by the mercies of God, to present your bodies as a living sacrifice, holy and acceptable to God, which is your spiritual worship. Do not be conformed to this world but be transformed by the renewal of your mind, that you may prove what is the will of God, what is good and acceptable and perfect.

For by the grace given to me I bid every one among you not to think of himself more highly than he ought to think, but to think with sober judgment, each according to the measure of faith which God has assigned him. For as in one body we have many members, and all the members do not have the same function, so we, though many, are one body in Christ, and individually members one of another. Having gifts that differ according to the grace given to us, let us use them: if prophecy, in proportion to our faith; if service, in our serving; he who teaches, in his teaching; he who exhorts, in his exhortation; he who contributes, in liberality; he who gives aid, with zeal; he who does acts of mercy, with cheerfulness.

—Romans 12:1–8

IN GOD'S PRESENCE, CONSIDER . . .

If I receive it and respond to it, the mercy of God can raise me into a new level of being. I want to use the gifts He's given me and embrace the gifts that others have. The same light that floods into me unites me with my brothers and sisters: we become one body united in love.

CLOSING PRAYER

Lord Jesus Christ, from the dawn of time You have held a splendid destiny for me as I am raised up from flimsy egoism into the fullness of Your Mercy. Draw me close to You, and in so doing, reveal to me the intimacy of communion with all Your loved ones.

The "Primacy of Mercy" for Confessors

In a strong teaching on confession, Pope Francis explains that the priest is called and gifted to participate in Christ's mission of divine love in the confessional, reflecting the Father's mercy "always, everywhere, and in every situation."

I will never tire of insisting that confessors be authentic signs of the Father's mercy. We do not become good confessors automatically. We become good confessors when, above all, we allow ourselves to be penitents in search of his mercy. Let us never forget that to be confessors means to participate in the very mission of Jesus to be a concrete sign of the constancy of divine love that pardons and saves. We priests have received the gift of the Holy Spirit for the forgiveness of sins, and we are responsible for this. None of us wields power over this Sacrament; rather, we are faithful servants of God's mercy through it. Every confessor must accept the faithful as the father in the parable of the prodigal son: a father who runs out to meet his son despite the fact that he has squandered away his inheritance. Confessors are called to embrace the repentant son who comes back home and to express the joy of having him back again. Let us never tire of also going out to the other son who stands outside, incapable of rejoicing, in order to explain to him that his judgement is severe and unjust and meaningless in light of the father's boundless mercy. May confessors not ask useless questions, but like the father in the parable, interrupt the speech prepared ahead of time by the prodigal son, so that confessors will learn to accept the plea for help and mercy pouring from the heart of every penitent. In short, confessors are called to be a sign of the primacy of mercy always, everywhere, and in every situation, no matter what.

—Pope Francis, *Misericordiae Vultus (The Face of Mercy)*, 17

IN GOD'S PRESENCE, CONSIDER . . .

What an awe-inspiring gift Christ plans for us all in the confessional, where through His priests He gives us access to our merciful Father.

CLOSING PRAYER

Father, in Jesus's name, I pray for a fuller outpouring of grace on all confessors! Strengthen and inspire them to a deeper awareness and acceptance of the awesome responsibility and privilege You have entrusted to them as ministers of Your mercy.

Meeting Christ Personally

*Confession is not about you and a priest; it's about you and Jesus. "When you go to confession," Jesus told St. Faustina, ". . . the Blood and Water which came forth from My Heart always flows down upon your soul. . . . I Myself am waiting there for you there" (*Diary, *1702).*

As I wrote in *7 Secrets of the Eucharist*, the priest, through his ordination, "is not merely authorized to represent Christ, but rather is uniquely and sacramentally identified with Him."

So what? So it's not just the priest who hears your confession; and it's not the priest who acts in your soul. It's Christ. As Pope John Paul II explains, "In the sacrament of Reconciliation we are all invited to meet Christ personally." He stresses that this is why individual confession is so necessary, because it provides each of us with the opportunity for "a more personal encounter with the crucified, forgiving Christ, with Christ saying, through the minister of the sacrament, . . . 'Your sins are forgiven; go and do not sin again.'" [Homily, September 29, 1979]

To meet Christ personally? I was never taught that. As a child, I was taught how to go to confession, and I was taught that, if I committed serious sin, then I had to go to confession. I learned all about the ritual and the rules, but I never heard anything about going to meet Jesus personally. And yet this is the most important thing for us all to understand!

As Fr. Raniero Cantalamessa explains, we need to learn to live confession not as a rite, a habit, or a canonical obligation, but as a personal encounter with the Risen One who allows us, as he did Thomas, to touch his wounds, to feel in ourselves the healing force of his blood and taste the joy of being saved.

—Vinny Flynn, *7 Secrets of Confession*

IN GOD'S PRESENCE, CONSIDER . . .

Have I collapsed Jesus's infinite love into a structure that masks the true power of His mercy and the personal nature of my encounter with Him in the confessional? Today, can I rediscover that Confession, and all the sacraments, draw me back to the font of life, the wounded heart of Jesus overflowing with love for me?

CLOSING PRAYER

Eternal Love, open my eyes to how tender, how living, how personal and intense Your love is for me, especially in the confessional, as I come to meet You personally and reveal to You my deepest self.

The Greatest Right to Mercy

God sees beyond behavior. He sees our weakness, our misery, our woundedness, and all that can lead us into sin. He knows that our sin weakens our relationship with Him, separates us from Him. So He responds with what Pope Francis calls "the judgment of mercy . . . the love that goes beyond justice."

I am mercy itself for the contrite soul. A soul's greatest wretchedness does not enkindle Me with wrath; but rather, My Heart is moved towards it with great mercy (1739). . . . With My mercy, I pursue sinners along all their paths, and My Heart rejoices when they return to Me. I forget the bitterness with which they fed My Heart and rejoice at their return (1728).

When a soul sees and realizes the gravity of its sins, when the whole abyss of the misery into which it immersed itself is displayed before its eyes, let it not despair, but with trust let it throw itself into the arms of My mercy, as a child into the arms of its beloved mother. These souls have a right of priority to My compassionate Heart, they have first access to My mercy. . . . No soul that has called upon My mercy has been disappointed or brought to shame (1541).

I am more generous toward sinners than toward the just. It was for their sake that I came down from heaven; it was for their sake that My Blood was spilled. Let them not fear to approach Me; they are most in need of My mercy (1275). . . . [Let] the greatest sinners place their trust in My mercy. They have the right before others to trust in the abyss of My mercy. . . . Souls that make an appeal to My mercy delight Me. To such souls I grant even more graces than they ask. I cannot punish even the greatest sinner if he makes an appeal to My compassion (1146).

. . . The greater the sinner, the greater the right he has to My mercy (723).

—St. Faustina, *Diary* (Christ's words)

IN GOD'S PRESENCE, CONSIDER . . .

Sinners are the ones who need God's mercy most. I should rejoice at this because I *am* a sinner! When others have more outwardly conspicuous sins, or simply different sins than mine, do I tend to respond with judgment, or do I try to look beyond their actions and respond with compassion?

CLOSING PRAYER

Lord, thank you for continually pursuing me with Your mercy to draw me out of my weakness and sin into a more faithful relationship with You. Give me Your Heart of mercy for others.

Mercy Through the Church

In one of his many well-known sermons, Newman speaks of the Church, the Holy Hill of Zion, as the means through which we can always access God's mercy, and also of the comforting and convicting spiritual world all around us.

Though you are in a body of flesh, a member of this world, you have but to kneel down reverently in prayer, and you are at once in the society of Saints and Angels. Wherever you are, you can, through God's incomprehensible mercy, in a moment bring yourself into the midst of God's holy Church invisible, and receive secretly that aid, the very thought of which is a present sensible blessing. Are you afflicted? You can pray; Are you merry? You can sing psalms. Are you lonely? Does the day run heavily? Fall on your knees, and your thoughts are at once relieved by the idea and by the reality of your unseen companions. Are you tempted to sin? Think steadily of those who may witness your doings from God's secret dwelling-place; Have you lost friends? Realize them by faith; Are you slandered? You have the praise of Angels; Are you under trial? You have their sympathy.

May thoughts like these, my brethren, sink deep into your hearts, and bring forth good fruit in holiness and constancy of obedience. Whatever has been your past life, whether (blessed be God) you have never trusted anything but God's sacred light within you, or whether you have trusted the world and it has failed you, God's mercies in Christ are here offered to you in full abundance. Come to Him for them; approach him in the way He has appointed, and you shall find Him, as He has said, upon His Holy Hill of Zion.

—St. John Henry Newman, Sermon 12,
"The Church a Home for the Lonely"

IN GOD'S PRESENCE, CONSIDER . . .

Saints and angels, gather around. Today I reject my familiar isolation, my trudging through each day as though I'm on my own. Today in faith I open my eyes to each of you, brothers and sisters who accompany on this path of happy destiny.

CLOSING PRAYER

Lord God of Hosts, You who gather the Bride of Christ from east and west, north and south: reveal to me the vast company of those who cheer me on, who delight in my advance, who embrace me in trial.

Knowing We Are Loved

Before we can love God with our whole heart, our whole soul, our whole mind, and our whole strength, we must first be fully aware of how we are loved.

Every saint is a lover. Elizabeth of the Trinity was no exception. Her life was a constant search, inspired by the words of the apostle Paul, *to live through love in his presence* (Eph 1:4). To love, and to be loved, is the deepest of all human needs; it alone gives meaning and a sense of fulfilment to our lives. A few days before her death, Elizabeth said to her sisters, *Everything passes! . . . In the evening of life love alone remains. . . .*

The first and the greatest of all the commandments is to love God with every fibre of our being. Yet, in a strange way, this presupposes something even more fundamental: to know how much we ourselves are loved. Love is a two-way relationship, a giving and receiving. It is the awareness of being loved that gives us our sense of worth and uniqueness; it helps us to realise that we are special, and awakens within us our sense of individuality. . . .

Fear had no part in Elizabeth's understanding of God: she knew herself to be a cherished daughter of her beloved Father. *It is love that makes His burden so light and His yoke so sweet*, she once said (L 22). It was a message she shared with others. As she wrote to a family friend: *if you knew how He loves you, how at every passing moment He wants to give Himself to you more! I am praying very much to Him, that He may carry out fully the dream of His love in you* (L 241).

—Eugene McCaffrey, OCD, *Let Yourself Be Loved*

IN GOD'S PRESENCE, CONSIDER . . .

"Everything passes! . . . In the evening of life love alone remains." How would my life change if I were truly aware of my belovedness? What things would cease to matter, and what would matter more?

CLOSING PRAYER

Father, I am cherished by You, and though I want to love You well, I realize that I can only do that because You loved me first. Thank you for that great mercy. "At every passing moment" You want to give Yourself to me more. I want to be fully aware of that and fully open to You.

Thanks for Everything

It's easy to be thankful when wonderful things happen, but St. Paul tells us to "give thanks in all circumstances; for this is the will of God in Christ Jesus for you" (1 Thes 5:18). St. Faustina teaches us how to put this into practice.

Father of great mercy, I desire that all hearts turn with confidence to Your infinite mercy. No one will be justified before You if he is not accompanied by Your unfathomable mercy. When You reveal the mystery of Your mercy to us, there will not be enough of eternity to properly thank You for it. . . .

Jesus, I thank You for the little daily crosses, for opposition to my endeavors, for the hardships of communal life, for the misinterpretation of my intentions, for humiliations at the hands of others, for the harsh way in which we are treated, for false suspicions, for poor health and loss of strength, for self-denial, for dying to myself, for lack of recognition in everything, for the upsetting of all my plans.

Thank You, Jesus, for interior sufferings, for dryness of spirit, for terrors, fears and incertitudes, for the darkness and the deep interior night, for temptations and various ordeals, for torments too difficult to describe, especially for those which no one will understand, for the hour of death with its fierce struggle and all its bitterness.

I thank You, Jesus, You who first drank the cup of bitterness before You gave it to me, in a much milder form. I put my lips to this cup of Your holy will. Let all be done according to Your good pleasure; let that which Your wisdom ordained before the ages be done to me. I want to drink the cup to its last drop, and not seek to know the reason why. In bitterness is my joy, in hopelessness is my trust. In You, O Lord, all is good, all is a gift of Your paternal Heart. I do not prefer consolations over bitterness or bitterness over consolations, but thank You, O Jesus, for everything!

—St. Faustina, *Diary*, 1122, 343

IN GOD'S PRESENCE, CONSIDER . . .

Do I thank God only when things are going well, or do I trust Him enough to give thanks even when things seem terrible? "Deo gratias" may have to become one of my constant phrases to remind my heart to thank Him in all things.

CLOSING PRAYER

Lord, help me to see everything as a gift from You even when I don't understand, trusting that You really will "turn all things to good for those who love You" (Rom. 8:28).

Our Weakness, His Mercy, and the Holy Spirit . . .

Fr. Philippe writes here of Peter's denial of Jesus and how our failures can lead to a "deep outpouring of the Holy Spirit" and stir up in us a deeper trust in God's mercy.

But the Holy Spirit sometimes impoverishes us. Peter's supreme experience of this kind was at the most terrible point in his life: his denial of Jesus. But through God's mercy that denial became the occasion of a deep outpouring of the Holy Spirit. The Prince of the Apostles wept for his own baseness and sin, but in his tears he received the hope of forgiveness. Peter's denial of his Lord was a terrible fall for him. He was the head of the Apostles. Jesus had chosen him for that. But all his noble sentiments and keen sense of responsibility toward the other disciples crumbled in just a few seconds. All it took was a servant girl in the High Priest's courtyard who asked: "Are not you also one of this man's disciples?" Three times Peter denied his Master . . . But the Holy Spirit, Father of the poor, made use of this terrible fall to touch the Apostle's heart again, very deeply. Peter met Jesus' eyes and understood the full horror of his betrayal. But at the same time he saw that he was not being condemned but loved more tenderly than ever. . . . And Peter broke down in tears, in which his heart was purified there and then. Judas, why did you avoid Jesus' eyes, and so trap yourself in your own despair? Right up until the very end the hope of salvation and forgiveness could have been yours. Your sin was no worse than Peter's.

In Jesus' gaze Peter received an outpouring of the Holy Spirit. One of those sorrowful outpourings that impoverish us but ultimately are infinitely profitable because they show us our powerlessness and oblige us from then on to trust exclusively in God's mercy and faithfulness.

—Fr. Jacques Philippe, *Interior Freedom*

IN GOD'S PRESENCE, CONSIDER . . .

Is there a time I have experienced the gaze of Jesus, thinking it would be (or should be) full of condemnation, and instead it was a look of tenderness and mercy? If so, I remember it now with gratitude and a resolution to love Him more. If not, I place myself in my weakness with Peter after the denial and allow the Lord to look on me.

CLOSING PRAYER

Jesus, I never want to be afraid of meeting Your gaze. If there is ever a resistant part of me that wants to avoid Your eyes, send the Holy Spirit to my poor and needy heart. Remind me that I need not fear my powerlessness and poverty. Convict me of Your love.

Renewed Like the Eagle

As Jesus said to St. Catherine of Siena, I am He who is, you are she who is not. Discovering God's mercy means discovering that He takes care of everything, and we are lifted up like soaring eagles.

Bless the Lord, O my soul;
and all that is within me, bless his holy name!
Bless the Lord, O my soul,
and forget not all his benefits,
who forgives all your iniquity,
who heals all your diseases,
who redeems your life from the Pit,
who crowns you with steadfast love and mercy,
who satisfies you with good as long as you live
so that your youth is renewed like the eagle's. . . .
The Lord is merciful and gracious,
slow to anger and abounding in steadfast love.
He will not always chide,
nor will he keep his anger for ever.
He does not deal with us according to our sins,
nor requite us according to our iniquities.
For as the heavens are high above the earth,
so great is his steadfast love toward those who fear him;

—Psalm 103:1–5, 8–11

IN GOD'S PRESENCE, CONSIDER . . .

Forget not all His benefits. How often do I pile onto my own shoulders the burden of my existence, my responsibilities, my needs and demands, forgetting the God of blessing and abundance, who is steadfast and trustworthy?

CLOSING PRAYER

Father of mercies, You never cease to pour forth Your renewal into the world; You redeem, You heal, You satisfy. Bring renewal into my life in whatever way I need it most, and let all within me bless Your holy name.

A Cry for the Mercy of God

Saint Pope John Paul II calls upon the Church—and each of us—to respond to the various forms of evil that threaten us today by imploring God's mercy for this generation.

At no time and in no historical period—especially at a moment as critical as our own—can the Church forget *the prayer that is a cry for the mercy of God* amid the many forms of evil which weigh upon humanity and threaten it. . . .

The more the human conscience succumbs to secularization, loses its sense of the very meaning of the word "mercy," moves away from God and distances itself from the mystery of mercy, the more *the Church has the right and the duty* to appeal to the God of mercy "with loud cries." (Cf Heb 5:7). . . . These "loud cries" should be the mark of the Church of our times, cries uttered to God to implore His mercy. . . .

Let us implore God's mercy for the present generation. . . . Let us offer up our *petitions, directed by the faith, by the hope, and by the charity* which Christ has planted in our hearts. . . .

In the name of Jesus Christ crucified and risen, in the spirit of His messianic mission, enduring in the history of humanity, *we raise our voices and pray* that the Love which is in the Father may once again be revealed at this stage of history, and that, through the work of the Son and Holy Spirit, it may be shown to be present in our modern world and to be more powerful than evil: more powerful than sin and death. We pray for this through the intercession of her who does not cease to proclaim "mercy . . . from generation to generation," and also through the intercession of those for whom there have been completely fulfilled the words of the Sermon on the Mount: "Blessed are the merciful, for they shall obtain mercy." (Mt 5:7).

—St. Pope John Paul II, *Rich in Mercy*, 15

IN GOD'S PRESENCE, CONSIDER . . .

Do I believe that the Father's love is more powerful than evil, sin, and death? How can I commit to pleading daily for mercy? And what can I do to make His love more present and visible in the world?

CLOSING PRAYER

Father, in Jesus's name, I add my voice to St. Pope John Paul II's and pray that the floodgates of Your mercy will be released upon the world. Help me to do my part by being merciful as you are merciful.

Entrust Judgment to the Mercy of God

Fr. Chris Alar shares important insights about the judgment of grave actions, including the Church's developed understanding of suicide.

The Church teaches that "although we can judge that an act is in itself a grave offense, we must entrust judgment of persons to the justice and mercy of God" (*CCC*, 1861). In other words, we can know that an act such as suicide is objectively grave . . . however, we cannot know that it is definitively a mortal sin. This is because we don't know exactly what someone knew or didn't know about the seriousness of the act, or if their will was entirely free when committing it.

Because we now better understand the mitigating circumstances surrounding suicide, the Church has recently turned to a more personalist view in discerning the path of pastoral care in these situations. The Church and society as a whole have begun to see suicide more often as an act of desperation, of surrender to a human condition that has made living unbearable, than as a cowardly, purely selfish act, or as the sin of despair that is a total rejection of God.

As a result, the Church now tends to look upon those who have taken their own lives with compassion, not condemnation, and with mercy, not judgment. Masses and prayers are now offered for the deceased, and they are often given full burial rites. In past times, it was commonly assumed that those who chose to take their own lives were acting freely, and psychological duress was not always taken fully into account. . . . Today, those mitigating factors are generally taken into account. Therefore, the *Catechism* now teaches the following:

> We should not despair of the eternal salvation of persons who have taken their own lives. By ways known to him alone, God can provide the opportunity for salutary repentance. The Church prays for persons who have taken their own lives (2283).

—Fr. Chris Alar, MIC, *After Suicide*

IN GOD'S PRESENCE, CONSIDER . . .

Suicide is such a painful reality to deal with. Do I pray for those affected by it and for all who struggle with mental health? In other areas of grave matter do I tend to a "judgment of persons" that belongs to God alone?

CLOSING PRAYER

Father, when I am tempted to render judgment, remind me that You alone know the depths of our minds and hearts and that Your mercy is great. I pray for Your peace and hope to descend on all those who need it most right now.

A Flicker of Good Will

In the fifth notebook of her Diary, *St Faustina records dialogues between the merciful Savior and five souls. One of the most powerful is this "Conversation of the Merciful God with a Despairing Soul."*

Jesus: O soul steeped in darkness, do not despair. All is not yet lost. Come and confide in your God, who is love and mercy.

But the soul, deaf even to this appeal, wraps itself in darkness.

Jesus calls out again: My child, listen to the voice of your merciful Father.

In the soul arises this reply: "For me there is no mercy," and it falls into greater darkness, a despair which is a foretaste of hell and makes it unable to draw near to God. Jesus calls to the soul a third time, but the soul remains deaf and blind, hardened and despairing. Then the mercy of God begins to exert itself, and, without any co-operation from the soul, God grants it final grace. If this too is spurned, God will leave the soul in this self-chosen disposition for eternity. This grace emerges from the merciful Heart of Jesus and gives the soul a special light by means of which the soul begins to understand God's effort; but conversion depends on its own will. The soul knows that this, for her, is final grace and, should it show even a flicker of good will, the mercy of God will accomplish the rest.

—St. Faustina, *Diary*, 1486

IN GOD'S PRESENCE, CONSIDER . . .

When I get weighed down by failure, weakness, or habitual sin, do I lose hope and sink into despair, or do I refocus on the Lord and entrust myself to His mercy?

CLOSING PRAYER

Father God, help me to remember that Your mercy is greater than my sin and that You are always seeking to forgive and restore and heal me, no matter what.

Interceding for Life . . .

Fr. Seraphim Michalenko offers a significant teaching about the "most fundamental act of mercy" and shares his insights about the Chaplet as a powerful prayer for life.

I asked you earlier to keep three things in mind: God is Mercy; He wants us to be merciful; and the most fundamental act of mercy is to give life. Now think of it: to be a human father or mother is to create just as God did, out of nothing, to call something from non-being into being by one's love, one's mercy. Understanding the intimate connection between the womb and mercy, is it any wonder that the one to whom God said, "I will make you and the woman irreconcilable enemies" (Gen 3:15), is bent on destroying mothers' wombs? In the Apocalypse we read, "the dragon stood before the Woman who was about to bear a child so that he might devour her child as soon as it was born" (Rev 12:4). Today, the devil can't even wait for the child to be born, but wants to destroy children in the womb.

From the Diary of Blessed Faustina, we learn that she was called to intercede in two ways for those committing the sin of abortion: by her personal suffering and by prayer. . . . What antidote did the Lord give her? The Chaplet of Divine Mercy. . . . I believe that the Chaplet of Divine Mercy is a powerful prayer for life, a prayer that the Lord has given us in order that we may fight the scourge of abortion and every other lack that His mercy alone can supply for.

Let us then, with utmost fervor and gratitude to God, as a recognition of His great mercy towards us and as a sign of our trust in Him, pray the Chaplet of Divine Mercy at every opportunity, especially for the dying, for those contemplating abortion, and for those who have, in any way, sinned against life.

—Fr. Seraphim Michalenko, MIC, "Wombs of Mercy"

IN GOD'S PRESENCE, CONSIDER . . .

In my daily march through life do I lose sight of the extraordinary gift God has bestowed on each person who exists? That just as He breathed life into Adam long ago in the garden, God shares His existence with us? Today I rejoice again in this wondrous gift and commit to praying for those who do not recognize the dignity of each precious life.

CLOSING PRAYER

Father of Mercy, Father of Love, You do not revoke Your heavenly gift, but continue to sustain us even when we depart from this realm. Help me to have a heart that values each life as You do, and to pray that every person who has Your breath of existence will be cherished.

Reparation for Abortion

St. Faustina records in her Diary *that, on at least three occasions, the Lord allowed her to suffer extremely violent pain for three hours in reparation for abortion. For this reason, the Chaplet, which she prayed most often, has become for many a prayer for life—for unborn children, and for those who have had or plan to have an abortion; and it is often prayed by people keeping vigil at abortion clinics.*

At eight o'clock I was seized with such violent pains that I had to go to bed at once. I was convulsed with pain for three hours; that is, until eleven o'clock at night. No medicine had any effect on me, and whatever I swallowed I threw up. At times, the pains caused me to lose consciousness. Jesus had me realize that in this way I took part in His Agony in the Garden, and that He himself allowed these sufferings in order to offer reparation to God for the souls murdered in the wombs of wicked mothers. I have gone through these sufferings three times now. . . . No medicine can lessen these sufferings. When eleven o'clock comes, they cease by themselves, and I fall asleep at that moment. The following day, I feel very weak. This happened to me for the first time when I was at the sanatorium. The doctors couldn't get to the bottom of it, and no injection or medicine helped me at all nor did I myself have any idea of what the sufferings were about. I told the doctor that never before in my life had I experienced such sufferings, and he declared he did not know what sort of pains they are. But now I understand the nature of these pains, because the Lord himself has made this known to me. . . . Yet when I think that I may perhaps suffer in this way again, I tremble. But I don't know whether I'll ever again suffer in this way; I leave that to God. What it pleases God to send, I will accept with submission and love. If only I could save even one soul from murder by means of these sufferings!

—St. Faustina, *Diary*, 1276

IN GOD'S PRESENCE, CONSIDER . . .

In what ways can I join Christ in His agony by offering my sufferings to Him in reparation for the sins of abortion? I consider praying the Chaplet (or praying it more often) specifically for this intention.

CLOSING PRAYER

Lord, Jesus, help me to follow Faustina's example and willingly accept whatever sufferings You send me, offering them up to You in reparation.

Mater Clementissima, Mother Most Merciful . . .

In this prayer of Pope Pius XII, one cannot help but feel the tender and merciful heart of the Blessed Mother towards us. When we come to her—she who is "full of grace" and espoused to the Spirit—we find a place in her heart, where our misery meets God's mercy.

Enraptured by the splendor of your heavenly beauty, and impelled by the anxieties of the world, we cast ourselves into your arms, O Immaculate Mother of Jesus and our Mother, Mary, confident of finding in your most loving heart appeasement of our ardent desires, and a safe harbor from the tempests which beset us on every side.

Though degraded by our faults and overwhelmed by infinite misery, we admire and praise the peerless richness of sublime gifts with which God has filled you, above every other mere creature, from the first moment of your conception until the day on which . . . He crowned you Queen of the Universe.

O crystal fountain of faith, bathe our minds with the eternal truths! O fragrant Lily of all holiness, captivate our hearts with your heavenly perfume! O Conqueress of evil and death, inspire in us a deep horror of sin . . . O well-beloved of God, hear the ardent cry which rises up from every heart. Bend tenderly over our aching wounds. Convert the wicked, dry the tears of the afflicted and oppressed, comfort the poor and humble, quench hatreds, sweeten harshness, safeguard the flower of purity in youth, protect the holy Church, make all men feel the attraction of Christian goodness. In your name . . . may they recognize that they are brothers, and that the nations are members of one family.

Receive, O most sweet Mother, our humble supplications, and above all obtain for us that, one day, . . . we may repeat before your throne that hymn which today is sung on earth around your altars: You are all-beautiful, O Mary! You are the glory, you are the joy, you are the honor of our people! Amen.

—A Prayer of Pope Pius XII

IN GOD'S PRESENCE, CONSIDER . . .

What an image: Mary bending "tenderly over our aching wounds." How many times in my life have I needed that kind of concern and care, but didn't receive it? I resolve to turn to her in all my future needs.

CLOSING PRAYER

Mary, merciful Mother of all mankind, be a mother to me in the places where I need mothering most—where I need comfort, growth, encouragement, guidance, wisdom.

To Touch His Wounds

Pope Benedict exhorts us to have hearts that are alert to the mercy of God all around us, the mercy of this "wounded God," who even in eternity retains the marks of His love.

The Spirit of Jesus Christ is the power of forgiveness. He is the power of Divine Mercy. He makes it possible to start all over again —ever anew. The friendship of Jesus Christ is the friendship of the One who makes us people who forgive, the One who also forgives us, raises us ceaselessly from our weakness . . . and instils in us an awareness of the inner duty of love. . . .

In the Gospel passage for today we also heard the story of the Apostle Thomas' encounter with the Risen Lord: the Apostle is permitted to touch his wounds and thereby recognizes him . . . in his true and deepest identity: "My Lord and my God!" (Jn 20:28).

The Lord took his wounds with him to eternity. He is a wounded God; he let himself be injured through his love for us. His wounds are a sign for us that he understands and allows himself to be wounded out of love for us. These wounds of his: how tangible they are! Indeed, time and again he allows himself to be wounded for our sake. What certainty of his mercy, what consolation! . . . And what security they give us regarding his identity: "My Lord and my God!" And what a duty they are for us, the duty to allow ourselves in turn to be wounded for him!

God's mercy accompanies us daily. To be able to perceive his mercy it suffices to have a heart that is alert. We are excessively inclined to notice only the daily effort that has been imposed upon us as children of Adam. If, however, we open our hearts, . . . we can be constantly aware of how good God is to us; how he thinks of us precisely in little things, thus helping us to achieve important ones.

—Pope Benedict XVI, Homily, St Peter's Square
Second Sunday of Easter, April 15, 2007

IN GOD'S PRESENCE, CONSIDER . . .

Where is my attention throughout each day? Am I inclined to notice only the fallen world and my experience of it? Or is my heart alert and open to *notice* and *receive* all the daily gifts of God's mercy, and respond to them in love?

CLOSING PRAYER

Wounded God, Your love for me is revealed in your Body and in the daily encounters with Your mercy. You make it possible for me to start all over again, each day, even each moment. Help me set my heart's gaze again and again on this gratuitous love flowing from your wounds—until I notice Your mercy everywhere.

With One Voice of Praise

Jesus sees you not as humans do, but with Divine love and insight. His compassion and mercy illuminate your heart to recognize each brother and sister as likewise called to a heavenly destiny far higher than their wildest dreams.

We who are strong ought to bear with the failings of the weak, and not to please ourselves; let each of us please his neighbor for his good, to edify him. For Christ did not please himself; but, as it is written, "The reproaches of those who reproached thee fell on me." For whatever was written in former days was written for our instruction, that by steadfastness and by the encouragement of the scriptures we might have hope. May the God of steadfastness and encouragement grant you to live in such harmony with one another, in accord with Christ Jesus, that together you may with one voice glorify the God and Father of our Lord Jesus Christ. Welcome one another, therefore, as Christ has welcomed you, for the glory of God. For I tell you that Christ became a servant to the circumcised to show God's truthfulness, in order to confirm the promises given to the patriarchs, and in order that the Gentiles might glorify God for his mercy. As it is written, "Therefore I will praise thee among the Gentiles, and sing to thy name".

—Romans 15:1–9

IN GOD'S PRESENCE, CONSIDER . . .

Is my life filled with the drudgery of the mundane, or with Isaiah do I hear the seraphim cry out, "Holy, Holy, Holy" and recognize that Divine Glory pierces this world? In my life here, I am meant to glorify God for His mercy in harmony with my neighbors. Today, I receive God's encouragement in the places where it is difficult for me to live in harmony and keep my eyes fixed on Him.

CLOSING PRAYER

Lord my God, while You are everywhere, I permit my thoughts to drag far too long in the shadows of forgetfulness. For Your glory, grant me a heart of welcome, that bears mercifully with people's failings, and abides always in a song of praise to You.

Prayer—Veronica Wipes the Face of Jesus

Caryll Houselander invites us to walk our own road to Calvary, opening our hearts to mercy.

Saviour of the world,
take my heart,
which shrinks
from the stark realism
and ugliness of suffering,
and expand it with Your love.
Open it wide
with the fire of Your love,
as a rose is opened
by the heat of the sun.

Drive me by the strength
of Your tenderness
to come close to human pain.
Give me hands
that are hardened
by pity,
that will dip into any water
and bathe any wound
in mercy.

Give me Your hands,
hands that heal the blind
by their touch,
hands that raise the dead
and are nailed to the cross;
give me Your hands
to tend the wounds of the body
and the wounds of the mind.

Give me Your eyes
to discern the beauty of your face,
hidden under the world's sorrow.
Give me the grace
to be a Veronica;
to wipe away
the ugliness of sin
from the human face,
and to see
Your smile on the mouth of pain,
Your majesty on the face of
dereliction,
and in the bound and helpless,
the power of Your infinite love.

Lord take my heart
And give me Yours.

—Caryll Houselander, *The Way of the Cross*, Ch. 6

IN GOD'S PRESENCE, CONSIDER . . .

Do I allow the suffering I encounter to expand my heart, or do I let it harden me? The strength of God's tenderness can draw me close to those in pain. What would it look like in my daily life if I allowed His grace to change me, causing me to see with His eyes and reach out with His hands?

CLOSING PRAYER

Lord, take my heart. Expand it with your love. Lord, take my heart. And give me Yours.

A Civilization of Love

During his apostolic visit to Poland in 2002, St. Pope John Paul II proclaimed that the hour has come for the message of mercy to resound throughout the world and "become the spark of a new civilization."

From the beginning of her existence the Church, pointing to the mystery of the Cross and the Resurrection, has preached the mercy of God, a pledge of hope and a source of salvation for man. Nonetheless, it would appear that *we today have been particularly called* to proclaim this message before the world. We cannot neglect this mission, if God himself has called us to it through the testimony of Saint Faustina.

God has chosen our own times for this purpose. Perhaps because the twentieth century, despite indisputable achievements in many areas, was marked in a particular way by the "*mystery of iniquity*". . . . Frequently man lives as if God did not exist, and even puts himself in God's place. He claims for himself the Creator's right to interfere in the mystery of human life. . . . In a variety of ways he attempts to silence the voice of God in human hearts; he wishes to make God the "great absence" in the culture and the conscience of peoples. . . .

In experiencing this mystery, man lives in fear of the future, of emptiness, of suffering, of annihilation. Perhaps for this very reason, it is as if Christ, using the testimony of a lowly Sister, entered our time in order to indicate clearly the source of relief and hope found in the eternal mercy of God.

The message of merciful love needs to resound forcefully anew. The world needs this love. The hour has come to bring Christ's message to everyone: to rulers and the oppressed, to those whose humanity and dignity seem lost in the *mysterium iniquitatis*. The hour has come when the message of Divine Mercy is able to fill hearts with hope and to become the spark of a new civilization: the civilization of love.

—St. Pope John Paul II, Beatification of Four Poles, August 18, 2002

IN GOD'S PRESENCE, CONSIDER . . .

It is easy to become discouraged or angry with the state of things in our world. But, I am called to help build a civilization of love, to counter the mystery of iniquity with the mystery of mercy. How is God calling me personally to do that?

CLOSING PRAYER

Father of Mercy, direct me to the particular ways You want me to spread Your message of mercy that will fill hearts with hope. Give me the guidance and the zeal I need to be a laborer for this civilization of love!

People of Hope

Sometimes we're like the disciples on the road to Emmaus, downcast, without hope, not recognizing Jesus. Or, like the disciples locked in the upper room, we find ourselves fearful, uncertain, discouraged. We might be like that with our suffering, our waylaid plans, or the news stories we hear every day. The author describes the struggle within and the path to hope.

One part of us says, "Hope. All will be well." And another part says, "Hope, really? Do you see what's going on? Do you remember what we've been dealing with? And do you not see that the world is in a time of utter chaos and destruction?" That voice can be dramatic and convincing! Sometimes that part wins out, and there we sit. Overwhelmed. Doubting. Afraid. Without hope. There are many different roads to Emmaus. And many locked upper rooms.

> *"But Jesus came and stood in their midst and said to them, 'Peace be with you.' And when he had said this, he breathed on them and said, 'Receive the holy Spirit'" (Jn. 20:21–22).*
>
> *"He was made known to them in the breaking of the bread" (Lk. 24:35). "Then they said to each other, 'Were not our hearts burning within us while He opened the scriptures to us?'" (Lk. 24:32).*

Breathing. Breaking. Opening. That's our life. It's the gift of each breath. It's the Holy Spirit, the Consoler. And Jesus, our Bread. He breathes into our brokenness: the broken world, the broken heart open to the touch of the Divine . . . and the Dawn from on high breaks upon us, filling us with Himself. That's our source of hope. No matter how broken or messy our lives are, no matter how messy the world is, hope springs eternal. Why? Because the Eternal entered time. Hope entered time. And now nothing is hopeless. No one is hopeless. And by this act of mercy, He showed us that there is a plan of love for each life, each person. A plan in time, and a plan for eternity. So each year, each day, each moment I have breath, I get to try to carry out that plan in time a little bit better, and see how it corresponds to that eternal plan of love.

—Erin Flynn

IN GOD'S PRESENCE, CONSIDER . . .

How often do I allow the circumstances of my daily life, the press of troubles, or the headlines from around the world to weigh me down and sap my hope?

CLOSING PRAYER

God, in Your mercy, breathe upon me a new spirit of hope. Help me recognize Your Presence in all things and stay close to You through all circumstances.

To Comfort the Afflicted

In the Scriptures Satan is called the Accuser, while the Holy Spirit is called the Advocate: the one who speaks on our behalf. The fundamental shift brought by God is from rejection to acceptance.

A person who lets himself be comforted by the Spirit becomes in turn a comfort. Saint Paul has a convincing text about this: He (God) "comforts us in all our affliction, so that we may be able to comfort those who are in any affliction, with the comfort with which we ourselves are comforted by God" (2 Cor 1:4).

If the Spirit comforts you, it is not only so that you will be comforted, but so that his comfort will be extended to others.

The world has perhaps never been in such great need of a "comforter." We ought to have a holy ambition to be a comforter like the Spirit. But we may not forget that we can only comfort "with the comfort with which we ourselves are comforted by God." If our comfort is of our own making, it will have no deep and lasting effect. If we are not ourselves reconciled with God and life, we cannot help others. Then our "comfort" will only be an agreement with the complaints and grumblings of others, and the result will be endless complaining and grumbling.

One becomes a true "comforter" when one mediates something of the acceptance he has himself experienced from God. "Welcome one another, therefore as Christ has welcomed you, for the glory of God" (Rom 15:7). Saint Paul also exhorts us to: "Bear one another's burdens" (Gal 6:2). We bear the burden of another person first of all by *accepting* him as he is. It is not things and circumstances that make up man's heaviest burden, it is he himself. Man is himself a burden by the fact that he does not want to be who he is.

If, then, a "comforter" comes along who accepts him, *with* his limitations, weaknesses, and failures, it will be easier for him to accept himself. If the "comforter" himself has received peace from knowing he is accepted and affirmed by God, he will be able to pass on that peace and say with Jesus: *My* peace I give to *you* (Jn 14:27).

—Fr. Wilfrid Stinissen, OCD, *The Holy Spirit: Fire of Divine Love*

IN GOD'S PRESENCE, CONSIDER . . .

What have I still kept in the shadows, unable to be seen or accepted; places where I do not want to be who I am? What do I hide from the light, in the fear that I will be the first to not be welcomed by God?

CLOSING PRAYER

Come Holy Spirit, open my heart to Your consolation. Lift me up into the light that overpowers all my shadows and holds me in Your safety. Let the comfort I receive flow out to those I meet. May my heart be a place of acceptance and welcome for others.

Past, Present, Future . . .

Fr. Philippe reminds us that all grace, all contact with reality is in the present moment alone. And because of God's infinitely merciful love, each moment allows for the possibility of rich blessings and communion.

All we have is the present moment. Here is the only place where we can make free acts. Only in the present moment are we truly in contact with reality. Someone might think it tragic that the present is so fleeting and neither the past nor the future really belongs to us. But, approached from the standpoint of Christian faith and hope, the present moment is rich in grace and holds immense reassurance. This is where God is present. "I am with you always, to the close of the age." God is the eternal present. Every moment, whatever it brings, is filled with God's presence, rich with the possibility of communion with God. . . . We should learn to live in each moment as sufficient to itself for God is there; and if God is there, we lack nothing. . . .

There is something very liberating in this understanding of the grace of the present moment. Even if the whole of our past has been a disaster, even if our future seems like a dead end, now we can establish communion with God through an act of faith, trust, and abandonment. God is eternally present, eternally young, eternally new, and our past and future are his. He can forgive everything, purify everything, renew everything. "He will renew you in his love." In the present moment, because of his infinitely merciful love, we always have the possibility of starting again, not impeded by the past, or tormented by the future.

—Fr. Jacques Philippe, *Interior Freedom*

IN GOD'S PRESENCE, CONSIDER . . .

It is easy to forget that I only have grace for the present moment. The past cannot be changed and belongs entirely to God's mercy. My future belongs to His providence, and I do not yet have the grace to handle what will come. Even if I am able to do things that will affect my future, I can only do them with God's grace here and now. Union with God, moment by moment, is the only thing necessary.

CLOSING PRAYER

Father, every moment, whatever it brings, is filled with Your presence, rich with the possibility of communion with You. Keep me focused on this reality: that if I unite myself with You, not only do I lack nothing, but it opens my heart up to something far greater than my life here in time.

Prayer Makes (God's) Mercy Present (in the World)

St. Pope John Paul II shows us the intimate connection between prayer and Divine Mercy.

Prayer in our time . . . marks a kind of challenge. We must look at the immensity of good that has sprung from the mystery of the Incarnation of the Word and, at the same time, not lose sight of the mystery of sin, which is continually expanding. Saint Paul writes that "where sin increased" ("ubi abundavit peccatum"), "grace overflowed all the more" ("superabundavit gratia"; cf. Rom 5:20).

This profound truth presents a perennial challenge for prayer. It shows how necessary prayer is for the world and for the Church, because in the end it constitutes the easiest way of making God and His redeeming love present in the world. . . .

The Church prays for the suffering. Suffering, in fact, is always a great test not only of physical strength but also of spiritual strength. Saint Paul's truth about "completing the sufferings of Christ" (cf. Col 1:24) is part of the Gospel. It contains the joy and the hope that are essential to the Gospel; but man will not cross the threshold of that truth without the help of the Holy Spirit. Prayer for the suffering and with the suffering is therefore a special part of this great cry that the Church and the Pope raise together with Christ. It is a cry for the victory of good even through evil, through suffering, through every wrong and human injustice. . . .

Prayer is a search for God, but it is also a revelation of God. . . . Through prayer God reveals Himself above all as Mercy—that is, Love that goes out to those who are suffering, Love that sustains, uplifts, and invites us to trust. The victory of good in the world is united organically with this truth. A person who prays professes such a truth and in a certain sense makes God, who is merciful Love, present in the world.

—St. Pope John Paul II, *Crossing the Threshold of Hope*

IN GOD'S PRESENCE, CONSIDER . . .

What would my daily life look like If I believed more fully that prayer really does have an effect in the world? Do I know deeply that my prayer is powerful in making God's merciful love present to a world entrenched in sin?

CLOSING PRAYER

Father of Mercy, Father of Love, I seek You in prayer and I also want to trust more deeply that through prayer we draw Your redeeming love down upon the whole world. Grant me the zeal I need to pray unceasingly for this suffering world and for the victory of good over evil.

True Faith in Divine Mercy

Fr. Jean D'Elbee speaks to our troubled and fearful hearts of how God's mercy continually extends its tenderness, despite our lack of faith.

What does Jesus lament most when He is with His Apostles? Their lack of confidence. "Men of little faith!" This is the main reproach He makes to them.

Jesus was crossing the lake of Tiberias in a boat with His disciples. He was asleep in the stern. A great windstorm blew up, and the waves poured in the boat. . . . Seized with anguish, the disciples awakened Jesus: "Lord, save us; we are perishing!" [Mt 8:25] And rising up, He reprimands the wind and says to the sea, "Peace! Be still!' And the wind abated." Then turning to His Apostles, He asks, "Where is your faith?" [Mk 4:39] I can hear Jesus scolding them with gentleness, but with pain, too: "Why is this? I was in the boat with you—I slept, but I was there—and you were afraid; you were terrified. You doubted either my omnipotence or my love. Do you not know after all who I am, and . . . with what tenderness my Heart watches over you continually?" It is truly such doubt that pains and offends Him most.

But you see, we have lost so completely the notion of entire confidence that He expects of us, that we sometimes make a prayer of the words for which He reproached His Apostles; "Lord, save us; we are perishing!" This is not how we should pray, but rather, "With You, Jesus, I cannot perish; You are always in the boat with me; what have I to fear? You may sleep; I shall not awaken You. My poor nature will tremble, oh yes! But with all my will I shall remain in peace in the midst of the storm, confident in You."

In hours of anguish, think of the Divine Master calming the violent storm with one word. This will be a tremendous source of comfort for you as you wait—peacefully—for Him to waken.

—Jean C.J. d'Elbee, *I Believe in Love*, pp. 40–41

IN GOD'S PRESENCE, CONSIDER . . .

What situations in my life have caused me to doubt God's omnipotence or His love? What keeps me from trusting that God's merciful Heart watches over me with unimaginable tenderness and that, even as I face suffering, His Presence and His will are all I need?

CLOSING PRAYER

"With You, Jesus, I cannot perish; You are always in the boat with me; what have I to fear? You may sleep; I shall not awaken You. My poor nature will tremble, oh yes! But with all my will I shall remain in peace in the midst of the storm, confident in You."

Under Her Cloak

As the Mother of Mercy, Mary's heart is a place of tenderness, with room for all her children.

Virgin Mary . . . I come to present to you the homage of faith and love of the holy people of God who live in this city and diocese. I come on behalf of families, with their joys and fatigue; of children and young people, open to life; of the elderly, full of years and experience; in a special way I come before you on behalf of the sick, the imprisoned, those who feel the way more difficult. As a Pastor I also come on behalf of all those who have come from distant lands in search of peace and work.

Under your cloak there is room for everyone, because you are the Mother of Mercy. Your heart is full of tenderness towards all your children: the tenderness of God, who became incarnate in you and has become our brother, Jesus, Savior of every man and woman.

Looking at you, our Immaculate Mother, we recognize the victory of Divine Mercy over sin and all its consequences; and the hope of a better life, free from slavery, rancor, and fear, is rekindled within us. Today, . . . we feel your mother's voice calling us all to walk towards that Door, which represents Christ. You say to everyone:

> Come, come closer with trust; come in and you will receive the gift of Mercy; do not be afraid, do not feel ashamed: the Father awaits you with open arms to give you his forgiveness and welcome you into his house. Come, everyone, to the fountain of peace and joy.

—Pope Francis, "Act of Veneration of the Blessed Virgin Mary"

IN GOD'S PRESENCE, CONSIDER . . .

How completely, like St John at the foot of the cross, have I accepted Christ's gift of Mary as my mother and taken refuge in her heart?

CLOSING PRAYER

Mary, help me to live under your cloak, your mantle of mercy and let you lead me to the Father's house.

Praying "Too Hard"

Sometimes, writes Fr. Chris Alar, we get too anxious and apprehensive when we pray: we "overdue it" and thus lose our peace and trust in God.

. . . Wait. Did I just say pray "too hard?" Is that even possible? Yes, it is. According to Jesus' words to St. Faustina, we actually can pray too hard and overdo it:

> After Holy Communion today, I spoke at length to the Lord Jesus about people who are special to me. Then I heard these words: My daughter, don't be exerting yourself so much with words. Those whom you love in a special way, I too love in a special way, and for your sake, I shower My graces upon them. I am pleased when you tell Me about them, but don't be doing so with such excessive effort (*Diary*, 739).

Pondering this amazing passage, we should be struck again with the immensity of Jesus' love and mercy. Here, He expresses His love for those whom Faustina loves and showers His graces upon them for her sake, showing how much He loves Faustina. We, too, should find hope and be consoled about the fate of those we love and have lost. Jesus loves those whom we love, and how much more? Remember the Gospel story of the four men and the paralytic (see Mt 9:1–8; Mk 2:1–12). That is why, if you have faith, even if the level of faith of your loved one is unknown, there is still hope!

Let's pray for those whom we have lost, then, but let's do so with peace, knowing that those we love in a special way are also loved by Jesus in a special way. We don't need to exert ourselves so much, causing ourselves anxiety and stress, wondering if we've said enough prayers for them or if our prayers were long enough. God steps in, and He provides the grace for those souls, even when we are tired and fatigued and sometimes unable to pray any more for them.

—Fr. Chris Alar, MIC, *After Suicide*

IN GOD'S PRESENCE, CONSIDER . . .

Do I sometimes try too hard to get God to answer my prayers, as if I don't quite trust that He cares, or as if I have to wrangle mercy out of Him?

CLOSING PRAYER

Lord, help me learn to pray for my loved ones with peace, trust, and joy, knowing that You love them and want to shower them with mercy.

The Antidote for Fear

The ever-joyful "Divine Mercy priest," Fr. George Kosicki, shares the healing remedy for the spiritual "poison" of fear.

Trust is a living faith in the Lord, faith that He is indeed Lord, that He is in charge, and that He loves us with an infinite merciful love.

Trust gives God permission to act freely so He can have mercy on all (see Rom 11:32). Lack of trust is the greatest obstacle to God acting, and it is what pains Him the most. Souls do not trust Him and so do not receive His mercy.

Our Lord told St. Faustina that "the greatest sinners would achieve great sanctity, if only they would trust in My mercy" (*Diary*, 1784). "If only" is the key. If only souls would trust, they would overcome the obstacles of the human condition and take steps to grow spiritually.

The greatest obstacle of our human condition is fear. Fear paralyzes us and keeps us in bondage. The list of the fears and anxieties that plague us would fill a book! Yet Our Lord said in the gospel: "Fear is useless. What is needed is trust" (Mk 5:36).

How do we trust in the midst of fears? How do we use trust as an antidote to our fears and as a stepping stone to sanctity?

We can repeat over and over again, from the heart, "Jesus, I trust in You!" That says it all. It is our way of living as Christians; it is our response to Jesus, who is mercy itself, who stands at the door of our hearts waiting for us to open them even a little bit (see Rv 3:20 and *Diary*, 1486, 1507). . . .

How can you grow in trust? Gaze upon the image of the Merciful Savior often. Carry it with you; place it in your home and office, and even on the dashboard of your car—and cry out from your heart each time you look at it: "Jesus, I trust in You!"

—Fr. George Kosicki, CSB, *Antidotes and Stepping Stones*

IN GOD'S PRESENCE, CONSIDER . . .

Saying "Jesus, I trust in You" even if there are parts of me that don't fully believe it, is itself an act of trust. By saying this prayer, I am exercising trust! So I will say it again and again until it resonates in my whole being.

CLOSING PRAYER

I pray for greater trust, Jesus, greater sanctity, greater freedom from all fear. Increase my trust in Your mercy. Jesus, I trust in You!

Visit to Purgatory

St. Faustina records several instances where she was visited by specific souls suffering in Purgatory, and on one occasion was led by her Guardian Angel into Purgatory itself, where she learned how deeply these souls are suffering and how much they need our prayers.

Shortly after this, I fell ill [general exhaustion]. The dear Mother Superior sent me with two other sisters for a rest to Skolimow, not far from Warsaw. It was at that time that I asked the Lord who else I should pray for. Jesus said that on the following night He would let me know for whom I should pray.

[The Next night] I saw my Guardian Angel, who ordered me to follow him. In a moment I was in a misty place full of fire in which there was a great crowd of suffering souls. They were praying fervently, but to no avail, for themselves; only we can come to their aid. The flames which were burning them did not touch me at all. My Guardian Angel did not leave me for an instant. I asked these souls what their greatest suffering was. They answered me in one voice that their greatest torment was longing for God. I saw Our Lady visiting the souls in Purgatory. The souls call her "The Star of the Sea." She brings them refreshment. I wanted to talk with them some more, but my Guardian Angel beckoned me to leave. We went out of that prison of suffering. [I heard an interior voice] which said, My mercy does not want this, but justice demands it. Since that time, I am in closer communion with the suffering souls.

—St. Faustina, *Diary*, 20

IN GOD'S PRESENCE, CONSIDER . . .

How close is my communion with the suffering souls in Purgatory? How often do I make time to pray for them?

CLOSING PRAYER

Jesus, I lift up to you the souls in Purgatory who are in most need of my prayers, tremendously. Fulfill their longing for you, Lord. And as you sent Faustina's guardian angel to accompany her, send mine to remind me to pray more often for those who have died.

A Living Tabernacle

One of the ways Jesus carries out His plan of mercy in us is through the Eucharist. But we don't receive Communion constantly . . . do we? Spiritual Communion is not just for when we can't receive sacramentally. It's also an anticipation or an extension of sacramental Communion through our desire to be united with God. Spiritual Communion helps keep us in a perpetual state of union with Him.

Two great modern saints of the Eucharist, St. Padre Pio and St. Faustina, each appear to have reached a state of continuous, uninterrupted spiritual Communion, flowing from their daily sacramental reception of the Eucharist. . . . Through her devotion to the merciful Heart of Jesus in the Eucharist, St. Faustina was able to enter into an unbroken relationship with God—a personal, moment-to-moment, heart-to-heart conversation with Jesus in the unity of the Trinity:

> "Jesus, when you come to me in Holy Communion, . . . I try to keep you company throughout the day. I do not leave you alone for even a moment" (*Diary*, 486).

Her diary entry for September 29, 1937, barely a year before her death, is a powerful witness of the great value of spiritual Communion:

> I have come to know that Holy Communion remains in me until the next Holy Communion. A vivid and clearly felt presence of God continues in my soul. . . . My heart is a living tabernacle in which the living Host is reserved (1302).

St. Padre Pio not only lived this way himself, but prescribed it for others as well:

> In the course of the day, . . . call on Jesus, even in the midst of all your occupations. . . . He will come and will remain always united with your soul by means of His grace and His holy love. Fly with your spirit before the tabernacle, when you cannot stand before it bodily, and there . . . embrace the Beloved of souls.

—Vinny Flynn, *7 Secrets of the Eucharist*

IN GOD'S PRESENCE, CONSIDER . . .

When I receive Eucharist, does my mind wander, or am I actively longing to unite myself with Jesus as He offers Himself to me? And what things can I do to remind myself to try to "keep Him company" throughout the day?

CLOSING PRAYER

Thank you, Jesus, that you are always present to me; Give me the grace to remain always present to You.

The Mystery of Trinitarian Love

In the Eucharist, says Pope Benedict, Christ doesn't give us a "thing," but offers us an encounter with the Trinity whereby we participate in the very life of the Father, the Son, and the Holy Spirit.

The first element of eucharistic faith is the mystery of God himself, trinitarian love. In Jesus' dialogue with Nicodemus, we find an illuminating expression in this regard: "God so loved the world that he gave his only Son, that whoever believes in him should not perish but have eternal life. For God sent the Son into the world, not to condemn the world, but that the world might be saved through him" (*Jn* 3:16–17). These words show the deepest source of God's gift. In the Eucharist Jesus does not give us a "thing," but himself; he offers his own body and pours out his own blood. He thus gives us the totality of his life and reveals the ultimate origin of this love. He is the eternal Son, given to us by the Father.

. . . The Eucharist reveals the loving plan that guides all of salvation history (cf. *Eph* 1:10; 3:8–11). There the Deus Trinitas, who is essentially love (cf. *1 Jn* 4:7–8), becomes fully a part of our human condition. In the bread and wine under whose appearances Christ gives himself to us in the paschal meal (cf. *Lk* 22:14–20; 1 Cor 11:23–26), God's whole life encounters us and is sacramentally shared with us. God is a perfect communion of love between Father, Son and Holy Spirit. At creation itself, man was called to have some share in God's breath of life (cf. *Gen* 2:7). . . . Jesus Christ, who "through the eternal Spirit offered himself without blemish to God" (*Heb* 9:14), makes us, in the gift of the Eucharist, sharers in God's own life. This is an absolutely free gift, the superabundant fulfilment of God's promises. The Church receives, celebrates and adores this gift in faithful obedience. The "mystery of faith" is thus a mystery of trinitarian love, a mystery in which we are called by grace to participate. We too should therefore exclaim with Saint Augustine: "If you see love, you see the Trinity" [*De Trinitate*, VIII, 8,12: CCL 50, 287].

—Pope Benedict XVI, *Sacramentum Caritatis (Sacrament of Charity)*, 7–8

IN GOD'S PRESENCE, CONSIDER . . .

Do I receive "the Host" as if it's just a thing, or do I recognize that not only is Jesus present, but the whole Trinity is there when I receive? I hold in my awareness today this awesome reality of deep communion with the divine life of the Trinity.

CLOSING PRAYER

Most Holy Trinity: Father, Son, and Holy Spirit, help me to enter into communion with You in every Sacrament with awe and thanksgiving, especially each time I receive the Eucharist.

Mercy Leads to Wonder

The intensity and intimacy with which God loves us in the interior of our soul is greater than any love we have ever or will ever experience on earth. And in Fr. Matthew's profound work on St. John of the Cross, we see that it is only mercy that allows for the all-powerful God to submit Himself in this way, "making the soul great in the kindness He shows her."

Traditionally, Grace comprises two dimensions: God's gift of his Spirit; and his empowering us to enter the Spirit's domain. When God gives, he does not bulldoze, or patronise. *He so loves as to make us capable of being part of his* love [emphasis added]. Faith, charity, is sharing God's life; not just receiving handouts and remaining a stranger.

> God communicates himself to the soul in this inner union with such a real love, that no mother has ever cherished or caressed her child so tenderly; with this love of God no brother's love or friends' friendship could compare. So tender and so real is the love of the all-encompassing Father that—how awesome this is, how amazing, what a wonder!—he truly submits himself to this humble, loving soul, so as to make her great, making her great in the kindness he shows her. It is as if he were her servant and she his Lord. . . . So profound is God's humility and gentleness! . . . "He will gird himself and have them sit at the table, and he will come and serve them" (SCB27:1; cf. Lk 12:37).

This is grace from the inside. For God to love is to give, to give himself, and so to share, and empower. And what this evokes in John is, precisely, wonder.

—Iain Matthew OCD, *John of the Cross: Seasons of Prayer*

IN GOD'S PRESENCE, CONSIDER . . .

The way God desires to be united to me, the fact that He considers me His beloved, and lavishes goodness and love upon me, should fill me with constant awe and wonder. When it doesn't, I have lost sight of the reality that each of these things is an incredible gift of mercy, so far beyond anything I could ever deserve.

CLOSING PRAYER

All-encompassing God, You give me Your grace, Your love, and in that You also empower me to enter into that love, so that I am not just receiving handouts and remaining a stranger. Fill me with wonder and the receptivity to let You be what You want to be: an intimate communion of persons, unsurpassed by anything else I could ever experience.

A Heart So Big . . .

"A new command I give unto you," Jesus tells us. "Love one another, as I have loved you" (Jn 13:34). St. Faustina gives a wonderful example of what this actually means.

My Jesus, penetrate me through and through so that I might be able to reflect You in my whole life. Divinize me so that my deeds may have supernatural value. Grant that I may have love, compassion and mercy for every soul without exception.

. . . O Jesus, I understand that Your mercy is beyond all imagining, and therefore I ask You to make my heart so big that there will be room in it for the needs of all the souls living on the face of the earth. O Jesus, my love extends beyond the world, to the souls suffering in purgatory, and I want to exercise mercy toward them by means of indulgenced prayers. God's mercy is unfathomable and inexhaustible, just as God himself is unfathomable. Even if I were to use the strongest words there are to express this mercy of God, all this would be nothing in comparison with what it is in reality. O Jesus, make my heart sensitive to all the sufferings of my neighbor, whether of body or of soul. O my Jesus, I know that You act toward us as we act toward our neighbor.

My Jesus, make my heart like unto Your merciful Heart. Jesus, help me to go through life doing good to everyone.

—St. Faustina, *Diary*, 1242, 692

IN GOD'S PRESENCE, CONSIDER . . .

In my everyday life, do I tend to be preoccupied with my own concerns and agendas or do I try to focus on others and make room in my heart for them?

CLOSING PRAYER

Lord of love, open and enlarge my heart so that I can see and love others as You do.

To Look with New Eyes

We are called to enter into the mystery of God's love and come to see and love others as He does.

Christ has taught us that man not only receives and experiences the mercy of God, but is also called "to practice mercy" towards others: "Blessed are the merciful, for they shall obtain mercy'" (*Mt* 5:7). . . .

In fact, love of God and love of one's brothers and sisters are inseparable. . . . This love can only be learned by penetrating the mystery of God's love. Looking at him, being one with his fatherly heart, we are able to look with new eyes at our brothers and sisters, with an attitude of unselfishness and solidarity, of generosity and forgiveness. . . .

Sr. Faustina Kowalska wrote in her *Diary*: "I feel tremendous pain when I see the sufferings of my neighbours. All my neighbours' sufferings reverberate in my own heart; I carry their anguish in my heart in such a way that it even physically destroys me. I would like all their sorrows to fall upon me, in order to relieve my neighbor" [see *Diary*, 1039] This is the degree of compassion to which love leads, when it takes the love of God as its measure! . . .

It is this love which must inspire humanity today. . . . The message of divine mercy is also implicitly *a message about the value of every human being*. Each person is precious in God's eyes; Christ gave his life for each one; to everyone the Father gives his Spirit and offers intimacy. . . .

This consoling message is addressed above all to those who, afflicted by a particularly harsh trial or crushed by the weight of the sins they committed, have lost all confidence in life and are tempted to give in to despair. To them the gentle face of Christ is offered; those rays from his heart touch them and shine upon them, warm them, show them the way and fill them with hope. How many souls have been consoled by the prayer "*Jesus, I trust in you*," which Providence intimated through Sr Faustina! This simple act of abandonment to Jesus dispels the thickest clouds and lets a ray of light penetrate every life. *Jezu, ufam tobie*.

—St. Pope John Paul II, Homily, Divine Mercy Sunday, April 30, 2000

IN GOD'S PRESENCE, CONSIDER . . .

Does my love for God reach out to all his other children? Is each person precious in my eyes?

CLOSING PRAYER

St. Faustina, intercede for me for a full measure of your compassion for others.

Extravagance

The sinful woman in Luke's Gospel gives Jesus the opportunity to teach us all that when we truly receive and recognize God's mercy, it will never leave us unchanged and will stir our hearts to great love.

One of the Pharisees asked him to eat with him . . . And behold, a woman of the city, who was a sinner . . . brought an alabaster flask of ointment, and standing behind him at his feet, weeping, she began to wet his feet with her tears, and wiped them with the hair of her head, and kissed his feet, and anointed them with the ointment. Now when the Pharisee who had invited him saw it, he said to himself, "If this man were a prophet, he would have known who and what sort of woman this is who is touching him, for she is a sinner." And Jesus answering said to him, "Simon, I have something to say to you." And he answered, "What is it, Teacher?" "A certain creditor had two debtors; one owed five hundred denarii, and the other fifty. When they could not pay, he forgave them both. Now which of them will love him more?" Simon answered, "The one, I suppose, to whom he forgave more." And he said to him, "You have judged rightly." Then turning toward the woman he said to Simon, "Do you see this woman? I entered your house, you gave me no water for my feet, but she has wet my feet with her tears and wiped them with her hair. You gave me no kiss, but from the time I came in she has not ceased to kiss my feet. You did not anoint my head with oil, but she has anointed my feet with ointment. Therefore I tell you, her sins, which are many, are forgiven, for she loved much; but he who is forgiven little, loves little." And he said to her, "Your sins are forgiven." Then those who were at table with him began to say among themselves, "Who is this, who even forgives sins?" And he said to the woman, "Your faith has saved you; go in peace."

—Luke 7:36–50

IN GOD'S PRESENCE, CONSIDER . . .

Throughout my day, do I find that I separate myself in my mind from others who have different sins than me? I truly cannot know how culpable they are, and it may be that I am actually much more culpable, even if their sins seem great. I resolve to focus on my own areas of sinfulness, and how God wants to change me with His mercy.

CLOSING PRAYER

Jesus, You are the great lover of mankind. Give me the courage to care nothing for what others think and to simply love You with extravagance. Help me to focus on the places in me that need Your mercy. How can I love You better; how can I love You more in my life? Let me hold nothing back.

Mercy (Not Reproach)

Reflecting on the Gospel story of Zacchaeus's encounter with Jesus, Fr. Cantalamessa provides us with a clear example of how God's mercy operates.

Zacchaeus, a chief tax collector, heard Jesus talked about as a prophet who is different from the others, so he wants to see him. . . . Since Zacchaeus is short, he cannot see much, so he climbs up a tree. Jesus arrives and looks up—from many hints in the Gospels, it seems that Jesus' eyes had a miraculous power and spoke more than his words—and he calls Zacchaeus by name. . . .

"Zacchaeus, make haste and come down; for I must stay at your house today" (Luke 19:5). The issue here is urgent: it has to happen now. He wants to spend time with Zacchaeus and not just go by his house to see where he lives. He wants to enter Zacchaeus' home, stay for a while, have a meal there, and perhaps spend the night. . . .

Zacchaeus, however, is able to read in Jesus' gaze the same love that Jesus elsewhere directed to the rich young man (see Mark 10:21), and that gaze affects him. It is more than enough to fill Zacchaeus with extraordinary joy. He welcomes this presence that lavishes him with unconditional love; he lets himself be swept away by this love. And it is precisely due to this love that he feels himself come back to life and become a human being again. . . .

And so, spontaneously, without Jesus asking anything of him, Zacchaeus announces that he will give half of his goods to the poor and will restore fourfold to anyone from whom he collected more taxes than were owed. . . .

Zacchaeus does not do this because of a condition imposed on him by Jesus in order to receive his love. It is instead a consequence of that love. Having been loved first, and freely, Zacchaeus feels the urge to turn toward others, toward those he has defrauded up to that time, and he learns to respect and love them. This is how God's mercy operates. Let us never forget it.

—Raniero Cantalamessa, *The Gaze of Mercy*

IN GOD'S PRESENCE, CONSIDER . . .

Mercy precedes change. I wonder how many times in my life I have looked for change, from others and even myself, without first showing kindness, understanding, love.

CLOSING PRAYER

Jesus, I want that extraordinary joy, basking in Your presence and unconditional love. Bring me back to life in new ways through Your miraculous gaze of love, and let me look on others with that love.

Mercy Is My Exclusive Task

The Lord assigned an extraordinary mission to St. Faustina, not only during her earthly life but also in the life to come: to reveal the goodness of God and encourage us to trust in His mercy.

After Holy Communion today, Jesus said, My daughter give Me souls. Know that it is your mission to win souls for Me by prayer and sacrifice, and by encouraging them to trust in My mercy (1690). . . .

O my God, . . . with every beat of my heart I want to praise Your unfathomable mercy. I want to tell souls of Your goodness and encourage them to trust in Your mercy. That is my mission, which You yourself have entrusted to me, O Lord, in this life and in the life to come (1325). . . .

O my Jesus, each of Your saints reflects one of Your virtues; I desire to reflect Your compassionate heart, full of mercy; I want to glorify it. Let Your mercy, O Jesus, be impressed upon my heart and soul like a seal, and this will be my badge in this and the future life. Glorifying Your mercy is the exclusive task of my life (1242). I shall sing before heaven and earth the song of the Lord's fathomless mercy. This is my work and the mission which the Lord has destined for me from the beginning of the world (825).

—St. Faustina, *Diary*

IN GOD'S PRESENCE, CONSIDER . . .

I want to glorify God and share this message of mercy. Yet, with the utmost kindness towards myself and without condemnation I consider this truth: I don't fully entrust everything to God, which means there are places within where I myself am not truly convinced of His goodness and love for me. It is an ongoing journey of surrender, and I invite Him to lead me deeper.

CLOSING PRAYER

Faustina, "lift the veils" that keep me from seeing how good and merciful God is, so that I will no longer wound His heart with any lack of trust. Intercede for me that I would be healed of any barriers, any self-reliance, any wounds in my life that keep me from this childlike abandonment to His loving will for me.

Sing of the Mercies of the Lord

The oldest prayer to Mary according to an early coptic manuscript prays, "We fly to your mercy, oh holy Mother of God . . . " So the more contemporary version of this prayer, "We fly to your patronage . . . " is a turning to her as a merciful mother. And Fr. Kosicki tells us that she is the one who teaches us to sing of the mercies of the Lord.

In her apparition to St. Juan Diego, Mary proclaims, "I am your merciful mother, the merciful mother of all of you who live united in this land, and all of mankind" (Dec. 9, 1531). Later, responding to Juan Diego's fears and anxiety, she tells him, "Am I not here who am your mother? Are you not under my shadow and protection? . . . Are you not in the folds of my mantle; in the crossing of my arms? Is there anything else that you need? (Dec. 12, 1531).

Pope John Paul II in his pilgrimage to the Shrine of Our Lady of Fatima (May 13, 1982) in thanksgiving for his life being spared, joined Mary in proclaiming the mercies of the Lord:

"I began this pilgrimage with the canticle of God's mercy in my heart; and, on my departure, I want to tell you that my soul is still vibrating with this canticle; and 'I will sing the mercies of the Lord' (Ps. 89 [88]:2) in the choir of the present generation of the Church, which has as first soloist the Mother of Divine Mercy.

What a marvelous way to honor Mary—Mother of Divine Mercy, the first soloist of the choir of the Church and Heaven!

John Paul II continued to sing of the mercies of the Lord as he went as a pilgrim to the Shrine of Divine Mercy in Poland "to take part in the unending hymn in honor of Divine Mercy. The psalmist of the Lord intoned it—'I will sing of the mercies of the Lord forever' (Ps 89)—expressing what every generation preserved and will continue to preserve as a most precious fruit of faith" (June 7, 1997).

We can also learn . . . to sing of the mercies of the Lord by turning to Mary, our Mother of Mercy.

—Fr. George Kosicki, OSB

IN GOD'S PRESENCE, CONSIDER . . .

Like St. Pope John Paul II, I want my soul to vibrate with the canticle of God's mercy. And I want to proclaim it even in times of hardship and suffering.

CLOSING PRAYER

Mary, Mother of Mercy, show me how to sing with my life a canticle of God's mercy. Be a mother to me, especially during those times when I need to remember His mercies and when I need to be drawn close to Jesus.

The Feast of Mercy

St. Faustina didn't invent the Feast of Mercy: it emerged "from the very depths" of Christ's tenderness as a "refuge and shelter" for all. He insisted on it, repeatedly telling Faustina to have the second Sunday of Easter established as "the Feast of Mercy" and to have the Divine Mercy Image displayed, solemnly blessed, and venerated.

I desire that there be a Feast of Mercy. I want this image, which you will paint with a brush, to be solemnly blessed on the first Sunday after Easter; that Sunday is to be the Feast of Mercy. . . . Ask of my faithful servant [Father Sopocko] that, on this day, he tell the whole world of My great mercy; that whoever approaches the Fount of Life on this day will be granted complete remission of sins and punishment. Mankind will not have peace until it turns with trust to My mercy. . . . No soul will be justified until it turns with confidence to My mercy, and this is why the first Sunday after Easter is to be the Feast of Mercy. On that day, priests are to tell everyone about My great and unfathomable mercy.

I desire that the Feast of Mercy be a refuge and shelter for all souls, and especially for poor sinners. On that day the very depths of My tender mercy are open. I pour out a whole ocean of graces upon those souls who approach the fount of My mercy. The soul that will go to Confession and receive Holy Communion shall obtain complete forgiveness of sins and punishment. On that day all the divine floodgates through which grace flow are opened. Let no soul fear to draw near to Me, even though its sins be as scarlet. My mercy is so great that no mind, be it of man or of angel, will be able to fathom it throughout all eternity. Everything that exists has come forth from the very depths of My most tender mercy. . . . The Feast of Mercy emerged from My very depths of tenderness. It is My desire that it be solemnly celebrated on the first Sunday after Easter.

. . . I am giving mankind the last hope of salvation; that is, recourse to My mercy. My Heart rejoices in this feast.

—St. Faustina, *Diary*, 49, 300, 570, 699, 998 (Christ's words)

IN GOD'S PRESENCE, CONSIDER . . .

Since Christ clearly wants us all to experience the great gifts of mercy He offers us on the Feast of Mercy, do I make it a priority to participate in the Mass and special devotions of that day and encourage others to do the same?

CLOSING PRAYER

Lord Jesus, thank you for Your tender mercy. Help me to prepare my heart to celebrate this Feast each year in the fullest way possible.

Shalom—The Gift of Mercy Sunday

Mercy Sunday! "This is the day the Lord has made"—— the day of days, the octave day of Easter, the last and greatest day of that greatest of all feasts, the day that celebrates the unconditional love of God for you and me and His desire to fill us with peace and joy.

I love the Gospel story of the first Easter Sunday and its octave day, which we celebrate as Divine Mercy Sunday. The disciples are confused and frightened. Christ had represented their deepest hopes, but all that had changed in the garden, in the court of the high priest, in the praetorium of Pilate, and on that awful hill of Calvary where most of them had not even dared to show themselves. After the torture and execution of Christ, all had seemed lost. So they had withdrawn into the upper room and locked the doors.

And suddenly He was there with them. (*In our fear we can try to lock Him out, but He is always with us.*) The first word He spoke was "shalom," which means not just "peace," but complete health and well-being in mind, body, and spirit.

Thomas wasn't there and refused to believe unless he could see the holes in Christ's hands and put his hand into the wound in his side. So, eight days later, Christ shows up again, offering Thomas the proof he needs. What a wonderful testimony to how far God is willing to go to reveal himself to each of us, personally, when we long to see Him!

Here we are, some 2000 years later. So many scripts that haven't worked out. So many dashed expectations. In my fear, how many rooms have I fled into to hide? *How many locked doors are there in my mind and heart?* How many times have I been afraid to trust, unwilling to believe, unable to receive?

Every day, but especially today, when we remember and celebrate His mercy, Christ stands before us (even in the deepest locked rooms of our being), offers us His "shalom," and invites us to receive His Spirit. And if we long to experience the reality of His presence and His love, He will reveal Himself to us.

—Vinny Flynn

IN GOD'S PRESENCE, CONSIDER . . .

Where are my "locked doors"? What fears do I need to let go of? What rooms in my mind and heart do I need to invite Christ to enter and fill with His peace?

CLOSING PRAYER

Lord, help me to let go of all fear today, trusting You to break through all the locked doors, heal all the wounds, and breathe Your "shalom" into my heart.

St. Pope John Paul II's Final Message of Mercy

On April 2, 2005, St. Pope John Paul II died peacefully on the eve of the feast he had established 5 years earlier as Divine Mercy Sunday. Before his death, he had prepared his Regina Caeli address and given explicit instructions that it was to be read after the celebration of the Holy Mass celebrated on Divine Mercy Sunday. It was his final gift to the world.

Today the glorious Alleluia of Easter resounds. Today's Gospel from John emphasizes that on the evening of that day he appeared to the Apostles and "showed them his hands and his side" (Jn 20:20), that is, the signs of the painful passion with which his Body was indelibly stamped, even after the Resurrection. Those glorious wounds, which he allowed doubting Thomas to touch eight days later, reveal the mercy of God who "*so loved the world that he gave his only Son*" (Jn 3:16).

This mystery of love is at the heart of the liturgy today, the Second Sunday of Easter, dedicated to the devotion of Divine Mercy.

As a gift to humanity, which sometimes seems bewildered and overwhelmed by the power of evil, selfishness and fear, the Risen Lord offers his love that pardons, reconciles and reopens hearts to love. It is a love that converts hearts and gives peace. How much the world needs to understand and accept Divine Mercy!

Lord, who reveal the Father's love by your death and Resurrection, we believe in you and confidently repeat to you today: Jesus, I trust in you, have mercy upon us and upon the whole world.

The liturgical solemnity of the Annunciation that we will be celebrating tomorrow urges us to contemplate with Mary's eyes the immense mystery of this merciful love that flows from the Heart of Christ. With her help, we will be able to understand the true meaning of Easter joy that is based on this certainty: the One whom the Virgin bore in her womb, who suffered and died for us, is truly risen. Alleluia!

—St. Pope John Paul II

IN GOD'S PRESENCE, CONSIDER . . .

How completely have I tried to understand and accept Divine Mercy in my life? Have I let the world confine and overwhelm me? Am I willing to allow the Lord to reopen my heart to a deeper, more unselfish love for others?

CLOSING PRAYER

Lord Jesus, I trust in you! Have mercy on us and on the whole world. Help me to grow in my understanding and acceptance of Your mercy.

Mercy Always

Our celebration of God's mercy, says author Mary Flynn, should not be limited to one day.

To me, Divine Mercy Sunday is, in a sense, like a birthday. It's an important day, and you don't want to miss it, especially because of God's great promise of "complete remission of sins and punishment" for those who go to confession and receive Holy Communion (*Diary* 300, 699, 1109).

But the whole point of a birthday is to celebrate a person, the person's life, all the beauty and goodness that person has brought to others, and to honor and acknowledge the person. It's similar to many other celebrations, like Mother's Day, Father's Day, Valentine's Day, Veteran's Day, etc. Just because there is a designated day to celebrate these various groups, doesn't mean we have to limit our celebration to one day! We should honor and cherish the people in our lives *every day*, not just on birthdays or other holidays. And so it is with God.

We ought to be thanking and praising God *daily* for His great mercy, honoring Him above anyone else in our lives. Because truly, since mercy is simply love that reaches down to the undeserving, everything that comes to us from God is mercy, and He is not stingy. God longs to open the floodgates of His mercy to each and every one of us; all we have to do is say, "Jesus, I trust in You. You know all my failings and just how much I need your mercy. I ask for as much of it as possible! Help me receive it, respond to it, and hunger for more."

God's mercy is *always* there—every day, every hour, every moment.

—Mary Flynn, *Musings*

IN GOD'S PRESENCE, CONSIDER . . .

Do I see everything that comes to me as an extension of God's mercy? I wonder what would happen in my life, and the lives of those I pray for, if I focus more and more on asking for and trusting in His mercy.

CLOSING PRAYER

Lord, let me never forget and always celebrate that you are the God of mercy, that your mercy is always there for me—every day, every hour, every moment.

One Thing Alone Sustains Me

In his encyclical letter Ecclesia de Eucharistia, St. Pope John Paul II wrote that his purpose in writing it was "to rekindle Eucharistic amazement," with the understanding that "the Church draws her life from the Eucharist." St. Faustina gives us a great example of the joy and strength that a Eucharistic spirituality can bring.

The most solemn moment of my life is the moment when I receive Holy Communion. I long for each Holy Communion, and for every Holy Communion I give thanks to the Most Holy Trinity (1804). . . . All the good that is in me is due to Holy Communion. I owe everything to it. I feel that this holy fire has transformed me completely. Oh, how happy I am to be a dwelling place for You, O Lord! My heart is a temple in which You dwell continually (1392). . . .

I find myself so weak that were it not for Holy Communion I would fall continually. One thing alone sustains me, and that is Holy Communion. From it I draw my strength; in it is all my comfort. I fear life on days when I do not receive Holy Communion. I fear my own self. Jesus concealed in the Host is everything to me. From the tabernacle I draw strength, power, courage and light. Here, I seek consolation in time of anguish. I would not know how to give glory to God if I did not have the Eucharist in my heart (1037). . . .

This Bread of the Strong gives me all the strength I need to carry on my mission and the courage to do whatever the Lord asks of me. The courage and strength that are in me are not of me, but of Him who lives in me—it is the Eucharist (91). . . . Here I obtain strength and light; here I learn everything; here I am given light on how to act toward my neighbor. From the time I left the novitiate, I have enclosed myself in the tabernacle together with Jesus, my Master. He himself drew me into the fire of living love on which everything converges (704).

—St. Faustina, *Diary*

IN GOD'S PRESENCE, CONSIDER . . .

Is the Eucharist just something I receive on Sunday, or is it "everything to me"? Have I learned to draw strength, courage, and consolation from the tabernacle?

CLOSING PRAYER

Draw me deeper into union with You, Eucharistic Lord. Help me to devote myself to regular Eucharistic devotion and "enclose myself in the tabernacle" with You.

A Host Lifted in Me

From Fr. Mateo Crawley-Boevey, founder of The Enthronement of the Sacred Heart, comes a beautiful post-Communion prayer to God the Father, asking Him to help us to not merely receive Christ's love but to take it with us into the world.

I came, with my sins, my troubles, my weakness, my limitations. I go with the life of Christ, with the Host in my soul; Let me go as a host, offered with Him and for the love of Him to all those I come in contact with today.

Let me be to them a Christ, loving with His love, not with sentimentality and selfishness, not asking for anything, but with my own heart an altar of sacrifice, where He shall be offered for them, in patience, in submission, in compassion, in service, in cooperation, in abnegation, in sacrifice, in wrestling with self, and, please God, in dying to self.

Let Him be a host lifted in me, in places where otherwise no Host comes. Let me show His beauty, His simplicity, His attractiveness, in laughter, in tenderness, in my interest in their affairs, in seeing the good in them, fostering their aspirations, making myself, my heart—not only the outside of me—accessible to them.

Let me reveal Him even when I fail; in humility, in acknowledging my faults without servility, without morbidity, without the vanity which is amazed by its own failure; but asking forgiveness and going on, trusting Him.

Let me work with His devotion to duty, to the will of God, and for the glory of God. Let my soul be His Nazareth. Let Christ in me, be among my fellow-workers, and be in ways I shall not know, light to them and strength. Let them be happier because in me, He has, with exquisite courtesy, chosen to be among them.

I have been this morning in Heaven, and Heaven has come to abide in me; let me take Heaven with me into the world.

—Fr. Mateo Crawley-Boevey, SS.CC., in *Mass & Adoration Companion*

IN GOD'S PRESENCE, CONSIDER . . .

After receiving Christ Himself, the Living God, do I spend at least a few moments in thanksgiving for this incredible gift, a few moments 'in communion with" Him? Or do I simply attend Mass, receive Communion, and leave immediately after the final blessing?

CLOSING PRAYER

Lord, Jesus, help me to welcome You into my mind, heart, and soul when I receive, and to spend time with You in person-to-Person conversation. Then stay with me as I go to bring heaven to the world and extend Your mercy to others.

The "Problem" with Divine Mercy

The devotional elements and practices found in the Diary *of St. Faustina can bring great grace—but they must touch our hearts as well as our lips.*

Because the devotion to Divine Mercy has spread so quickly and has borne such wonderful fruit in people's lives . . . it has led some people to an almost superstitious focus on the devotional practices themselves. Anything, even something good, can become an idol if it draws our focus *to itself* instead of to God. The Divine Mercy Image, for example, can be an icon—like a window leading us into a deeper relationship with God—or an idol, as if the painting itself has some kind of magic power. . . .

Are these devotional practices wrong? Is it wrong to hang the Image on my wall? Wrong to pray the Chaplet? Wrong to celebrate the Feast of Mercy? Of course not! But we need to understand the real meaning and purpose of these outward practices, so that our *devotions* will lead us to deeper *devotion.*

Devotion means dedicating yourself, giving yourself completely to something or someone. In a religious context, it means completely dedicating yourself to God, belonging to Him, caring about Him and the things He cares about. It means allowing Him to touch your heart and give direction *to the way you live.*

Devotion to Divine Mercy involves a commitment to *live the message* of Divine Mercy. It's a decision to trust more and more in God, to accept His mercy with thanksgiving, and to be merciful as He is merciful. . . .

There are two Scripture passages that help me to remember who I want to be, help me to refocus and rededicate myself to mercy in action:

1. This people honors me with their lips, but their hearts are far from me (Mt 15:8, NABRE).
2. Blessed are the merciful, for they shall obtain mercy (Mt 5:7).

If the Lord were to talk about you, which of these would you like to hear Him say?

—Vinny Flynn, *7 Secrets of Divine Mercy*

IN GOD'S PRESENCE, CONSIDER . . .

The Pharisees practiced daily devotions. They did all the "right stuff," said all the right prayers, performed all the proper rituals. But it didn't seem to touch their hearts or led to a deeper, lived-out relationship with God. Am I a Pharisee or a disciple? Do I live what my lips profess, or do I say one thing and do another?

CLOSING PRAYER

Lord, fill my heart with Your mercy and help me to put it into practice in my daily life.

Eternal His Merciful Love

Psalm 100 gives us the perfect reflection on who God is; and it shows us the proper disposition we should have as we place ourselves in His Presence each morning in prayer, as we enter into Holy Mass, and as we cross the threshold of heaven.

Cry out with joy to the Lord, all the earth.
Serve the Lord with gladness.
Come before him, singing for joy.

Know that he, the Lord, is God.
He made us, we belong to him,
we are his people, the sheep of his flock.

Go within his gates, giving thanks.
Enter his courts with songs of praise.
Give thanks to him and bless his name.

Indeed, how good is the Lord,
eternal his merciful love.
He is faithful from age to age.

—Psalm 100, *The Liturgy of the Hours*

IN GOD'S PRESENCE, CONSIDER . . .

I meditate individually on these truths, especially those where I feel my heart particularly moved: You are God. You made me. I belong to You. I owe You thanks and the glory due Your Name. You are good. Your merciful love is for eternity. You are faithful.

CLOSING PRAYER

Lord, You are sovereign and You are so good. Let me give my life back to You with joy and serve You with gladness. Help me to have a grateful heart, in awe of You and Your merciful love. You are forever faithful, and I want to be unwavering in my whole-hearted devotion to You.

The "Annunciation" to Faustina

Like Our Lady, St. Faustina had an "annunciation" experience, during which the Lord revealed the unique mission He had chosen for her; and, in spite of the suffering she knew it would bring, she, too, freely responded with an unconditional "fiat."

A vision passed before the eyes of my soul; it was like the vision Jesus had in the Garden of Olives. First, the physical sufferings and all the circumstances that would increase them; [then] the full scope of the spiritual sufferings and those that no one would know about. Everything entered into the vision: false suspicions, loss of good name. I've summarized it here, but this knowledge was already so clear that what I went through later on was in no way different from what I had known at that moment. My name is to be: "sacrifice." When the vision ended, a cold sweat bathed my forehead. Jesus made it known to me that, even if I did not give my consent to this, I could still be saved; and He would not lessen His graces, but would still continue to have the same intimate relationship with me, so that even if I did not consent to make this sacrifice, God's generosity would not lessen thereby.

And the Lord gave me to know that the whole mystery depended on me, on my free consent to the sacrifice given with full use of my faculties. In this free and conscious act lies the whole power and value before His Majesty. Even if none of these things for which I offered myself would ever happen to me, before the Lord everything was as though it had already been consummated. At that moment, I realized I was entering into communion with the incomprehensible Majesty. I felt that God was waiting for my word, for my consent. Then my spirit immersed itself in the Lord, and I said, "Do with me as You please. I subject myself to Your will. As of today, Your holy will shall be my nourishment, and I will be faithful to Your commands with the help of Your grace. Do with me as You please. I beg You, O Lord, be with me at every moment of my life.

—St. Faustina, *Diary*, 135–136

IN GOD'S PRESENCE, CONSIDER . . .

How consciously do I use my free will to say a full yes to God? Am I ready to stay faithful through whatever sacrifices He may ask of me?

CLOSING PRAYER

Lord, help me to hear Your "annunciations" to me and to make my life a continual "fiat" to You.

The Measure of Mercy

In showing us mercy, says St. Pope John Paul II, Christ also calls us to be witnesses of that mercy in the world.

"This is my commandment,
that you love one another as I have loved you" (Jn 15:2).

Dear Brothers and Sisters!

The words of Jesus which we just heard are closely related to the theme of today's liturgical assembly in Błonie in Kraków: "God, rich in mercy". This phrase in a way captures the entire truth about the love of God which has redeemed humanity. "God, who is rich in mercy, out of the great love with which he loved us, even when we were dead through our trespasses, made us alive together with Christ" (Eph 2:4–5). The fullness of this love was revealed in the sacrifice of the Cross. For "greater love has no man than this, that a man lay down his life for his friends" (Jn 15:13). Here is the measure of God's love! Here is the measure of God's mercy!

Once we recognize this truth, we become aware that Christ's call to love others even as he has loved us calls all of us to that same measure. We feel in some sense impelled to make our lives a daily offering by showing mercy to our brothers and sisters, drawing upon the gift of God's merciful love. We realize that God, in showing us mercy, calls upon us to become witnesses to mercy in today's world.

—St. Pope John Paul II, August 18, 2002

IN GOD'S PRESENCE, CONSIDER . . .

How do I measure up? Have I let God's mercy to me "impel me" to show that same mercy to others?

CLOSING PRAYER

Lord, help me to be a more faithful witness to Your mercy, recognizing the extent of Your love and seeking to love others in You.

Mercy Is the Garment of Light

On Mercy Sunday, in 2007, Pope Benedict reaffirmed St. Pope John Paul II's call to "have faith in Divine Mercy."

The Holy Father, John Paul II, wanted this Sunday to be celebrated as the Feast of Divine Mercy: in the word "mercy," he summed up and interpreted anew for our time the whole mystery of Redemption. He had lived under two dictatorial regimes, and in his contact with poverty, neediness and violence he had a profound experience of the powers of darkness which also threaten the world of our time.

But he had an equally strong experience of the presence of God who opposed all these forces with his power, which is totally different and divine: with the power of mercy. It is mercy that puts an end to evil. In it is expressed God's special nature—his holiness, the power of truth and love.

Two years ago now, after the First Vespers of this Feast, John Paul II ended his earthly life. In dying, he entered the light of Divine Mercy, of which, beyond death and starting from God, he now speaks to us in a new way.

Have faith, he tells us, in Divine Mercy! Become day after day men and women of God's mercy. Mercy is the garment of light which the Lord has given to us in Baptism. We must not allow this light to be extinguished; on the contrary, it must grow within us every day and thus bring to the world God's glad tidings.

—Pope Benedict XVI, St. Peter's Square, Second Sunday of Easter, April 15, 2007

IN GOD'S PRESENCE, CONSIDER . . .

Is my faith in Divine Mercy strong enough to enable me to live as a man or woman of God's mercy?

CLOSING PRAYER

Lord, help me to clothe myself with mercy every day as in a garment of light, so that I can be a beacon of Your Presence in the world.

Selected Bibliography

Alar, Fr. Chris, MIC, and Lewis, Fr. Jason, MIC. *After Suicide: There's Hope for Them and for You.* Stockbridge, MA: Marian Press, 2019.

Ambrose. "As I Approach Your Banquet," *Mass & Adoration Companion.* TAN Books.

Ancient Homily for Holy Saturday *Liturgy of the Hours.* Vol II.

Augustine NEW ADVENT SERMONS Sermon 6 on the New Testament. On the Lord's Prayer in Matthew 6:9, etc. to the Competentes. First Series, Vol. 6. Translated by R.G. MacMullen. From Nicene and Post-Nicene Fathers, Edited by Philip Schaff. Revised and edited for New Advent by Kevin Knight. Buffalo, NY: Christian Literature Publishing Co., 1888. https://churchlifejournal.nd.edu/articles/forgive-us-our-debts-a-catechesis-of-mercy-in-the-early-church/#_edn20.

Balthasar, Hans Urs von. *Heart of the World.* Ignatius Press.

Barron, Robert. *Daily Reflections on the Gospel.* 2021.

Basil. *Mass & Adoration Companion.* TAN Books.

Boylan, Eugene. *This Tremendous Lover.* Catholic Way Publishing, 1946.

Butler, Alban. *The Lives of the Fathers, Martyrs and Other Principal Saints.* Vol. III. Nabu Press, 1946.

Cantalamessa, Raniero. Contemplating the Trinity. Word Among Us Press, 2007.

———. *The Gaze of Mercy.* Word Among Us Press, 2015.

Catherine of Siena. *The Prayers of St. Catherine of Siena.* Paulist Press.

Chaput, Charles J., "A Jubilee Year of Mercy," Article at First Things.

Chesterton, G.K. *St. Francis of Assisi.* Empire Books, 2012.

Chevrot, Georges. *The Prodigal Son.* Scepter Press.

Claude de la Columbiére, *The Spiritual Direction of Saint Claude de la Colombière.* Translated and arranged by Mother M. Philip, IBVM. Ignatius Press, 2018.

Crawley-Boevey, Mateo, in *Mass & Adoration Companion,* TAN Books.

Cyril of Jerusalem. *Catechetical Lectures, II: 5–6.* The Oxford translation of Mr. Church, then fellow of Oriel College; revised by Edward Hamilton Gifford, D.D., formerly Archdeacon of London, and Canon of S. Paul's.

de Caussade, Jean-Pierre, SJ, *Abandonment to Divine Providence.* Reverend J. Ramiere S.J. Catholic Way Publishing.

d'Elbee, Jean C.J. *I Believe in Love.* Sophia Institute Press.

Diary of St. Maria Faustina Kowalska: Divine Mercy in My Soul. Stockbridge, MA: Marian Press, 1987.

Doherty, Catherine de Hueck. *Grace in Every Season.* Edited by Mary Bazzett. Madonna House Publications, 2001.

———. *The Gospel Without Compromise.* Ave Maria Press, 1967.

Donne, John. "Occasional Mercies," *Sermons preached on Christmas Day.* Vol. II. *Sixteenth Century to the Restoration.* Henry Craik, ed. English Prose, 1916. https://www.bartleby.com/lit-hub/english-prose-an-anthology-in-five-volumes/john-donne-15721631-16/.

Dziwisz, Stanisław. Homily at Beatification of Blessed Sopocko. Translated by Father Kazimierz Chwalek, MIC, director of Evangelization and Development for the Congregation of Marians at the National Shrine of The Divine Mercy, Stockbridge, Mass. https://www.marian.org/news/Father-Michael-Sopocko-Our-New-Blessed-3368.

Flynn, Erin. *Mass & Adoration Companion*, TAN Books, 2017.

Flynn, Mary. *A Study Guide for 7 Secrets of Divine Mercy*, MercySong, 2016.

Flynn, Vinny. *7 Secrets of Confession*, MercySong, 2013.

———. *7 Secrets of Divine Mercy*, MercySong, 2015.

———. *7 Secrets of the Eucharist*, MercySong, 2006.

———. *21 Ways to Worship*, MercySong, 2012.

———. *Mass & Adoration Companion*. TAN Books, 2017.

Francis de Sales, Francis. *The Art Of Loving God*. Sophia Institute Press.

Francis of Assisi. *The Writings of Saint Francis of Assisi.* Newly translated into English with an Introduction and Notes by Father Paschal Robinson. Philadelphia: The Dolphin Press, 1906.

Gallagher, Timothy M. *Overcoming Spiritual Discouragement: The Wisdom and Spiritual Power of Venerable Bruno Lanteri.* EWTN Publishing, 2019.

Gregory Nazianzen. Bishop and Doctor of the Church. (Oratio 14, De Pauperum Amore, 38. 40: PG 35, 907. 910).

Guardini, Romano. *The Lord*. Gateway Editions, 1996.

Hahn, Scott. *Lord Have Mercy*. Image Books, 2003.

Houselander, Caryll. *The Way of the Cross*. Liguori Publications, 2015.

Ildephonsus. *Crown of the Virgin*. TAN Books.

John Climacus. *The Ladder of Divine Ascent*. Translated by Archimandrite Lazarus Moore. Harper & Brothers, 1959.

John Eudes. *The Sacred Heart of Jesus*. Preserving Christian Publications, 1977.

John of Kronstadt (Archpriest John Iliytch Sergieff). *My Life in Christ.* Grand Rapids, MI: Christian Classics Ethereal Library.

Kosicki, Fr. George, CSB, with Flynn, Vinny. *Now is the Time for Mercy*. Stockbridge, MA: Marian Press, 2010.

———, with Came, David. *Faustina: Saint for Our Times. A Personal Look at Her Life, Spirituality, and Legacy*. Stockbridge, MA: Marian Press, 2010.

Lewis, C.S. *The Weight of Glory*. New York: Simon & Schuster, 1996.

Matthew, Iain, OCD. *John of the Cross: Seasons of Prayer*. Teresian Press, 2014.

Maximilian Maria Kolbe, His Life, Apostolate, and Spirituality. Kolbe Publications.

McCaffrey, Eugene, OCD. *Let Yourself Be Loved*. Teresian Press, 2016.

Michalenko, Seraphim, MIC, "Wombs of Mercy," *Marian Helpers Bulletin*, Marian Fathers, Stockbridge, MA, Summer, 1995.

Moloney, Daniel. *Mercy: What Every Catholic Should Know*. Ignatius Press, 2020.

Nectarios of Aegina. See Bigorski Monastery. https://bigorski.org.mk/en/our-mission/the-holy-fathers-for-the-mercy/.

Nouwen, Henri. *Life of the Beloved*.Crossroad.1995.

"Mary in the Writings of St. Proclus of Constantinople." : https://www.homeofthemother.org/en/resources/virgin-mary/fathers/8909-st-proclus.

Philippe, Jacques. *Interior Freedom.* Scepter Publishers.

———. *Searching for and Maintaining Peace*. Society of St Paul, 2002.

———. *Time for God*. Scepter. 2008.

Pope Benedict XVI. *Jesus of Nazareth*. Ignatius Press.

Pope Francis, "Act of Veneration of the Blessed Virgin Mary" on the occasion of the Feast of the Immaculate Conception, December 8, 2015, coinciding with the opening of the Jubilee Year of Mercy.

Pope Francis. General Audience. Wednesday.

———. Homily at first Vespers for Divine Mercy Sunday. 2016.

———. Mercy Sunday Homily.

Pope John Paul II. Beatification of Four Poles. Błonie, Kraków.

———. Błonie, Kraków.

———. *Crossing the Threshold of Hope*. Knopf, 1995.

Proclus. Archbishop of Constantinople, from Rev. Alban Butler. Volume X: October. *The Lives of the Saints*, 1866.

Sri, Edward. *Into His Likeness*. Ignatius Press/Augustine Institute, 2018.

Sopocko, Blessed Michael. Excerpts from an article first published in the Spring. *Marian Helpers Bulletin,* Marian Fathers, Stockbridge, MA, 1958. https://www.thedivinemercy.org/articles/picture-merciful-christ.

———. *Marian Helpers Bulletin,* Marian Fathers, Stockbridge, MA. https://www.thedivinemercy.org/articles/peace-and-mercy-god.

Stackpole, Robert. *Divine Mercy: A Guide from Genesis to Benedict XVI.* Stockbridge, MA: Marian Press, 2001.

———. "What is the Meaning of the Rays?" TheDivineMercy.org, Oct. 11, 2010. https://www.thedivinemercy.org/articles/what-meaning-rays.

Stinissen, Wilfred, OCD. *Bread That is Broken*. Ignatius Press.

———. *Into Your Hands, Father*. Ignatius Press, 2017.

———.*The Holy Spirit, Fire of Divine Love*. Ignatius Press, 2017.

The Divine Mercy. "The Priest Who First Believed Faustina." http://www.thedivinemercy.org. /articles/priest who first believed faustina.

The Letters of Saint Faustina. Misericordia Publications.

Thomas Aquinas. "Prayer before Communion." *Mass & Adoration Companion*. TAN Books.

Vivaldelli, Carlo. "Rainbow," *On Discovering Mercy*,, Marian Press, 1988.

Von Balthasar, Hans Urs. *Heart of the World*. Ignatius Press, 1980.